# The Hertfordshire Yeomanry Regiments, Royal Artillery

*An Illustrated History*

*Other titles by the author*

Published by the Hertfordshire Local History Council:

Hertfordshire's Soldiers (1969)

Published by the Hertfordshire Yeomanry and Artillery Historical Trust:

Hertfordshire Yeomanry and Artillery Roll of Honour (1972)
Hertfordshire Yeomanry and Artillery Honours and Awards (1976)
Hertfordshire Yeomanry and Artillery Uniforms, Arms and Equipment (1980)

Published by Samson Books Ltd.:

'For Gallantry in the Performance of Military Duty' (1980)

Published by Hart Books, Welwyn:

'Hazardous Work' (1985)
A Guide to the History of the Bedfordshire and Hertfordshire Regiment (1987)
The Hertfordshire Yeomanry – An Illustrated History 1794–1920 (1994)
The Hertfordshire Batteries, Royal Field Artillery – An Illustrated History 1908–1920 (1996)

Published by Castlemead Publications:

The Hertfordshire Regiment – An Illustrated History (1988)

This book is dedicated to all those who have contributed
to the achievements of the Hertfordshire Yeomanry Regiments
of the Royal Regiment of Artillery in peace and war
but especially to those who gave their lives serving with
86th, 135th and 191st Field Regiments, Royal Artillery in
the Second World War, 1939–1945.

"The moril of this story, it is plainly to be seen:
You 'avn't got no families when servin' of the Queen –
You 'avn't got no brothers, fathers, sisters, wives, or sons –
If you want to win your battles take an' work your bloomin' Guns!"

Rudyard Kipling

Frontispiece *Sexton self-propelled 25-pdr. of C Sub-Section, C Troop, 342 Field Battery moving through the ruined town centre of Écouché while in support of 11th Armoured Division during the battle to close the 'Falaise Gap', 19th August 1944. Detachment* (L.–R.) *– Sergeant R.T. Stackwood, Gunner J. Leese, Lance-Bombardier F.G. Smith* (partly obscured), *Lance-Bombardier F.W. Wrench, Gunner G.W. Goard; the driver, Gunner S.C. Turner, cannot be seen.*

(I.W.M. – B 9460)

# The Hertfordshire Yeomanry Regiments, Royal Artillery

## *An Illustrated History*

### Part 1: The Field Regiments 1920–1946

Lieutenant-Colonel J. D. SAINSBURY, O.B.E., T.D., F.S.A.

HART BOOKS, WELWYN

First Published 1999 by
Hart Books, Welwyn for the
Hertfordshire Yeomanry and
Artillery Historical Trust



British Library Cataloguing-in-Publication Data

A catalogue record for this book is available
from the British Library

ISBN 0–948527–05–6

Set in 11/12 Palatino

Printed and bound in Great Britain by

Stephen Austin and Sons Ltd., Hertford

# Preface

I first heard of the Hertfordshire Yeomanry from Stan Day, a Hitchin postman I worked with as a Christmas temporary in 1955. The 6-wheeler G.P.O. Telephones lorry we used for the parcel round was, Stan told me, just like the one he drove at the outbreak of war, and he went on from there with stories of the campaign in Malaya and Singapore. I was properly impressed when he removed his false teeth to demonstrate that he had lost all his own while a prisoner of the Japanese. Stan's stories came back to mind when I joined the regiment three years later, especially his admonition not to believe the one that 135th Field Regiment had 'walked off the ship into the arms of the Japanese'. Then Joe Baker, Arthur Chappell, Joe Robinson, Ron Saunders and Ted Sharp took over – in the bar at the Welwyn Garden City drill-hall – and I learned of the 86th and 191st Field Regiments as well. Their eye-witness accounts were later supplemented by conversations with Chic Bullen and Reg Munt, both of 86th and the 'Information, Intention and Execution' from the officers' point of view was explained patiently to me in conversation and correspondence by Major-General George Fanshawe, Major Garton Ash and Major Robert Kiln of 86th Field Regiment, Brigadier Sir Philip Toosey and Lieutenant-Colonel Peter Halford-Thompson of 135th and Brigadier Maurice Hope of 191st. Fortunately also, each regiment produced its own contemporary diarists, among whom Major Stephen Perry and Captain Sydney Beck of 86th, Bunny Austin of 135th and David Lamb of 191st stand out. My debt to those I have named is immense but I hope that my many friends from the three regiments who shared with me their memories and experiences will know that, although space prevents me listing them, this history would have been the poorer without their contributions and that I am grateful to them all.

To some people this volume will be 'too much, too late'. But the intensity of personal memory is apt to unbalance the whole story and I remain convinced that it was necessary, in the interests of a proper balance between the histories of such a variety of units over two centuries, to produce the volumes in chronological order. If emotion had triumphed over logic and the volume covering the Second World War had appeared first, I have little doubt that the rest of the series would never have reached the printers. Now we can see that the generous financial support of those who served in the Second World War and of their post-war successors has more than secured the first three volumes and the Trustees feel justified in extending their appeal to selected businesses with long-standing connections with Hertfordshire and with the regiment in order that the series may be concluded.

I must, as previously, record my thanks to the organisations listed later. Among the individuals who have contributed to this volume through their knowledge, expertise and patience, I am especially indebted to Brigadier Ken and Mrs Bridget Timbers at the Royal Artillery Institution; Colonel Paddy de Burgh and Lieutenant-Colonel John Payne of the Badley Technical Library at the Royal School of Artillery; Joan Wanklyn, whom we all thank for her superb additions to our series of water colours; and the staff of the Departments of Photographs and of Film at the Imperial War Museum, whose skilled and cheerful help over many years has enabled me to put together an extraordinary pictorial record of the Hertfordshire Yeomanry in the Second World War.

Professor Ian Beckett read Chapter I in draft and made suggestions for which I am grateful, but I must point out that, unless attributed to others, the opinions expressed and the judgments made in this volume are my own, as are any mistakes or omissions. Those seeking to expand on the detail, or perhaps to rectify the omissions, are referred to the Bibliography and Guide to Sources. Those who deplore the absence of maps are asked to try to understand the additional work and expense that the inclusion of satisfactory maps would have entailed. They should note, however, that the campaigns in North-West Europe can be followed on Michelin motoring maps, which I had to hand while writing, and that the Official Histories contain excellent maps.

The manuscript was typed entirely by volunteers, among whom Lilian Smith and Oriel Brownjohn must be mentioned, and thanked, by name. The ladies of Room 3/14 will recognise their contribution, for which I am equally grateful, too.

Finally, I will again point out to past and present members of the regiment the extent to which my wife has contributed in many ways to the eventual appearance of these volumes and offer her my renewed thanks.

J. D. Sainsbury
Welwyn, Hertfordshire
February 1999

# Acknowledgements

The author and the trustees of the Hertfordshire Yeomanry and Artillery Historical Trust record their thanks to the following:

Bank of England Libraries

Commonwealth War Graves Commission

Corporation of London – Guildhall Library

Hertfordshire Archives and Local Studies

Imperial War Museum – Departments of Art, Photographs, Film and Printed Books

Ministry of Defence – Military Secretary's Department, Army Medal Office and Central Library

Royal Artillery Institution

Royal School of Artillery

They also express particular appreciation to:

The Trustees of the Imperial War Museum for permission to reproduce photographs, stills from films and drawings, all of which are accompanied by their reference numbers.

The Proprietors of the *Illustrated London News* for permission to reproduce drawings by Bryan de Grineau on the cover and at Plate 114.

The Controller of Her Majesty's Stationery Office for permission to reproduce Colour Plate III and extracts from the Official History, other Crown Copyright material and material in the Public Record Office.

Curtis Brown Ltd., London, on behalf of the Estate of H. St. G. Saunders for permission to reproduce extracts from *The Red Beret* (Copyright H. St. G. Saunders) (see Bibliography).

Athlone Press Ltd. and Dr. P. N. Davies for permission to reproduce extracts from *The Man Behind the Bridge* (see Bibliography).

The Regimental Lieutenant-Colonel Coldstream Guards for permission to reproduce extracts from *The Coldstream Guards, 1920–1946* (see Bibliography).

The Executors of the late David Lamb for permission to reproduce extracts from *View from the Bridge* (see Bibliography).

Stephen Alexander for permission to reproduce extracts from *Sweet Kwai Run Softly* (see Bibliography).

The Proprietors of *After the Battle* for permission to reproduce extracts from Edition No. 26.

Joan Wanklyn for the skill and care with which she extended her series of paintings of Hertfordshire's Gunners by Coloured Plates I, II, IV and V.

# Contents

# Coloured Plates

*Plate* *facing page*



# Cover

'Overloon Sector of Nijmegen Salient – British Second Army troops pressing out eastwards of the Eindhoven–Nijmegen road towards Overloon and Venray' – From a composite drawing by Bryan de Grineau published in the *Illustrated London News* of 21st October 1944. The section 'Sexton self-propelled 25-pdrs. firing towards Overloon' was drawn from notes made during a visit by the artist to 86th Field Regiment.

Plate 1 *Gunner W. T. Norris of 343 Battery, 86th Brigade, R.F.A. at his first annual camp in 1921. He is wearing 'T./R.F.A.' shoulder titles; the title 'Y./R.F.A.' was not authorised until December 1922.* (Regimental Collection)

Chapter 1

# *Historical Background to the Territorial Artillery, 1920–1945*

*The transition from the Territorial Force to the Territorial Army, 1920–1922*

Recruiting for the post-war Territorial Force opened in February 1920, after about a year of discussion within the War Office, between the War Office and County Associations (at a series of three conferences presided over by the Secretary of State for War, Winston Churchill),[1] and in Parliament. Much of the debate concerned the revised terms of service that the experience of the past ten years had shown were necessary. The order of battle, too, underwent substantial change. The 'conferences', punctuated by periods of more detailed discussion, seem to a great extent to have been confrontational in character, owing to the government's determination to revise terms of service so that Territorials could be employed abroad on embodiment. It was also proposed to reorganise the force so that it consisted of 'Imperial' divisions, i.e., infantry divisions conforming to a standard order of battle that would be similar in the British Regular and Territorial Armies and in the armies of the dominions.[2] At the final conference, at the end of January 1920, it was announced that in recognition of the greatly diminished requirement for horsed cavalry only sixteen out of the 55 regiments of Yeomanry would retain their mounted role. The remainder would be converted to artillery or to armoured car companies of the Royal Tank Corps or to a signals role, while retaining their Yeomanry titles and

Plate 2 *An 18-pdr. with 6-horse team* (Top) *and a riding horse* (Bottom) *of 342 Battery, 86th Brigade, R.F.A. at annual camp at Trawsfynydd, North Wales, 1922. Some former members of Yeomanry regiments joined the Gunners in order to remain mounted but mechanisation was only a few years away and the last horses would be struck off strength by the early 1930s.* (Regimental Collection)

traditions. There were very few other specific references to artillery during the consultation period, though it was clear that additional artillery units would be needed and that, in reflection of the standard order of battle, Territorial batteries would have to be established for the same number of guns (normally six) as Regular batteries.

The final part of the January 1920 conference was devoted to the government's proposals for new terms of service, as follows:

> "... First, that the purpose of the Territorial Army shall be Imperial Defence, including our obligations to France and Flanders. Secondly, that the Territorial Army shall be embodied only when a Royal Proclamation has called out the Reserves and when Parliament has been duly informed of this grave state. Thirdly, that when the Territorial Army has been embodied, it shall only be sent beyond the seas if a fresh Act of Parliament has been passed authorising its despatch to a theatre of war."[3]

These proposals, together with an outline of the new organisation (fourteen infantry divisions
[2] "approximating as closely as possible to the Regular divisions of the Army", with corre-

Plate 3 *Morris-Commercial 6-wheeler gun towers of 86th Field Brigade at Hitchin, early 1930s. Territorial field batteries began to mechanise in 1927, generally with much more enthusiasm than the Regulars, but only one towing vehicle was provided for each battery. Week-end training relied on the pooling of all four of the brigade's vehicles to move a single battery, as here.* (Regimental Collection)

sponding corps and army troops and "complementary cavalry formations composed of Yeomanry units"), a statement of the purpose of the 'Territorial Army' and some details of revised rates of pay and bounty, were incorporated in a leaflet issued in February 1920 to clarify the obligations incurred by recruits.[4] The leaflet contained the important statement that:

> "The Territorial Army, when embodied by Royal Proclamation and despatched abroad by Act of Parliament, will not be used for the purpose of supplying drafts for the Regular Army. They will serve together as regimental or corps units, and, if opportunity arises, as brigades and divisions. That is to say, officers and men of the Territorial Army . . . will serve in their own units and with their own comrades . . .
>
> When, in the stress of emergency a man may, as a purely temporary measure, be attached to a unit other than his own, he will be reposted to his own Territorial Army unit as soon as possible."

It further confirmed that all the conditions of service set out would stand unless modified by Act of Parliament. The undertaking not to send Territorials abroad until so authorised by Act of Parliament, and then not to use Territorials as drafts or individual reinforcements, became known as 'the Pledge'. It was to be challenged at intervals by the policy makers in the War Office but stoutly defended by the Territorial Associations and it would only be on the outbreak of war (see below) that the Army Council would gain what they saw as the necessary flexibility in the employment of the embodied reserves.

Some immediate legislation was required to give effect to the broader concepts underlying the reorganisation. This was passed as the Territorial Army and Militia Act, 1921[5] to come into effect on 1st October 1921. Under this Act, the title 'Territorial Force' was changed to 'Territorial Army' and, by repeal of earlier legislation, the Territorial Army became the only authorised auxiliary military force in the United Kingdom, apart from the Militia (formerly the Special Reserve), which was not re-formed after the war. (It was accordingly necessary to introduce new legislation to cover the raising of the Home Guard in 1940.)

It had been envisaged, even early in the consultative process that preceded the opening of recruitment, that it would take two years for the new order of battle to become effective. In practice, most of the required conversions and amalgamations took place very quickly, but it was not until December 1922 that full details were published.[6] The divisional artillery of each of the fourteen infantry divisions comprised three brigades, each with three 18-pdr. batteries and one 4.5-in. howitzer battery, and the Territorial component of 2nd Cavalry Division included one 3-battery brigade of Royal Horse Artillery. Included in 'Army Troops' were sixteen field brigades, some of four batteries and some of two, one 3-battery pack brigade and eleven 4-battery medium brigades of the Royal Garrison Artillery. Field Force units thus accounted for 168 batteries. Additionally, there were eighteen coast defence units which were not at first sub-divided into batteries (see below).

An outline scheme for the designation of artillery units of the Territorial Force after reorganisation had been promulgated in September 1920 "with a view to preventing confusion from the duplication of numbers".[7] The scheme provided for Territorial brigades of both the Royal Field Artillery and the Royal Garrison Artillery to be "numbered from 51 upwards and batteries from 201 upwards". Divisional artillery brigades took 51st–92nd and their batteries 201–368, following the numerical order of their divisions (42nd–44th and 46th–56th); the eleven medium brigades took 51st–61st and their batteries 201–244. The designations of army troops brigades, R.F.A. and pack and coast brigades, R.G.A. were not made known at this stage. Full details of designations, including historic or local titles where applicable, were set out in the pamphlet *Titles and Designations of Units of the Territorial Army*.[8] This confirmed the early detail of divisional and medium brigades and allotted 93rd–108th to army troops brigades, with 369–430 to their batteries. The single pack brigade was designated 13th and the pack batteries 49–51. The coast brigades had titles describing the areas they defended. The seeds of future confusion were sown by the repeated use of series which began with the same numbers, but it must be pointed out that the same possibilities of confusion existed amongst Regular brigades and batteries and, as will be seen, it was not until after the Second World War that a system was devised that gave unmistakable designations to Regular and Territorial units. The *Titles and Designations* ... pamphlet also authorised Yeomanry batteries and brigades to wear the shoulder title 'Y. – R.F.A.' instead of the usual 'T. – R.F.A.'

### *The formation of the first Territorial anti-aircraft units, 1922–1923*

During 1922 it was decided that anti-aircraft units of the Royal Garrison Artillery and the Royal Engineers would be formed in the Territorial Army. First appointments to these units were made in August 1922 but the build-up was slow and they were not included in the details of the Territorial Army's order of battle published in December 1922 (see above). Rather, their organisation and designations were announced separately in July 1923.[9] The expansion of the Anti-Aircraft Branch of the Royal Artillery and the Royal Engineers to an eventual seven anti-aircraft divisions under Headquarters Anti-Aircraft Command will be fully recorded in a further volume. To follow the development of the Field Branch of the Royal Artillery in the Territorial Army it need only be noted that between 1932 and 1938 nine field and five medium brigades and several individual batteries were transferred to the expanding Anti-Aircraft Branch.

### *The reorganisation of the Royal Regiment of Artillery in 1924 and consequent changes in nomenclature*

In January 1924, the separate horse, field and garrison 'categories' of artillery were abandoned in favour of a single 'Royal Regiment of Artillery'.[10] The designations to be adopted by the various types of unit were not announced until May the same year,[11] when it became clear that the title 'Royal Horse Artillery' would continue in use in both the Regular Army and the Territorial Army – though there was at the time only one Territorial brigade of the Royal Horse Artillery.[12] All brigades and batteries of the Royal Artillery would in future incorporate in their designation a description of their role, e.g., 51st Field Brigade, 205 Medium Battery, etc. The expression 'brigade' was at the time in common use to describe two totally different groupings – a brigadier's command of three or four battalion-sized units of armour, cavalry or infantry, and a lieutenant-colonel's command of two, three or four batteries of artillery. The possibilities for confusion to which this double meaning of 'brigade' gave rise were not addressed for nearly fifteen years, and even then there were different effective dates for the Regular and Territorial Armies. In May 1938[13] it was announced that, in order to bring the nomenclature of Regular Royal Artillery formations, units and sub-units more into line with that used in other arms, a lieutenant-colonel's command, formerly a brigade, would be known as a 'regiment'. The major's command would still be known as a battery but it would be divided first into 'troops' and then into sections and sub-sections, rather than, as previously, directly into sections. The only formation title then used within the Royal Artillery was 'group'; it would in future be replaced by 'brigade'. Similar changes were made in the Territorial Army some months later (see below).

Plate 4 *Sergeant-Major Chettleborough, who joined 342 Field Battery as permanent staff instructor in 1930 – obviously a force to be reckoned with! The energy and enthusiasm of the permanent staff had an extremely important influence on the efficiency and morale of Territorial units, especially in the lean years between the wars.* (Regimental Collection)

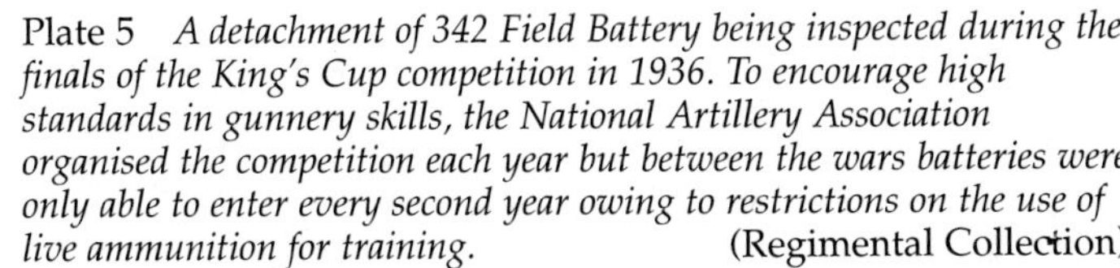

Plate 5 *A detachment of 342 Field Battery being inspected during the finals of the King's Cup competition in 1936. To encourage high standards in gunnery skills, the National Artillery Association organised the competition each year but between the wars batteries were only able to enter every second year owing to restrictions on the use of*
[5] *live ammunition for training.* (Regimental Collection)

*Coast Artillery, 1920–1939*

As reconstituted after the First World War, the Territorial contribution to the artillery component of 'Coast Defence Troops' consisted of twelve coast brigades and six unbrigaded coast batteries. The brigades carried local designations, e.g., Clyde Coast Brigade, Royal Garrison Artillery, from the start but battery designations, from a series beginning 150 and in order of the recognised precedence of brigades, were not allocated until December 1923.[14] As a consequence of the amalgamation of the Royal Field Artillery and the Royal Garrison Artillery in 1924, Coast Brigades, R.G.A. were redesignated Heavy Brigades, R.A. – an indication that the personnel could, if required, man mobile heavy guns.

In 1926, it was decided that Regular heavy batteries would no longer be used in the coast defences of England, Scotland and Wales. All the guns would in future be manned by Territorials, but a Regular headquarters staff would be retained at all the defended ports, as would a 'District Staff', responsible for providing certain specialists, but above all for the maintenance of the guns. This decision was put into effect early in 1927 but the consequent reorganisation took more than five years to complete. It was announced in May 1932 that a scheme for the reorganisation of coast defence arrangements at home had been approved, "under which the general responsibility for the land coastal defence of Great Britain will be undertaken by the Territorial Army".[15] Most of the details of the reorganisation and the consequent changes in designation were announced in October the same year, with a follow-up in March 1934.[16] A total of thirty batteries were now organised in fourteen brigades. As a result of the raising of three more brigades and the addition of batteries to existing brigades, the order of battle on mobilisation comprised forty batteries in seventeen regiments.[17]

*Reorganisation of the Field Force, 1938*

By the summer of 1938, conversion to the anti-aircraft role (both gun and searchlight) had accounted for two of the fourteen infantry divisions reconstituted in 1920.[18] Planned further conversions were such that the remaining divisions could not stay on their present order of battle (each three infantry brigades of four battalions) but they were, in any case, becoming recognisably 'old-fashioned' compared with Regular divisions. It was accordingly promulgated by War Office Letter dated 10th October 1938 that:

> "It has been decided to reorganise the Field Force portion of the Territorial Army on the lines of the new Regular Army organisation.
>
> The object has been, without raising any additional units or any appreciable increase to establishments and with the least possible dislocation to existing units or areas, to produce a General Purpose Army, organised on modern lines and capable of providing support to the Regular Army in any major emergency necessitating the embodiment of the Territorial Army."

The Territorial Army's Field Force would in future consist of one mobile division (comprising the equivalent of three brigades, two of which would be armoured), nine infantry divisions (each of three 3-battalion brigades) and three motor divisions (of two 3-battalion brigades). Additionally, sixteen regiments of Yeomanry or Scouts would remain horsed, and there would be corps and army troops, notably from the Royal Armoured Corps, Royal Artillery and Royal Engineers.[19]

The effect of this reorganisation on the Royal Artillery was considerable. Units were ordered to adopt the nomenclature which had been in use in the Regular component of the Royal Regiment since May. Thus, with effect from 1st November 1938, brigades became regiments, and batteries were split into troops, sections and sub-sections. Field batteries were reorganised to consist of three 4-gun troops and there were only two batteries in a field regiment, which, at war establishment, totalled the same 24 guns as the old 4-battery field brigade.

The reorganised Field Force required 37 field regiments as divisional artillery; a further six were designated as army troops. The divisional artillery of the mobile division and each of the infantry divisions (but not the motor divisions) was augmented by the addition of a 4-battery anti-tank regiment. Ten new anti-tank regiments were accordingly required, of which five were formed by conversion of field artillery brigades and five from infantry battalions. They followed earlier precedent by taking their numbers from a series beginning 51st and their batteries were numbered from 201, thus adding to the potential for confusion between units with similar designations. As corps and army troops, there were, in addition to the six field regiments, four new 3-battery light anti-aircraft regiments for the protection of the Field Force after deployment, seven medium regiments which had their origins in 1920, and two survey regiments, which were to be expanded from two survey companies raised in 1937. The new light anti-aircraft regiments were to be raised by conversion of two field artillery brigades and two infantry battalions. They too would be numbered from 51st, with their batteries starting at 151.

The decision to reorganise the Field Force and convert units 'without the option' was communicated to Home Commands, Territorial Field Force units and Territorial Associations in the War Office Letter previously quoted, which regretted that the Army Council had found it impracticable to invite Lords Lieutenant, G.O.Cs. and Association representatives to London for the (by implication) normal discussions on the future of units, "in view of the urgency of implementing the scheme". The War Office Letter was marked 'Not to be published' but this did not prevent the issue of a substantial official press release (without any detail of the units involved) or a speech made by the Secretary of State for War, Leslie Hore-Belisha, at a dinner at the Mansion House on the evening of 10th October.[20] The reorganisation was accompanied by the intention – only partly put into effect before the outbreak of war just under a year later – to re-equip Field Force units with modern weapons and vehicles (see Chapter 2). Frederick (see Bibliography) gives the effective date of conversion of Field Force artillery units as 28th November but no Army Order or Army Council Instruction detailing their new roles and designations was published.

## *'Duplication' of the Field Force, 1939*

The reorganised Field Force had had very little time in which to face up to its new organisation and revised role, and, importantly, had not been to annual camp, before further widespread changes were announced. In a final effort to avert conscription, increasingly demanded by the press following the German occupation of the rest of Czechoslovakia, but still firmly rejected by the Labour Party and the Trade Unions, the Prime Minister had accepted a spur-of-the-moment suggestion from Hore-Belisha that if conscription was out of the question the Territorial Army should be doubled. A War Office Letter, dated 31st March 1939,[21] the essential details of which had been announced in Parliament on 29th March,[22]

Plate 6 *Display by 344 Field Battery in St. Mary's Square, Hitchin during recruiting for the expanding Field Force of the Territorial Army, April 1939. Although the battery had the opportunity of showing off some of the new vehicles that were beginning to reach the Territorial Army, their 4.5-in. howitzers were of First World War vintage.*
(Hertfordshire Pictorial Archives – Hitchin Museum)

Plate 7 *Recruits for 344 Field Battery start gun drill at Bearton Camp, Hitchin, April 1939. The influx of keen young men presents a wry contrast with the antiquated iron-tyred guns and limbers.*
(Hertfordshire Pictorial Archives – Hitchin Museum)

stated that, "an expansion of the T.A. Field Force by duplicating . . . units" had been decided upon. All 'teeth arms' units except those mounted on horses would go through a three-stage process of expansion. The first stage involved the formation of the cadres required as unit training centres on mobilisation and the raising of all ranks to war establishment. The second stage provided for the nucleus of a '2nd Line' unit to be raised and the third stage for that nucleus to be expanded to a full-strength unit at war establishment. Although the expression '2nd Line' was used in the War Office Letter, it was explained that the function and status of the new units would, "on their assuming a separate identity (third stage of expansion) be in all respects similar and equal to the 1st Line units". It will be seen, therefore, that the 1939 'expansion by duplication' was in no sense similar to the expansion which took place after mobilisation in 1914 and gave rise to true 2nd Line units. The expression 'duplicate unit' came into general use to describe those raised in 1939 and is a much more apt description. No time limit for the expansion was given in the original letter but there were some pressures on young men to join the Auxiliary Forces (see below). The flow of recruits was accordingly such that many units went to camp in 1939 at a strength close to that necessary to provide two full-strength units, and generally had plans to give the duplicate unit its own independence and identity immediately after camp. This process became mixed up in the preparations for mobilisation and many units did not genuinely stand alone until after the outbreak of war.

The duplicate units of the Royal Artillery were numbered from the same series as their original units, and in the same order. Royal Horse Artillery and field regiments were numbered 109th–150th (with the duplicate regiment of the Honourable Artillery Company becoming 12th R.H.A.), medium regiments 63rd–69th, light anti-aircraft regiments 55th–58th, anti-tank regiments 61st–70th and survey regiments 5th and 6th. Batteries followed the same pattern. No published announcement of the roles and designations of duplicate artillery units was made but they are clear (with some errors as to batteries) from the 'Security Edition' of the September 1939 *Monthly Army List*. They are fully accounted for by Frederick, who indicates that the finally agreed designations were not promulgated until February 1942.

*Further legislation, 1939*

[8] The deterioration in relations with Germany that culminated in the so-called 'Munich Crisis'

in the autumn of 1938 led to the declaration of a State of Emergency and the mobilisation of anti-aircraft units for some three weeks from 23rd September. This period of full-time service at war stations confirmed serious deficiencies in armament and other equipment, notably transport, but equally demonstrated that it was realistic to base the anti-aircraft defence of Britain on part-time volunteers. However, under the existing legislation it was not possible to call out a limited part (e.g., anti-aircraft units only) of the Territorial Army. In any case, Territorials could not be embodied before the call-out of the First Class of the Army Reserve. This difficulty had been temporarily overcome by inviting the personnel of anti-aircraft and coast defence units to undertake to assemble in an emergency before general mobilisation. In April 1939, however, the government decided that they could not continue to rely on the willingness of volunteers and an additional Reserve and Auxiliary Forces Act[23] was passed to permit the call-out of "all or any" members of the Reserves, once the Secretary of State was satisfied that their services were urgently required to ensure the defence of the United Kingdom against external threat.

At the same time as they had taken steps to secure the anti-aircraft and coast defences in advance of general mobilisation, the government, deeming it unwise to continue to rely exclusively on volunteers for the Army (either Regular or Territorial) decided to introduce a measure of conscription. The Military Training Act, 1939,[24] which became law on 26th May 1939, made temporary provision for men aged twenty to be called up for four years' service in a reconstituted Militia. Only six months of their engagement would be spent in full-time training, after which they would be posted to Territorial units with a continuing liability for part-time service, and, of course, embodiment. Such shortages as there might be in the expanded Field Force would be made good and anti-aircraft units could be kept up to war establishment with soldiers who had experienced the considerable benefit of six months' full-time basic and 'trade' training. In practice, the full effect of the Military Training Act, 1939 was never felt, partly because of the outbreak of war in September 1939 but to a much greater extent because of the flood of recruits into the Territorial Army in the period March–April 1939. This flood was caused initially by genuine feelings that 'something must be done' to counter the growing menace of Hitler's Germany – a mixture of quiet patriotism and the Government's measures to encourage 'National Service' – and units that had started waiting lists for recruits before the expansion were able to open their books again to considerable effect. However, the Military Training Act itself was responsible for a further inrush of volunteers. It excluded from call-up for full-time training men who had enlisted, or been commissioned, into any of the Reserve Forces before 27th April 1939 and was thus responsible for directing into Territorial units many twenty-year-olds who quickly chose a voluntary part-time engagement in preference to full-time service. Eighteen to twenty-year-olds joined too, of course, partly as 'genuine' volunteers, sucked along by the tide of enthusiasm, and partly because they saw some form of military service as unavoidable and preferred to soldier voluntarily, locally and with their friends, rather than await call-up.

Two further Acts, the Armed Forces (Conditions of Service) Act[25] and the Military and Air Forces (Prolongation of Service) Act[26] were introduced while embodiment and mobilisation were taking place. The first had the effect of creating a single national army and suspended

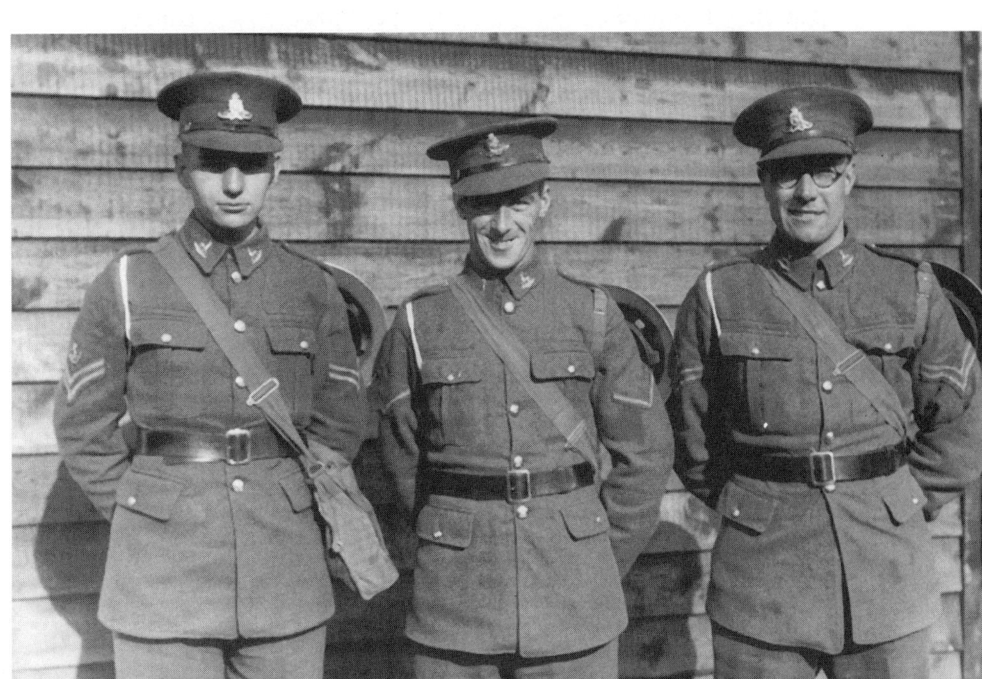

Plate 8 *Bombardiers Dimond, Ferguson and King of 86th Field Regiment on mobilisation in September 1939. Apart from the recent substitution of trousers for breeches in the Royal Artillery, the uniform was the same as that worn in August 1914.* (Regimental Collection)

Plate 9 *The splendid Rolls-Royce used by Lieutenant-Colonel Sir Patrick Coghill, Bt., commanding 86th Field Regiment, carrying his 'Z' sign, early 1940. The severe shortage of vehicles on mobilisation led to widespread requisitioning to bring units up to a workable strength and some requisitioned vehicles remained in service for as much as two years.* (Regimental Collection)

for the duration of the war the separate status of the Territorial Army, removing any remaining restrictions to 'general service' and to transfer between arms of the service or units. (One of its effects was to suspend the appointment of officers to Territorial commissions; instead, officers commissioned during the war received 'Emergency' commissions into the Royal Regiment of Artillery, rather than commissions into individual Territorial units, as had been the case for most of the First World War.) The second Act quite simply extended all terms of service entered into before embodiment for the duration of the war. (This, too, was in contrast to the First World War, when, in theory at any rate, Territorial enlistments 'ran out' and, before the introduction of conscription in 1916, men had to be persuaded to re-engage while on active service.) Taken together, the Acts that became law in 1939 put an end to 'the Pledge' (see above).

*The Second World War, 1939–1945*

War was actually declared on 3rd September 1939 but from the Territorial Army's point of view there had been a steady build-up since the introduction in May of the anti-aircraft 'couverture' (i.e., the partial manning of the anti-aircraft defences by call-out under the Reserve and Auxiliary Forces Act, 1939). Full-scale call-out of the anti-aircraft and coast defences took place on 24th August, followed a few days later by call-out of the National Defence Companies (responsible for guarding vulnerable points in the United Kingdom), then by 'key parties' of remaining Territorial units and finally by embodiment of the Territorial Army as a

Plate 10 *A 25-pdr. of 135th Field Regiment training in Scotland, March 1941. The arrival of the 25-pdr. more than a year after mobilisation marked the end of the re-equipment programme begun in the autumn of 1938.* (I.W.M. – H 7703)

Plate 11
*Covenanter O.P. tanks of 42nd Armoured Divisional Artillery on exercise, September 1942. O.P. parties were equipped with tanks when supporting armoured units, giving them similar cross-country performance to the 'supported arm' and enabling them to present a similar appearance.*
(I.W.M. – H 24095)

whole and recall of officers from the Territorial Army Reserve of Officers on 1st September.

Some 400,000 Territorials in all were embodied, of which the Royal Regiment of Artillery accounted for just over 120,000. On mobilisation there were in all 240 Territorial artillery units. One hundred field (including R.H.A.) and medium regiments, twenty anti-tank, eight light anti-aircraft and four survey regiments were in the Field Force, which comprised 26 divisions (many still in course of formation). In addition, there were 51 heavy anti-aircraft, thirty light anti-aircraft and nine searchlight regiments in seven divisions under Anti-Aircraft Command, which also included a further 41 searchlight regiments, most of them in the Royal Engineers but some still nominally Infantry. These numbers were to be considerably expanded during the war. Between February and May 1940, six field and six medium regiments were added by conversion of six Yeomanry regiments that had started the war with horses, and in August 1940 all Territorial searchlight units of the Royal Engineers and Infantry were transferred to the Royal Artillery. Circumstances were such in September 1940 that large-scale changes in the coast artillery order of battle were considered necessary. As a result, the original seventeen unnumbered pre-war heavy regiments were reorganised and redesignated as 35 numbered coast regiments, later expanded to 39. At intervals later in the war, Territorial infantry battalions were transferred to the Royal Artillery and converted to field, anti-tank or light anti-aircraft regiments. The bulk of war-formed heavy and light anti-aircraft batteries and searchlight batteries were raised around cadres drawn from existing (and thus Territorial) regiments in Anti-Aircraft Command. The extent to which these batteries, which legally were not part of the Territorial Army, reflected their Territorial heritage varied. Some which returned to their original regiments were for practical purposes indistinguishable from 'the real thing'. The formation of new regiments of the Field Branch from Territorial cadres was less usual. A notable exception was 191st Field Regiment (see Chapter 6).

As the war progressed, it was necessary from time to time, starting with the conversion of field regiments to heavy regiments late in 1939, to re-equip and re-role Territorial artillery units within the Royal Regiment. None were converted from artillery to other arms while the war continued, but the shortage of infantry and parallel redundancy of heavy and light anti-aircraft, searchlight and coast regiments led to the conversion of 38 Territorial Gunner units into an infantry role – initially designated as 'garrison' regiments, later simply as 'regiments', numbered from a series beginning 600th. Shortage of infantry, again in parallel with redundancy of anti-aircraft units, was the major factor leading to the dispersal of artillery units from 1944 onwards by the posting of suitably fit personnel to infantry and the rest to artillery units remaining in the order of battle.

Care was taken that no pre-war Territorial unit should be disbanded during the war. Instructions were issued in December 1943[27] that, "should it prove operationally essential to break up a . . . T.A. unit, the unit will not be disbanded but will lapse into 'suspended animation' ". Under this procedure the unit retained its identity with no posted strength and its property and plate were not disposed of but held in suspense. The unit could be reconstituted

Plate 12
*Disbandment parade of 191st Field Regiment in Holland, 5th December 1944. Territorial units which were no longer required during the Second World War were placed in 'suspended animation' but war-formed units like 191st Field Regiment were disbanded.*
(I.W.M. – B 12475)

at any time to carry on its history and traditions. The War Office Letter detailing the reorganisation of the Territorial Field Force (see above) had contained a paragraph which had probably been largely ignored but stated:

> "The adoption by the Territorial Army of the modern organisation for the artillery makes it necessary that the 'unit' should no longer be the 'battery', but the 'regiment'."

In pursuance of this directive the instructions covering suspended animation repeated the idea that "in the case of T.A. units, the identity is incorporated in the regiment" and stated that as long as the regimental headquarters remained in being (albeit in suspended animation), there was no objection on historical grounds to the disbandment of a Territorial battery. In practice, the dispersal of all pre-war Territorial regiments of the Royal Artillery, either during the war or on demobilisation, resulted in units being placed in suspended animation, with any thought of their future postponed until the eventual reconstitution of the Territorial Army.

NOTES

1. *Report of Proceedings at a Conference between the Secretary of State for War and Representatives of the Territorial Force Associations – 1st April 1919*
2. *Report of Proceedings ...... 1st May 1919*
3. *Report of Proceedings ..... 30th January 1920*
4. *Reorganisation of the Territorial Force* (Leaflet printed for the War Office, February 1920)
5. 11 & 12 Geo.V c.37 (see Appendix 1). The change of title to 'Territorial Army' was promulgated in Army Order 396/1921.
6. Army Order 482/1922
7. A.C.I. 594/1920
8. Army Order 481/1922
9. Army Order 264/1923
10. Army Order 1/1924
11. Army Order 164/1924
12. 11th (Honourable Artillery Company and City of London Yeomanry) Brigade
13. *The Times*, 16th May 1938 and Army Order 204/1938
14. Army Orders 481/1922 and 463/1923 (see also Frederick)
15. Army Order 75/1932
16. Army Orders 176/1932 and 55/1934
17. *Monthly Army List* (Security Edition), September 1939 (see also Frederick)
18. The two London divisions (47th and 56th) were amalgamated following the formation of 1st Anti-Aircraft Division (Army Order 215/1933). Most of the units of 2nd Anti-Aircraft Division were formed by conversion of units of 46th Division, which was then disbanded.
19. W.O.L. 20/Gen./5689 (T.A.1) of 10th October 1938
20. *The Times*, 11th October 1938
21. W.O.L. 79/Mob./2778 (T.A.1) of 31st March 1939
22. *The Times*, 30th March 1939
23. 2 & 3 Geo.VI c.24 (see Appendix 1)
24. 2 & 3 Geo.VI c.25 (see Appendix 1)
25. 2 & 3 Geo.VI c.68 (see Appendix 1)
26. 2 & 3 Geo.VI c.90 (see Appendix 1)
27. W.O.Ls. 20/Inf./3334(A.G.1a) of 9th December 1943 (reproduced in *Royal Artillery Notes*, April 1944), 30th November 1944 and 12th February 1946

Chapter 2

# *The Development of Field Artillery Tactics, Organisation and Equipment, 1920–1945*

*Introduction – The Legacy of the First World War*

This book is concerned only with what are now termed 'close support' units of artillery. The key functions within a close support unit were defined during the First World War and remain valid today. They are:

1. Target acquisition and observation of fire.
2. Reconnaissance, selection and occupation of gun positions, and control of the guns in action.
3. The 'means of delivery' of the shell, i.e., the guns themselves, together with their ready-use ammunition.
4. Immediate resupply of ammunition, and, since mechanisation, fuel.
5. Administration and logistics.

Throughout the nineteenth century and in the early years of the twentieth, the battery was considered the tactical fire unit of the field artillery. As the First World War continued, however, techniques were necessarily evolved for grouping larger numbers of guns, often of different calibres, in both offensive and defensive operations and for counter-battery work. The emphasis on the battery as the tactical unit accordingly diminished, while the significance of larger units – the existing 'brigade' of three or four batteries, the ad-hoc 'group' of as many as six to eight batteries, or the whole of the divisional artillery – increased. This placed extra demands on signal communications and survey, and called for larger staffs and enhanced fire direction systems in command posts at all levels.

The development of artillery weapons and equipment, in common with those of other arms, was hampered during the 1920s and early 1930s by what became known as the 'ten-year rule' – the continuing government policy that there would be no major war for ten years. The effect of this policy, which was not abandoned until the later 1930s, was not only to minimise budgetary provision for development of new weapons and equipment, and for their eventual procurement, but to remove any great sense of urgency towards the innovations that new technology would have made possible. Against this background, and despite the efforts of the School of Artillery, dedicated members of the Gunnery Staff and a few far-sighted regimental officers, it proved difficult even to preserve the systems and skills that had been perfected in the later years of the First World War. It could even be said that there was a distaste for 'technical' gunnery in the 1920s and '30s, especially for survey. Although funds for development and procurement gradually increased, these difficulties were not fully overcome, and then again by necessity, until the early years of the Second World War. Perhaps the most important factor in enabling the Royal Regiment of Artillery to face the requirement for the vital skills of survey and more complex command post procedures was the huge infusion of well educated men, of which the Territorials, of course, formed a large part, in the critical early stages. Shortcomings in signalling in the later 1930s were due more to financial stringency preventing the development of suitable wireless sets, than to lack of interest or willingness to set aside

Plate 13 *The Mk. II 18-pdr. Q.F. gun* (Top)*, its limber* (Bottom left) *and ammunition wagon* (Bottom right)*. The Mk. II 18-pdr. was the standard British and Commonwealth field gun of the First World War. Its maximum range was restricted to 6,525 yards by the pole trail.*

(Royal Artillery Institution)

traditional methods. Again, though, the pressures of war speeded up progress and the pre-eminence of artillery communications had become a by-word before the opening of the campaign in North-West Europe in 1944.

Another lesson of the First World War, which lapsed in large part until revived through the early experiences of the Second, was the system of 'permanent affiliation' in action of a single battery with an infantry battalion. The presence of known Gunner faces – the battery commanders' and forward observation officers' parties – amongst the infantry did much to foster mutual trust and confidence and it would seem strange to the present-day Gunner, who has been brought up with the concept of 'direct support', as permanent affiliation became known, that methods had ever been different.

Whatever steps were taken to establish and improve higher levels of command, and tactical and fire control, the battery remained the key unit. Within the Royal Regiment of Artillery it is the lowest level of command capable of operating independently from all tactical and administrative points of view. Indeed, while in the cavalry and infantry a lieutenant-colonel's command (regiment or battalion) is sub-divided into squadrons or companies commanded by majors, in the Royal Regiment major's commands (batteries) are grouped into regiments (prior to 1938, brigades) commanded by lieutenant-colonels. Batteries have distinctive designations and are the focal point for all aspects of morale, including history and tradition.

Plate 14 *The 4.5-in. Q.F. howitzer used by howitzer batteries of field brigades during and after the First World War* (Top), *with its limber* (Bottom left) *and ammunition wagon* (Bottom right). *The box trail allowed an elevation of 45 degrees and a maximum range of 7,300 yards.* (See also Plate 24) (Royal Artillery Institution)

*The closing years of the horse-drawn era, 1920 to the early 1930s*

On reconstitution in 1920, brigades of the Royal Field Artillery forming part of the divisional artillery of Territorial divisions were placed on a standard establishment which would provide three 6-gun 18-pdr. batteries and one 6-gun 4.5-in. howitzer battery on mobilisation. However, batteries held only four guns in peace-time. The guns and their first-line ammunition wagons were horse-drawn and the battery staff mounted.

Despite the lessons of the First World War, batteries were established to provide only one observation post (O.P.), manned by the battery commander (B.C.), who had a small staff – technical assistant, rangetaker and signallers. Additional forward observation officers (F.O.Os.) and their teams were drawn from the gun position as the operational situation dictated, but at the expense of some capability, or at least, flexibility, at the 'gun end'. Communication between the observation posts and the gun position was normally by telephone and the establishment provided for teams of operators, known as 'terminals', and line maintenance parties. Equipment for flag, lamp and heliograph signalling was held and these methods were used as appropriate instead of, or as back-up to, line.

On deployment, the general area of the gun position was selected by the battery commander, who would indicate it, together with the line of fire, to the gun position officer (G.P.O.), either visually or by map reference, and move on to his observation post position. The gun position officer then marked the position of the 'pivot' gun, the alignment of the line of guns and the direction of the line of fire. The 'battery leader' (a subaltern officer) brought the guns

Plate 15 *The Mk. IV 18-pdr. gun on Mk. IV box-trail carriage. The Mk. III and Mark IV carriages were of box-trail, rather than pole-trail design, with the recoil system below the barrel. Maximum range was increased to 9,300 yards (Mk. III) and 10,600 yards (Mk. IV) through the greater elevation possible with the box trail.*
(I.W.M. – MH 12550)

on to the position to come into action at twenty-yard intervals from the pivot gun, in a straight line. The rudimentary command post was set up behind the gun line or to a flank. Fire orders from the battery's own O.P. were sent in a form that could be directly applied to the gun sights, but map co-ordinates of targets received through the artillery communications network could be converted into 'gun data' by the command post staff, using an artillery board, on which both gun position and target were plotted and bearing and range could thus be deduced.

The guns were organised in sections of two, each commanded by a subaltern officer known as the 'section commander'. He was responsible for command and supervision of his section in action and for its training in peace-time but was also qualified to work as G.P.O. or as a forward observation officer as necessity arose. A sub-section consisted of one gun (6-horse team, limber and gun with detachment) and its associated ammunition wagons (two at war establishment – usually only one for training). These first-line wagons were attached to a limber similar to that used with the gun and pulled by a 6-horse team, so that in the event of casualties there was plenty of spare gun-pulling power. Guns travelled with one ammunition wagon under immediate command and this wagon was dropped beside the gun as part of the drill for coming into action. As it became exhausted, the next wagon was brought on to the position and the first taken away for replenishment. The gun limber carried a certain amount of ammunition but, contrary to modern misconception, in horse-drawn units this was used only

Plate 16 *The Morris-Commercial Series D six-wheeled lorry used to tow guns and howitzers following the mechanisation of Territorial field batteries from 1927. The four rear wheels were driven and could be fitted with chain tracks for use on difficult ground.* (I.W.M. – KID 1567)

in emergency. Gun teams and wagons not required on the gun position were withdrawn to the wagon lines – an area well away from the gun position, giving some protection from counter-battery fire. The wagon lines were commanded by the battery captain, the only captain on the establishment, who was in signal communication with the gun position and could supervise immediate resupply of ammunition, etc.

As the smallest artillery unit organised and equipped to function independently, the battery held its own administrative and repair personnel – gun fitters, farriers and shoeing-smiths, saddlers, wheelers, cooks, clerks, etc. Those who were not at any given time actually working on the gun position were normally grouped in a battery administrative area even further away than the wagon lines and under the local command of the battery quartermaster-sergeant.

### *Mechanisation, 1927–1933*

Mechanisation, as put into effect between the wars (in the Territorial Army between 1927 and 1933), was carried out as a replacement of the horse by the motor vehicle, with little change in tactics and organisation and hence in the character of the battery or brigade. Cross-country performance was not always improved. In the Regular Army the move was towards tracked vehicles (known as 'Dragons') but funds did not stretch to the issue of Dragons to Territorial batteries. Instead, they used Morris-Commercial 6-wheeler trucks for towing and, when battery staffs were eventually mechanised, 2- and 4-seater cars of civilian pattern. Remodelling of gun carriages and limbers did not keep pace with the introduction and further development of towing vehicles. Regular batteries were slow to receive pneumatic-tyred equipments and relied to a great extent on the traditional wooden wheels with solid rubber tyres. The Territorial Army lagged even further behind and retained iron tyres, which restricted the towing speed to eight miles per hour.

The battery establishment was reduced as drivers, horse-holders and some ammunition numbers became redundant but the only significant change on the gun position was in first-line ammunition supply. Some ammunition was carried on the towing vehicle and the limber – readily unhooked – was now used for immediate needs. The supply was topped up from motor lorries which were no longer under the immediate command of the gun detachment commanders but rather, classified as section ammunition vehicles.

### *Reorganisation and re-equipment, 1938–1939*

During 1938 there was a sweeping reorganisation of Field Branch artillery with a view both to providing a heavier weight of fire on a target without going above battery level, and to increasing the battery's capability to observe ground and direct fire in the close support role. Both Regular and Territorial brigades were placed on the same War Establishment, retaining

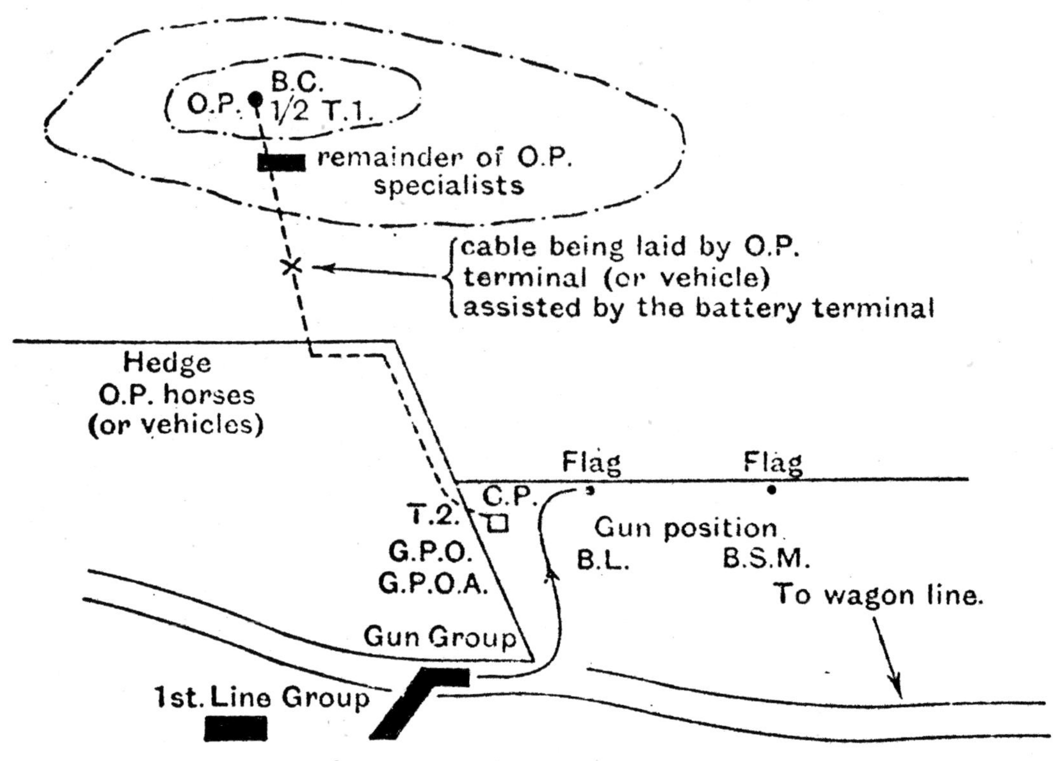


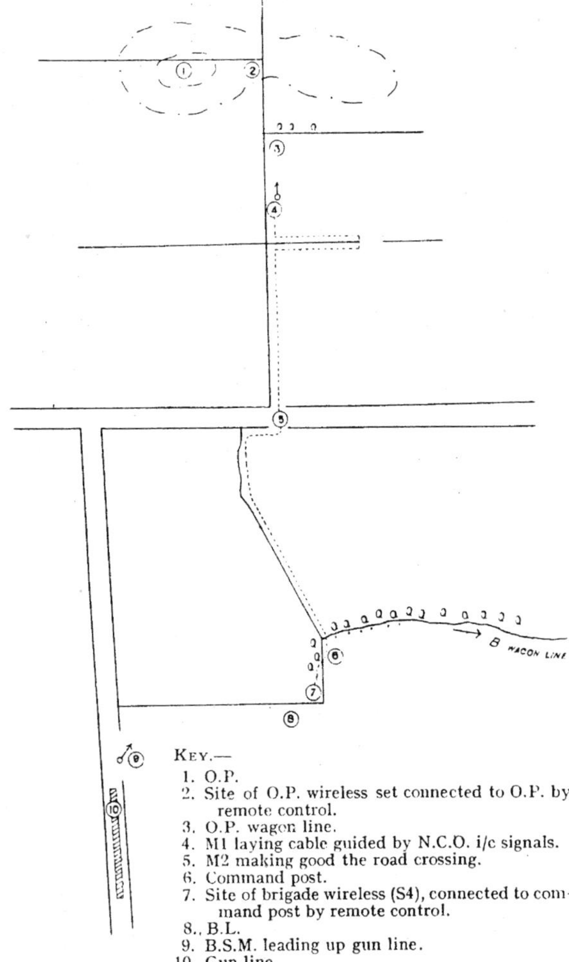


Plate 17 *Diagrams from pamphlets in the 'Artillery Training' series showing the process of occupying O.P. and gun position. In the diagram from 'A.T. Vol. I – Drill'* (Top), *published in 1932, the gun position officer (G.P.O.) has marked the gun line with flags and sited the command post (C.P.). The guns are being led on to the position by the battery leader (B.L.) and the battery sergeant-major (B.S.M.) is waiting to take the horses and limbers, or the towing vehicles, away to the wagon lines. Meanwhile, the battery commander (B.C.) has occupied his O.P. with one signaller (½ T.1), leaving his specialists (rangetaker and O.P. assistant) under cover on the reverse slope for the time being. The second O.P. signaller (½ T.1) and the two signallers forming the C.P. terminal (T.2) are laying the telephone cable between O.P. and C.P. Where circumstances permit, visual communication (lamp or flag) will also have been established. The diagram from 'A.T. Vol. I, Pamphlet No. 2 – Battle drill and manoeuvre for the reconnaissance and occupation of positions ...'* (Bottom), *published in 1938, illustrates much the same situation but shows two wireless sets, deployed at O.P. and C.P. Wireless communication is reinforced by cable, laid by two line-maintenance parties in vehicles M1 and M2. Comparison with Plate 9 of 'The Hertfordshire Batteries, R.F.A.' will show that diagrams lost a great deal of artistic merit, elegance and interest between the First and Second World Wars.*

(Royal School of Artillery)

Plate 18 *The Morris-Commercial CDSW 6 × 4 Field Artillery Tractor. Developed from the Series D tractor* (Plate 16), *the CDSW was issued in limited numbers to Territorial field batteries in 1938–39.* (I.W.M. – KID 2607)

the same total of 24 guns, but they now consisted of only two batteries rather than four. Each battery was sub-divided into three troops of four guns, with the important new appointment of a captain to command each troop, and with the necessary technical and signals assistance to provide two of the troop commanders with full-time forward observer capability. It was under this organisation that field artillery units (a lieutenant-colonel's command was redesignated a regiment as part of the wider changes) were mobilised in September 1939.

In the late 1930s, re-equipment of the Field Branch, including its Territorial component, began at last; not before time, for apart from some increase in range, little had changed, as far as guns were concerned, since before 1914. The pole-trail Mk. II 18-pdr. had been discarded by both Regular and Territorial batteries in the 1920s, though stocks were retained in store. Regular 18-pdr. batteries were now equipped with the Mk. IV gun on both the Mk. IV box-trail carriage – a development of the Mk. III giving a maximum range of 10,600 yards – and the Mk.V split trail, designed in the early 1920s for stability and quick traverse when engaging tanks. It is difficult to be precise about the marks of carriage used in the Territorial Army during the 1930s. They appear, from a limited survey of photographs, to have been exclusively of box-trail type, with the Mk. III predominating, at least until 1936–37. Meanwhile, all howitzer batteries of field brigades soldiered on with the Mk. I gun on Mk. I carriage, as it first saw service in 1909. As indicated earlier, pneumatic tyres and higher towing speeds were the exception, rather than the rule. Some excellent guns and vehicles were in prospect however, and began to trickle into service during 1938 and 1939.

The veteran 18-pdr. guns and 4.5-in. howitzers were replaced by the multi-purpose 25-pdr. gun/howitzer, which offered greater weight of shell, considerably increased maximum range,



Plate 19 *Truck, 8-cwt., 4 × 2, F.F.W.* (Left) *and Truck, 15-cwt., 4 × 2, G.S.* (Right). *These two vehicles, built by Morris-Commercial as models PU and CS8, were available in 'fitted for wireless' (F.F.W.) and 'general service' (G.S.) versions, which began to reach Territorial units in 1938 to replace civilian-pattern cars for B.Cs., O.Ps. and battery staff. The 15-cwt., also built by other manufacturers, remained in service until well after the Second World War.* (I.W.M. – KID 2584/1466)

Plate 20 *The 18/25-pdr., and the new limber designed to carry 25-pdr. ammunition. The Mk. I 25-pdr. barrel was mounted on a refurbished and 'pneumatised' 18-pdr. Mk. IV carriage. The limber – 'Trailer, Artillery, No. 27' – carried 32 rounds in pull-out trays.* (I.W.M. – MH 12774–5)

at 13,400 yards, and a variety of charges, enabling the elevation to be varied for 'crest clearance'. Early production of 25-pdr. Mk. I barrels was mounted on 18-pdr. carriages – both the box-trail Mk. IV and the split-trail Mk. V – resulting in a gun popularly known as the 18/25-pdr. None of these had reached the Territorial Army before mobilisation. The combined effect of the outbreak of war and the loss of many guns in France in 1940 was to increase to a crash programme the fitting of existing wooden-wheeled/iron-tyred guns and limbers with pneumatic-tyred wheels for 'high speed' towing. This programme was greatly assisted by the import of 'pneumatisation sets' from the United States. It was entirely necessary to 'make do and mend' in this fashion. Production of 'real' 25-pdrs. (Mk. II on Mk. I Carriage) did not begin to keep pace with demand until mid-1941 and 4.5-in. howitzers were still in action against the enemy in the early months of 1942.

The search for a wheeled field artillery tractor to replace both the Dragon and the 6 × 4 Morris-Commercial Series D ended as the war was about to begin with the 4-wheel drive 'Quad', soon to be universally known. Meanwhile, efforts had been made to modernise the towing vehicle used in the Territorial Army, resulting in a very rugged and useful descendant of the original 6-wheelers – the Morris-Commercial 6 × 4 'CDSW'. This vehicle began to reach Territorial batteries early in 1939 but was quite quickly replaced by the Quad as units moved on to full war establishment in 1940–41. Cars, 2- and 4-seater, never very satisfactory in a front-line military role, also began to be replaced by a new range of 8-cwt. and 15-cwt. vehicles in 1938–39. Supply to the Territorial Army was, however, very restricted and units mobilised with more than half their vehicles requisitioned from civilian sources. Fortunately, though, the decisions on some basically sound designs had been made, and production facilities laid down, before the outbreak of war.

Wireless signalling was still in its infancy as far as field artillery was concerned in 1938–39 and sets had not been issued to the Territorial Army. Nevertheless No.1 and No.11 sets were available for annual training in 1939 and early faltering steps were made to introduce what was to become a crucial feature of field artillery in its war role. In particular, the systems and skills of operating more than two stations on one frequency, forming a 'net', that by 1943–44 were taken for granted, had not been developed. In the early stages, field artillery radio links merely replaced the bilateral links provided hitherto by flag, lamp, heliograph or line and, indeed, units mobilised more ready to signal with these obsolescent means than with wireless.

Plate 21 *The first 'real' 25-pdr. – 'Ordnance Q.F. 25-pdr. Mk. II on Carriage, 25-pdr. Mk. I' – on its firing platform* (seen carried on top of the limber in Plates 20 and 22). *The 25-pdr. had four different charges and a maximum range, with Charge Super, of 13,400 yards.* (I.W.M. – MH 12938–40)

Plate 22 *One of the great institutions of the Second World War – the 'Quad, limber and 25-pdr.' The original Quad, shown here, was built by Morris-Commercial, but similar vehicles were also built in Canada by Chevrolet and Ford.* (I.W.M. – H 8241)

*Developments during the War, 1940–1945*

Early experience in action, particularly in North Africa, and trials and exercises at home showed that the three-troop battery was unwieldy and did not provide the means of bringing sufficient guns to bear swiftly on a single target. Further, the fact that one troop was on a lower establishment of vehicles and technical assistants and signallers meant that the third troop commander was prevented from functioning as a full O.P. and virtually relegated to reserve. A new organisation of 8-gun batteries, each divided into two troops and grouped in regiments of three batteries (so that a lieutenant-colonel's command was still 24 guns), was provisionally adopted in the autumn of 1940 and confirmed in March 1941. It proved to have all the expected advantages over the previous organisation. The fire of both troops in a battery could easily and swiftly be brought down on a single target and, if eight guns were insufficient, regimental survey and communications now put three batteries at the disposal of O.Ps. with very little more difficulty or delay. Three batteries was also a convenient number, because the armoured or infantry brigades to which regiments were deployed in direct support generally consisted of three units, and batteries could be affiliated to each unit in training and placed in direct support on operations. Within the two-troop battery, each troop commander was fully established with an O.P. party and with an armoured vehicle (a tracked carrier or tank depending on the role of the supported unit) – a big advance on the earlier vehicle establishment which had provided only one carrier in each battery. Field regiments had at last reached the point where they were more than the old horsed field brigades on wheels. True mobility, in the sense of swiftness of reaction, as well as better cross-country movement, had been achieved.

Partly as a result of two years' experience of war, and partly due to the changes in battery organisation, deployment drills had evolved considerably from those briefly described above, which had held good for some twenty years. The battery commander now always deployed to the tactical headquarters of the infantry battalion or armoured regiment which the battery was supporting. The two troop commanders would normally join the forward companies or squadrons but their attachment depended on the tactical situation and would be decided between the battalion commander and his artillery adviser, the B.C. If required, a third O.P. or F.O.O. could be found from the gun position for relatively short periods.

At the gun end, the second-in-command of the regiment would allocate an area to the senior subaltern, or command post officer (C.P.O.) of each battery. The C.P.O. would recce the area with a view to siting the two 4-gun troops of his battery and his own battery command post. The troop G.P.O.s would do their own recces, selecting individual gun platforms, which were no longer in a straight line. To improve survival against air attack or counter-battery fire, the guns were staggered and the troop frontage increased from eighty yards to 100–120 yards. The stagger had the added advantage of giving some depth to the fall of shot. The track plan for vehicles entering and moving round the gun position was important in contributing to an overall camouflage and concealment plan, and it, too, would have to be worked out during the recce, as would a plan for the local defence of the troop position. Local defence of the bat-

Plate 23 *The 18-pdr. Mk. II on Carriage Mk. II PA – a 'pneumatised' version of the 18-pdr. using United States-manufactured axle and wheels. After service with field regiments in Britain until replaced by the 25-pdr., this gun remained in use for training well into 1944.*
(I.W.M. – MH 12892)

Plate 24 *The 4.5-in. howitzer on Mk. I carriage after conversion by the substitution of United States-manufactured pneumatic-tyred wheels for the original iron-tyred, spoked wheels. This carriage was known as 'Mk. I PA'.* (Compare with Plate 14) (I.W.M. – MH 12780)

tery area was co-ordinated by the C.P.O. and relied not only on the guns themselves, which now had armour-piercing solid shot for use against tanks, but on a generous issue of Bren light machine-guns, as well as each man's personal weapon – rifle or sub-machine-gun.

On arrival at the troop position, led by the troop leader but guided on to their platforms by the troop sergeant-major, who had taken part in the recce, the guns came into action and were at once placed in the zero line – a bearing calculated to go through the centre of the area in which targets were likely to occur – by the troop director. By this time, the troop director was usually in sympathy with the battery director, which would have passed 'battery line' to each troop. 'Regimental line', which would place all three batteries of the regiment in sympathy, would next be passed to the battery director and onwards to troop directors and to the guns, then divisional line, and so on. Meanwhile, the troop G.P.Os. would have worked out the grid reference of their troop centre, using the relatively primitive survey methods of compass, calibrated pace, and elementary map-reading skills. Once the troop position was known and troop line passed, the troop was able to report to its O.P. that it was ready to fire on 'troop grid'. More sophisticated survey, first by the C.P.O., then by the regimental survey party would improve the state of survey, first to battery grid, which, with battery line, enabled the two troops to shoot fully in sympathy, then regimental grid, and so on, up to theatre grid, which would ensure that the artillery of neighbouring divisions would be able to shoot together. Fire orders for 'troop targets' would reach the troops directly from their own troop commander, by wireless over the battery net or by line. 'Battery targets' would also be called for on the battery net and could thus be heard by the two troops. Regimental (or Mike) and higher targets (Division = Uncle; Corps = Victor; Army = William)were ordered through the regimental wireless net, which extended only to battery command posts, and so had to be passed on to the troops by telephone.

The 'echelon' system of describing the role of the various components of a fighting unit came into use during the Second World War and needs explanation here. The Fighting (or 'F') Echelon comprised all those immediately concerned with carrying the fight to the enemy. In a field battery, F Echelon was further sub-divided for tactical movement into 'groups'. The Recce Group comprised the B.C., B.K. and C.P.O., i.e., all those necessary for establishing the outline of the battery position and wagon lines and who needed to be first on the scene in order to carry out reconnaissance, select areas and pass on orders to the follow-up groups. The H.Q. Group was divided into two parties – the 'O' Party consisting of the O.P. officers, whose place in action was with the supported unit, and the 'G' Party, made up of the G.P.Os. and

Plate 25 *The 'famous French 75-mm. Gun'. The 75-mm. guns used in Britain had originally been supplied to the United States Army, which knew the 'pneumatised' version as '75-mm. Gun M1897 on Carriage M1897 A4'. The sighting system was very complicated compared with that of the 18-pdr. or 25-pdr.; maximum range and weight of shell were comparable to the 18-pdr. Mk. IV.*
(I.W.M. – MH 12944–5)

Plate 26 *An O.P. party from a field regiment on exercise in south-east England, June 1942. The O.P. officer's assistant, or 'ack'* (Background, left) *studies the map, while the troop commander* (Centre) *and his signaller are apparently struggling to get through on the wireless – probably on the set in their vehicle, which has a 'remote' headset in the O.P., rather than the No. 18 manpack set* (Foreground, right).
(I.W.M. – H 20996)

Plate 27 *The 'Bishop' self-propelled 25-pdr. The 25-pdr. and its recoil system were mounted in a primitive armoured box on top of a Valentine tank. Restricted elevation limited the range of the gun to 6,400 yards.* (I.W.M. – MH 4356)

other personnel involved in the detailed preparation of the troop gun positions. The guns of each troop, under the command of their troop leaders (T.Ls.), the section ammunition vehicles, the battery command post and signals vehicles not required during the reconnaissance formed the Gun Group. The fourth group – the Ammunition Group – is formally described in pamphlets but was at least as much part of 'A' Echelon – the muster of ammunition and fuel resupply vehicles, often under regimental control, which worked between regimental ammunition and fuel points and the batteries in action. The 'administrative tail' or 'B' Echelon under the battery quartermaster-sergeant was normally grouped with the other batteries' B Echelons in an area under the command of the quartermaster.

The remaining important step in the development of field artillery tactics, organisation and equipment was the move towards self-propelled artillery. Early trials with self-propelled 18-pdr. guns had not resulted in their adoption in the British Army, largely owing to the financial stringency of the inter-war years. Now, experience in action re-awakened the idea and the primitive 25-pdr. Mk. II on Carrier, Valentine, 25-pdr., or 'Bishop', was produced, principally for use in North Africa, in 1942. By the opening of the campaign in North-West Europe in June 1944, self-propelled artillery was generally available for the support of armoured formations, and more units were held at higher levels (Corps or Army) for assignment as needed. The principles and tactics were hardly different from towed field artillery but there were important differences in equipment which recognised the need for cross-country mobility and armoured protection. Not only were the guns themselves on tracked armoured vehicles, but forward observer parties had enhanced scales of vehicles depending on the regiment's role, and command posts, and some line-signalling and first-line ammunition vehicles were also tracked and armoured.

Plate 28 *The U.S. '105-mm. Howitzer Motor Carriage M7', known in the British Army as 'Priest'. The gun, which fired a 33-pound shell to a maximum range of 12,200 yards, was mounted on a modified Medium Tank M3 (Lee/Grant).* (I.W.M. – STT 5230)

Plate 29 *The principal armoured vehicles used by self-propelled field regiments in North-West Europe.*
Top – *The 'Sexton' self-propelled 25-pdr. The Mk. II or III 25-pdr. barrel on a modified recoil system was mounted on a Canadian-built chassis, based on components of the 'Ram' tank – the Canadian equivalent of the U.S. M3 (Lee/Grant), which was later developed towards the standard of the M4 (Sherman). Maximum range was similar to the towed 25-pdr.*
(I.W.M. – MH 4130)
Centre – *The Sherman O.P./C.P. tank – a standard M4 Sherman with the gun removed and replaced by a dummy to allow extra radios to be installed.*
(I.W.M. – B 7424)
Bottom – *The U.S.-built M14 half-track. Half-tracks were first issued to self-propelled artillery units as section ammunition vehicles but as supplies increased the establishment was changed to provide for their use as command posts and recce vehicles.*
(Regimental Collection)

Plate 30 *Two Jeeps of 86th Field Regiment – the Medical Officer's* (leading) *and the Signals Officer's – negotiating floods at Kranenburg, just across the Dutch–German border, February 1945. The Jeep, officially known as 'Car, 5-cwt., 4 × 4' was imported from the United States or built in Britain to U.S. specification and was used throughout the British Army, replacing the 8-cwt. 4 × 2* (Plate 19) *in a variety of command and reconnaissance roles in units of the Royal Artillery.* (I.W.M. – B 14536)

In self-propelled regiments, the Bishop was phased out in favour of the Canadian-built 'Sexton' – a 25-pdr. mounted on a modified Ram tank chassis – and the American 'Priest' – a 105-mm. howitzer on M3 medium tank chassis. (Self-propelled guns in British service have generally been named after office-holders in the Church.) Forward observers graduated from the Covenanter tank, used only in training, to the Crusader, which was replaced shortly before the landings in Normandy by the Sherman, the O.P. version of which had its main armament removed to make room for extra radio equipment and a plotting table. When operating with units that were not equipped with the Sherman, forward observation officers were usually able to draw appropriate tanks – frequently Churchills – for temporary use. Troop vehicle establishments were often augmented locally to provide a tracked carrier (Carrier, Armoured Observation Post in theory but sometimes Carrier, Universal in practice) for use when supporting infantry. The remaining high-mobility, partially armoured vehicle was the American M14 half-track, originally issued as a section ammunition vehicle, then for command post and signals use.

The introduction of the Car, 5-cwt., 4 × 4 or 'Jeep' from 1942 was a further major feature in promoting mobility. In towed as well as self-propelled regiments, it was invaluable as a replacement for civilian pattern cars, light utility vehicles and the 8-cwt. truck (which had never had 4-wheel drive). Load-carrying vehicles improved considerably as the war pro-



Plate 31 *Two of the workhorses of the later war years – the Truck, 3-ton, 4 × 4, G.S., Bedford QL* (Left) *and the Truck, 3-ton, 4 × 4, G.S., Austin K5* (Right). *These trucks and a similar 3-ton built by Fordson were widely used in ammunition- and cargo-carrying roles throughout the Royal Artillery.* (I.W.M. – KID 3037/1427)

Plate 32 *An artillery surveyor using a director, 1938. Superficially similar to a theodolite, the director incorporated a magnetic compass and was capable of measuring horizontal as well as vertical angles. Once aligned towards north, either by its own compass, or by means of an angle passed by another director or measured from a surveyed reference object, a system of fixed and sliding scales enabled angles to be passed to the dial sight of a gun, which could in turn be aligned in any chosen direction. The colour of the fabric 'skirt' on the director tripod indicated the battery within the regiment.* (I.W.M. – 17/29)

gressed, culminating, as far as field regiments were concerned, with the introduction of the Truck, 3-ton, 4 × 4, G.S. in good time for the campaign in North-West Europe. Field regiments made no use of the various special purpose bodies that were supplied on 15-cwt. and 3-ton chassis, other than the Truck, 15-cwt., 4 × 2, Water Tank. Trailers were issued for 3-ton vehicles (Trailer, 1-ton) and 15-cwt. trucks and Jeeps (Trailer, 5-cwt.). They were extensively used in 'B' Echelons, and used, though not always enthusiastically, by command posts, T.S.Ms., etc., in the 'F' Echelon.

On the signals side, wireless was increasingly used as the No.19 set became available and scales of issue were increased. An important development was the system of 'rebroadcasting' from a manpack set carried by a forward observer party, through a receiving station in their vehicle and then automatically into the battery or regimental net. This freed the observers from any reliance on line during an advance and enabled them to be constantly available to the commander of the supported arm and constantly in touch with either troops or batteries to pass back not only calls for fire but the situation and intelligence reports which became such a feature of Gunner nets and upon which commanders came to rely. Despite the advances in wireless communication, line remained a vital link. It was laid between O.P. and gun position in all but the fastest moving situations and within the regimental area provided the all-important links between troop, battery and regimental command posts. Alongside these advances, the historic methods of flag, lamp and heliograph – the latter never particularly well suited to operations in North-West Europe – died hard and, indeed, came back into their own from time
[28] to time in such difficult theatres as Burma and Malaya.

**SECRET**

5 Feb.45.

# OPERATION "VERITABLE"

## R.A. 30 CORPS FIRE PLAN : BARRAGE

Ref. Maps. Holland 1:25.000. Sheets 12N.W.(East). 4102. 4202.

Issued in conjunction with Task Tables 33a, 33b, 33c.

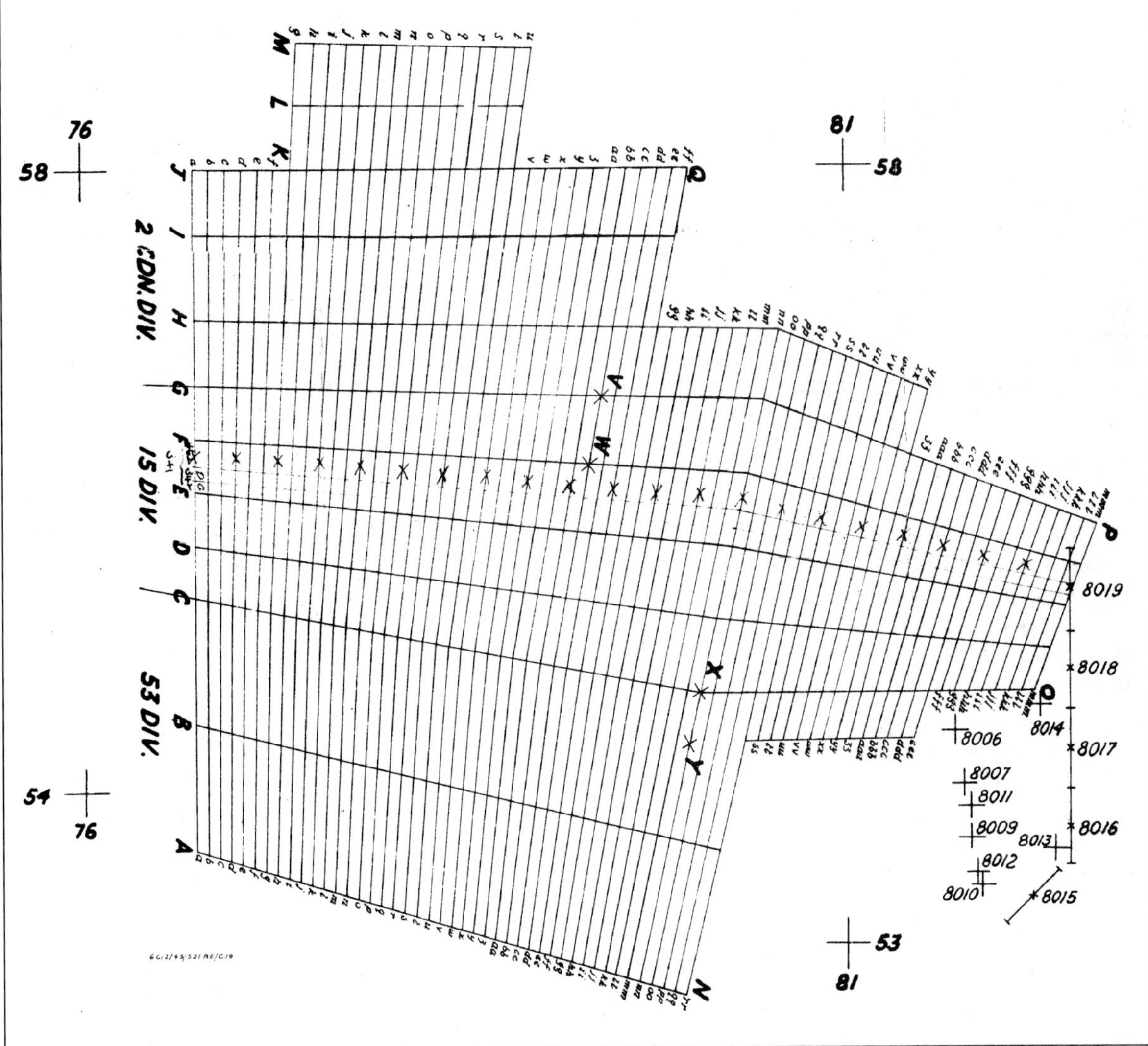


Plate 33 *Barrage trace for Operation 'Veritable', 8th February 1945* (see page 132). *The arrival of orders for the artillery support of a major operation such as 'Veritable', which frequently included a barrage, presaged intense activity at all levels in the regiment. In battery and troop command posts, usually in cramped conditions and in poor light, officers and 'acks' had first to calculate 'map data' for each line of the barrage after pinning to their artillery boards a trace, drawn at 1:25,000 scale, which was received from the headquarters controlling the operation – in this case H.Q.R.A.. XXX Corps. Additional corrections for atmospheric conditions and to take account of the 'displacement' of guns from the troop centre were effected and the resulting 'gun data' transferred to printed 'task tables' for issue to individual guns. This trace was issued to 342 Battery, who fired on the right-hand half of the regimental lane. The left-hand lane was covered by 462 Battery, while 341 Battery's fire was 'superimposed' across both halves.* (Regimental Collection)

Plate 34 *Lieutenant-Colonel Geoffrey Lawrence, D.S.O., who was appointed to command 3rd East Anglian Brigade, R.F.A. (later 86th Brigade) in February 1920 and held command until March 1926. His four years in command of A Battery, 270th Brigade, R.F.A. in Egypt and Palestine would have been invaluable in enabling him to choose experienced field artillery officers as the brigade formed, and to lay down sound, and successful, principles for training and administration.* (Photograph, in the Regimental Collection, of the oil painting by Sir William Orpen)

# Chapter 3

# *Between the Wars, 1920–1939*

*The Hertfordshire Batteries re-formed, 1920*

In the two preceeding volumes the return of the Hertfordshire Yeomanry from Egypt and India, and of 270th Brigade, R.F.A. (originally 4th East Anglian Brigade) from Egypt, was recorded. It was without ceremony or celebration, as the squadrons and batteries had been run down by demobilisation abroad and only cadres, consisting, in the case of 4th East Anglian Brigade's Peterborough Battery, for example, of "two men and a stationery box, commanded by a Canadian officer who had never served in the battery", returned to home stations. Unsurprisingly, those released from active service gave little thought to the reconstitution of their units as they struggled to return to civilian life. In Whitehall, however, plans for a new Territorial Army were being made even as the troops returned. The first of three conferences between the War Office, headed by the Secretary of State for War, Winston Churchill, and representatives of the Territorial Associations took place on 1st April 1919. Others followed on 1st May 1919 and 30th January 1920.[1] The President of Hertfordshire Territorial Association, Brigadier-General Viscount Hampden and the Chairman, Lieutenant-Colonel The Rt. Hon. T. F. Halsey attended all three conferences and the Association took action as necessary as the future of the force gradually became clear. On learning at the first meeting with the Secretary of State that a War Office Board was to visit each command in order to select future commanding officers of Territorial units, Hertfordshire Association appointed a sub-committee on 9th April 1919 to deal with the board but there is no evidence of further action until the Association meeting of 29th September. It was then reported that the G.O.C. East Anglian Division had been appointed and that Major J. H. Drake, O.B.E., M.C. and Major Geoffrey Lawrence, D.S.O. were recognised as the 'interim' commanding officers of the Hertfordshire Yeomanry and 4th East Anglian Brigade, R.F.A., respectively. The Association resolved to recommend Major Lawrence for command of 4th East Anglian Brigade on re-raising but concluded that no decision could yet be made on a future commanding officer for the Yeomanry. At the third War Office conference, on 30th January 1920, it was announced that recruiting for the reconstituted Territorial Force, to be called the Territorial Army, would begin on 16th February and, indeed, instructions to this effect reached Hertfordshire Territorial Association, who decided that no action could be taken until the future of the Hertfordshire Yeomanry was known.

The future of the Yeomanry and the Royal Field Artillery of the county were, in fact, inextricably linked. The Secretary of State had announced on 30th January that only a small number of the existing 55 regiments of Yeomanry – it turned out to be sixteen – would be retained in their traditional mounted role. The remainder would be required to re-form as armoured car units of the Royal Tank Corps or in the Royal Field Artillery. A conference under the chairmanship of Major-General Sir Charles Harrington, Deputy Chief of the Imperial General Staff, would assemble at once to consider how, "with the least inconvenience and the greatest advantage, the necessary duties [*could*] be divided up". It had already been made clear that Territorial brigades of the Royal Field Artillery would follow, but with a reduced peace establishment, the new four-battery organisation for divisional artillery, though non-divisional (i.e., 'Army') brigades could consist of only two batteries. Clearly, therefore, Hertfordshire was going to have to move fast to assure one further major unit, in addition to the infantry of the Hertfordshire Regiment, within the county, and the threat of cross-border amalgamation was considerable.

It was perhaps predictable that, following Sir Charles Harrington's meeting, which was held

Plate 35 *Members of B Sub-Section, 342 Battery with their Mk. II 18-pdr. gun on Mk. II carriage (identifiable by the pole trail, on which the sub-section's designation is painted), probably 1921. The gun may recently have required attention from the battery's gun fitter* (second from left); *artificers and gun fitters were 'badged R.A.' and full members of the battery until many were transferred to the Royal Electrical and Mechanical Engineers in 1942.*
(Regimental Collection)

on 4th February, Hertfordshire Territorial Association would start by "strongly disapproving" of the scheme "for the drastic reduction of the Yeomanry . . . and the consequent loss of traditions and esprit de corps" and a resolution to this effect, urging the government to allow the Association to continue to raise the Hertfordshire Yeomanry was passed at an Association meeting on 6th February and given wide publicity. More pragmatically, however, a meeting of officers of the Hertfordshire Yeomanry was called for 1st March "on the subject of the future of the regiment". It was subsequently postponed to 19th March when the points for discussion were:

"1. The possibility of re-forming the Hertfordshire Yeomanry as suggested by the Secretary of State for War.

2. Taking into consideration the fact that under the conditions published in the Daily Press the regiment, if re-formed, will be liable in two years' time, if not sooner, to be changed into another Branch of the Service, whether it would not be better to come into line at once with the wishes of the General Staff and form with the two Hertfordshire Batteries of the late 4th East Anglian Brigade, R.F.A. one complete brigade of the Royal Field Artillery to bear the name of the county: the title of 'Yeomanry' to be borne by at least two batteries of the brigade."

At the next meeting of Hertfordshire Territorial Association, held on 12th April, it was reported that the conference of Yeomanry officers had unanimously agreed that it would be better to proceed at once with the raising of a complete (i.e., four-battery) field artillery brigade from the Yeomanry and the two Hertfordshire batteries, and that application to the War Office for authority to do so had been made as early as 20th March – the day following the conference. The application included a request that the name of the county should be included in the title of the new unit and that the traditions of the Yeomanry should be carried on by the use of the title 'Yeomanry' in some form or other. By this means a whole unit (i.e., a lieutenant-colonel's command) would be retained in Hertfordshire in defiance of two proposals that would have meant sharing a unit with another county. One, said to have been favoured by the War Office, would have resulted in a four-battery Army field brigade with two batteries from the Hertfordshire Yeomanry and two from the Bedfordshire Yeomanry. The other would have kept the Hertfordshire batteries in the East Anglian Divisional Artillery but in a brigade that would have had headquarters and two batteries in Hertfordshire and two batteries (originally forming 3rd East Anglian Brigade) in Suffolk. The fate of the Herts Yeomanry under the second proposal was not disclosed.

By 14th June 1920, the date of the Association's next meeting, it was known that before the end of March the War Office had approved the application for a complete divisional artillery brigade to be raised in Hertfordshire. Major Geoffrey Lawrence was recommended for command and his appointment, and promotion to lieutenant-colonel, had been gazetted on 1st April, with an effective date of 16th February – the date on which recruiting for the reconsti-

Plate 36 *Another sub-section of 342 Battery, with a Mk. IV 18-pdr. gun on Mk. III box-trail carriage, probably 1921. The box trail permitted much greater elevation than the pole trail and hence a maximum range of 9,300 yards, rather than 6,525 yards. By 1927, at the latest, all pole-trail guns had been withdrawn from 86th Brigade and replaced by box-trail. The split-trail Mk.V carriage was never used by the brigade.* (Regimental Collection)

tuted Territorial Army had started. Under the revised order of battle for a Territorial infantry division, the divisional artillery comprised only three four-battery brigades, compared with the four brigades of the pre-war order of battle. In the East Anglian Division, which retained the designation 54th, under which it had fought throughout the war, 1st and 2nd East Anglian Brigades, from Norfolk and Essex respectively, were reorganised to the four-battery establishment and retained. The old divisional howitzer brigade, 3rd East Anglian, from Suffolk, became a two-battery army field brigade. The vacant designation '3rd East Anglian' was then allocated, provisionally, as things turned out, to the new brigade raised in Hertfordshire from the Hertfordshire Yeomanry and 1st and 2nd Hertfordshire Batteries. Accordingly, it was to command of 3rd East Anglian Brigade, R.F.A. that Lieutenant-Colonel Lawrence was appointed.

It was at first thought that two of the batteries of 3rd East Anglian Brigade would carry on the traditions of the Hertfordshire Yeomanry, and at their meeting on 14th June 1920 it was reported to Hertfordshire Territorial Association that the stations of the batteries and their provisional titles had been approved as follows:

| | |
|---|---|
| 1st Hertfordshire Battery | St. Albans |
| 2nd Hertfordshire (Yeomanry) Battery | Hertford |
| 3rd Hertfordshire Battery | Watford |
| 4th Hertfordshire (Yeomanry) Battery | North Herts |

The decision was quickly made that 4th Herts Battery would be centred on Hitchin and two officers of the Hertfordshire Yeomanry joined the brigade on 6th July 1920 – Major Reginald Halsey to command 2nd Herts Battery and Major Barré A. H. Goldie to command 4th Herts. The Yeomanry were further represented in the new brigade by Lieutenants S. C. Albany and R. G. Harradence, both of Ware, who had served in the ranks and been commissioned into the regiment during the war, and later by Lieutenant G. W. Dixon, who would have been well placed to carry on the traditions of both predecessor units, having served in the ranks of the Hertfordshire Yeomanry before being commissioned in 4th East Anglian Brigade. There is, unfortunately, no record of how many former non-commissioned officers and men of the Hertfordshire Yeomanry joined the new brigade. Some fifty years after the amalgamation of the Hertfordshire Yeomanry and 4th East Anglian Brigade, Colonel Geoffrey Lawrence, by then Lord Oaksey, confided to the regimental historian that uppermost in his mind as he selected officers for 3rd East Anglian Brigade had been the intention that the brigade should place the highest priority on developing and maintaining the skills of gunnery. (This far-sighted view contrasted with the way some field artillery brigades were more concerned with the horse, the demise of which was predictable throughout the Regular and Territorial Armies, than the gun.) Accordingly, Colonel Lawrence was careful to select two experienced Field Gunners as the battery captains of the Yeomanry batteries – Captain E. J. T. Lutyens, formerly of 1st Herts Battery, who now joined 2nd Herts, and Captain W. R. D. Robertson, M.C. who joined 4th Herts. Command of 3rd Herts Battery went to Major J. M. Currie, who had been commissioned in 4th East Anglian Brigade but spent most of the war in 'extra-regimental

Plate 37 *Annual camp at Shorncliffe, Kent, September 1921.* Left – *General view of the camp.* Right – *Other ranks of 343 Battery relaxing in their dining area.* (Regimental Collection)

employment' and had commanded a battery in France. Major Currie rejoined in November 1920 but it was to be several more months before Major G. S. Church, M.C., who had not previously served with either unit, arrived to command the St. Albans battery.

Meanwhile, instructions had been issued on 1st September 1920 that Territorial field artillery brigades and their constituent batteries were to be renumbered "with a view to preventing confusion from the duplication of numbers".[2] The divisional artillery of 54th (East Anglian) Division was allocated 84th–86th for its three brigades and 333–344 for their batteries. The provisionally-designated 3rd East Anglian Brigade accordingly became 86th Brigade, R.F.A. and the four batteries became 341, 342, 343 and 344 Batteries, R.F.A. The instructions provided for any additional designation of a brigade or battery to be placed in brackets immediately after the number but at this stage no such designations were approved for 86th Brigade or its batteries. However, the first indications that the whole brigade, rather than just 342 and 344 Batteries, might be seen to trace part of its ancestry to the Hertfordshire Yeomanry, appeared during the autumn of 1920, when Hertfordshire Territorial Association resolved to apply for the hart collar badge of the Yeomanry to be worn in khaki service dress – by officers in bronze on the shoulder strap and by other ranks in brass "on the upper arm" – apparently regardless of the battery to which officers or men belonged.

### *On horsed establishment, 1920–1926*

There was, as yet, no question of mechanisation of the Territorial field artillery and 86th Brigade was required to recruit to a peace establishment of 26 officers and five hundred other ranks.[3] Three of the batteries – 341, 342 and 343 – were armed with the 18-pdr. gun and one – 344 – with the 4.5.-in. howitzer, in accordance with the same establishment, which provided for only four guns to each battery, to be expanded to six on mobilisation. Recruiting for 86th Brigade had actually started early in June 1920 and was at first very disappointing – a strength of only four officers and eighty men was reported to the September meeting of Hertfordshire Territorial Association – but it picked up considerably in the autumn and an end-year strength of twelve officers and 312 other ranks was achieved. Horses were required too, of course, and Hertfordshire Territorial Association resolved in September to buy one riding horse and six light draught horses for each battery, at not more than £75 for riding horses and £80 for light draught, as soon as suitable custodians had been found. These, lent between batteries as necessary and supplemented by such horses as officers and men could themselves bring or borrow, would suffice for evening or week-end training; large numbers would have to be hired for annual camp. Six months later it was reported that the full complement of 28 horses had been bought and the Association Horse Committee (see *The Hertfordshire Batteries, R.F.A. – An Illustrated History*) resurrected.

The year 1921 brought the peculiar difficulty of the formation of the Defence Force, which was hastily raised against the possibility of widespread breakdown of public order. Units of the Defence Force were based on major units of the Territorial Army, and 86th Brigade R.F.A. (Defence Force) was raised for three months' full time service between April and July (see Appendix 4). As a result of transfers to the Defence Force, the strength of the Territorial brigade fell to two officers and 165 other ranks. Nevertheless, shortly after the stand-down of

Plate 38 *Gunner H. Edgar of 342 Battery shows off his 'horse, riding', at camp at Trawsfynydd, 1922. Bridle and head-collar, head-rope and saddle are all of War Department pattern.* (Regimental Collection)

the Defence Force 86th Brigade went to their first annual camp at Shorncliffe in Kent with a strength of fourteen officers and 361 other ranks, the full establishment of guns and wagons, and 221 horses, of which 27 were Association horses. The headline over a report of camp in the *Hertfordshire Mercury*, "A Jolly Time at Shorncliffe", belies the amount of serious training which took place, but correctly places some emphasis on the need for Territorials to enjoy camp. In this case excellent weather and a full programme of sport and off-duty entertainment helped balance the hard work. As the year ended, the brigade strength was returned as seventeen officers and 459 other ranks – a shortfall of nine officers and 41 against establishment – and Hertfordshire Territorial Association took up with the War Office the possibility that part of 342 Battery should be accommodated at Barnet, a southern extremity of the county that was well populated and had before the First World War been the headquarters of a squadron of the Hertfordshire Yeomanry.

The peace establishment of a Territorial field artillery brigade was reduced in March 1922 from 26 officers and five hundred other ranks to 22 officers and 418 other ranks.[4] The number of guns was unchanged at four to each battery but the considerable saving in man- and horse-power was achieved by reducing the number of first-line ammunition wagons in each battery to what might be described as the 'theoretical minimum' – one 4-horse wagon to each gun. While this may well have been adequate for the very limited amounts of ammunition used in peace-time training, it would certainly not have worked in war and the gap between the peace and war establishments which would have to have been made good on mobilisation was fur-



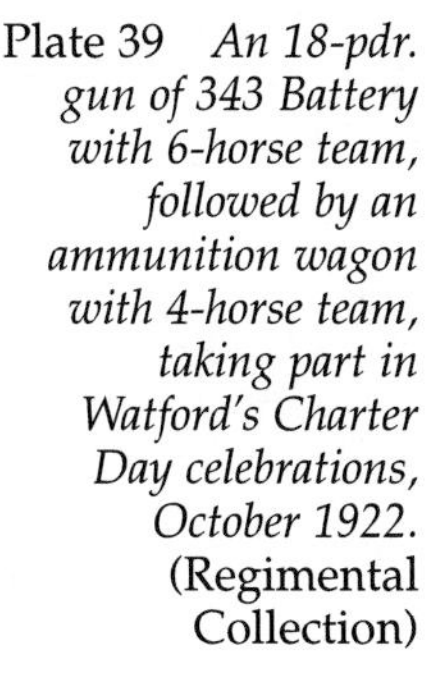

Plate 39 *An 18-pdr. gun of 343 Battery with 6-horse team, followed by an ammunition wagon with 4-horse team, taking part in Watford's Charter Day celebrations, October 1922.* (Regimental Collection)

Plate 40 Left –*The hart cap and collar badge worn by other ranks of the Hertfordshire Yeomanry between 1901 and 1920 that was authorised for wear on the service dress jacket by other ranks of 86th Brigade. It was originally worn on the shoulder strap but was moved to the collar in 1925. Gilding metal – actual size 1½ in × 1⅜ in.* Right – *The bronze-finish cap and collar badge worn by officers of the Hertfordshire Yeomanry between 1901 and 1920 that was authorised for wear on the service dress jacket by officers of 86th Brigade. It was worn below the rank badges on the shoulder strap and the bronze grenade badge was worn on the collar. Some officers of Hertfordshire Yeomanry units of the Royal Artillery managed to continue wearing their bronze harts throughout the war. Actual size 1⅝ in. × 1⅛ in.* (Regimental Collection)

ther widened. The reduction was probably welcome, though, in 86th Brigade, which on 1st March 1922 had a strength of fourteen officers and 458 other ranks, resulting in a shortfall of eight officers against the new establishment and an overbearing of forty other ranks, which was to be allowed to run off through 'natural wastage'. The new establishment was implemented in time for 86th Brigade's first firing camp, which was held at Trawsfynydd in North Wales in June 1922. Again, the *Hertfordshire Mercury* emphasised the holiday aspect of camp, even headlining its report of the second week "Herts R.F.A. in Camp – An Enjoyable Holiday", but the reports did also dwell on the excellence of the shooting – "especially at the moving tank" – and commented on the high standards in the gun-laying and turn-out competitions. Association horses were particularly well thought of and brought due credit to their 'custodians' as well as to those riding them at camp. After describing the batteries' homeward journey by overnight train the report concluded with the statement that "the men detrained guns and horses and proceeded home, having spent a very enjoyable fortnight's holiday, coupled with good soldiering". The report on the brigade by C.R.A. 54th Division was excellent and showed what a sound foundation Lieutenant-Colonel Geoffrey Lawrence had laid by his careful selection of officers and attention to gunnery skills.

Two Army Orders issued in December 1922 promulgated at last the titles and designations of units of the Territorial Army, the allotment of units to counties and the order of battle.[5] Thus, after nearly three years of provisional titles, it was confirmed that 86th Brigade was indeed the lineal descendant of the Hertfordshire Yeomanry and Headquarters 4th East Anglian Brigade, R.F.A., 1st and 2nd Hertfordshire Batteries and two sections of 4th East Anglian Brigade Ammunition Column. The full title of the brigade was to be 86th (East Anglian) (Hertfordshire Yeomanry) Brigade, Royal Field Artillery, properly reflecting both predecessor units. The batteries would each take the bracketed designation 'Hertfordshire' without any reference to the Yeomanry. Finally, in common with all brigades and batteries with Yeomanry forebears, the other ranks of 86th Brigade would wear the brass shoulder titles 'Y. – R.F.A.' in khaki service dress, rather than 'T. – R.F.A.' as worn by units of 'pure Gunner' descent. This last order gave rise to an almost immediate change of shoulder title in 86th Brigade, who had been wearing 'T. – R.F.A.' since formation in 1920. The Northamptonshire Battery of 4th East Anglian Brigade, together with one section of the brigade ammunition column joined the reconstituted Territorial Army as the howitzer battery of 84th Brigade, originally 1st East Anglian Brigade. It was still based at Peterborough, while the other three batteries of the brigade were recruited in Norfolk, and its title was now confirmed as 336 (Northamptonshire) Battery, R.F.A.

Plate 41 *The other ranks' shoulder titles 'Y.' and 'R.A.' in gilding metal which replaced the 'Y.' and 'R.F.A.' authorised by Army Order 481 of 1922, following the amalgamation of the Royal Field Artillery and the Royal Garrison Artillery to form the Royal Artillery in 1924. The 'Y. – R.A.' title was worn until after mobilisation in 1939.* (Regimental Collection)

The convention, which soon attained the status of a rule, that Territorial artillery units would fire live ammunition at camp only every second year had evidently not started to operate by 1923, since 86th Brigade went to Salisbury Plain in August. The *Hertfordshire Mercury's* reports, perhaps by a different correspondent, placed rather more emphasis on the "strenuous life essential to the training of the artilleryman" and the fact that "the men stood the strain well, although some of the younger personnel of the brigade confessed to a feeling of tiredness in some cases after such a long day in the saddle" – the latter after a day which had begun at 04.30 a.m. and continued well after the return to camp at 5.00 p.m. All the hard work was worth while, however, for at the October meeting of Hertfordshire Territorial Association it was reported that a letter had been received from G.O.C. 54th Division congratulating the Association on the achievements of the brigade, which was "among the few units in the division that was up-to-strength and second to none in efficiency". The G.O.C.'s remarks were borne out by the fact that 344 Battery had been selected from the Salisbury Plain 'pool' to go forward to the final of the King's Cup competition and had taken third place, while 342, 341 and 343 Batteries, in that order, had taken 1st, 2nd and 3rd prizes for batteries practising on 

Plate 42 *Major E.J.T. Lutyens at the head of the four guns of 342 Battery, probably 1923. Territorial batteries maintained a peace establishment of four guns (compared with a war establishment of six guns) until reorganisation late in 1938. Note the battery commander's trumpeter, standing to the right* (as seen) *of the battery commander, and the two section commanders* (in light coloured breeches). (Regimental Collection)

Plate 43 *Gunner W.T. Norris, 343 Battery, with a riding horse at camp, 1923 or 1924. He is wearing the shoulder titles 'Y.– R.F.A'. surmounted by the hart badge, which was moved to the collar in 1925.* (Regimental Collection)

Salisbury Plain but not reaching the final. At the same meeting Colonel Lawrence reported that 285 horses had been available for camp – 27 Association horses, three belonging to officers and the rest hired. While the hired horses had been distinctly better than those provided in 1921 and 1922, they were still not entirely satisfactory. They had evidently found the work a great strain and nine had died or had to be destroyed as a result of accidents. The Association accordingly resolved that "taking into consideration the fact that the stamp of the horses available on hire was not entirely satisfactory for horsing guns and wagons, the secretary should be authorised to purchase ten more light draught horses . . ."

Lieutenant-Colonel Geoffrey Lawrence was asked by Hertfordshire Territorial Association to extend his tour in command of 86th Brigade (from 1st January 1924 86th Field Brigade, Royal Artillery) for a further two years, to finish at the end of March 1926, and agreed to do so. He was, accordingly, in command at two further camps, in 1924 and 1925. That for 1924 was held at Hatfield Park and was marked by the attendance of a strong team of officers and non-commissioned officers who were attached from 86th Field Brigade's affiliated Regular unit, 17th Field Brigade, R.A. and from the Army School of Equitation at Weedon. The fortnight spanned the Whitsun week-end and a large number of visitors were able to attend the open-air service on Whit Sunday and the brigade sports and turn-out competitions, which took place during the following week. Unusually, the sports afternoon concluded with a musical drive by a gun team from each battery, which ended with "a spectacular repulse of a cavalry attack". No doubt the visiting instructors had been hard at work!

An inspection report presented to Hertfordshire Territorial Association in November 1924 recorded that a high standard of general efficiency had been reached in 86th Field Brigade but also noted that, while the state of clothing and personal equipment was satisfactory, "the varied patterns of jackets and caps issued militate against the general smartness of the turnout".

 This comment should have struck home within the Hertfordshire Association, for they were

Plate 44 *A smartly turned-out 18-pdr. of 342 Battery in the drill-hall yard at Hertford. The lead driver is wearing the hart badge on the collar, indicating that the photograph was taken between 1925 (when the badge was moved to the collar) and 1929 (after which gun draught was fully mechanised).* (Regimental Collection)

PLATE I Annual camp at Hatfield, 1924 – The competition for best turned-out gun and team
*(From the water-colour specially painted for this work by Joan Wanklyn, 1999)*

Annual camp in 1924 was a non-firing camp held in Hatfield Park during the fortnight which included the Whitsun bank-holiday week-end. It is apparent from press reports that great effort went into the brigade sports and turn-out competitions and that large numbers of visitors attended. The scene in the arena includes the winners of the best turned-out gun and team competition – a 4.5-in. howitzer from 344 Battery at Hitchin – whose No.1 (centre) is shown receiving the trophy. The runners-up, with an 18-pdr. gun and team, stand to the left of the winners, while a horse-holder waits with the battery commander's horse in the right foreground.

This plate has generously been sponsored by McMullen and Sons Limited, supporters of Volunteers and Territorials in Hertfordshire for well over a century.

Plate 45 *The officers of 344 Battery in blue undress uniform c.1925.* Seated (L.–R.) *Captain W.R.D. Robertson, M.C., Major B.A.H. Goldie, Lieutenant T.L.L. Green;* Standing (L.–R.) *Lieutenant M.A.U. Heathcote, Lieutenant C.F.W. Banham. Note the shoulder chains and hart collar badge on what was otherwise an orthodox pattern of Royal Artillery officers' uniform.* (Regimental Collection)

responsible for contracting with approved suppliers for the provision of uniforms and would have been solely responsible for such mis-matches as had caught the inspectors' eyes. Whether steps were taken to correct matters over succeeding years is, unfortunately, not on record. The same report also noted that the brigade had on charge six 18-pdr. Mk. II guns and two Mk. I 4.5-in. howitzers, all with ammunition wagons. There is no reason to doubt that the batteries each had their full complement of four guns, so it may be assumed that comparison is being drawn here between holdings of the now-obsolete Mk. II 18-pdr. and the box-trail 18-pdr. Mk. IV on carriage Mk. III. Indeed, there may have been plans for replacement of pole-trail guns by box-trail, which could have begun as early as 1925 and was certainly complete by 1927, perhaps earlier. It is not possible to distinguish from the available photographs the minor variations in the 4.5-in. howitzer that may have led to the replacement of one gun by another. Essentially, the Mk. I howitzer on Mk. I carriage was used throughout the inter-war period.

Late in 1924 the neighbouring Essex Territorial Association raised for the first time the question of 'cross-border recruiting'. Essex had been tasked with forming some of the earliest anti-aircraft searchlight units and, noticing that there was an absence of any 'technical arm' of the Territorial Army in the eastern part of Hertfordshire, suggested that a section of 309 Anti-Aircraft Company, Royal Engineers should be based at Bishop's Stortford. The proposal met with outright refusal by Hertfordshire, who, strangely, showed more inclination to accept part of an Essex field artillery battery when the question was raised again the following year. In 1926, however, grudging acceptance was recorded that the Essex searchlight group should recruit from the 'skilled artisan classes' in the Bishop's Stortford area. Thereafter, the question of cross-border recruiting came to prominence from time to time, but it was not until the threat of air attack, and hence the need for anti-aircraft counter-measurers, were much more evident, in the late 1930s, that anything approaching co-operation was accorded to Essex.

As 1925 – the final year of Colonel Lawrence's command – began, 86th Field Brigade was for the first time noticeably under establishment, with a strength of eighteen officers and 360 other ranks. However, a very large proportion – eighteen officers and 339 other ranks – attended firing camp at Okehampton, Devon, during August. In the absence of Colonel Lawrence, who was abroad, Major Barré Goldie of 344 Battery was in command of the brigade during camp. (The establishment post of second-in-command of a field artillery brigade did not then exist.) The Okehampton camp was remarkable for the appearance on parade for the first time of the brigade band. Application had been made to Hertfordshire Territorial Association late in 1924 for funds to support a band, but without success. Nevertheless, a band was recruited at Hitchin, largely through the enthusiasm of Major Barré Goldie, and by August 1925 was evidently both large enough and sufficiently skilled to play at the open-air church parade and for the march-past which followed. An entry in the officers' mess orders book (see page 47) dated 31st July 1925 confirms that for the purposes of rations and discipline the band would be attached to 344 Battery and states that during camp all members of the

Plate 46 *'Watford Terriers' – 343 Battery's football team, 1925* (Regimental Collection)

band would receive training in stretcher duties, first aid and hygiene from the brigade medical officer. (By long-standing practice bandsmen acted as stretcher bearers on active service.) Late in 1925 Major Barré Goldie announced that the band would "shortly be supplied with blue uniforms", though it is not clear whether they were, in fact, issued. Griffith (see Bibliography), writing early in 1927, recorded that "despite the greatest difficulties, due to the fact that artillery units get no financial aid from Army Funds for the purpose, the brigade possesses a very flourishing band", and it is clear from press reports that the band, which throughout its existence was under the direction of Bandmaster W. Burch, continued at least until camp in 1927. Shortly thereafter the "difficulties" quoted by Griffith evidently overcame enthusiasm, for there are no further reports of the band.

An important change in uniform, the only authority for which is the officers' mess orders book, took place in August 1925. Brigade Orders dated 31st July and obviously looking forward to the beginning of camp on 8th August, included the following:

> "*Dress*
>
> Service Dress, Marching Order will be taken. Steel helmets will also be taken. Owing to complaints that the regimental badge (the hart) is liable to breakage when worn on the shoulder straps, it is now ruled that this badge be worn on the collar of the jacket as follows:- Badge horizontal and mid-way between top and bottom of the collar, nose of hart one inch from commencement of collar. The title (Y. with R.F.A. beneath) will continue to be worn on the shoulder strap."

It should be noted that since January 1924 the authorised shoulder title had been 'Y. – R.A.'. While it may have taken some time for stocks of the new titles to reach 86th Field Brigade, it is curious that the title should still appear in orders as 'Y. – R.F.A.'. The position of the officers' bronze hart badge was not changed.

In the autumn of 1925 authority was obtained for the opening of a detachment of 341 Battery at Harpenden. As a result, 86th Field Brigade attained its widest spread of coverage of the county through battery drill-halls and detachments. Only 342 Battery at Hertford was without outlying drill-stations, the attempt to 'colonise' Barnet having evidently failed or been abandoned. While Watford remained the principal station for 343 Battery, a detachment was maintained at Berkhamsted, and 344 Battery at Hitchin had detachments at Letchworth and Royston. The idea of convenience of attendance at a nearby drill-station did not persist for much longer, however. The Letchworth and Royston detachments were closed early in 1928 and the Berkhamsted and Harpenden detachments appear not to have lasted beyond the very early 1930s.

On 1st April 1926, Lieutenant-Colonel Barré Goldie took over command of 86th Field Brigade from Lieutenant-Colonel The Hon. Geoffrey Lawrence, who was promoted to colonel and joined 'Commands and Staff, Territorial Army' with the seniority – 16th February 1924 – that he would have had if he had not stayed on for a further two years with the brigade. The new commanding officer must have been disappointed at the run of events in his first few months in command.
 Annual camp, which had been planned for Shorncliffe, was cancelled, to the great disappoint-

Plate 47 *The officers of 86th Field Brigade at camp at Ashridge Park, July 1926.* Back row (L.–R.) – *2nd Lieuts. H.D. Barré Goldie, G. Keane, Lieuts. G.L. Guthrie, T.W.W. Gooderidge, N.B. Henderson, M.A. Unwin Heathcote, R.J. Norbury.* Centre row – *Captains G.N. Bushman, S.C. Albany, F.N. Richardson, Major A.L.P. Griffith (Adjutant), Captain T.L.L. Green, Lieut. H.W.O. Ellery, Lt.-Col. E.E. Charles (Herts T.A. Association).* Front row – *Majors W.R.D. Robertson, G.S. Church, Major-General J. Duncan (G.O.C. 54th Division), Lt.-Col. Barré A.H. Goldie, Colonel O.M. Harris (C.R.A. 54th Division), Major S.M. Noakes, Major E.G. Gidley-Kitchin (H.Q. 54th Division).* Absent (Inset. Clockwise from top left) – *Major E.J.T. Lutyens, Captain A. Gregson Williams, R.A.M.C., Rev. E.F.W. Ames, C.F., Lieuts. E.F.W. Besly, F.J. Mullane, R.A.V.C.* (Regimental Collection)

ment of all ranks. Local press reports attributed the cancellation to "grounds of economy" but it may not have been coincidence that the General Strike had only just finished. Unwilling to forego camp altogether, the brigade swiftly made alternative arrangements and, according to the *Hertfordshire Mercury*, "It was immediately decided to hold a voluntary week-end camp at Ashridge Park instead". Despite the short notice, all officers and some 75 per cent of other ranks attended. Four 18-pdrs. and one 4.5-in. howitzer were taken, with one hundred horses, and the amount of training and sports that took place suggests that it must at least have been a 'long' week-end. Both the C.R.A. and G.O.C. of 54th Division visited the camp and the G.O.C. took the salute at a march-past which was filmed and subsequently shown at the Castle Cinema, Hertford. The film of the march-past was not the only appearance before the camera for many members of the brigade, since the Stoll Picture Co. Ltd. were in course of filming 'Boadicea the Warrior Queen' nearby and asked for men to take part in battle scenes once camp had finished. About two hundred volunteered and of these, half took part as cavalry – either British or Roman – and the rest "either as Roman legionaries or almost naked early Britons". [41]

*Mechanisation, 1927–1932*

By May 1927 it was known that 86th Field Brigade would carry out its next firing camp, during the second half of July, as a 'partially mechanised' brigade, i.e., two batteries would have mechanised gun draught, while two would remain fully horsed. The camp was to be at Okehampton and the batteries chosen for mechanisation were 343 and 344. The 6-wheeled Morris-Commercial lorries which were used as tractors were hired from G. N. Transport Ltd. and made their mark at once, for on arrival at Okehampton by rail the brigade was, according to the *Hertfordshire Mercury* "met by a convoy of six-wheeled tractors . . . and with the aid of these vehicles the business of transporting guns, stores and men up the steep hill to the camp was greatly facilitated". On the second day of camp the following appeared in brigade orders:

> "*Morris Tractors*
>
> Every possible care is to be taken with the Morris tractors on charge to batteries. Only the drivers passed out by the Morris representatives are to drive. Tractors will not be used except by the order of O.C. Battery. Drivers will turn into the gun park at all stable parades and will grease, oil and clean their tractors under the supervision of the Morris representative."

The principal press comment on camp was concerned with the atrocious weather, though it was clear that a great deal of effort was put into the live-firing exercises. The brigade strength now stood at 410 all ranks against an establishment of 440 and 330 attended camp, together with the brigade's affiliated section of 54th Divisional Signal Company. Only eleven Association horses went to camp and 177 were hired from the usual contractor, Canham's. The hired horses were much the best that the brigade had had. They were described as "of a very good stamp" in the Association minutes, which also included the following report, from which the evident enthusiasm for the tractors can be gauged:

> "Two batteries were equipped with Morris 6-wheel tractors in lieu of gun and wagon teams. These tractors, which pull the gun and also carry the ammunition and the gun detachment, were an unqualified success. They can go anywhere a team of horses can go, they move quicker and they are no more conspicuous. The draught hook and catch need strengthening but this is a very minor detail."

In the previous two firing years, 1923 and 1925, 344 Battery had come third and second, respectively, in the King's Cup competition for the best Territorial field battery. They again reached the final in 1927 and, as the only mechanised battery competing, set off from Hitchin to Salisbury Plain during the afternoon of Friday 6th October, as the *Hertfordshire Mercury* described:

> "The men [*were*] travelling in the Morris 6-wheel tractors with which the guns were to be drawn in the competition and they had only gone a few miles when an accident occurred which appeared to have ruined their chances of winning the cup. The front tyre of one of the tractors burst, causing the tractor to overturn. Nine men had to be taken to hospital, four being detained, the others taken to their homes after treatment. The only other two men riding in this tractor, Sergeant Tooley and Gunner Varney, although bruised and cut about the face, pluckily decided to continue the journey and take part in the competition. Efforts were made to obtain men to replace the casualties, but only three could be got, therefore the battery was handicapped at the start by being six men short, and among these were four of the principal men in the battery, i.e., the battery commander's assistant, the gun position officer's assistant, the non-commissioned officer in charge of signals and one of the gunlayers. However, another tractor was obtained from London and the battery eventually arrived at Larkhill at 3.00 a.m. on the day of the competition."

The same report goes on to describe how the battery drew last place in the order of firing – 1.30 p.m. on Sunday 8th October – and so must have had some time to reorganise. The battery commander, Major W.R.D. Robertson, M.C. received his orders and the guns moved off under the command of the battery captain, Captain T.L.L. Green. The *Hertfordshire Mercury* continued:

> "When the battery position and the observation post had been selected and occupied, the target, which was an oblique trench, was pointed out to the battery commander by the chief umpire and firing commenced. The range to the target was quickly found and a very effective shoot was carried out, the drill at the guns and the communications being well-nigh

Plate 48 *Major W.R.D. Robertson, M.C., Officer Commanding 344 Battery, receives the King's Cup for 1927 from the Lord Mayor of London. The battery was the only one with mechanical draught to reach the finals of the competition, which they won again in 1931.* (Regimental Collection)

perfect, the rearranged battery working practically as well as if there had been no casualties. An advance now had to be made to take up a fresh position. The move was carried out with speed and quietness. The target this time was a machine-gun post, represented by a patch of gorse, and Captain Green, who had now taken over the duties of battery commander, quickly ranged on to this, and when he had commenced to fire for effect the majority of the rounds fell well into the target.

The ammunition allotted now having been expended, the battery were taken out of action and proceeded back to camp. Before arriving in camp the battery commander was informed by the chief umpire that his battery had won the cup by a margin of forty points . . ."

Referring once more to the Morris tractors, the report went on:

"A great deal of interest was taken in the Morris six-wheelers supplied by G.N. Transport Ltd. These vehicles gave every satisfaction, both at the preliminary competition at Okehampton, and also in the final at Larkhill and the fact that the firm supplied another tractor so promptly after the accident was greatly appreciated by all concerned."

In its report of the final of the King's Cup competition, the *Daily Telegraph* noted that sixteen out of 66 field batteries taking part in the competition in 1927 were mechanised and reported Colonel Armitage, Commandant of the School of Artillery and Chief Umpire, as having said that it was noticeable that the battery which did not have horses to attend to during their annual training, and thus had more time to devote to gunnery, had won the prize. It was probable, the *Daily Telegraph* concluded, that next year the use of six-wheel vehicles in the competition would be considerably extended.

Major Robertson received the King's Cup for 1927 from the Lord Mayor of London at 

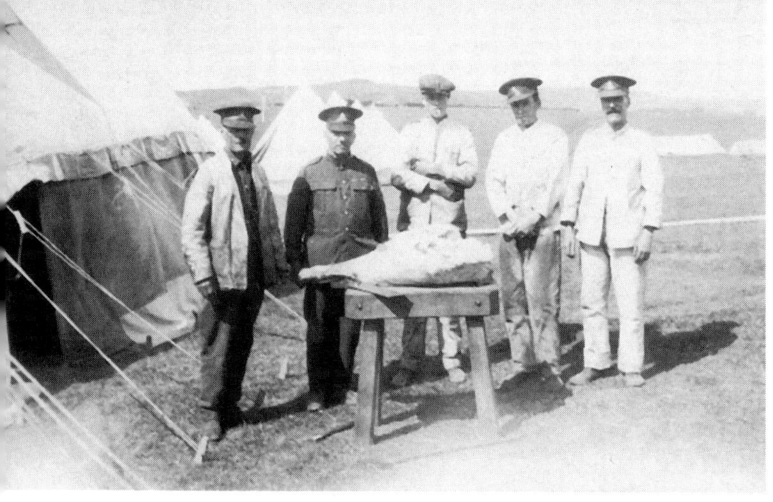

Plate 49 *342 Battery's cookhouse staff consider how to tackle a delivery of fresh rations at camp at Seaford, 1928. The battery establishment provided for two cooks, who were assisted by fatiguemen nominated each day. The cookhouse was supervised by the battery quartermaster-sergeant.* (Regimental Collection)

Guildhall on 28th October – a well deserved tribute to the success of 344 Battery despite the odds, and a high point to which they had steadily made their way through the post-war firing camps. With hindsight, it was clear to many that 1927 marked a turning point, most obviously in the willing, and successful, adoption of mechanised draught. It was a point of sadness, though, that there had been no Yeomanry officers at camp in 1927. Colonel Barré Goldie had been absent through sickness and the stalwart Captain Albany, though still on the books, had reached the age limit and was awaiting retirement. However, while things might never be the same, they would certainly not be worse.

Despite the enthusiasm, and evident success, with which the Territorial artillery in general and 86th Field Brigade in particular had taken up mechanisation, it was to be a further five years before Territorial units would be fully converted to mechanised establishment and would mobilise as mechanised units. Throughout 1928 and 1929 the only establishment in force was the horsed establishment (22 officers and 418 other ranks) introduced in 1922. That mechanised draught was used at all during these two years was due to ingenuity in financial accounting – the annual grant for the hire of horses for training was simply used to hire vehicles!

In July 1928, 86th Field Brigade had a strength of 21 officers and 360 other ranks, of which 19 officers and 260 other ranks did the full fifteen days' training, 53 other ranks did reduced training of eight days and three officers and 47 other ranks were granted leave of absence. The non-firing camp was at Seaford in Sussex and if the *St. Albans Times* is to be believed:

> "The camp was voted the most successful and most enjoyable spent since the formation of the brigade and though the weather was largely responsible for this happy state of affairs, the whole-hearted co-operation of all ranks greatly assisted in ensuring a good time for everybody . . .
>
> The camp was situated above the town and within easy walking distance from it and the sea, and the site itself was admirably suited for an artillery brigade . . . The weather was very nearly perfect, only one wet afternoon marring an otherwise gloriously hot and bright fortnight. As the wet evening, however, coincided with a brigade dance held in the town, it was really a blessing in disguise."



Plate 50 *342 Battery in the early days of mechanisation, 1928–29. The four batteries of 86th Field Brigade were provided with only one Morris-Commercial 6-wheeler gun tower each and were obliged to borrow from each other to put the whole battery into the field for local training. Initially, guns were hooked directly to the tower but by 1934* (see Plate 56) *an ammunition wagon was used in place of the limber and was dropped beside the gun in action.* (Regimental Collection)

Plate 51 *Easter training for 342 Battery at Hertford, 1929.* Left – *Parade in the drill-hall yard.* Right – *Gun drill on Hartham Common.* (Regimental Collection)

After this useful reminder that Territorials need to enjoy annual training, the report continued with a more prosaic description of training, competitions and sports that was echoed in Colonel Barré Goldie's report to Hertfordshire Territorial Association. He stated that the unit had been equipped with four 6-wheel Morris tractors per battery, again hired from G.N. Transport Ltd., instead of gun and wagon teams. The time saved from not having to 'team' the horses and accustom them to the work was enormous and in consequence training could proceed from the very first day in camp. Battery staffs were, of course, mounted and 25 horses had been hired as usual from Canham's for each battery. The brigade had been greatly assisted by a team of extremely efficient and helpful Regular instructors from 2nd Field Brigade, R.A. at Shorncliffe.

Lieutenant-Colonel Barré A. H. Goldie retired on 1st April 1929, handing over command to Lieutenant-Colonel Sir Geoffrey Church, Bt., M.C. who had been in command of 341 Battery since March 1921. It was to Sir Geoffrey Church that the brunt of the work of full conversion to mechanised establishment would fall. Meanwhile contact was not lost with Colonel Barré Goldie, who was appointed C.B.E. in the Birthday Honours of 1930. In February the following year he succeeded Colonel Abel H. Smith, who had been killed in the hunting field in November 1930, as one of the two Honorary Colonels of 86th Field Brigade – the other being the Marquess of Salisbury, who had been Honorary Colonel of 4th East Anglian Brigade between 1909 and 1920.

Following a conference between the Director-General, Territorial Army and representatives of the Territorial Associations in February 1929, it was announced that medium brigades and army field brigades of the Territorial Army would train and mobilise on a mechanised establishment, while divisional artillery would be 'allowed' to train mechanised, but would revert to horsed establishment and organisation on mobilisation.[6] To facilitate this curious state of affairs, which was due almost totally to underfunding, it was the policy of the Army Council to form a pool of War Department-owned vehicles that would be available both to Regular and to Territorial units for peace-time training but which would be allocated to the Regulars on mobilisation. No new establishments had been issued by the time 86th Field Brigade went to firing camp on Salisbury Plain in 1929. It is perhaps possible to distinguish more attention to 'technical gunnery' in Sir Geoffrey Church's subsequent report, which lists "shooting by observation from an O.P., shooting by survey methods, shooting with observation by a F.O.O., and shooting at tanks" as having been practised by the brigade, which was some twenty officers and 260 other ranks strong in camp, with mechanised draught and mounted battery staff. Reports in the local press were nothing if not enthusiastic, describing the training quite fully and maintaining an air of quiet confidence that one of batteries would reach the final of the King's Cup again. The *Hertfordshire Mercury* report included the following:

> "Of many interesting shoots, the one that caused greatest interest was the tank shoot. These tanks consist of wooden frames covered with canvas and look the real thing when on the move. There was great excitement in the gun detachments when eight tanks appeared over the crest about a thousand yards in front and advanced upon the battery. Some very effective shooting was carried out by the Hertford battery on this target, one tank being completely destroyed and five others having direct hits registered upon them. The Gunnery Staff remarked that the brigade was up to the standards of any Regular brigade that had fired at Tilshead this year".

The *Hertfordshire Express* chose to highlight a different type of shoot, and apparently one that Sir Geoffrey Church omitted in his report:

> "Of the many interesting shoots, one that caused great interest was that carried out in conjunction with an aeroplane, the observer in which calls the battery up by wireless and reports the observation of the bursts to the battery."

The optimism that one of the batteries would reach the final of the King's Cup was not misplaced. Once more it was 344 Battery but this time they were placed third. Interestingly, *The Times*, which between the wars invariably found space for an account of the finals, remarked that "the tests this year were more exacting than on any previous occasion".

Early in 1930, the arrangements for 'allowing' Territorial brigades to train with mechanised draught were placed on a more formal basis and new peace establishments were issued for a fully mechanised brigade and for a partly mechanised brigade (i.e., with mounted battery staffs but mechanised draught).[7] Colonel Sir Geoffrey Church at once proposed to Hertfordshire Territorial Association that the partly mechanised establishment should be adopted and it was agreed that it should be implemented with effect from 1st April 1930. While 86th Field Brigade were at non-firing camp at Shoreham in August, however, new instructions were issued by the War Office.[8] These required all Territorial field brigades to move to the fully mechanised establishment in accordance with a three-year programme over the period 1931–33. The three brigades of 54th Divisional Artillery were scheduled to go fully mechanised on 1st April 1932, including adjusting their strengths to conform to the new establishment – 22 officers and 341 other ranks. Each battery would be issued with one 6-wheel tractor and the tractors of a brigade would, when pooled, be sufficient for one battery to carry out fully-manned weekend-, or other out-of-camp training. However, since brigades were required to hand over their tractors for a summer-long 'camp pool', any battery out-of-camp training would have to take place well before the camp season opened. There were no immediate plans to issue vehicles for use by battery staff and the present system of hire, both for local training and at camp, would continue.

With all these arrangements in prospect, 86th Field Brigade went to camp in 1930 without any of their own gun tractors and with the battery staff mounted. During the first week gun-towing vehicles were supplied by a Regular unit of the Royal Army Service Corps. These were reported later to have been unsuitable as they were too big and heavy. In the second week Morris-Commercial 6-wheelers were hired "as usual" from G.N. Transport Ltd. but these vehicles had had "such a buffeting at previous camps that some of them were very uncertain all week". An interesting feature of camp training was a one-day exercise with infantry which was reported to Hertfordshire Territorial Association as the first time the brigade had had the opportunity of co-operating with other arms.

June 1930 saw the publication of Standing Orders for 86th Field Brigade, apparently for the first, and only, time between the wars. Paragraph 1, entitled 'Nomenclature' sets out first the full title of the brigade as authorised by Army Order 481 of 1922 but unfortunately goes on to state that "for ordinary purposes the brigade is known as 86th (Herts Yeo.) Field Brigade, R.A. (T.A.). This unauthorised shortening of what is, admittedly, a cumbersome title is apparent from press reports over several years prior to 1930 but it is to be regretted as the first step towards the eventual removal from the title of evidence of 4th East Anglian Brigade as half of the 'parentage' of 86th Field Brigade, which took place in 1947. The Standing Orders also set out, without authority, new bracketed designations for the batteries, viz.:

341 (St. Albans) Field Battery

342 (Hertford) Field Battery

343 (Watford) Field Battery

344 (Hitchin) Field Battery

It was not, in fact, until 1934 that the War Office indicated that it would be sympathetic to amplifications of unit titles throughout the Territorial Army and Hertfordshire Territorial Association applied for the batteries' titles to be amended as shown above. Consideration of the vast number of applications took a very long time, however, and approval of the new titles, as part of a consolidated list, was not promulgated until July 1937.[9]

Plate 52 *342 Battery's drill-hall, St. Andrew Street, Hertford, 1930.*
Left – *A 'ride' under instruction. By now, only the battery staff were mounted and orders would be received during the year for 86th Field Brigade to become fully mechanised in time for camp in 1932.*
Right – *The gun park. All four guns are 18-pdr. Mk. IV on carriage Mk. III. The last pole-trail guns were withdrawn before 1927.* (Regimental Collection)

As far as uniform and badges were concerned, the new Standing Orders seem simply to confirm practices already authorised, or at any rate to confirm actions in the spirit of the authority. The wearing of the bronze hart on the shoulder strap by officers and the brass hart on the collar by other ranks was confirmed but, interestingly, while showing that blue patrol uniform, rather than mess dress, was worn by officers, the Orders provide for the hart badge to be worn on the collar of the patrol jacket and not on the Yeomanry-style shoulder chains. Another point of great interest is the instruction that "the P.S.I. on duty, when reading orders in the Officers' Mess, will wear blue uniform". The custom of ensuring that the officers of the brigade were conversant with orders for the following day apparently originated in the Hertfordshire Yeomanry and Major Reginald Halsey presented a handsome vellum-bound, silver-mounted book to the mess in time for annual camp in 1914, at which time it may simply have been placed in an appropriate position for officers to read it. By repute, a commanding officer in the 1920s, having witnessed the failure of officers to comply with brigade routine orders, gave instructions that they should be read out at dinner, so that officers would have no excuse for failing to carry them out. This custom carried on until the outbreak of war – there is no record of whether orders were ever read during the war – and was revived, for formal dining-in nights only, in 1948. It continued until 1967, but has been difficult to keep in being since the successors to 86th Field Brigade were reduced to a single battery. The original orders book, covering the period 1913–1966, is now in the Regimental Collection at Hertfordshire Archives and Local Studies.

Camp in August 1931 was again a firing camp and once more on Salisbury Plain. It became notorious among the inter-war camps for the appalling weather; the *Hertfordshire Mercury* reported that "in fact very little fine weather was experienced during the whole period". Battery staffs were still mounted and the guns were again pulled by R.A.S.C. vehicles. Colonel Sir Geoffrey Church later repeated his opinion that these vehicles were unsuitable as field artillery tractors and remarked that, since only ten were available for sixteen guns, training was "difficult at times", despite, on this occasion, "the wholehearted co-operation of the R.A.S.C. drivers". In the face of these difficulties, 344 Battery won the West Down pool of the King's Cup competition and thus entry to the final, to be held the first weekend in October.

Plate 53 *'Capes, groundsheet' being worn with some humour during the notoriously bad weather of annual camp on Salisbury Plain in 1931. The only waterproof garment available to other ranks, the cape guaranteed that the wearer would be soaked from the knees down and got in the way of every activity. It continued in use long after the Second World War.* (Regimental Collection)

Plate 54 *Silver statuette of a draught horse presented to 86th Field Brigade by Captain D.A.J. Bowie, R.A., 1931. Captain Bowie served as adjutant from April 1927 to September 1931, the period during which mechanisation of the brigade took place. Although the inscription does not say so, it is safe to assume that the presentation was intended to commemorate the passing of the horse as the means of moving the guns.* (Photograph by Boris Mollo in the Regimental Collection)

*The Times* reported the finals in some ten column-inches but with very little detail of 344 Battery's performance in an 'advance to contact' setting. However, the battery "looked particularly smart at the rendezvous and took up the two positions in good style and time" and "their work generally was of a high standard" – high enough for them to be declared winners, with a total score of two hundred points and a margin of seventeen points over B Battery, H.A.C. Major Robertson received the cup from Prince Arthur of Connaught at Guildhall in the City of London on 30th October.

### *Four years of financial stringency, 1932–1935*

Even as preparations were being made, in September 1931, for the final of the King's Cup competition, depressing news about the following training year reached 86th Field Brigade. Instructions issued by the War Office on the grounds of the "urgent need for national economy" cancelled annual camp during the year beginning 1st April 1932 and imposed a recruitment ceiling for the Territorial Army which would hold the overall strength at the 1931 level; in effect, only wastage could be made good. Additionally, the clothing upkeep grant was reduced. These restrictions provided an inauspicious start to the year in which the brigade was due to reach mechanised establishment and hold its first fully mechanised camp. As the training year opened, Hertfordshire Territorial Association gave instructions for the disposal of the remaining Association horses and, determined not to let the momentum of the change to mechanised establishment slip, 86th Field Brigade made plans to get round the ban on annual camp. They were successful, as Colonel Sir Geoffrey Church later reported to the Association. The brigade managed to arrange a week in barracks at Colchester as guests of 17th Field Brigade, who "did everything possible to make the camp a success". Fourteen officers and 210 other ranks attended – whether or not they were paid is not on record – and a good deal of centralised training was carried out, presumably with the help of additional instructors from the host brigade. There was, of course, no firing, but on field training exercises towards the end of the week two batteries deployed fully mechanised for the first time, using borrowed lorries to transport the battery staff and the B.C.'s party, while the other two batteries borrowed riding horses for what amounted to a 'farewell to the horse'. Continuing to press for high standards in technical gunnery, Sir Geoffrey ensured that each battery carried out a 'survey scheme'. Given this enthusiastic approach to mechanisation and the brigade's efforts to carry out the required changes successfully, despite considerable difficulty,
 the instruction received in December 1932 that divisional artillery would in future mobilise

Plate 55 *Warrant and non-commissioned officers form a guard of honour as Lieutenant R.D. Cribb of 342 Battery leaves church with his bride, 1934. Other ranks' blue undress uniform similar in pattern to that of the Royal Artillery was provided at individuals' expense. The hart collar badge was only worn by Territorial members of 86th Field Brigade.* (Regimental Collection)

mechanised[10] must have come both as an encouragement and a relief.

Early in 1933, Hertfordshire Territorial Association asked Sir Geoffrey Church to extend his tour as commanding officer of 86th Field Brigade by one further year – to the end of March 1934 – and Sir Geoffrey agreed to do so. No doubt owing to continuing financial difficulties, there was no firing camp in 1933, as might have been expected in the normal two year cycle. For their first fully mechanised camp, therefore, 86th Field Brigade assembled in July at Swingate Camp, Dover. The four brigade gun towers were once more made up to full strength by R.A.S.C. vehicles and the few staff cars then on strength supplemented by borrowing. According to a report specially contributed to the *Hertfordshire Mercury*, fifteen officers and 285 other ranks went to camp and they were accommodated alongside the four battalions of 163 Infantry Brigade, who took it in turns to wake the whole camp each morning with bugles and drums. Some 150 officers and men of 86th Field Brigade had already attended a four-day Easter camp at Woolwich in April, which had concentrated on specialist individual training for gunners, drivers, signallers and battery staff, so batteries were well able to cope with the first week of individual training and battery exercises. Brigade exercises followed in the second week, during which some attention was paid to camouflage and the Royal Air Force flew photographic sorties over the gun positions. The final exercise took advantage of the presence in camp together of both the infantry and artillery and involved the creation, for demonstration purposes of a battalion of infantry and its affiliated battery at full war establishment. The composite 6-gun battery with full battery staff and administrative echelon proved quite an 'eye opener', according to the *Hertfordshire Mercury's* report, and was perhaps a useful reminder that, although they would no longer have to contend with horses on mobilisation, a fifty per cent increase in fire-power, with attendant increases in personnel of all trades, would bring its own problems. On the last Friday of camp the Sergeants' Mess made the first of a series of farewells to the remarkable R.S.M. W. Paines, M.M., who had joined 86th Brigade on formation in 1920 as P.S.I. of the St. Albans battery, had served as regimental sergeant-major since his promotion in 1922, and was due to retire in January 1934. R.S.M. Paines evidently was held in the highest regard throughout the brigade, with which he spent well over half his entire military career. He was among several outstanding characters who served as P.S.Is. between the wars and, both individually and collectively, made a huge contribution to the continuing efficiency, skill and spirit of the brigade.

During the autumn of 1933 instructions for further financial savings in the training year 1934–35 reached 86th Field Brigade. These moved Sir Geoffrey Church, who, in fact, was to stay in command for an additional three years rather than the one additional year recorded above, to write formally to Hertfordshire Territorial Association pointing out the results likely to arise from a £300 reduction in funds made available to 86th Field Brigade and his special concern at the reduction in travelling expenses for drill nights. By their December meeting, Hertfordshire Association were gloomily concluding that the War Office was no longer con-

Plate 56 *Week-end exercise by 342 Battery at Tonwell, near Ware, June 1934.* Top – *Guns and vehicles waiting for the order to move. The battery staff are now mounted in civilian cars, which were hired or borrowed for training.* Bottom – *An 18-pdr. fires a round of blank ammunition. Note the 18-pdr. ammunition wagon in the foreground. Its short perch, which already had a towing eye, made it suitable for use as a mechanised-draught limber.* (Regimental Collection)

cerned at the strength, or even the state of training, of the Territorial Army but simply thought of units that were steadily declining in numbers as a framework for eventual expansion.

Although the fortunes of the Territorial Army as a whole may have been at their lowest in 1934, 86th Field Brigade seem to have soldiered on with some confidence. Each battery was allowed two paid exercises before camp, when the full complement of towing vehicles and staff cars were provided for local training and with the co-operation of landowners realistic training was carried out, even to the extent of firing blank ammunition (see Plate 56). Annual camp was held at Okehampton in the last fortnight of July. This time the brigade took none of their own guns or vehicles and relied completely on equipment drawn from the camp pool. Sixteen officers and 195 other ranks attended for the full two weeks, with a further three officers and sixty other ranks able to attend for one week only, so a very large percentage of the brigade strength completed the minimum obligatory in-camp training. Despite the poor weather – "rain and mist one day, mist and rain the next", according to a report in the *Hertfordshire Mercury* – which curtailed the firing programme, 344 Battery once more qualified for the final of the King's Cup competition, which was held on Salisbury Plain in late September. A correspondent of *The Times* recorded that the scheme, based on a withdrawal, was "much more difficult and elaborate" than the previous year. The very diverse weather conditions led to some difficulty in allocating marks and after declaring winners and runners-up, the umpires placed the remaining three batteries, 344 Battery among them, equally in third place. No doubt 344 Battery were disappointed, but they had completed a remarkable run of appearances in all six finals available to them between 1923 and 1934, and, of course, had won the cup twice.

The spring of 1935 was dominated, as far as 86th Field Brigade was concerned, by the Silver Jubilee of King George V and Queen Mary, which was celebrated nationally on 6th May. The batteries took part in local celebrations by firing salutes and the commanding officer, two sergeants and one gunner received the Silver Jubilee Medal. (For details see *Hertfordshire Yeomanry and Artillery Honours and Awards.*) Camp was at Newhaven in July. No accounts seem to have appeared in the local press but in his usual autumn report to Hertfordshire Territorial Association, Sir Geoffrey Church mentioned the extremely cramped living conditions in Newhaven Fort and the useful training that had taken place, including the occupation of gun positions by night in order to support a dawn attack with a barrage. Night occupations and dawn barrages had become commonplace during the First World War (see *The Hertfordshire Batteries, Royal Field Artillery – An Illustrated History*) and predictably would have

Plate 57 *Silver Jubilee celebrations, May 1935.*
Top – *An 18-pdr. of 342 Battery at Hertford. The regulation vehicle marking '342 Fd. Bty., R.A. (T.A.)' and the vehicle's War Department number, L19068, are contained in the circle to the upper left of the towing vehicle's spare wheel.*
(Regimental Collection).

Bottom – *4.5-in. howitzers of 344 Battery firing a salute in Priory Park, Hitchin. Note how the 4.5-in. ammunition wagon* (see also Plate 14) *is now in use as a limber.* (Hertfordshire Pictorial Archives – Hitchin Museum)

Plate 58 *342 Battery taking part in the finals of the King's Cup competition, September 1936.*
Top – *Gunners manhandle a limber to its position beside the gun while signallers, Lance-Bombardier Manser and Gunner Allen, receive orders by lamp from the O.P.*
Centre – *D Sub-Section's gun, under the command of Sergeant Willson, at full recoil, with the No.2 about to open the breech and eject the spent cartridge case.*
Bottom – *Another view of Sergeant Willson's gun. The battery were placed second in the competition.*
(Regimental Collection)

been so again following any future mobilisation. It is accordingly strange that these skills appear not to have been practised before – they are certainly not mentioned in any previous press reports or commanding officers' statements to the Association.

*Signs of revival, 1936–1938*

Command of 86th Field Brigade changed again on 1st April 1936, when Lieutenant-Colonel W.R.D. Robertson, M.C., T.D., who had served for ten years as battery commander of 344 Battery, took over from Sir Geoffrey Church. At the same time it became clear that the Territorial Army was at last pulling out of the trough into which it had fallen during the years of financial stringency, 1932–35. Money was still tight but evidence of an increasing potential threat from Germany led the Under-Secretary of State for War to emphasise the urgent need for increased numbers of Territorials. Hertfordshire Territorial Association lost no time in circulating details of the statement to local employers. It is unlikely that the appeal had immediate effect but camp attendance figures were better than for several years, with nineteen officers and 220 other ranks doing two weeks and one officer and more than fifty other ranks the authorised reduced period of eight days. Shortage of vehicles meant that only two batteries could fire on the same day but Colonel Robertson ensured that all officers conducted one shoot from the O.P. and the R.A.F. put in another appearance, this time to direct the fall of shot, rather than to take photographs. For the first time a limited number of firing platforms were available and each battery used them for anti-tank shooting. At last, 344 Battery's long run of successes in reaching the final of the King's Cup competition was broken and 86th Field Brigade's representatives in the 1936 final were 342 Battery – a triumph for their P.S.I., B.S.M.(I.G.) J. W. Olney, who had been posted to the battery in 1934 and was to prove a tower of strength and another of the great P.S.I. 'characters'. The battery, now under the command of Major Sir Patrick Coghill, Bt., achieved second place and were featured in a remarkable series of photographs taken by an *Evening News* photographer, many of which appear in this volume.

The year 1937 opened on an encouraging note, for in the debate on the Army Estimates in mid-March it was announced that funding for the Territorial Army would be increased. Other ranks would in future be issued with shirts, socks and, very importantly for mechanised units, canvas overalls. Battery staff vehicles would at last be issued, rather than hired, and re-equipment of the Territorial Army with up-to-date guns and vehicles would, as far as could possibly be achieved, proceed in step with the Regular Army.[11] Then, on 12th May, the coronation of Their Majesties King George VI and Queen Elizabeth took place. It was at once noticeable that awards of the Coronation Medal were on a more generous scale then the 1935 Jubilee Medal. Not only did the Honorary Colonel and the Commanding Officer of 86th Field Brigade each receive one, but it proved possible so to interpret the issue formula as to allow the remaining four medals to go one to each battery! (For details see *Hertfordshire Yeomanry and*

Plate 59 *Lieutenant R.D. Cribb, G.P.O. of 342 Battery, gives orders to the guns during the final of the 1936 King's Cup competition. His G.P.O. 'ack', Lance-Bombardier Boughton works at the artillery board while the Battery Signals Sergeant supervises the arrival of a telephone cable laid from a borrowed tracked vehicle.* (Regimental Collection)

FORM C.E. 1.

# HERTFORD TERRITORIAL ARMY.

UNIT 343 Field Battery RA — No. 632

**LIST OF CLOTHING AND EQUIPMENT IN POSSESSION OF**

No. ........ *Rank and Name* Gnr F Ryder

*Full Address* 4 Park St Berkhampstead

This Form to be completed in DUPLICATE and the *second* copy handed to the Soldier at the time of issue of the articles enumerated below.

| ARTICLE. | NO. | ARTICLE. | NO. |
|---|---|---|---|
| **CLOTHING.** | | **EQUIPMENT.** | |
| Badges, Cap ... | 1 | Bandoliers, 50 rds. ... | |
| Bags, Kit ... | 1 | Belts, Waist, W.E. ... | 1 |
| Bits, G.M., S.D. ... | | Braces, with Buckle ... | |
| Boots, Ankle ... | 1 | Braces, without Buckle ... | 1 |
| Buttons, R.A.F.S., Lea, Small ... | | Carriers, 75 cartridge rds. R. ... | |
| Caps, S.D., Soft ... | | Carriers, 75 cartridge rds. L. ... | |
| Caps, S.D., Stiff ... | 1 | Carriers, Water-bottle ... | 1 |
| Chevrons, S.D. -bar ... | | Carriers Imp. Intr. Heads ... | |
| Chevrons, G.C. -bar ... | | Carriers Imp. Intr. Helves ... | |
| Coats, Warm, M.S. ... | 1 | Covers, Mess Tin, D.S. ... | |
| Drums, G.M., S.D. ... | | Covers, Equipment, M.T., M.S. ... | |
| Great Coats ... | | Frogs, Bayonet ... | |
| Guns, G.M., S.D. right arm ... | | Haversacks, G.S. ... | |
| Guns, G.M., S.D. left arm ... | | Haversacks, O.S. ... | 1 |
| Jackets, S.D. ... | 2 | Implements Intrenching Heads ... | |
| Knives, Clasp... | | Implements Intrenching Helves ... | |
| Lanyards ... | 1 | Lanyards, Pistol ... | |
| Pantaloons, cord ... | 1 | Packs ... | |
| Puttees, pairs... | 2 | Slings, Rifle, Web ... | |
| Rings, Split, Small ... | | Straps, Great Coat, B.E. ... | |
| Shoes, G.M., S.D. ... | | Straps, Mess Tin ... | |
| Spurs, Jack ... | 1 | Straps, supporting ... | |
| Trousers, S.D. ... | 1 | Tins, Mess, D.S. ... | |
| Trumpets, G.M., S.D. ... | | Tins, Mess, M.S. ... | |
| Titles, Shoulder, ~~sets~~ ... R As ... prs | 2 | Water-bottles, Mk. VI. ... | 1 |
| Wheels, G.M., S.D. ... | | Whistles, Art ... | |
| Crowns, G.M., S.D. ... | | Whistles, Inf. ... | |
| Stags, ~~No.~~ ... prs | 2 | | |
| Y.'s, ~~No.~~ ... prs | 2 | | |

*I certify that I received a copy of this Form at the time of issue of the above-named articles.*

*Station* Watford — *Signature of Soldier* F L Ryder

*Date* 26-10-36 — *Signature of Issuing Officer* [illegible]

**NOTES.**—1. Should any article not be available for issue at the same time as the other articles enumerated, the word "NIL" will be inserted opposite the article in question, and an ADDITIONAL Form used when the article, or articles, are subsequently issued.

2. Where an article is not applicable to the Unit concerned, this will be ruled through in RED ink previous to the issue of the duplicate copy of the Form to the Soldier.

**UNIFORM, etc., is to be worn on MILITARY DUTY ONLY.**

Plate 60 *Hertfordshire T.A. Association's Form C.E.1 recording the initial issue of clothing and equipment to Gunner F. Ryder on enlistment, October 1936. The issue of pantaloons (breeches), puttees and spurs would shortly be discontinued in favour of a second pair of trousers, and 'canvas' overalls would be introduced, but the minimal issue of equipment, which would have been quite inadequate for active service, was not improved until battledress and 1937-Pattern web equipment were issued some months after mobilisation.* (Regimental Collection)

PLATE II Week-end training at Nomansland Common, Wheathampstead, c.1935 – 18-pdrs. and Morris-Commercial 6-wheelers of 341 Field Battery
*(From the water-colour specially painted for this work by Joan Wanklyn, 1999)*

In order to exercise a section of two guns, 341 Battery have borrowed an additional gun-towing vehicle – each battery had only one – and have borrowed or hired open-topped civilian cars as reconnaissance and signals vehicles. The two guns have just been ordered into action and their limbers – originally 18-pdr. ammunition wagons – are being manhandled into position while the vehicles move away to the wagon lines. In the foreground the brigade adjutant, a Regular Officer of the Permanent Staff, takes notes. He is accompanied by one of the Permanent Staff warrant officers who is an assistant instructor in gunnery (right of centre with white-topped cap). The two schoolboys look as if they will just be old enough to volunteer for service with 341 Battery in the big expansion of the Territorial Army's Field Force which will take place in the spring of 1939.

This plate has generously been sponsored by McMullen and Sons Limited, supporters of Volunteers and Territorials in Hertfordshire for well over a century.

*Artillery Honours and Awards.*) The batteries each provided a party of seven non-commissioned officers and men to make up the brigade's contribution to the coronation procession and for street-lining duties in Trafalgar Square, and each man in the 'Coronation Detachment' was issued with the new blue uniform. Salutes were fired as part of the celebrations in Hertfordshire. In their battery scrapbook, now in the Regimental Collection, 342 Battery recorded the day's events in some detail. All four guns were taken into the grounds of Hertford Castle where "the battery fired a salute of 21 guns, punctuated after each seven rounds by a feu-de-joie from the Hertfordshire Regiment and followed by the Royal Salute and three cheers for Their Majesties . . . In the afternoon C Sub-Section, with gun, lorry and detachment complete, Sergeant R. J. Street i/c, turned out and took part in the procession through the town to Balls Park".

Meanwhile, instructions had been issued in March 1937 that the programme of 'mechanisation' of 18-pdr. guns and 4.5-in. howitzers by fitting them with solid rubber tyres on the original wooden wheels was to be abandoned. Instead, Territorial brigades were to reorganise to an establishment of two 18-pdr. batteries and two 4.5-in. howitzer batteries and await "the impending mechanisation of artillery equipments by the fitting of pneumatic tyres".[12] The implementation of the new establishment did not take place until later in the year, so 86th Field Brigade went to non-firing camp at Newhaven on the existing establishment of three 18-pdr. batteries (341, 342 and 343 Batteries) and one 4.5-in. howitzer battery (344 Battery). Living conditions at Newhaven Fort had obviously not changed. They were again reported as "cramped" but in Colonel Robertson's eyes the advantages outweighed the disadvantages, though he did not give details to Hertfordshire Territorial Association. New features of annual training in 1937 included a demonstration of gun drill in respirators, given by 343 Battery, a continuous 24-hour exercise and the Brigade Survey Party. The brigade's 'fitness for role' was suspect, however, since Colonel Robertson drew attention to the absence of any water carts or trailers on the establishment and the fact that, since batteries held no portable cookers, most meals had to be brought into the field from the camp cookhouse. Figures for camp attendance have not survived but they were evidently good, as the following extract from a circular letter to officers of the brigade, dated 28th June 1937, indicates:

> "*Annual Training in Camp – Blankets*
>
> According to Regulations blankets are not drawn for officers. Blankets are drawn for the full establishment of other ranks, irrespective of whether they all go to camp or not.
>
> In previous years when only 40 or 50 other ranks per battery have attended camp out of an establishment of 79, there have been sufficient spare blankets for officers.
>
> This year batteries are going to camp at practically full strength. Therefore there will be very few blankets spare and if officers use the men's blankets as previously the men will be short. Will officers, therefore, please take their own blankets, sheets, etc."

Detailed instructions for the change in brigade establishment foreshadowed in March (see above) were issued in October 1937 in a letter which made clear that the intention to convert at least some units to the new establishment had been promulgated as early as August 1936.[13] According to the present letter, ten field brigades, including 86th, had been "selected for reorganisation" and within 86th Brigade it was 342 Battery that would change from the 18-pdr. to the 4.5-in. howitzer. Howitzers and stores were to be demanded at once and 18-pdrs. returned to the Royal Arsenal, Woolwich, without delay, since they were "urgently required for another service". (In fact, it seems most likely that they were to be converted to 18/25-pdrs. – see Chapter 2.)

At the beginning of 1938, which proved to be an eventful year both for the Territorial Army as a whole and for 86th Field Brigade in particular, Colonel Robertson was attached to the Imperial Defence College as a student – the first Territorial officer to attend the college. Since the course allowed sufficient time for him to continue to carry out his duties with 86th Field Brigade, there was no change of command. Early in the year, too, the four battery drill-halls were surveyed by Hertfordshire Territorial Association with a view to establishing their fitness as battery centres. The survey concluded that the accommodation provided was generally inadequate, especially when the number of vehicles in course of issue was taken into account. Plans may well have been made to rectify the deficiencies but they would have been overtaken by continuing increases in the Territorial Army in Hertfordshire throughout 1938–39 and finally by mobilisation.

Plate 61 *86th Field Brigade parading inside Newhaven Fort during annual camp in 1937. Officers and some senior non-commissioned officers are wearing blues, indicating that Church Parade is about to take place. The primitive other ranks' accommodation, described by the commanding officer as 'cramped', and evidently converted from the fort's original stores, can be seen in the background.*
(Regimental Collection)

A small collection of papers relating to 341 battery assembled by Lieutenant A. J. J. Cory-Wright and now in the Regimental Collection throws some interesting light on the period before camp in 1938. A letter from the P.S.I. to the battery captain and subalterns gives details of brigade and battery exercises to take place during April, ending, "I am to state, Sir, that it is hoped that you will be able to attend most of these exercises". On Good Friday, 15th April, there was a battery staff exercise to be attended by full staff of officers and signallers with specialists as detailed. Easter Sunday was devoted to a "Full battery exercise – Staff and guns", as was the following Sunday but, whereas the instructions for the first are annotated "not enough lorries for all the guns", the next exercise was "with use of all lorries of the brigade". Early in May, 86th Field Brigade received new instructions on dress, which were duly forwarded for the information of the officers by the P.S.I. The instructions covered both ceremonial dress and dress for training "pending the issue of battledress and a decision on a new pattern of dress for ceremonial and walking out". The final paragraph of the War Office letter states that:

> "Officers and other ranks will wear spurs for training only when actually required to be mounted, but spurs will be worn by those entitled to wear spurs for ceremonial, with mess dress, undress and walking-out dress, when breeches or overalls are worn."

In May 1938 a suit of 'canvas' was issued to each man and canvas was taken into use for all drills. Evening drills during May included anti-gas training, and battery orders for 8th June detailed not only that canvas would in future be worn on all exercises but that respirators would be carried as well. The same orders give an indication that 'caps, field service, drab', which are incorrectly referred to as 'caps, forage', had been issued, for non-commissioned officers and men were ordered to cease wearing the gun cap badge in this headdress and wear instead the left-hand hart collar badge. The two-piece canvas suits were not issued to officers, who were required instead to wear 'suits, overall, combination, brown' – or 'boiler suits' – which were made available on repayment through the Association supply channels at five shillings and eleven pence for a suit. In the event that the suits were supplied without shoulder straps, these were to be made and sewn on, together with cloth badges of rank, the adjutant instructed all officers in a letter dated 10th June. The same letter advised officers to obtain their suits "on the large size" as they would shrink with washing. To guard against the ultimate in ridiculous appearance, it was also ordered that "Sam Browne belts will not be worn with the suits"!

The instructions regarding spurs which are referred to above were evidently prompted by War Office Letters circulated in April and May 1938.[14] These were cancelled in August 1938 when a new letter[15] promulgated the interim measures that had been approved "as regards the leg wear of Regular Army personnel at home stations . . . and also the Territorial Army and Supplementary Reserve", pending decisions on the future dress both for ceremonial and walking out, and for active service and training. The new instructions provided for service dress trousers to be worn without puttees, both by officers and other ranks, for ceremonial, walking out and training. In 86th Brigade, spurs would in future be worn only with blue undress uniform, but there would be some competion by 'those in possession' to appear to be 'old sweats' by wearing breeches and puttees for as long as possible, just as in the period after the formation of the Territorial Force in 1908, their predecessors of the Hertfordshire Yeomanry had made every effort to keep in wear the scarlet collar and 'H.I.Y.' shoulder titles of the Hertfordshire Imperial Yeomanry.

Plate 62 *Okehampton Camp, July 1938.*
Top – *A camp guard mounted by 343 Battery. Their service dress uniform and rifles are indistinguishable from those of their predecessors, 1st Herts Battery, before and during the First World War, except that spurs are no longer worn. Instructions for breeches (known as 'pantaloons, Bedford cord') to be replaced by serge trousers were issued in August 1938.*
Bottom – *Gun detachments of 341 Battery wearing the new 'canvas' two-piece working dress parade for gun drill in respirators. Note the regulation marking 'D 341' on the trail of the nearest gun.* (Regimental Collection)

Plate 63 *The officers of 86th Field Brigade at Okehampton, July 1938 – the last camp at which all four original batteries of the brigade were present.* Back row (L.–R.) – *2nd Lieuts. J.S. Crisfield, K.S. King, K.G. Swann, J.A. Briggs, A.J.J. Cory-Wright, D.W. Cherry, R.S.W. Higgens, J. Carew Jones, T.P. Halford-Thompson.* Centre row – *Lieuts. J.L.G. Weall, E.D. Wells, W.E. Boyes, Captains R.H. Mortis, R.A.M.C., J.B. Morgan Smith, J.B.S. Tabor, R.D. Cribb, Lieut. R.N. Hanbury.* Front row – *Rev. C.T.R.C. Perowne, C.F., Captain G.D. Fanshawe (Adjutant), Majors C.F.W. Banham, T.L.L. Green, Lt.-Col. W.R.D. Robertson, Majors Sir Patrick Coghill, Bt., I.W.G. Barry, Captains G. Keane, F.D.E. Fremantle.*
(Regimental Collection)

Annual camp in 1938 was a firing camp and took place at Okehampton in the second half of July. It would be the last of the 'traditional' camps of the inter-war years, though this was not yet apparent. All four batteries were close to their peace-time establishment and numbers attending as a percentage of strength were probably the best ever. Press reports are sparse but agree that the weather was indifferent, while refraining from forecasting whether 86th Field Brigade would once more be represented in the final of the King's Cup competition. In fact, the brigade did win the Okehampton pool and again selected 342 Battery as representatives in the final, which took place in September, with 342 Battery gaining third place.

### *The formation of 79th Anti-Aircraft Brigade, July–November 1938*

The unusual lack of recorded detail of camp in 1938 and of the King's Cup results may be due to the general atmosphere of upheaval which beset 86th Field Brigade from mid-1938 until the outbreak of war just over a year later. By letter dated 18th July 1938, which is said to have reached the brigade at camp, the War Office announced, apparently without any prior consultation with Hertfordshire Territorial Association or with 86th Field Brigade that:

> "An anti-aircraft brigade consisting of headquarters and three batteries will be raised in Hertfordshire from the nucleus of 343 Field Battery of 86th (East Anglian) (Hertfordshire Yeomanry) Field Brigade. The anti-aircraft brigade so formed will be known as 79th Anti-Aircraft Brigade. The numbers allotted to the batteries are 246, 247 and 248.
>
> The provisional distribution is:
>
> | | |
> |---|---|
> | Headquarters and two batteries | Watford |
> | One battery | Welwyn Garden City |
>
> Titles are provisional only and T.A. Associations are to report whether provisional titles are agreed to. Similarly, in the case of new units, recommendations may be submitted to include a Territorial designation within the title."[16]

Plate 64 *Major T.L.L. Green, T.D., Officer Commanding 341 (St. Albans) Field Battery, who was selected to command the anti-aircraft brigade to be formed at Watford and Welwyn Garden City in the autumn of 1938. The photograph shows in detail officers' blue uniform as worn in 86th Field Brigade and the Royal Artillery pattern of officers' sword with three-bar hilt.* (Regimental Collection)

The formal date of formation of 79th Anti-Aircraft Brigade was provisionally fixed for 1st November 1938 and Colonel Robertson wrote at once to Hertfordshire Territorial Association to recommend that Major T. L. L. Green, T.D., commanding 341 Battery, should be appointed to command the new unit. The Association supported this nomination and, in putting it forward to the War Office, asked for 'Hertfordshire Yeomanry' to be included in 79th Anti-Aircraft Brigade's title. Major Green's promotion and appointment to command were gazetted with effect from 1st October 1938 and the following officers were transferred from 86th Field Brigade to 79th Anti-Aircraft Brigade on 1st November:

| | |
|---|---|
| Major I. W. G. Barry | 343 Battery |
| Captain F. D. E. Fremantle | 342 Battery |
| Captain J. B. Morgan Smith | 343 Battery |
| Lieutenant J. L. G Weall | 343 Battery |
| Lieutenant R. N. Hanbury | 342 Battery |
| 2nd Lieut. J. S. Crisfield | 344 Battery |

All other ranks of 343 battery were transferred but it is not known whether any from the other batteries volunteered, as had some officers, to provide a cadre for the Welwyn Garden City battery. The history of 79th Anti-Aircraft Brigade, later 79th (Hertfordshire Yeomanry) Heavy Anti-Aircraft Regiment, will be told in a following volume. Here it need only be recorded that instructions for the return of 343 Battery's 18-pdrs. to the Royal Arsenal, Woolwich were received before the end of October[17] and, on a happier note, that the officers of 86th Field Brigade resolved to present to 79th Anti-Aircraft Brigade a silver salver of the type customarily given to officers of 86th Brigade on marriage, though "in this case the salver will commemorate a divorce, not a union" (Cory-Wright papers). The presentation duly took place and the salver is among the principal pieces held by 201 (Hertfordshire and Bedfordshire Yeomanry) Battery, present-day successors to both brigades.

*Reorganisation and re-equipment, November 1938–February 1939*

Instructions for the reorganisation of the Field Force component of the Territorial Army, the general effect of which has already been noted in Chapter 1, were promulgated on 10th October 1938.[18] Among the 'Principal Changes' introduced were the adoption by Royal Artillery units of the Territorial Army of the nomenclature introduced for Regular units in May 1938 and the reconstitution of units from the four-battery field brigade to the field regiment, consisting of only two batteries, each of three troops. It was made clear in the appendix showing the detail of 54th (East Anglian) Division that the division would reorganise as an infantry division with three three-battalion infantry brigades, retaining the traditional designations 161–163, and that the divisional artillery would be reconstituted as follows:

| *New Unit* | *To be formed from* |
| --- | --- |
| 85th (East Anglian) Field Regiment | 85th Field Brigade |
| 86th (East Anglian) (Hertfordshire Yeomanry) Field Regiment | 86th Field Brigade |
| 105th (Bedfordshire Yeomanry) Field Regiment | 105th Field Brigade (formerly Army Troops) |
| 55th (Suffolk and Norfolk Yeomanry) Anti-Tank Regiment | 108th Field Brigade (formerly Army Troops) |

Noting that within the divisional area 84th Field Brigade (less 336 Battery) and 343 Battery of 86th Field Brigade were in course of conversion to the anti-aircraft role, the same appendix directs that "336 Field Battery will join 86th Field Brigade to replace 343 Field Battery". Thus, 86th Field Brigade would be restored to the old four-battery establishment and able to comply with the instruction that "Field brigades which are required to become divisional field regiments will be reorganised into headquarters and two batteries, each of three troops, by merging pairs of existing batteries into one battery". The effective date of this far-reaching reorganisation, which, as the War Office letter made clear, was both imposed and without consultation, was to be 1st November 1938, though in practice it was to take much longer for the fine details to be implemented, and by then yet more reorganisation would have overtaken Associations and units.

Colonel Robertson was faced with the impossible task of selecting two out of the existing four batteries (341, 342, 343 and the recently-joined 336) to continue as the reconstituted batteries of the new regiment. For reasons which have not been recorded, he decided to set aside the designations 336 and 341 and the new unit was organised and located as follows:

*86th (East Anglian) (Hertfordshire Yeomanry) Field Regiment, R.A.*

| | |
| --- | --- |
| Regimental Headquarters | Hertford |
| *342 Field Battery, R.A.* | |
| Battery Headquarters and A Troop | Hertford |
| B and C Troops | St. Albans |
| *344 Field Battery, R.A.* | |
| Battery Headquarters and D Troop | Hitchin |
| E and F Troops | Peterborough |

Major W. A. Ramsay, commanding 336 Battery, five officers and all other ranks of the battery were transferred from 84th (1st East Anglian) Field Brigade to 86th Field Regiment with effect from 1st November 1938. Major Ramsay was appointed to the new post of second-in-command of the regiment, while the rest of the old Peterborough battery were re-formed as E and F Troops of 344 Battery. Distance and differing traditions did nothing to encourage the proper integration of the Peterborough component into the overwhelmingly Hertfordshire 86th Field Regiment, despite the fact that the Territorial batteries of Hertfordshire and

Northamptonshire had, between 1908 and 1920, been linked in 4th East Anglian Brigade, R.F.A. (see *The Hertfordshire Batteries, Royal Field Artillery – An Illustrated History*). Now, as previously, only embodiment, mobilisation and the common purpose of war would properly suppress the antipathies between the two 'ends' of the regiment.

It will be recalled that 86th Field Brigade consisted of two 18-pdr. batteries (341 and 343) and two 4.5-in. howitzer batteries (342 and 344) immediately prior to 1st November 1938 and that 343 Battery's 18-pdrs. had been returned to Ordnance when the battery converted to the anti-aircraft role. As at 1st November 1938, therefore, 86th Field Regiment held four 18-pdrs. and eight 4.5-in. howitzers in Hertfordshire. Instructions were received in mid-December that the regiment would retain the four 4.5-in. howitzers held by 336 Battery and would take over four more howitzers previously held by 84th Field Brigade, at the same time disposing of the remaining four 18-pdrs.[19] As a result, 86th Field Regiment would be armed with sixteen 4.5-in. howitzers – an unsatisfactory number, if only for the reason that they could not be shared equally between the six troops. The instructions on the redistribution of the elderly 4.5-in. howitzers had in fact been preceded by details of the scale and arrangements for issue of the new equipment which had been foreshadowed in the debate on the Army Estimates nearly two years previously.[20] As a 'scattered' unit, 86th Field Regiment would be entitled to the following scale:

| | |
|---|---|
| 25-pdr. guns | 16 |
| Field artillery tractors | 13 |
| 8-cwt. trucks (wireless) | 10 |
| 8-cwt. trucks | 3 |
| 15-cwt. trucks | 14 |
| Motor-cycles | 10 |
| Bren guns | 8 |
| Anti-tank rifles | 8 |
| Wireless sets (No. 1 or No. 11) | 10 |

The converted 25-pdrs. ('18/25-pdrs.') would not be available for issue until some time between November 1939 and February 1940, since priority was to be given to the replacement of 18-pdrs. still in the hands of Territorial batteries so that they could be returned for conversion and re-issue. Four-wheel drive field artillery tractors, or 'Quads', would not be available before June 1939, but in the meantime units would be able to draw additional 6-wheeled vehicles (of unspecified type). Units already held their entitlement of 8-cwt. trucks, G.S. and would be complete to scale with 15-cwt. trucks by March 1939 and 8-cwt. F.F.W. by May 1939. Issues of Bren guns and anti-tank rifles would take place during the summer of 1939 but the full scale of wireless sets would not be available "for a considerable time" and meanwhile units would have to make do with only two each. All this must have come as encouraging news to 86th Field Regiment, which, in the space of a single year was scheduled to leap from the iron-tyred guns of the First World War and a very limited holding of 1920's wheeled vehicles to the conspicuously modern 'families' of guns, vehicles and wireless sets that would make them almost indistinguishable from their Regular counterparts. Small wonder, too, that accommodation for vehicles in battery drill-halls had been found wanting earlier in the year.

In January 1939, Lieutenant-Colonel Robertson, who had just been appointed O.B.E. in the New Year Honours, left 86th Field Regiment on posting to the War Office (T.A.1). He was succeeded by Lieutenant-Colonel Sir Patrick Coghill, Bt., who had been in command of 342 Battery since January 1935. Sir Patrick took over at a time when a period of stability was much to be desired, to allow the reconstituted unit to settle down, new equipment to arrive and new skills to be mastered, culminating, of course, in a successful summer camp, planned for the second half of July. The peace establishment of a Territorial field regiment, at thirty officers and 348 other ranks, differed little, in total, from that of a field brigade (24 officers and 342 other ranks) but early in 1939 regiments were directed to recruit other ranks to 120 per cent of peace establishment. The strength of 86th Field Regiment on 1st March 1939 was reported as 24 officers and 357 other ranks – a shortfall of six and sixty, respectively, against the new targets, but with recruiting relatively buoyant, one that the unit could reasonably expect to make good within the year, even if not before camp.

*The duplication of the Field Force and preparations for war, March–August 1939*

All thought of stability and consolidation combined with a steady inflow of recruits must have been set aside, however, when the news broke at the end of March 1939 that the Field Force component of the Territorial Army was to be doubled. There is no indication in Hertfordshire Territorial Association records or in papers in the Regimental Collection of any prior warning of the announcement, which was made in the House of Commons on 29th March. Detailed instructions to units were promulgated by War Office letter dated 31st March,[21] which set out a three-stage process, as follows:

> *Stage 1*
>
> The formation of a training cadre (nine officers and 64 other ranks, mainly non-commissioned officers, for a field regiment) to form the unit training centre on mobilisation; the appointment of additional staff within units to deal with the influx of recruits and to prepare for expansion; the raising of all ranks to war establishment (27 officers and 555 other ranks for a field regiment) plus the training cadre.
>
> *Stage 2*
>
> The raising within the original unit of the nucleus of the duplicate unit. For a field regiment this nucleus was defined as a battery headquarters and two troops (eleven officers and 195 other ranks), which would expand to form regimental headquarters and two batteries.
>
> *Stage 3*
>
> The duplicate unit to be raised to war establishment around the nucleus formed during Stage 2.

During Stage 1 the commanding officer-designate of the duplicate unit was to be selected, so that he could be appointed to command the nucleus as a major and be promoted to lieutenant-colonel at the opening of Stage 3. The War Office letter unfortunately used the terms '1st Line' and '2nd Line' rather than 'original' and 'duplicate' and was obliged to conclude with the following paragraph:

> "Although duplicate units have been referred to as '2nd Line', their [*function and*] status will, on assuming a separate identity (Stage 3), be in all respects similar and equal to 1st Line units."

The words 'function and' were included in the original letter but deleted by an amendment dated 3rd April 1939 – an indicator, perhaps, that events were moving so fast that some of the implications of policy decisions necessarily made quickly, and at short notice, had not been fully assessed.

Recalling the events of the spring of 1939 some thirty years later, Sir Patrick Coghill wrote:

> "When the doubling of the Territorial Army was ordered the War Office gave no clue whether speed or a long-term policy had prior claim. In the event I decided that expansion could only be based on the existing drill-halls – Hertford, St. Albans, Hitchin and Peterborough – and that quality was more important than quantity. The four battery stations were the only foundation on which to build. Also . . . it was always possible that the War Office might order a first-line regiment to be handpicked . . . leaving a weak second-line regiment."

The likelihood that many units would find it most convenient to split geographically – the natural result of Sir Patrick's plan to expand on existing battery centres – seems not to have been taken into account in the elaborate, three-stage War Office plan outlined above and there is no evidence that 86th Field Regiment went formally through the stages required. Before there could be any assessment of quality, volunteers would have to appear at the drill-halls in considerable numbers, and most of the month of April was taken up by a Government-backed campaign for recruits that ran in parallel with other appeals for volunteers for 'National Service', notably the Air Raid Precautions Service (later to become 'Civil Defence') and the Special Constabulary, which then included the Observer Corps. There was huge support for this campaign in the local press, both throughout Hertfordshire and in Peterborough. Statistical tables, some quite elaborate, concentrated on 'Volunteers needed'. A table published in the *Hertfordshire Mercury* on 21st April showed, for instance, that as at 1st April, 86th Field Regiment had required 202 to reach war establishment (probably including an over-bearing for the training cadre) and a further 581 to meet the increased requirement under the expansion programme. Advertisements in the press, open days and public demonstrations all emphasised the technical interest of the modern Territorial Army and the new weapons and vehicles that were steadily coming in. It was, perhaps, unfortunate that 86th Field Regiment's ageing 4.5-in. howitzers, still with the iron tyres of the horse-drawn era, should be described as 'new' in more than one local newspaper, but their recently-received Morris-Commercial CDSW tractors looked the part, for all that they were stop-gaps until Quads became available. Recruits flocked in. It is no longer profitable to argue whether they were genuine volunteers, 'conscience-conscripts' or seeking to avoid call-up. The important thing was that they did enlist, and in sufficient numbers to indicate that two field regiments at war establishment was a viable proposition, even with competition from anti-aircraft units, both gun and searchlight, and the local infantry battalions, not to mention the civilian services. Taking St. Albans alone as an example, the *Hertfordshire Advertiser* reported on 5th May 1939 that 270 men had enlisted for 86th Field Regiment within the previous fortnight and went on almost to excuse the poor local response by explaining that, "It must not be overlooked that a large number of young men living in St. Albans work in London, and many of them have joined London units . . ."

The War Office letter giving instructions on the raising of duplicate units required Territorial Associations to forward their recommendations for the location of original and duplicate units by 20th April. Accordingly, at their meeting on 17th April Hertfordshire Territorial Association resolved to reply:

> ". . . provided recruiting comes up to what is expected, the Association's policy with regard to 86th Field Regiment is as follows:
>
> 1. To increase the two troops at Peterborough to form one complete battery there.
> 2. To increase the two troops at St. Albans to form one complete battery there. A new drill hall will be required.
> 3. To form one full battery divided between Hitchin and Hertford.
> 4. To form one full battery at Barnet, where part of the site now occupied by 334 Anti-Aircraft Searchlight Company may be utilised for units and a drill-hall."

On seeing these proposals, C.R.A. 54th Division responded giving approval in principle but continuing:

> "I think . . . it should be considered whether it is not possible to take this opportunity . . . to remove the Peterborough Artillery from their recently-formed connection with Hertfordshire, as the distances involved are really too great for efficiency. It is understood there would be little difficulty in raising a new complete battery in Cambridge, and if this is so, that battery, with Peterborough, would form the second-line regiment, while the whole of the first-line regiment would remain in Hertfordshire; in this case St. Albans and Barnet would have to produce only one battery between them."

That there was merit in the C.R.A.'s observation was confirmed by a report made by the adjutant of 86th Field Regiment to the Financial and General Purposes Committee of Hertfordshire Territorial Association on 12th May. He had, he said, just returned from a visit to Peterborough with Sir Patrick Coghill and "it was very evident that all concerned in Peterborough were only too ready to sever the connection with Hertfordshire". All thought of losing the Peterborough battery was abandoned, however, when the War Office replied on 16th May that it was "regretted that it is not possible to group the Peterborough battery with another situated nearer to that town and therefore this battery must remain part of 86th Field Regiment or its duplicate unit".[22] The letter went on to approve the provisional distribution of headquarters and batteries as follows:

*86th Field Regiment*

| | |
|---|---|
| Regimental Headquarters | Hertford |
| Half-battery | Hertford |

Plate 65 *Recruiting for the doubled Field Force at Hitchin, April 1939.*
Top – *Demonstration by 344 Battery in St. Mary's Square. The near-antique 4.5.-in. howitzers are in sharp contrast to the new Morris-Commercial CDSW gun towers and 8-cwt. trucks that were reaching the battery and can also be seen in the arena.*
Bottom – *Potential recruits hear details of the 4.5-in. howitzer at 344 Battery's drill-hall at Bearton Camp.*
(Hertfordshire Pictorial Archives – Hitchin Museum)

| | |
|---|---|
| Battery and half-battery | St. Albans |
| *Duplicate Unit* | |
| Regimental Headquarters | Hitchin |
| Battery | Hitchin |
| Battery | Peterborough |

Confirmation of the geographical distribution of the two regiments enabled Hertfordshire Territorial Association to proceed with the acquisition of sites for new drill-halls or hutted accommodation. Suitable sites were identified at Hertford (in North Crescent), St. Albans (off Holywell Hill) and Hitchin (opposite the existing drill-hall in Bedford Road) but of these only the Holywell Hill site was secured before the outbreak of war. What amounted to a technical adjustment of battery locations, again because it was not properly implemented before mobilisation, was introduced in June 1939, when it was decided that a whole battery, rather than the half-battery approved, should be stationed at Hertford.

The War Office list of provisional designations for duplicate regiments and batteries dated 1st June 1939[23] took no account of the geographical distribution or the long-standing traditions of 86th Field Regiment and its duplicate, now designated 135th Field Regiment. Hertfordshire Territorial Association replied at once saying that it seemed "a pity to separate stations from the battery numbers with which they have been associated for many years" and asking for the designations to be confirmed as:

| | |
|---|---|
| *86th Field Regiment* | |
| 341 Battery | St. Albans |
| 342 Battery | Hertford |
| *135th Field Regiment* | |
| 336 Battery | Peterborough |
| 344 Battery | Hitchin |

In response to an invitation to propose "titles which it is desired shall be included in the designations of regiments and batteries in addition to numbers", the Association explained that prior to 1871 there had existed in Hertfordshire two separate Yeomanry units – the North Hertfordshire Yeomanry and the South Hertfordshire Yeomanry – and asked for the designations of the two field regiments to reflect this historical division as 86th (South Hertfordshire Yeomanry) Field Regiment and 135th (North Hertfordshire Yeomanry) Field Regiment. The 'East Anglian' part of their heritage, which applied to both units, would have been officially extinguished, rather than simply unofficially discarded, if these designations had been approved, but embodiment and mobilisation were to intervene and there is no evidence that the King's approval was ever obtained. Certainly the War Office publication *Revised Titles and Designations of Units of the Territorial Army*, issued in 1952 as the authority on the succession of units from the inter-war to the post-war years, keeps to the old 'East Anglian – Hertfordshire Yeomanry' designation.

The organisation and designations of duplicate formations – divisions and brigades – of course needed to be proposed and agreed, as well as those for units. A War Office letter dated 22nd May 1939[24] laid down the principle that the areas of the original divisions would be split geographically but pointed out that divisional troops would not necessarily fall clearly, and in the necessary numbers, into the areas which had been selected purely on the basis of the infantry components of the new divisions. Accordingly, a comprehensive scheme for the allocation of divisional troops would be drawn up and no account was to be taken of these units in planning the geographical split of the infantry. It was recognised that this arrangement would cause some difficulty but, in the event of mobilisation in the near future, the original division would be reconstituted and would be given "absolute call" on all or any personnel. The new divisions were to be numbered either to correspond with analogous 2nd Line Territorial divisions of the First World War or were to take the numbers of the 'New Army' divisions from the same area. Infantry brigades would be numbered appropriately within divisions and both divisions and brigades would be able to apply for local designations. The effective date of reorganisation was not to be later than 1st November 1939 but could be put off until the close of the summer training season. The recommendations of Commander-in-Chief Eastern Command for the organisation and designations of the two infantry divisions raised in the old 54th Divisional Area were approved on 17th August 1939[25] as follows:

*54th Division* (Original Formation)

| | |
|---|---|
| Divisional Headquarters | Hertford |
| 161 Infantry Brigade (1/4th, 1/5th and 2/5th Essex) | Brentwood |
| 162 Infantry Brigade (1st and 2nd Herts, 6th Bedfs/Herts) | Hertford |
| 163 Infantry Brigade (2/4th Essex, 5th and 7th R. Berks) | Ilford |

*18th Division* (Duplicate Formation)

| | |
|---|---|
| Divisional Headquarters | Norwich |
| 53 Infantry Brigade (5th, 6th and 7th R. Norfolks) | Norwich |
| 54 Infantry Brigade (4th R. Norfolks, 4th and 5th Suffolk) | Ipswich |
| 55 Infantry Brigade (5th Bedfs/Herts, 1st and 2nd Cambs) | Cambridge |

The duplicate division was designated in accordance with the instruction permitting the use of the numbers of locally-raised New Army divisions, the 18th Division of the First World War having been raised principally in East Anglia. Reorganisation in accordance with the War Office letter of 17th August was ordered to be complete by 1st November. The allocation of divisional troops appears to have been overtaken by mobilisation but worked out as follows, as far as the divisional artillery were concerned:

*54th Divisional Artillery*

85th (East Anglian) Field Regiment

86th (East Anglian) (Hertfordshire Yeomanry) Field Regiment

134th (East Anglian) Field Regiment

55th (Suffolk Yeomanry) Anti-Tank Regiment

*18th Divisional Artillery*

105th (Bedfordshire Yeomanry) Field Regiment

135th (East Anglian) (Hertfordshire Yeomanry) Field Regiment

148th (Bedfordshire Yeomanry) Field Regiment

65th (Norfolk Yeomanry) Anti-Tank Regiment

Necessary as all the arguments over titles and new peace-time organisation may have been, officers and men of 86th Field Regiment had much more pressing matters on their minds as they went to annual camp at Chiseldon, near Swindon on the edge of Salisbury Plain, for the last fortnight of July. Partial, but full-time, manning of the anti-aircraft defences had been in effect since May and the drive to progress preparations for war was intensifying, rather than slackening. An advance party of four officers and seventy other ranks – huge by all previous standards – erected 211 bell tents, fifteen store tents and sixteen marquees, not to mention cookhouses and latrines, for occupation by more than sixty officers and nearly 1,100 other ranks who attended camp. Most of those recruited in the previous three months had been issued only with 'overalls, combination' (boiler suits) and until two or three days before setting off for camp it was believed that they would have to make do on this minimal scale. However, by some miracle, the supply system delivered huge quantities of clothing just in time, and all was well[26]. It was fortunate that the latest-joined were kitted out, for all sources

Plate 66 *86th Field Regiment's last camp before mobilisation – Chiseldon, July 1939.*
Top – *Newly-commissioned Second Lieutenant Stephen Perry in the field training dress laid down for officers and based on a dark brown one-piece overall* (above left); *'Mixed dress' in a 4.5-in. howitzer detachment – the No. 1* (back to camera) *has old-style service dress, with trousers, rather than breeches, while the rest of the detachment have newly-issued overalls and khaki field service caps* (above right); *a Morris-Commercial six-wheeler Series D, of 1920s vintage, leads two new CDSWs away from a gun position* (below).
Bottom – *A vehicle park with a mixture of modern Morris-Commercial and Guy 8- and 15-cwt. trucks in the foreground* (above); *Guy 15-cwt. in use as 'Y1' (a battery C.P.O.'s vehicle) making an effort to appear inconspicuous without the benefit of a camouflage net* (below).
(Regimental Collection)

Plate 67 *Battery staff at Chiseldon, July 1939.*
Top – *Signallers contact the O.P. by wireless, while the G.P.O. exercises 'voice control' over the guns in the traditional manner.*
Bottom – *A battery command post in a 'non-tactical' setting.*
(Regimental Collection)

agree that the weather was appalling, with torrential rain and seas of mud, throughout the first week and well into the second. The two eventual regiments went to camp organised and administered as a single unit – 86th Field Regiment – with two batteries – 342 Battery (A, B and C Troops) and 344 Battery (D, E and F Troops). A quartermaster had only just been added to the establishment of a Territorial field regiment and two of the regiment's P.S.Is. had been selected for commissioning and appointment – B.Q.M.S. P.E. Felstead of 344 Battery, who was commissioned on 10th June with a view to becoming quartermaster of 135th Field Regiment and was quartermaster at camp, and R.S.M. J. W. Olney, who remained R.S.M. for camp but was due to be commissioned as quartermaster of 86th Field Regiment in October. Quartermasters, commissioned or otherwise, and storemen, must have been at a premium at Chiseldon, for not only was the regiment vastly over establishment in men who were training in adverse weather, but there were sufficient vehicles and instruments for only one fully equipped battery to exercise. A pool system had therefore to be operated both for individual training, which took place during the first week, and battery training during the second. Visitors to the regiment in camp included Lieutenant-Colonel J. Hudson, M.C., T.D., at the time on the Territorial Army Reserve of Officers (General List, Royal Artillery). Colonel Hudson was shortly afterwards selected for command of 135th Field Regiment – in defiance of the instructions that the officer selected for command of the 2nd Line unit should command the nucleus under Stage 2 – and was appointed back to the active list as a lieutenant-colonel with effect from 18th August 1939.

Colonel Sir Geoffrey Church, Bt., M.C., T.D., who was promoted to brigadier in May 1939 as C.R.A. 54th Division, kept an account of events in 86th Field Regiment between 1938 and 1940 which is now in the Regimental Collection. His diarist, for it seems unlikely that he
[68] assembled the detail himself, gives no account of the final parade at camp from which the

original and duplicate regiments are said to have marched off to their separate futures. He does record, however, that, "It was decided to complete the split at our leisure in October". Once again, reasonable plans were overtaken by the urgency of impending war, for Sir Geoffrey's account continues, "On 24th August advance parties were mobilised and started preparations for general mobilisation at battery stations". Full mobilisation was ordered on 1st September, two days in advance of the actual declaration of war, and 135th Field Regiment cut the ties with 86th and assumed independent existence on 7th September 1939.

The histories of the two units must now be followed separately.

NOTES

1. *Report of proceedings at a Conference between the Secretary of State for War and Representatives of the Territorial Force Associations – 1st April 1919, 1st May 1919 and 30th January 1920*
2. A.C.I. 594/1920
3. *Peace Establishments, Part II.* See also Appendix 2.
4. *Peace Establishments, Part II.* See also Appendix 2.
5. Army Orders 481 and 482/1922
6. W.O.L. 20/Artillery/4577 (A.G.1) of 20th March 1929
7. W.O.Ls. 20/Artillery/4798 (A.G.1) of 9th January and 7th March 1930 and *Peace Establishments, Part II,* 1929-30. See also Appendix 2.
8. W.O.L. 57/Vehicles/1311 (T.A.1) of 16th August 1930
9. W.O.L. 20/General/5457 (A.G.4d) of 27th July 1937 and Army Order 168/1937
10. W.O.L. 79/Mobn./885 (S.D.2) of 16th December 1932
11. *The Times* 17th and 22nd March 1937
12. W.O.L. 20/Artillery/5017 of 8th March 1937
13. W.O.L. 54/Artillery/1110 (M.G.O.2) of 12th October 1937
14. W.O.Ls. 54/General/8118 (A.G.4c) of 25th April and 3rd May 1938
15. W.O.L. 54/General/8118 (A.G.4c) of 9th August 1938
16. W.O.L. 20/A.-A./146 (T.A.1) of 18th July 1938. Confirmation of the formation of 79th Anti-Aircraft Brigade and the designations of brigade and batteries were promulgated in A.C.I. 344/1939.
17. W.O.L. 54/Artillery/1110 (M.G.O.2) of 24th October 1938
18. W.O.L. 20/General/5689 (T.A.1) of 10th October 1938
19. W.O.L. 54/Artillery/1110 (M.G.O.2) of 13th December 1938
20. W.O.L. 57/General/9129 (S.D.2) of 1st December 1938
21. W.O.L. 79/Mob./2778 (T.A.1) of 31st March 1939
22. W.O.L. 9/Herts/562 (T.A.1) of 16th May 1939
23. W.O.L. 20/Artillery/5492 (T.A.1) of 1st June 1939
24. W.O.L. 20/General/5733 (T.A.1) of 22nd May 1939
25. W.O.L. 20/Misc./1335 (T.A.1) of 17th August 1939
26. The clothing issued was service dress, with trousers. W.O.L. 54/General/7874 (M.G.O. 7b) of 31st March 1939 had announced the approval of a new form of active service dress, known as 'battle dress', which was to be issued to the Regular Army "during the summer of 1939". No date for issues to the Territorial Army was forecast and they did not, in fact, begin until some months after mobilisation. Throughout 1939 and the first few months of 1940, photographs show a considerable variety of dress.

Army Form E.518

# RESERVE AND AUXILIARY FORCES ACT, 1939.
# TERRITORIAL ARMY.

## CALLING OUT NOTICE.

To—

Name ..........SAUNDERS . R. J...........

Rank..........Gnr.............................. Army Number.896707..

Regt. or Corps.342 Battery . R.A. (T.A.)..........

In pursuance of directions given by the Secretary of State for War in accordance with an Order in Council made under Section 1 of the above-mentioned Act, you are hereby notified that you are called out for military service commencing from

25 · 8 · 1939 and for this purpose you are required to join the

..........Above Unit..........

at.....28. St Andrews St.............on that day.

Should you not present yourself on that day you will be liable to be proceeded against.

342nd FIELD BATTERY R.A. (T.A.)
25 AUG 1939
No...................
86th FIELD REGIMENT R.A. (T.A.)

*Stamp of Officer Commanding Unit.*

*Place*..............................................................

*Date* ..............................................................

You should bring your Health and Pensions Insurance Card and Unemployment Insurance Book. If, however, you cannot obtain these before joining you should write to your employer asking him to forward these to you at your unit headquarters. If you are in possession of a receipt (U.I. 40) from the Employment Exchange for your Employment Book bring that receipt with you.

You will also bring your Army Book 3, but you *must not fill* in any particulars on page 13 or the " Statement of family " in that book, and the postcards therein *must not be used.*

**[5/39] (393/2397) Wt. 21114 750M 7/39 H & S Ltd. Gp. 393 (2242) Forms E518/1**

Plate 68 *Army Form E.518 – 'Calling Out Notice' – giving notice of call-out and embodiment to Gunner R.J. Saunders of 342 Battery. Gunner Saunders lived at Hoddesdon and was employed in the Surveyor's Department of Hoddesdon Urban District Council. He was a member of 342 Battery's 'Key Party' and as such was called out on 25th August 1939. The calling out notice was brought to him at work and he left at once – to serve throughout the war with 86th Field Regiment.*
(Regimental Collection)

Chapter 4

# *The Original Unit – 86th Field Regiment, R.A., September 1939–April 1946*

*With 54th Infantry Division, September 1939–June 1942*

Orders for mobilisation reached Regimental Headquarters of 86th Field Regiment – at that time still responsible for 135th Field Regiment – at Hertford at 3.15 p.m. on 1st September 1939. Steps were at once taken to call out and embody all ranks and Major E.J.T. Lutyens, former battery commander of 342 Battery and veteran of the Egypt–Palestine campaign with 1st Hertfordshire Battery, R.F.A., and four other officers were immediately recalled from the regimental list of the Territorial Army Reserve of Officers. By the time war was declared on 3rd September, the combined 86th and 135th Field Regiments boasted 73 Territorial officers and one Regular officer of the Royal Artillery, together with two Territorial medical officers and a Territorial chaplain. The war establishment of a field regiment required 27 officers of the Royal Artillery, including one quartermaster, and one attached medical officer, but preparation for war throws up all kinds of miscellaneous officer appointments which units are called upon to fill. The combined regiments lost six officers at once – three to Headquarters 54th Division and three to the artillery training organisation – so the overbearing was welcome, especially when the inexperience of so many officers is taken into account.

When the two regiments achieved independence from each other on 7th September, Regimental Headquarters of 86th Field Regiment remained at Hertford with Lieutenant-Colonel Sir Patrick Coghill in command and Major J.C. Chaytor as second-in-command. Major J.B. Morgan Smith was battery commander of 341 Battery (A, B and C Troops) at St. Albans, with Major R.D. Cribb commanding 342 Battery (D, E and F Troops) at Hertford. Some three weeks after mobilisation the regiment was brought up to war establishment in other ranks (555) by a draft of 'Army Class I' militiamen. For the first two months of the war batteries remained at their home stations, arranging such training as they could with the limited guns, vehicles and equipment at their disposal, and overflowing from their drill-halls into billets, with some soldiers who lived close by going home each night.

On 20th October advance parties left for Leicestershire, where it was planned that the whole of 54th Division would concentrate for training and re-equipment. The regiment would have been billeted in the area Coalville–Ashby-de-la-Zouche but "a sudden East Coast scare changed all this" (Church) and in conformity with the 'Julius Caesar' plan, briefly described by Collier (see Bibliography), the division was ordered to a counter-invasion deployment on the Suffolk coast. Some idea of the hand-to-mouth arrangements that were commonplace in the early weeks of the war is conveyed by the complete absence of officially-supplied maps of the deployment area. On ascertaining that none were available, Sir Patrick Coghill turned upside-down the stationers and bookshops in Hertford and secured two half-inch-to-the-mile maps of the East Coast. He turned out to be just a little better equipped than the brigade commander he was to support, who had a motoring map with the whole of England on one sheet! Less than 24 hours after the regiment had received orders to place a two-troop battery, both troops of which had to be capable of operating independently, under command of 163 Infantry Brigade, 341 Battery (eight 4.5-in. howitzers) moved to Redgrave Hall, near Diss in

Plate 69 *Gunners* (L.–R.) *Stevenson, Millard, Waldren, Dudley and North of 342 Battery in the drill-hall yard at Hertford, reputedly on the'first night of the war', September 1939. The small differences in dress – headgear, collar badges, belts, boots – may reflect the supply position or the men's unfamiliarity with standing orders and the fact that the battery sergeant-major has not yet seen them! Note also the precarious sandbagging balanced on the exterior window ledges. Gunner Stevenson was later to receive a United States decoration for gallantry as an O.P. signaller.*
(Regimental Collection)

Norfolk. On 5th November the guns deployed forward more than twenty miles to Westleton to cover possible landings in the Dunwich area under command of 163 Infantry Brigade, while 342 Battery moved into Redgrave Hall and Regimental Headquarters to Yoxford, some five miles inland and three miles from Westleton. The Yoxford–Westleton–Redgrave Hall layout held good until mid-January 1940, when Redgrave Hall was abandoned in favour of Sudbourne Hall, Orford, about ten miles south of Yoxford. The eight guns deployed on the coast by 341 Battery were the only serviceable guns the regiment had, so throughout the period November 1939–early February 1940, according to Sir Geoffrey Church's diary, "341 and 342 shuttlecocked to and fro between Westleton and Redgrave Hall or Sudbourne Hall" in relief of each other at roughly fortnightly intervals.

An intake of 150 'Army Class II' militiamen, recorded in Sir Patrick Coghill's diary as "all from Hertfordshire", began arriving on 12th December. In order to train these men, and a fur-



Plate 70 *The officers of 342 Battery at Hertford shortly after mobilisation, September–October 1939.* Standing (L.–R.) *2nd Lieuts. D.C. McClintock, J.A.S. Cleminson, M.R. Norman, S.D. Perry, R.T. West, P.A. Turner.* Seated (L.–R.) *2nd Lieuts. W.A. Anderson, K.G. Swann, Captain J. Carew Jones, Major R.D. Cribb, Captains W.E. Boyes, R.J. Norbury, 2nd Lieut. H.A.R. Powell.*
(Regimental Collection)

Plate 71 *On the Suffolk coast during the winter of 1939–40.* Left – *A 4.5-in. howitzer dug in. Expanded metal sheets have been laid on the floor of the gun-pit in an effort to prevent the iron-tyred wheels sinking into the sandy soil.* Right – *The ammunition shelter to the rear of the same gun-pit. Note that smoking should not have been permitted anywhere near ammunition.* (Regimental Collection)

ther fifty or so from 85th Field Regiment, to a standard at which they could be posted to batteries, a training battery was formed at Redgrave Hall, staffed jointly by officers and non-commissioned officers of 85th and 86th Field Regiments and under the command of Captain J. Carew Jones of 86th Field Regiment. The trainees, who came directly from civilian life, were successfully put through an eight-week course and were ready for posting to batteries on 10th February. In 86th Field Regiment's case, the draft was split approximately equally between the two batteries, which became substantially over establishment in both officers and men. Perhaps with this overbearing in mind, 86th Field Regiment was instructed during December to select a cadre of seven officers, seventeen non-commissioned officers and fifty gunners around which a new regiment would be raised. The cadre would, in theory, carry the spirit of the Hertfordshire Yeomanry into the off-spring, which might, for instance, have worn the hart badge and incorporated 'Hertfordshire Yeomanry' into its designation. The possibility remains theoretical, however, since orders to cancel the cadre were received in April 1940.

There were losses of individuals in January and February 1940 which will serve to illustrate the steady turnover of personnel that was to be a feature of the next four years. Major Chaytor was posted to a staff appointment in the Middle East and succeeded as second-in-command by

Plate 72 *A 4.5-in. howitzer of B Troop, 341 Battery dug in on the coast at Dunwich, Suffolk, winter 1939–40.* (Regimental Collection)

Major Morgan Smith, whereupon Captain J.B.S. Tabor was promoted to the command of 341 Battery. Three officers volunteered for service with a ski battalion that was to be sent to Finland. Eventually only one was accepted but Finland capitulated before the battalion could finish its training, so in the end all three volunteers returned. Posting and volunteering were not the only ways out of the regiment as far as officers were concerned, though, for Sir Patrick Coghill recorded in his diary in February, "painful interview with ..... to explain he was n.b.g. and must go". The drain of other ranks began in December 1939, when the first five were selected for training for War Emergency Commissions and posted to an officer cadet training unit. Later there would be calls for those with special skills – Gunners Burgess and Searl, both of 342 Battery would get as far as the regimental office after a call for those with electrical experience, but their ploy to escape the grind of service in England came to nothing when it was discovered that, though employed by a local electricity board, their experience was limited to digging holes in the road to allow their more highly qualified colleagues to work on the cables! The Commandos, the Army Air Corps (later the Parachute Regiment) and any number of 'funnies' and specialist requirements would make their appeals to officers and men as the war went on and the out-take of experienced personnel would be made good with newly-commissioned officers, and men fresh from basic training. As a result of this turnover, the number of pre-war Territorial officers and men – once one hundred per cent of unit strength – was steadily eroded, but there were always enough to ensure that the newcomers, who were, of course, from all parts of the British Isles, swiftly adopted the *esprit de corps* of the Hertfordshire unit whose badges they wore.

The regiment handed over the forward deployment at Westleton to 134th Field Regiment early in February and moved into billets in Chelmsford. The move was made without regret, for the weather had been appalling and for much of January large parties of men had been placed at the disposal of the local authorities to assist in clearing roads blocked by several feet of snow. The exceptionally hard winter and poor billets, especially at Westleton, might have made for poor health and poor morale but Sir Geoffrey Church records the contrary:

> "... the health of the men was remarkably good and the regiment escaped the flu epidemics which ravaged other units. Nothing could have exceeded the kindness of the people living round the areas where the regiment was, nor their hospitality, from the highest to the lowest. This made a vast difference to the happiness and morale of all."

Once at Chelmsford and relieved of immediate responsibility for artillery defence of the coast, the regiment could attempt 'collective training'. This was easier said than done, for according to Sir Geoffrey Church's diary:

> "Little training was possible, as the regiment had only twelve 4.5-in. howitzers, four of which were 'D.P.' [*'for demonstration purposes only'*], seven 8-cwt. and seven 15-cwt. trucks and some shocking hired transport. It was generally short of all equipment. However, by the beginning of April it succeeded in doing skeleton regimental 'schemes'."

Sir Geoffrey's diarist failed to record the event which years later is the principal memory of the regiment's time in Chelmsford – the regulations covering vaccinations and inoculations could no longer be avoided and every man was given eight 'jabs'!

Following orders that 54th Division was to move complete to Northumberland, recce parties left Chelmsford on 30th March and an advance party on 6th April. The main body left by train on 16th April, to arrive at Newcastle the following morning and continue their journey on the branch line through Morpeth. They were deposited at Ponteland Station, rather than Angerton, as planned, but there they were met by eighteen 'charabancs' (according to Sir Patrick Coghill) instead of the five that had been ordered, so they finished the journey in some style. Regimental Headquarters and the Light Aid Detachment, R.A.O.C. were billeted at Whalton, while 341 Battery occupied Belsay Castle and 342 Battery Capheaton Hall. The coming of spring may have heightened perceptions, but Sir Geoffrey Church's diarist recorded that the new locations were "all very comfortable and with most kind and hospitable neighbours and delightful country – mostly grass and good for training". Despite the lack of guns and equipment, the pace of training was indeed stepped up and a note at the end of 342 Battery's scrapbook records that there were now "regimental exercises and divisional exercises each week and two-day exercises including night occupations". Purpose would no doubt have been added to the training as the 'Phoney War' turned into a shooting war and the British Expeditionary Force first advanced into Belgium and then retired on Dunkirk. The same scrap book records:

Plate 73 *342 Battery at Capheaton, Northumberland, spring 1940.* Top – *Guard mounting. The guard commander* (far left) *is Bombardier R.T. Stackwood. Full web equipment was not issued until June 1940, hence the absence of belts, braces and ammunition pouches.* Bottom – *'Spud bashing'.* (Regimental Collection)

"Owing to the gravity of the situation in Europe, all leave was cancelled on 11th May, one leave party having to be recalled. Patrols were sent out each dawn and dusk during these days of crisis, chiefly to guard against the enemy landing troops by parachute. These patrols were withdrawn within a week."

To make best use of the regiment in the counter-invasion or counter-raid role, all serviceable guns – by now only five 4.5-in. howitzers – were concentrated in 342 Battery and 341 Battery became a 'rifle battery'. The regiment was placed on six hours' notice to move, and, as if to mark the new earnestness by giving 86th Field Regiment the highest possible degree of self-sufficiency, the regimental signal section, until now under training with 54th Divisional Signals, joined, and an 'O.M.E.' (Ordnance Mechanical Engineer) officer was at last posted in to take command of the L.A.D.

"Great news", Sir Patrick Coghill had recorded in his diary towards the end of May, "four 18/25-pdr. guns due to arrive soonest". These long-awaited guns reached the regiment on 6th June 1940, preceded by the unit's full complement of 'Trailers, Artillery, No. 27' – the 25-pdr. 

Plate 74 *A Guy 'Ant' 15-cwt. of 342 Battery at Capheaton, Northumberland, May 1940. The recently-adopted formation sign of 54th Division is on the right-hand front mudguard. The blue monogram 'J.P.' on a red circle was derived from the initials of the divisional commander, Major-General J.H.T. Priestman.* (Regimental Collection)

Plate 75 *Sergeant W. Rist in command of a 4.5-in. howitzer of 342 Battery on exercise in Northumberland, summer 1940. Gas capes have now been issued and are carried tied across the shoulders. Note the 'mechanised' wheels with solid rubber tyres, indicating that the howitzer has reached the regiment after mobilisation.*
(Regimental Collection)

limber. The commanding officer lost no time in booking some range days and Sir Geoffrey Church's diary records that:

> "On 10th and 11th June these four guns and the five serviceable 4.5-in. howitzers went to Redesdale and fired four rounds per gun . . . The O.M.E. is making the remaining three D.P. 4.5s fit to fire. They were duly fired out to sea at a target provided by the Navy, which was hit by Morgan Smith. So the regiment now disposes of four 25-pdrs. and eight 4.5-in. howitzers".

In fact, the firing out to sea did not take place until some days later, by which time the howitzers had been dug in on the beach at Druridge Bay, but the diarist can perhaps be forgiven for allowing his accuracy to be affected by the arrival of modern guns and the first time the regiment had fired its guns since mobilisation. More prosaically, the 342 Battery scrapbook states that, "This was the first time many of the gunners had fired a gun or had even heard one being fired" and goes on to record the issue of complete webbing equipment on 8th June.

The policy of meeting a seaborne invasion or raid on the beaches, rather than in a more mobile encounter away from the shoreline, led to the regiment's move on 19th–20th June to
[76] Linden Hall, Longhorsley, near Morpeth, where they were both nearer the coast and concen-

Plate 76 *Signallers of 342 Battery training with the No. 11 wireless set* (Left) *and the daylight signalling lamp* (Right) *at Capheaton, April–May 1940.* (Regimental Collection)

Plate 77 *Captain J. Carew Jones* (Left) *and Major J.B.S. Tabor* (Right) *in Northumberland, summer 1940. Major Tabor is apparently wearing an early version of the 'Austerity' pattern of service dress jacket in which cloth is saved by having no pleats in the breast pockets and by placing the lower pockets in the lining, rather than having the 'expanding' type worn by Captain Carew Jones.* (Regimental Collection)

trated in one place, from which it was originally intended that guns could be deployed as required. There was, however, an increasing tendency towards incorporating guns in fixed beach defences and, in the absence of more suitable weapons on fixed mountings, 4.5-in. howitzers were gradually removed from their mobile role and dug in. By the end of June six guns had been lost to these 'singleton' positions, which covered more than fifteen miles of coast between Alnmouth and Blyth, though two were then relieved by 18-pdrs. from 85th Field Regiment and returned to regimental control. Six U.S.-manufactured 'pneumatisation sets' (see Chapter 2) arrived early in July and the dug-in 4.5s were rendered more mobile, though there was no intention that they should be moved!

During July, as part of an overall plan that battle-experienced officers and men from the now-withdrawn British Expeditionary Force should pass on their new experience and skills to troops that had remained at home, 86th Field Regiment was involved in an exchange of personnel with 19th Field Regiment, which had served in France and Belgium with 1st Infantry Division. Major Cribb, two other officers and some fifty warrant officers, non-commissioned officers and men left 86th Field Regiment, to be replaced by a similar number from 19th Field Regiment. Major Morgan Smith took over command of 342 Battery from Major Cribb and was succeeded as second-in-command by Major W.S. Wingate Gray, M.C., who led the party from 19th Field Regiment.

The last days of July and the months of August and September were marked, according to Sir Geoffrey Church's diarist, by "endless changes in guns and positions". At the beginning of August, 86th Field Regiment was organised as:

| | | |
|---|---|---|
| 341 Battery: | A Troop | Four 4.5-in. howitzers |
| | B Troop | Infantry |
| | C Troop | Infantry |
| 342 Battery: | D Troop | Four 4.5-in. howitzers |
| | E Troop | Infantry |
| | F Troop | Four 18/25-pdrs. |

In the next two months all the 4.5-in. howitzers were withdrawn. They were replaced by stopgaps while the regiment continued to wait for 25-pdrs., having only one further delivery, of four guns, in mid-September. During August, two troops were re-equipped with two First World War-vintage 60-pdr. medium guns each, reportedly 'trophy guns' removed from parks in Scotland, and at the end of the month eight 75-mm. guns arrived, variously described as "with no equipment of any sort" (Church) or "without limbers, sights or ammunition" (Coghill). These guns were the original French-made 1897 model and had come over from the United States under lease-lend, which probably accounted for the fact that the only range tables that came with them were for the later American-made gun. On 1st October 1940 the regiment was equipped and deployed to defend the beaches of Alnmouth Bay and Druridge Bay as follows:

Plate 78 *A First World War-vintage 60-pdr. gun of B Troop, 341 Battery at Ulgham Park, Northumberland, August–September 1940.*
(Regimental Collection)

| | | |
|---|---|---|
| Regimental Headquarters | | Acton House, Felton |
| L.A.D. and 'B' Echelon | | Campbell's Farm, Old Felton |
| 341 Battery: | Battery Headquarters | Widdrington Station |
| | A Troop (4 × 75-mm.) | Northsteads Farm |
| | B Troop (2 × 60-pdr.) | Ulgham Park |
| | C Troop (4 × 75-mm.) | Houndalee Farm |
| 342 Battery: | Battery Headquarters | Eastfield Hall |
| | D Troop (2 × 60-pdr.) (under command 341 Battery) | Easthouses Farm |
| | E Troop (4 × 18/25-pdr.) | Eastfield Hall |
| | F Troop (4 × 18/25-pdr.) (under command 162 Infantry Brigade Mobile Column) | Swarland |

The four 60-pdrs. were handed over early in October, leaving B and D Troops without guns for some weeks. Meanwhile, the towing vehicle situation was improving just a little better than the gun situation. The first delivery of 'Quads' (seven vehicles) was received early in August. They were, according to Sir Patrick Coghill, "a great advance on impressed gun towers but the 6-wheel field artillery tractor [*Morris Commercial CDSW*] is better". Five more Quads arrived in mid-September and the balance to complete the full establishment of 36 vehicles trickled in over several months. Each battery was entitled to one tracked armoured carrier (or 'T truck'), to be passed around among the O.P. officers as required. These also arrived in August but seem not to have excited so much attention as the Quads.

By mid-October 1940, thoughts were turning to 'winter quarters'. The Rothbury area was allocated to the regiment, which was by now expecting to reorganise to the new three-battery establishment. Regimental Headquarters was accordingly established at Rothbury and three battery locations were identified at Cragside, Thropton and Harbottle. F Troop was released from the 162 Brigade Mobile Column on 20th October and moved into Cragside well ahead of the other troops. On the same day Major Morgan Smith returned to Regimental Headquarters as second-in-command, an appointment which had been vacant since Major Wingate Gray had left on promotion in mid-September, and Major Carew Jones took over command of 342 Battery. The provisional three-battery organisation for a field regiment was adopted on 8th November 1940. The two original batteries each lost a troop to the new battery, as follows:

Plate 79 *342 Battery's first 'T truck' at speed in the snow at Rothbury, Northumberland, winter 1940–41. Carriers, in this case 'Carrier, Universal, Mk. I', were issued on a scale of one to each battery in the summer of 1940. As supplies increased the scale was improved to one to each troop and eventually a specially-fitted version – 'Carrier, Armoured Observation Post' reached units.* (Regimental Collection)

| *Old Designation* | *New Designation* |
|---|---|
| A Troop, 341 Battery | A Troop, 341 Battery |
| C Troop, 341 Battery | B Troop, 341 Battery |
| E Troop, 342 Battery | C Troop, 342 Battery |
| F Troop, 342 Battery | D Troop, 342 Battery |
| B Troop, 341 Battery | E Troop, '343' Battery |
| D Troop, 342 Battery | F Troop, '343' Battery |

Majors Tabor and Carew Jones remained in command of 341 and 342 Batteries, respectively, while Captain R.S.W. Higgens was appointed to command the new battery which was for the time being known unofficially as '343' – the number of the old Watford battery of 86th Field Brigade, which had been converted to the anti-aircraft role in 1938 (see Chapter 3). All the war-formed third batteries of field regiments were, however, numbered when the three-battery organisation was confirmed in January 1941, from a series which continued the pre-war Territorial field battery series and placed each new battery in seniority reflecting its parent regiment. The third battery of 86th Field Regiment was accordingly allocated the number 462.

The tactical role of the regiment while in winter quarters was to man the three coast defence positions – Houndalee Farm, Northsteads Farm and Eastfield Hall – now in support of 202 Infantry Brigade, while maintaining the capability, in the absence of a whole battery's worth of guns, of deploying as a two-battery regiment for operations inland. For this purpose the regiment would deploy with 341 Battery (two troops, each 4 × 75-mm.) and 342/462 Battery (two troops, each 4 × 18/25-pdr.). 'Manning the coast defence positions' meant, in some cases, actually remaining in them until necessary construction works had been completed at the new battery locations. Huts in course of construction were blown down by a gale in mid-November and Sir Geoffrey Church's diary refers to "the appalling dilatoriness and inefficiency of the contractors and the supervising Royal Engineers". The last troop did not leave the coast until 17th December, by which time life had quietened down a good deal. During November there had been "several two-day exercises under X Corps and 54th Division – rather unconvincing and untidy battles, which proved to be the



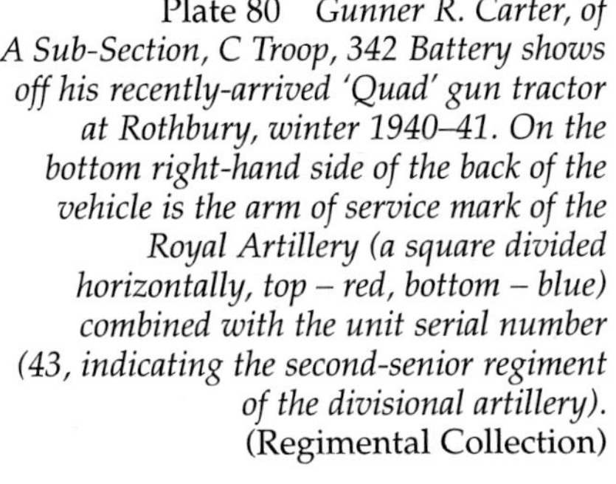

Plate 80 *Gunner R. Carter, of A Sub-Section, C Troop, 342 Battery shows off his recently-arrived 'Quad' gun tractor at Rothbury, winter 1940–41. On the bottom right-hand side of the back of the vehicle is the arm of service mark of the Royal Artillery (a square divided horizontally, top – red, bottom – blue) combined with the unit serial number (43, indicating the second-senior regiment of the divisional artillery).* (Regimental Collection)

Plate 81 *18/25-pdrs. of 342 Battery at Rothbury during the winter of 1940–41.*
Top – *Guns deployed along a hedgerow.*
Bottom – *The gun and limber – Trailer, Artillery, No.27 – which was normally positioned to the left of the gun* (Left); *a troop waiting in the position of assembly before moving away from a gun position* (Right). (Regimental Collection)

last dying spasms of 'Higher Training' before the winter finally closed in". With a little more time available and a state of preparedness for war which was ruled more by lack of guns, vehicles and equipment than by the state of training, the regiment could settle down to enjoy the second Christmas of the war. Interested officers even formed a syndicate to take a thousand-acre shoot, confident, perhaps, that the regiment would not move before the seasons ended.

The syndicate's confidence turned out to be justified, for the regiment did not move until the last week of March 1941. Intelligence assessments had concluded in October that "a major landing within the next five months could be discounted except in the south-east" (*Official History*) and that "elsewhere, only small diversionary expeditions need be feared". General Sir Alan Brooke, who had taken over as Commander-in-Chief Home Forces in July 1940 was determined to break away from the earlier policy of 'linear defence' and favoured 'mobile offensive action', but before his plans could be fully implemented, formations needed to be brought up to establishment in vehicles and in field- and anti-tank guns and other equipment, and then trained. This took many months and the vulnerable south-east corner of England was given priority. General Brooke's plans for reaching proficiency in modern mobile operations included withdrawing divisions from the coastal defences and placing them in 'G.H.Q. Reserve', generally well to the west of the expected area of operations, where they could give priority to mobile training. Before this could be done, it was necessary to place the immediate defence of a large part of the threatened coastal strip in the hands of the 'County Divisions', which were formed for static defence and were composed almost entirely of infantry. These nine divisions, stretching round the coast from Northumberland to Devon and Cornwall were in position by February–March 1941 to form the first line of defence against seaborne attacks.
 'Full-scale' (though not yet, in fact, fully equipped) divisions were available in each corps area

Plate 82 *342 Battery's O.P. carrier on exercise, summer 1941. Gunners Bottom (signaller) and Bousted (O.P. ack) are with Captain Perry in the right hand picture, with the carrier driver behind.* (Regimental Collection)

as corps reserve. With these measures in place, a proportion of the full-scale divisions that could be spared from corps reserves were available to be rotated through G.H.Q. Reserve, where they were put through "a much-needed course of training in mobile warfare", including "learning to go into action immediately after completing forced moves of up to two hundred miles in mechanised transport or forty miles on foot" (*Official History*).

On 21st March 1941, 54th Division left X Corps, under which they had served in the defence of north-east England since July 1940, and moved into G.H.Q. Reserve in Gloucestershire. The regiment was billeted in the Tewkesbury area, with Regimental Headquarters at Southwick Park. Neither the War Diary nor personal diaries are precise as to the regiment's gun and vehicle state at the time of the move. It seems probable that 462 Battery, who had spent most of the winter without guns, had received their first four 18/25-pdrs. in February, but equally probable that they moved as a four-gun battery and that the regiment did not finally reach its full establishment of 24 guns until some time well into the spring of 1941. Even then, eight guns, all held by 341 Battery, were the obsolete French 75-mm. The first large-scale divisional exercise, in which the division practised its new operational role with brigades moving long distances to a concentration area along separate routes, took place between 21st–25th April. From then until the division left the Tewkesbury area at the beginning of July, higher level exercises alternated with regimental 'dry' training (i.e., without ammunition) and periods at the practice camps on Salisbury Plain and at Sennybridge, near Brecon. The furthest distance covered under the "forced moves of up to two hundred miles" policy took place early in June during an exercise under Headquarters VIII Corps, when the regiment found itself well inside Devon. Here, for much of the 'gun end', the exercise ground to a halt in the narrow lanes. In between these exercises, on 12th May 1941, Lieutenant-Colonel Sir Patrick Coghill left the regiment. The War Office had at last caught up with his familiarity with the Middle East and his knowledge of Turkish and Arabic and he was promoted colonel and posted to command the British Security Mission in Syria and Lebanon. Lieutenant-Colonel R.S. Wade assumed command of 86th Field Regiment on 28th May.

The warning order for the move of 54th Division to a new area, in Buckinghamshire, still in G.H.Q. Reserve, reached the regiment on 6th July and on 27th July they occupied tented accommodation at Hazlemere Park, High Wycombe, with guns and vehicles concealed in nearby woods. Higher level exercises continued, with the division under command of XI Corps (responsible for the defence of the Essex–Suffolk coastline) for three days towards the end of August. Then, at the end of September, the widespread exercise 'Bumper' took place.

Plate 83 *'Pneumatised' French 75-mm. gun of A Sub-Section, A Troop, 341 Battery at Tewkesbury, summer 1941. A Sub have just won the Inter-Sub-Section Cup, which can be seen towards the top of the 'shadow board' holding the gun stores. 341 Battery was armed with the 75-mm. gun from September 1940 to late-1941.* (Regimental Collection)

For this exercise 86th Field Regiment was placed under command of 162 Infantry Brigade and the 'brigade group' acted as the invading enemy force. According to the War Diary, the 'invaders' were finally brought to battle on the River Lee south of Luton, so it may be presumed that the old Territorials derived some advantage – and not necessarily just tactical advantage – from fighting across their home county. 'Bumper' was the last of the large-scale exercises in which the regiment participated while in G.H.Q Reserve but regimental training continued in the High Wycombe area until orders were received for another move. The move was not before time, for by early autumn much of the regimental area had become a sea of mud. Hard standings for guns and vehicles had to be laid and lorry-loads of rubble from bombed areas of London were brought in to be rolled into place by steamroller. Some Nissen huts were even put up before the regiment left – just as the first snow was falling.

In the middle of November 1941, 54th Division left G.H.Q. Reserve and was placed under command of XI Corps, reinforced with an additional coast defence brigade – 212 Infantry Brigade – and allocated a sector of the East Anglian coast stretching approximately from Lowestoft southwards to Felixstowe, The regiment was placed in support of 163 Infantry Brigade, which was responsible for beach defence from Dunwich to Aldeburgh. By 22nd November, Regimental Headquarters was established in Yoxford and the batteries deployed close to Westleton, familiar from the previous East Coast deployment (341), Leiston (342) and Snape (462). No sooner had the batteries settled in their new locations than Major Tabor was 'Y-Listed' (struck off strength as long-term sick and to be replaced). Major Carew Jones moved from 342 Battery to command 341 and Captain W. A. Anderson was promoted to command 342. The winter routine of December 1941–January 1942 included the manning of O.Ps. on the coast at night. One was on the water-tower at Thorpeness. Another, in a pillbox on the marshes further north, was more popular – Captain Ash recalled many years later that among the 'allied activities' here were "shooting duck in the evening light and rats during the later watches". It is not recorded in the War Diary how the regiment came, in January, to be in support of 10th Glosters and 9th Royal Sussex, both of 212 Infantry Brigade, which held the sector south of 163 Infantry Brigade, including Felixstowe. However, 212 Brigade had no integral artillery and it may simply be that 86th Field Regiment's responsibilities for support were extended southwards to cover the neighbouring brigade frontage. Remembering that by now invasion was considered unlikely but there remained a threat of enemy raids, and that a corps reserve division and an army tank brigade stood behind the immediate coast defences, this does seem a likely explanation for what would undoubtedly have been recognised as inadequate artillery support.

Lieutenant-Colonel Wade relinquished command of 86th Field Regiment on 17th January 1942, the day before the first batch of 'real' 25-pdr. guns, delivered earlier that month, were due to be calibrated. They had replaced the 75-mms. in 341 Battery; the 18/25-pdrs. in 342 and 462 were replaced by succeeding deliveries over the next few weeks. New guns were followed, to the delight of all who had known him as adjutant before the outbreak of war, by the posting of Lieutenant-Colonel G.D. Fanshawe to command of the regiment on 10th February. The new commanding officer marked his arrival not only by a round of the searching 'administrative inspections' for which he became well known, but also by presiding, in company with the commander of 163 Brigade and his battalion commanders, over the registration of all the regiment's S.O.S. tasks. He also encouraged the gun detachments to greater efforts in the construction of their new 25-pdr. gun-pits, work on which continued throughout the rest of February, hampered by the very cold weather. During March there were two more exercises with 163 Brigade, in which the guns fired live ammunition on coastal and seaward targets. The S.O.S. tasks alone were fired on 3rd March; then on 10th–11th March a practice stand-to was held and the 'defensive fire' ('D.F.') targets were fired as well as the S.O.S., with the infantry's mortars and medium machine-guns joining in. Major Anderson handed over command of 342 Battery to Major E.G. Scammell on 19th March, and at the end of the month 462 Battery moved from Snape to Aldeburgh.

The regiment remained in support of 163 Infantry Brigade in the coast defence role for a further ten weeks and then, apparently without notice or explanation, was transferred from 54th Infantry Division to 42nd Armoured Division on 10th June 1942. This division was in course of reorganisation, having just lost its original two armoured brigades and taken under command 30 Armoured Brigade and 71 Infantry Brigade. There had not previously been any divisional artillery and the necessary two field regiments were both found by transfer. 'Opposite

Plate 84 *A gunner of 86th Field Regiment in 1942–43. His battledress blouse is 1937-pattern, with pleated breast pockets which have concealed buttons. On his left sleeve are the red and white diamond sign of 42nd Armoured Division and the red and blue 'arm of service strip' of the Royal Artillery. The coloured field service cap with hart badge was worn only when walking out.* (Regimental Collection)

numbers' to 86th Field Regiment were 147th (Essex Yeomanry) Field Regiment, the duplicate regiment of 104th (Essex Yeomanry) Field Regiment, which, like 86th Field Regiment, had its origins in the powerful combination of a county Yeomanry regiment and an artillery unit (in this case Royal Horse Artillery) raised on the formation of the Territorial Force. The characters of the two regiments promised an efficient and happy divisional artillery for 42nd Armoured Division.

### *With 42nd Armoured Division, June 1942–April 1943*

Joining 42nd Armoured Division entailed a move, which took place between 10th–12th June, from the Suffolk coast to Hovingham and Slingsby in Yorkshire, where the regiment were accommodated partly in billets and partly in a Nissen hut camp. Immediately before the move, Major Carew Jones left for India and was succeeded in command of 341 Battery by Major G.A. Loveday. Life was energetic from the start, and very different from static defence of a coastline. An armoured division, especially its armoured brigade (three armoured regiments, all in tanks, and a mechanised infantry battalion) is capable of moving fast, and in suitable country is not tied to roads or tracks. The Yorkshire moors provided an ideal training ground and the O.P. parties were soon mounted in tanks, not only so that they could keep up with the armoured regiments they were supporting, but so that they did not present a substantially different target from their 'friends', as the supported arm was guardedly referred to on the wireless net, and thus invite special attention from the enemy. 'Dry' exercises with the armoured and infantry brigades of the division were alternated with frequent live-firing practice on the nearby Spaunton Moor range. Here, too, to the great satisfaction of the signallers, the No. 11 wireless sets were replaced by the No. 19, which was to become the much-loved mainstay of Gunner communications in North-West Europe and elsewhere.

The requirement for additional field artillery regiments led, on 21st December 1942, to all officers and the great majority of other ranks of 462 Battery (only 25 per cent of signallers and 'specialists' – C.P. and O.P. assistants – were retained) being transferred to form 533 Battery of the newly-raised 191st Field Regiment (see Chapter 6). Captain J.B.S. Tabor, who had rejoined from the Y List and served for six months as adjutant, was promoted to take command of the 'new' 462 Battery, which had to be re-formed with all possible speed from personnel transferred from the other batteries or drafted in as reinforcements. No sooner had this huge change been put into effect, than the regiment moved to Scarborough for a two-month spell in winter quarters. Some were lucky enough to be billeted in sea-side guest houses; all the sig-

Plate 85 *Bombardier R.C. Couzins* (Left), *commanding A Sub-Section of A Troop, 341 Battery, with Gunners Emslie, Brown and Burgess, servicing their 25-pdr. gun at Hovingham, Yorkshire, September 1942. The first 'real' 25-pdrs. were issued to 341 Battery in January 1942 to replace French 75-mm. guns. Later deliveries replaced 18/25-pdrs. in 342 and 462 Batteries.* (Regimental Collection)

nallers remember that it was here that they had to master Morse code by wireless.

Towards the end of January 1943, 42nd Armoured Division, which had been under command of Northern Command since reorganisation at the end of June 1942, came under command of Headquarters VIII Corps. It was accordingly as part of VIII Corps that 86th Field Regiment moved out of Scarborough on 28th February for the two-week Exercise 'Spartan'. Those who took part in 'Spartan' have recalled – for the War Diary includes no detail – that there was a great deal of movement, initially in an advance southwards, with 342 Battery forming part of a 'flying column' charged with seizing the bridge over the Thames at Hungerford after a night-time dash, and then a long fighting withdrawal to a defensive stand in a 'box' near Raunds in Northamptonshire. When the exercise ended on 15th March the regiment moved into Upton Lovell Camp, near Codford in Wiltshire, rather than return to Yorkshire. At the same time, 42nd Armoured Division left VIII Corps and was placed under command of Southern Command.

### *A year of preparation for D-Day, May 1943–May 1944*

While 86th Field Regiment was not actually replaced in 42nd Armoured Divisional Artillery, by 191st Field Regiment, until early May 1943, it does seem as if the regiment's arrival at Codford coincided with its selection for an important role in the preparation for the eventual invasion of Europe. Many years later Colonel Fanshawe recorded in a memoir:

> "One day [*20th March 1943*] I had a message from the station master that 24 tanks had arrived by train addressed to the regiment and would I please send someone to take them over. Not unnaturally, we thought a mistake had been made, as no warning or notification had been received by anyone. However, it was found that they were intended for us and were self-propelled guns. Fortunately we had recently had a subaltern posted to us who had been in a tank regiment, so he went down to the station, only a few hundred yards away, and drove all 24 guns to the camp – and so the Herts Yeomanry were the first, or almost the first, field regiment to become self-propelled."

The regiment had indeed been selected for conversion to a self-propelled field regiment and 24 'Bishop' self-propelled guns (25-pdr. gun on Valentine tank chassis – see Chapter 2) had arrived by rail. The "subaltern . . . who had been in a tank regiment" was Lieutenant N. M. Pickford; he drove each Bishop off the train but then handed over to a Quad driver – none of whom had ever driven a tank. After a few words of explanation of the controls, the driver set off on the journey back to camp with Lieutenant Pickford shouting advice and instructions! The whole process may have taken something over two days but no disasters were recorded and more formal instruction in driving and maintenance could then begin.

The myths surrounding these great events die hard. Another eye-witness report that it took a week to get all the Bishops from the station to camp seems to be false but there may be a grain of truth in the story that a despatch rider was sent to Hertford to bring back the gun-drill book from the horse-drawn era, on which some of the self-taught gun drill and deployment drills are said to have been based. One fact is beyond dispute. On 4th April 1943 black berets (then the prerogative of the Royal Armoured Corps) were "taken into wear" (War Diary). Colonel Fanshawe declared many years later, "Well, *we* were an armoured unit", and

Plate 86 *The badge adopted by officers of 86th Field Regiment for wear in the black beret, early summer 1943.* (White metal, frosted silver finish; actual size 1⅜ in. × 1⅜ in.) (Regimental Collection)

described how he personally had arranged for the supply of the berets, which, against all the dress regulations of the time, were worn by 86th Field Regiment until early in 1946. Perhaps even more important than the introduction of the black beret was the instruction, again formulated within the regiment, that the hart badge should be worn. This instruction was well within the spirit of dress regulations as applied to head-dress other than the service dress peaked cap and the hart badge had, indeed, been worn by other ranks in the field service cap (see Plate 84). However, there was no precedent for officers wearing the hart badge and, rather than make use of the cap badge worn by officers of the Hertfordshire Yeomanry prior to 1920, the bronze version of which was worn on the shoulder strap of officers' service dress (see Chapter 3), a new white metal badge was introduced (see Plate 86). The black beret and the hart badge swiftly became a distinguishing mark for all ranks of 86th Field Regiment and a feature which makes members of the regiment instantly recognisable in photographs, even in the most difficult circumstances (see especially Plate 91).

While these details of dress were of some importance, the technicalities of self-propelled gunnery were uppermost in everyones' minds during April and May 1943. Live firing practice had taken place before the end of March. Unfortunately, no photographs have survived but practice instructions noted in the War Diary even specify "Ammunition: 32 rounds in S.P. and 32 rounds in trailer", confirming what now seems a curious idea – that each gun towed its own limber. O.P. tanks were now on the regimental establishment, and troop commanders of the time recall "haring around Salisbury Plain in Crusader tanks", so great progress must have been made in driver training! Progress in all specialities was indeed such that on 28th May 86th Field Regiment reported that it was fully reorganised to its new establishment and, in present-day terms, was 'up-and-running' as a 'Field Regiment, R.A. (25-pdr. S.P.)'. During this period of intense activity it was discovered that there was a danger of all the Bishops being 'off the road' at the same time owing to excessive wear in the bearings of the return rollers – the rollers supporting the tracks at their furthest point from the ground. It was taken as an indicator of the importance of the regiment's work when Colonel Fanshawe was able to obtain a requisition directly from the War Office and, ignoring the 'usual channels', to despatch the technical adjutant straight to the manufacturers near Birmingham, whence he returned with crates full of bearings – sufficient to repair all 24 guns.

Meanwhile, the first indications of the purpose for which the regiment had really been selected had become apparent earlier in May, when 341 and 342 Batteries went into camp at Blandford, Dorset, "for training in beach landings" (War Diary). There was indeed much to be learned about 'Combined Operations', and specifically about an opposed landing on an enemy-held beach. Allied landings of all arms would take place in Sicily and Italy during 1943 and vital experience, especially of the organisation of the beach and beach-head and of ship-to-shore bombardment, would be gained. There was no attempt in the Mediterranean, however, to make use of the fire-power of Army guns embarked in landing craft as the invading force approached the beach. The planning staff for the invasion of North-West Europe realised, according to a report written within 86th Field Regiment after the Normandy Landings, that "the fire which could be produced by the embarked self-propelled artillery regiments would provide a valuable addition to the naval bombardment if it could be put down with sufficient accuracy not to endanger the assaulting infantry". It fell to 86th Field Regiment to develop and pioneer the techniques of shooting from landing craft approaching the shore, and, in effect, to write the handbook *S.P. Artillery in an Assault Landing* that covered all aspects of the 'run-in shoot' and subsequent landing and deployment.

The early exercises at Blandford and on the Dorset coast had concentrated on the non-firing aspects of an assault landing. Drills had to be evolved for the loading of the regiment's guns and vehicles into 'landing craft, tank' (L.C.T.), which could only be entered in reverse through the bow ramp. Replica L.C.Ts. were staked out on the ground at Blandford and many hours spent placing the guns accurately, especially in relation to the centre line of the vessel, and working out how every inch of space could be used, for the guns themselves ('deployed' one troop to a L.C.T, so that the regiment was carried in six L.C.Ts., and within each craft as two sections 'forward' and 'aft'); for the vehicles needed on the gun position (especially the G.P.O.'s tank, the wireless sets of which were needed to control the run-in shoot); and O.P. tanks and carriers, which would land with the guns and be called forward as required to meet the F.O.O. teams that had landed without vehicles with the assault waves of infantry. The first experiments in actually shooting on to the shore were carried out by 341 and 342 Batteries in Studland Bay, near Poole, in the second half of July and the first half of August 1943. Here it was established that 'line' (i.e., the direction in which the gun was pointed) would have to be a naval responsibility. The G.P.O. would align his guns to the centre line of the vessel and apply any 'switch' necessary to compensate for sailing 'up-tide', but the vessel's heading, which was the captain's responsibility, would determine the direction in which the shells departed. (The captain had some help; all six L.C.Ts. travelled in a tight group on a common heading dictated by a radar-equipped motor-launch which accompanied the group.) Range was set on the gun sights in accordance with a 'range clock', which was synchronised to a speed of six knots (200 yards per minute). A high degree of co-operation and understanding between the Royal Navy crews of the L.C.Ts. and the regiment, especially the troop G.P.Os., was essential and was achieved, despite the fact that the Gunners did not begin to train with the craft from which they would actually land in Europe until a few weeks before the invasion. By the time all the necessary trials and training were finished, it was, according to the regiment's report quoted earlier, "proved to everybody's satisfaction that a self-propelled regiment loaded by troops in six L.C.T. Mk. IV could produce a concentration covering an area 300 yards

Plate 87 *A 105-mm. Priest self-propelled gun of 86th Field Regiment secured on the tank deck of a tank landing craft during run-in shoot trials and demonstrations in Kilbride Bay, Scotland, autumn 1943.* (Regimental Collection)

square under the worst weather conditions in which an invasion could be carried out".

While 341 and 342 Batteries had been occupied on the South Coast, Regimental Headquarters and 462 Battery moved to Scotland, where 462 Battery began run-in shoot trials at Tighnabruaich. Major K.J. Underwood took over command of 462 Battery from Major Tabor on 18th July, on posting from the School of Artillery, perhaps with the idea of bringing technical expertise to the regiment, though in fact he only stayed until the end of August. Captain K.J. Swann was then promoted to command of 342 Battery and Major Scammell moved to command of 462. The other two batteries rejoined the regiment at Kilmarnock in mid-August and a few days later the rather make-shift 'Bishop' S.Ps. were withdrawn and the United States-manufactured 105-mm. S.P. known as 'Priest' (see Chapter 2) was issued. In less than four weeks, on 17th September 1943, the regiment reported that reorganisation to 105-mm. 'Priest' establishment was complete. Training continued during October, beginning with a four-day exercise for which the regiment was trimmed down to 'assault scale'. The first regimental run-in shoot, with all three batteries taking part, was fired in Kilbride Bay on 15th October. Then, as the Scottish winter approached, there was a final four-day exercise between 9th–12th November and the regiment moved with 70 Infantry Brigade of 49th Division for a month at Walberswick, on the Suffolk coast. This was 86th Field Regiment's third visit to the area but for the first time their thoughts were directed towards attacking the coast, rather than defending it.

In the middle of December 1943, the regiment moved into winter accommodation in Norwich, apparently with a brief rest from large-scale training between the move and the Christmas–New Year period. It was here that the first honours received since mobilisation were announced. In the 1944 New Year List Lieutenant-Colonel Fanshawe was appointed O.B.E. and Captain (Q.M.) P.E. Felstead, who had served as quartermaster since annual camp in 1939, was appointed M.B.E.

Plate 88 *An early edition, probably the first, of Combined Operations Pamphlet No. 7(b) 'S.P. Artillery' approved in November 1943 and issued in January 1944. Much of the pamphlet was based on trials carried out by 86th Field Regiment in the summer of 1943.* (Regimental Collection)

**RESTRICTED**

**The information given in this document is not to be communicated, either directly or indirectly, to the Press or to any person not holding an official position in His Majesty's Service.**

**COMBINED OPERATIONS**

**PAMPHLET No. 7 (b)**

# SP ARTILLERY

**1943**

Issued under the direction of
The Chief of Combined Operations

November, 1943.

**THIS DOCUMENT MUST NOT FALL INTO ENEMY HANDS**

**This Pamphlet, when issued to Naval holders, will be known as ~~BR7 (b)~~**
**BR 640 (7(b))**

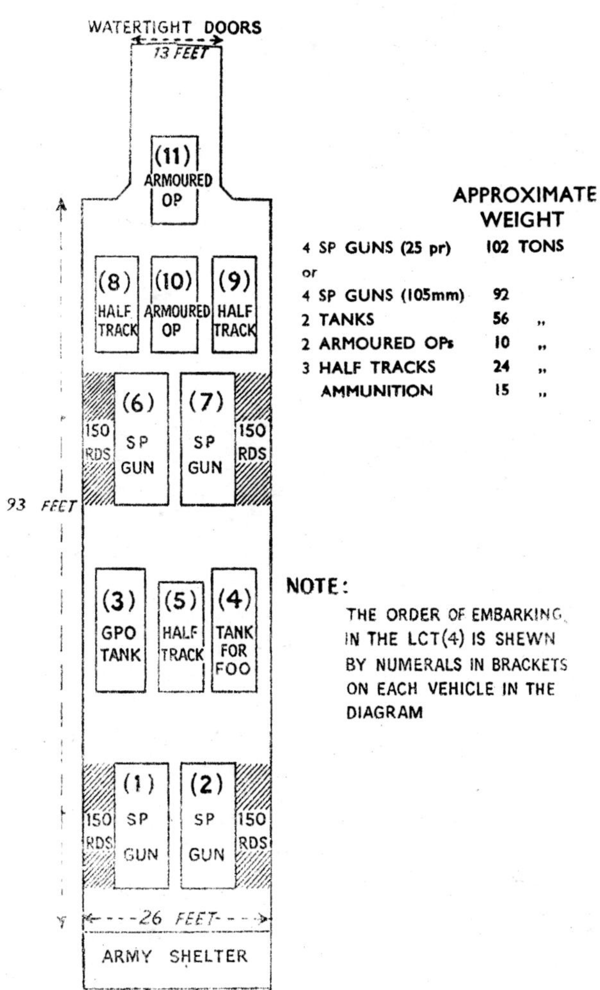

Throughout January and into February 1944, 86th Field Regiment remained under command of 49th Division and exercises with 70 Infantry Brigade and 33 Tank Brigade, which was also under command, continued. Early in February, the regiment received orders to reorganise on War Establishment II/190A/1 with effect from 7th February. The change to 'a Field (S.P.) Regiment, R.A. – 25-pdr. Ram' involved yet another swift handover of all the regiment's guns. This time the 105-mm. 'Priest' was replaced by the 25-pdr. 'Sexton', sometimes classified as 'Ram' because it was mounted on the Canadian Ram tank body (see Chapter 2). Not far from Norwich, 90th Field Regiment, of 50th Divisional Artillery, was converting directly from towed 25-pdr. to Sexton S.P. and instructors from 86th Field Regiment joined 90th in order to pass on their experience of all aspects of self-propelled artillery, being careful to make proper allowance for the fact that the S.P. gun of the future was the Sexton, rather than the mechanically similar Priest, on which some of the instruction had to take place. This first contact with 50th Division was significant, for although 86th Field Regiment paraded with 49th Division for inspection by General Montgomery, Commander-in-Chief Twenty-First Army Group, on 16th February, it must have been around this time that it was decided that 49th Division, with which 86th Field Regiment had been training for more than three months, would not be one of the assault formations for the invasion of Europe. A number of divisions had been brought back from the Mediterranean theatre late in 1943 in order to give a leavening of battle experience to the untried force of British and Canadian troops that was fast changing its role from the defence of the home base to the reconquest of occupied Europe. The 50th Division was an 'original' Territorial infantry division raised in North-East England – the initial letters of the main rivers of the area, Tyne and Tees, were used as the formation badge – and it had seen action with the British Expeditionary Force in 1940, in the Middle East and North Africa, and, most recently, in the assault landings in Sicily in July 1943 and the eventual capture of the island. On returning to England the division was quartered in the area Bury St. Edmunds–Thetford–Sudbury. It was decided quite early in the planning stages of Operation 'Overlord' as the assault landings on the Normandy coast were known, that 50th Division would be the assault formation of the British XXX Corps and that the division would land on a two-brigade frontage. Since each assault brigade would require the support of a self-propelled field artillery regiment, and since there was only one such regiment (90th) integral to 50th Divisional Artillery, a further regiment would need to be placed under divisional command for the assault phase of the operation. Headquarters Second Army held a pool of units, known as 'Second Army Troops' for use when reinforcements or specialist troops were required by subordinate formations and 86th Field Regiment had for some time been designated Second Army Troops. Before the end of February the regiment was placed under command of 50th Division for the assault phase of the landings and early in March affiliation with one of the assault brigades – 69 Infantry Brigade – was established. Thereafter, all exercises were conducted according to the order of battle that would be in force when 'D-Day' eventually came.

Two steps were taken at the end of February 1944 that showed that the 'count-down' to the invasion of Europe, then expected to take place early in May, was in earnest. The regiment was ordered to adopt the overseas system of pay accounting on 26th February and on the following day to mobilise on W.E. II/190A/1 by 10th March. The process of mobilisation involved bringing the regiment up to full strength, including immediate reinforcements, in both men and guns and vehicles, and ensuring that all personnel and vehicles were fit for front-line service. The war establishment for a Sexton S.P. battery, as amended in May 1944 (W.E. II/190A/2) and on which the batteries of 86th Field Regiment should have gone into action, is shown in Appendix 2. It needs to be said, however, that it is impossible to reconcile some of the contemporary evidence, particularly photographs, with the published establishment, especially in Tanks, O.P./C.P., which always seem to appear in greater numbers than provided for, and in addition to Carriers, Armoured O.P. Crusader O.P. tanks were replaced by Sherman Mk. V (M4A4); Jeeps were introduced; and some M14 half-track vehicles, though apparently not the full establishment, arrived, all as part of the mobilisation process (see Chapter 2).

By the middle of March, the naval force which was to carry 50th Division across the Channel, and give supporting fire as the assault went in, was beginning to assemble in the Southampton–Portsmouth area. The now well known code names for the five beaches on which the Allied invasion force would land had been allocated – 'Utah' and 'Omaha' to those which the United States forces were assaulting and 'Gold', 'Juno' and 'Sword' to the British

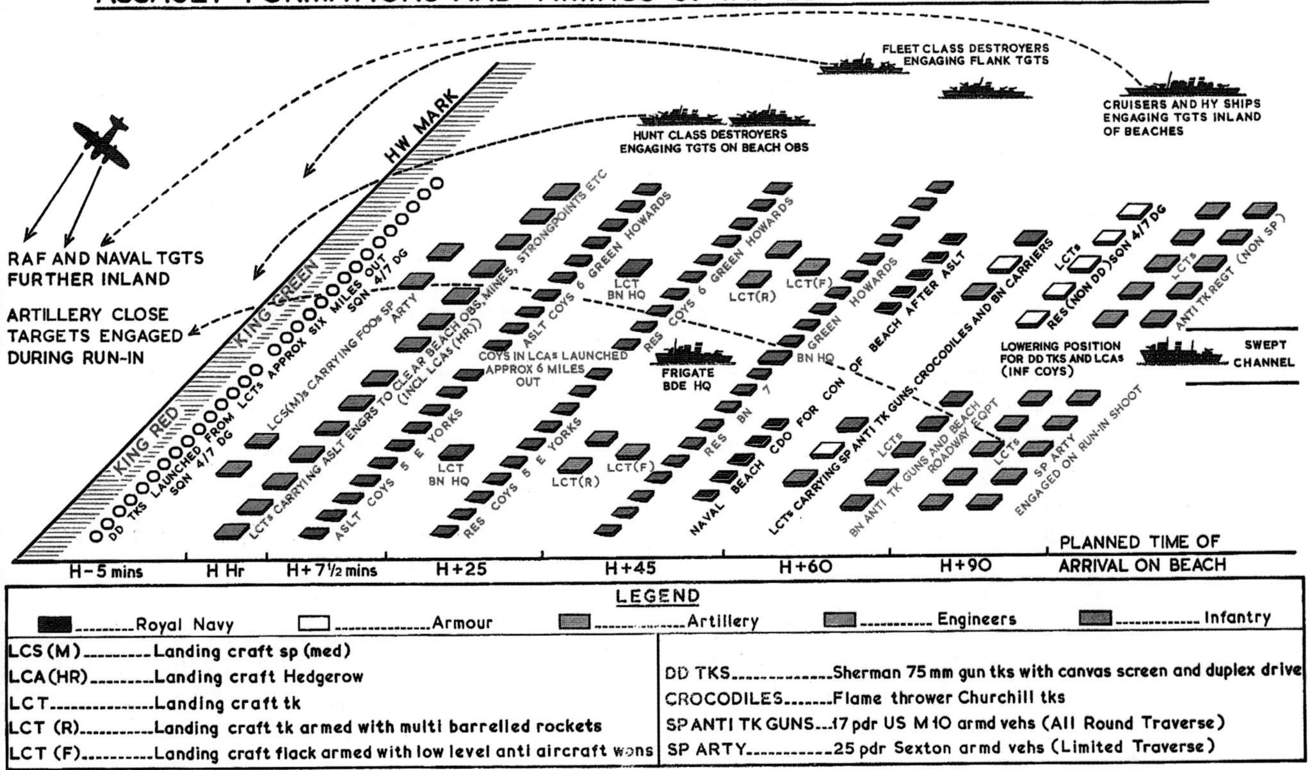


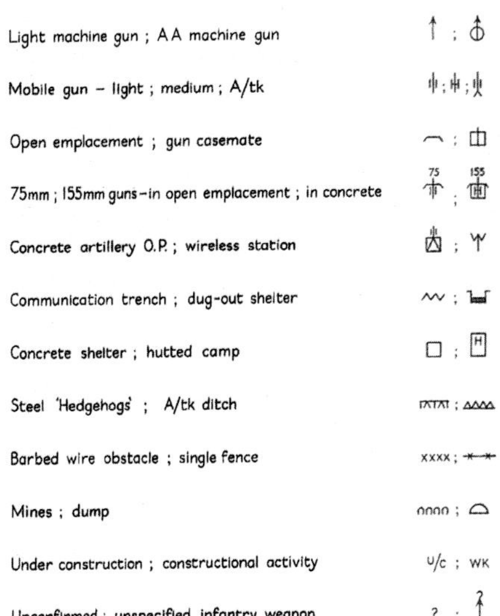


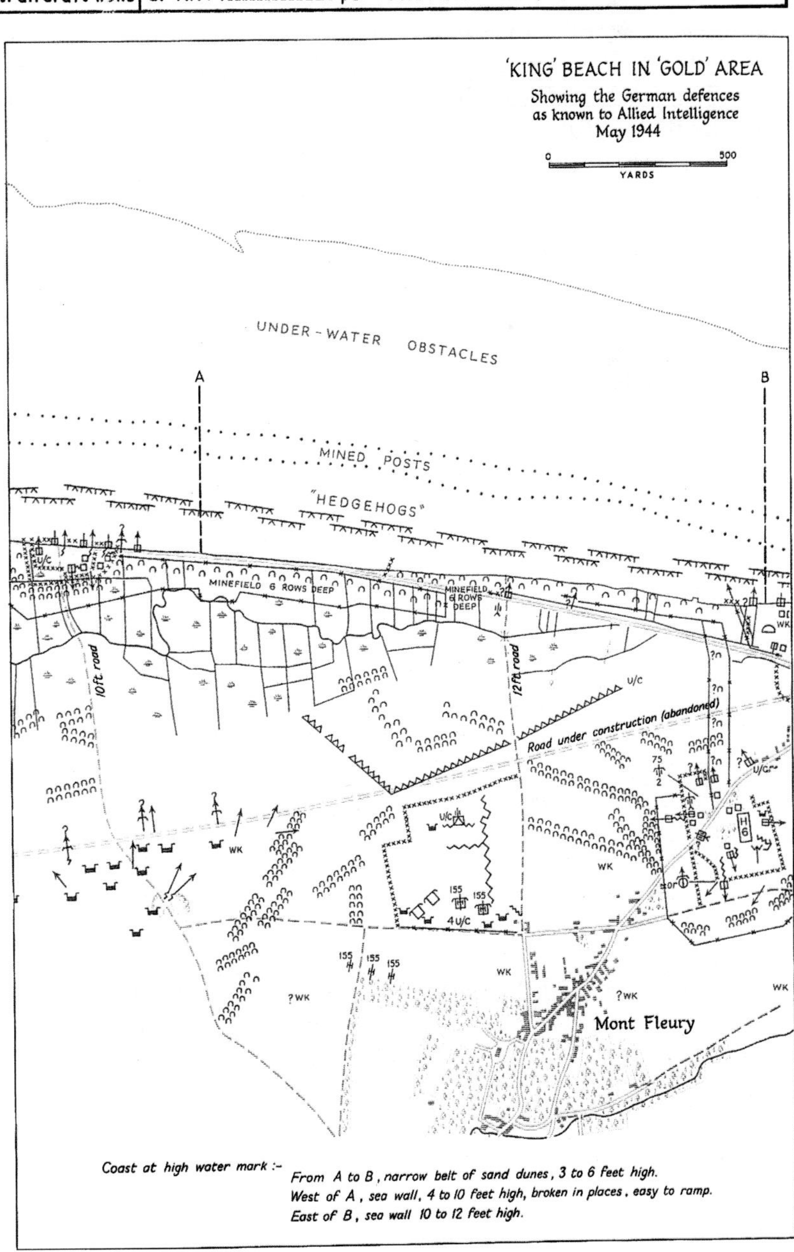


PLATE III King Beach

Top – Assault formations and timings (from a Staff College battlefield tour handbook)

Bottom – Intelligence assessment of the German defences (from the *Official History*)

Plate 89 *Exercise 'Smash I', Studland Bay, Dorset, March 1944. Troops of 69 Infantry Brigade land while the supporting bombardment, including rockets fired from landing craft, continues. All three 'Smash' exercises were preceded by a live run-in shoot by 86th Field Regiment.* (Pen and wash drawing by Anthony Gross) (I.W.M. – LD 3954)

and Canadian beaches. Separate naval forces were responsible for each beach. They were designated by the initial letter of their beach, so it was with Force 'G' that 50th Division would carry out all further training and eventually sail on Operation 'Overlord'.

Close co-operation with Force 'G' was achieved by moving 50th Division to Hampshire in the third week of March 1944. The regiment was quartered at Bournemouth and it was from there that they set out on 26th March to load into L.C.Ts. at Poole Hard for the first of three full-scale invasion exercises, known as 'Smash I–III', in which, after a run-in shoot, 50th [89]

Plate 90 *Landing exercises in Studland Bay, Dorset, April 1944. Z/1147, the commanding officer's tank of 86th Field Regiment drives on to the beach.* (I.W.M. – FLM 1077)

Division would land in Studland Bay. By now, forward observer parties from the towed field regiments of 50th Divisional Artillery were exercising with the S.P. regiments. They would provide valuable extra 'eyes and ears' and, on D-Day itself, one extra forward observer party from 124th Field Regiment would land with each battery of 86th. Further additions to the potential firepower of the regiment also made their appearance during the 'Smash' exercises – Forward observer bombardment' (F.O.B.) parties, composed of Royal Artillery officers and O.P. assistants and Royal Navy telegraphists (signallers, in Army terms) who would land with the assault waves in order to control ship-to-shore bombardment, which could be used in the same way as artillery for the support of forward troops; and Centaur tanks of the Royal Marine Armoured Support Regiment, which carried a 95-mm. gun firing high-explosive shells and were capable of either direct or indirect fire in close support.

On 23rd April, in common with other units of 50th Division, 86th Field Regiment moved into the specially prepared marshalling area for assault troops leaving from Portsmouth and Southampton. This consisted of a large number of camps – all fenced with barbed wire – dispersed throughout the New Forest. The regiment was in camp C 14, near Romsey, and it was from here that they set off on 29th April for the final exercise – in effect the 'dress rehearsal' prior to D-Day. Exercise 'Fabius' involved the whole of Force 'G' and all assaulting units of 50th Division. The landings took place across the beaches of Hayling Island early on the morning of 4th May. With the final exercise completed, it was necessary to undertake all manner of preparatory chores. The guns returned to Salisbury Plain for final calibration between 12th–14th May and the opportunity was taken to practise once more with personal weapons. Back in C 14, waterproofing of all vehicles began on 16th May. Extensions were fitted to exhaust pipes and air intakes, screens increased the 'wading depth' of carriers and S.P. guns, and waterproofing compound was applied liberally to cracks and openings and to electrical wiring – all under the supervision of the L.A.D. and the select few Gunners who had done the waterproofing course. Thanks to them, there were no serious problems when it was all put to the test but there are strong indications that the Sextons' wading screens, which can be seen in photographs taken in C 14, did not stand up to the blast of the run-in shoot and were dumped overboard as they began to disintegrate beyond repair. Briefing for *Exercise* 'Overlord' began on 28th May. The fiction of yet another exercise was maintained for as long as possible but the proliferation of air photographs and models, albeit with towns, villages and other features described by code-names, convinced everybody that this time it was 'the real thing'. A regimental diarist recorded soon after the event:

"... Stores of all sorts were issued, equipment was tested, and for the third and last time all vehicles were waterproofed. As D-Day grew near, the camp was sealed, no one was allowed in or out, and briefing began. This could hardly have been done more thoroughly. We saw air photos of the beach and the coastal defences, maps and charts of the minefields, underwater obstacles, anti-tank ditches, weapon pits and gun emplacements. We also saw 'going'

Plate 92 *In the New Forest waiting for D-Day, May 1944. Lieutenant-Colonel G.D. Fanshawe, O.B.E., commanding 86th Field Regiment, Captain R.R. Thornton, Adjutant and R.S.M. T. Lightfoot.* (Pen and wash drawing by Anthony Gross) (I.W.M. – LD 3942)

maps, which showed the kind of ground we would have to cross after the landing. The plan of attack of the whole brigade was explained time and again to everyone. Code-names were given to all the features so that the whole operation could be explained and memorised without giving away the actual place. Everyone knew which boat they were to sail on and where, and when, they were supposed to land."

Plate 93 *F.O.B. party supporting 69 Infantry Brigade, April–May 1944. This party, commanded by Captain J.G. Corke, worked closely with the O.Ps. of 86th Field Regiment on D-Day and immediately after. Captain Corke was later posted to the regiment to command 341 Battery. He was killed as the regiment crossed from France into Belgium early in September 1944.* (Pen and wash drawing by Anthony Gross) (I.W.M. – LD 3956)

Plate 94 *Scenes in Camp C 14, near Romsey, Hampshire, as 86th Field Regiment waited for D-Day, May 1944* – Top left – *Sherman O.P./C.P. tanks Z, X/341 and H/341 get yet another 'final check' of the waterproofing. Motor cycles are secured to the engine deck of each tank and Z has a .5-in. machine-gun mounted on top of the turret.* (I.W.M. – A70-021 1).

 Bottom left – *Further down the column of 341 Battery's vehicles. The two half-tracks are Y (battery command post) and*

*probably M1 (signals). They are followed by a universal carrier, the Sherman GA and the first of A Troop's guns.* (I.W.M. – A70-021 2). Top right – *A universal carrier of 5th East Yorkshire Regiment passing A Troop's guns. Note the wading screens fitted all round the fighting compartment.* (I.W.M. – A70-021 3). Bottom right – *Q staff of 86th Field Regiment* (black berets, backs to camera) *issuing 24-hour ration packs to troops of 69 Infantry Brigade.* (I.W.M. – A70-33-2-1) 

As became clear when sealed orders were opened on board ship, 50th Division's 'Gold' beach stretched for some 5,500 yards from La Rivière on the eastern (or left) flank to Le Hamel on the west (right). The beach was divided into two approximately equal sectors, knows as 'Jig' and 'King', and 69 Brigade was assigned to King Sector – the eastern half of Gold Beach. The 5th Battalion The East Yorkshire Regiment would assault 'King Red', where the enemy had made use of the few buildings (largely seaside houses) in his defences and added several concrete gun emplacements, including 88-mm. guns that enfiladed the beach. Once ashore, 5th East Yorkshires were to capture the defended area around the lighthouse some six hundred yards to the south, on rising ground, and then move on to Ver-sur-Mer and beyond. On their right, 6th Battalion The Green Howards would assault across 'King Green', which was dominated from its western end by a strong complex of pill-boxes at Hable-de-Heurtot. Their first objective was the Mont Fleury battery (4 × 155-mm. guns) on the same feature as the lighthouse and about eight hundred yards from the beach. The assault battalions would each be supported by a squadron of D.D. (or 'swimming') Sherman tanks of 4th/7th Royal Dragoon Guards and by 'breaching teams' equivalent to a squadron in strength and provided by C Squadron, Westminster Dragoons in Sherman mine-clearing 'flail' tanks and 81 Assault Squadron, Royal Engineers, whose Churchill tanks carried a variety of devices designed to overcome obstacles, as well as the 'Petard' mortar, which fired a massively powerful 'concrete-busting' bomb designed to destroy, or at least neutralise, heavily defended gun emplacements. Forward observer parties from 86th Field Regiment would land with the assault companies, ready to direct supporting fire as soon as their guns were landed. Further fire support would be available from the battery of 1st Royal Marine Armoured Support Regiment that was to land on King Beach, and from forward observer bombardment parties directing the fire of naval guns.

D-Day was by now fixed for 5th June and 'tactical loading' demanded that the regiment be split up, not only into ship-loads for those going in the first wave but also into follow-up parties, the last of which might land as much as three weeks after the assault. The batteries had been affiliated to battalions for direct support, 341 Battery to 7th Green Howards, 342 Battery to 6th Green Howards and 462 Battery to 5th East Yorkshires. The B.Cs.' and O.P. parties and the attached F.O.Os. from 124th Field Regiment were first to leave, on 31st May, to join their battalions and embark, according to their position in the assault, in the landing ships *Empire Mace*, *Empire Halberd*, *Empire Lance* and *Empire Rapier*. The commanding officer was to sail with Headquarters 69 Infantry Brigade on the headquarters ship H.M.S. *Kingsmill* and the battery captains of 341 and 342 Batteries would, with their signallers, provide another essential link between the naval force and the troops on shore from the smaller headquarters craft controlling the landings on Red and Green Beaches, respectively. Guns and other assault-wave vehicles drove to Southampton on 3rd June to embark on six L.C.Ts. of the 24th L.C.T. Flotilla. Then, according to the unidentified diarist quoted previously:

> "Tanks and guns, Jeeps and carriers, half-tracks and even hand-carts were fitted in, till not an inch of deck-space was unused. Everything was chained down in case of rough weather and when all was finished sixty or seventy men began looking around for bed spaces. Some of us slept in the fo'c's'les, some slung hammocks between the tanks, but most of us just crawled under a vehicle and slept on the iron deck. It was a bit hard, maybe, and if you got up too quickly you bumped your head, but it kept the wind and rain off you, and that was something. Of course we cooked our own rations on the deck, which kept us amused, and we had bags to eat – more than you could manage, especially when it got a bit rough in the Channel. We sailed on Sunday morning [*4th June*] and got well down the Solent before we turned back; it was too rough. It seemed worse on Monday morning but we sailed again and this time we did not turn back – we just got sick. The worst time was just off the Needles, where we seemed to lie for hours wallowing in the waves, but it was pretty bad all the way over and I think most of us were glad to set foot on shore."

The O.P. parties enjoyed comparative luxury on their L.S.Is. – some small compensation for several hours very rough weather while on the L.C.As. during the run-in to the beach.

### *D-Day and the Battle of Normandy, June–August 1944*

The landings had indeed been postponed for 24 hours and H-hour on Gold Beach was fixed

Plate IV D-Day, 6th June 1944 – Sexton self-propelled 25-pdrs. of A Troop, 341 Field Battery land and deploy on the beach
*(From the water-colour specially painted for this work by Joan Wanklyn, 1999)*

A, C and E Troops of 86th Field Regiment landed about thirty minutes ahead of their intended schedule and came into action on the beach at La Rivière at approximately 08.30 on 6th June. Each gun towed ashore a 'Porpoise', a sledge-like sealed container full of ammunition and fuel. The Sexton in the right foreground – A Sub-Section of A Troop – has just been ordered into action. A Sub's signaller, Gunner Beavis, whose job it was to plant the aiming posts, is reaching up as they are handed down by another member of the detachment. Gunner Beavis had sprained his left ankle on the assault course a few days previously and almost missed D-Day. His pleas that he was fully fit were eventually accepted by the medical officer but he was 'excused boots, left foot' and landed wearing one boot and one 'shoe, P.T.'!

This plate has generously been sponsored by McMullen and Sons Limited, supporters of Volunteers and Territorials in Hertfordshire for well over a century.

Plate 95 *Crossing the Channel, 6th June 1944. A gunner of 86th Field Regiment on a tank landing craft loaded with second or third priority vehicles.* (I.W.M. – FLM 1079)

for 07.25 on 6th June. The run-in shoot began on time at H−35 with the guns still seven miles from the beach. Their first target – one of thirteen in the bombardment plan, all of which were named after pieces of household furniture – was 'Stool', the beach at La Rivière. The two observers, Major Loveday and Captain Hall, in small craft ahead of the main force, had no need to correct the fall of shot and the guns kept up a steady four rounds per minute until H−7 when they transferred to 'Cupboard', the heavily defended position around the lighthouse, which was engaged until H+15, ten minutes longer than planned, as the assault craft carrying the infantry took longer than expected to reach the shore. The L.C.Ts. then turned about to leave the area of the beach clear for the assaulting troops. They were scheduled to return after 'marking time' offshore for about an hour and a half.

Now, according to the *Official History*:

"The Green Howards, landing to the west of La Rivière, quickly cleared the strong-point at Hable-de-Heurtot, where they were closely supported by engineer tanks. When four pill-boxes had been reduced with the help of petards, two of the tanks charged over the sea wall and routed the rest of the garrison who had been firing and throwing grenades from behind [95]

Plate 96 *'Low-level oblique' air reconnaissance photograph of King Red beach taken just before D-Day. Behind the sea wall are the substantial sea-side houses, some of which were incorporated in the defences. The lighthouse strong-point is on the skyline just to the right of the centre, while 'Lavatory-Pan House', which was just inside the left-hand boundary of King Green, can be seen, also on the skyline, at far right.* (I.W.M.)

Plate 97 *Gold-King beach early on D-Day. The boundary between the two assaulting battalions ran through the gap between the two woods on the skyline* (centre and right). *The left-hand battalion (5th East Yorkshires on King Red) had to clear buildings and woods from the beach to beyond the lighthouse* (visible on skyline, centre), *while the right-hand battalion (6th Green Howards on King Green) had to advance across marshy ground and up the slope to 'Lavatory-Pan House'* (visible, extreme right) *before reaching its main objective, the Mont Fleury Battery* (just off picture to right). (I.W.M. – A 23910)

it. The advance was quickly resumed and the Green Howards next took the battery position near Mont Fleury. It had been struck by the bombers and H.M.S. *Orion* had registered twelve hits. There was no sign that its four guns had ever fired a shot and the gun crews, cowed by the bombardment, offered no resistance.

The East Yorkshire landed near the outskirts of La Rivière and for a short time were pinned down by fire under the sea wall. They called for naval support, and destroyers and support craft closed the shore and shelled the position heavily. A flail of the Westminster Dragoons silenced an 88-mm. gun in a concrete emplacement and the East Yorkshire cap-
[96] tured the position, taking 45 prisoners. Even so it needed several hours' fighting to clear the

Plate 98 *The assault companies of 5th Battalion The East Yorkshire Regiment, with tanks of 4th/7th Royal Dragoon Guards and specialist armoured vehicles from the Westminster Dragoons and 81 Assault Squadron, Royal Engineers fighting their way off King Red beach at La Rivière, D-Day, 6th June 1944. Despite heavy casualties amongst the leading platoons, the battalion had cleared the village by soon after 9.00 a.m. and had begun to push inland while the build-up on the beach began. The lighthouse strong-point, which was the battalion's next objective after the beach can be seen on the skyline to the left.* (Pen and wash drawing by Edward James) (I.W.M. – LD 4600)

Plate 99 *Gold Beach, King Red at approximately 10.30 a.m. on 6th June 1944. L.C.T. 502 has just landed B Troop, 341 Battery.* (I.W.M.)

whole village and its capture cost, in killed and wounded, six officers and 84 other ranks. The rest of the battalion had gone on to capture the strong-point at the lighthouse near Mont Fleury. From there they took two guns and thirty prisoners and then moved on towards Ver-sur-Mer."

This short account belies considerable gallantry by the assaulting companies and their accompanying armour. The difficulties on King Red were shared by Major Scammell and his O.P. parties, who lost Lance-Bombardier Johnson and Gunner Priest killed and several wounded but were instrumental in bringing naval gunfire on to the gun emplacements along the sea wall. On King Green the forward observers of 342 Battery were witnesses of the great bravery of Company Sergeant-Major Hollis while clearing two pill-boxes in front of the Mont Fleury



Plate 100 *Two Sexton self-propelled guns of 86th Field Regiment, led by a carrier, making their way towards an exit from King Red on the morning of D-Day. Their 'Porpoises' – sealed sledges loaded with ammunition and fuel – can just be distinguished being towed behind each gun.* (I.W.M. – FLM 1080)

Plate 101 *Sergeant W. Rist's gun of C Troop, 342 Battery moving away from King Red towards the first regimental gun position near the Mont Fleury battery during the morning of 6th June 1944.* (I.W.M. – A70-33-02 2)

battery – an action which, together with his gallantry later in the day at Crépon, would result in the award of the Victoria Cross.

The first wave of guns – A, C and E Troops – landed about half an hour early. C Troop's log book records:

> "We were due to land at H+90 but this has now been shortened by thirty minutes. Land eventually at 08.35 approx. Robbie [*the L.C.T. captain*] did a good job here and put us down, in spite of obstacles and a strong sea, in about four feet of water. Unloading satisfactory and fairly fast. Jeeps both drowned, also Y. Survey's Jeep recovered but F.O.B.'s has had it . . . The porpoises – those misbegotten children of the 'War House' proved to be quite amenable to a wet landing and all were landed without any trouble. Perhaps this was the result of the language used on them previously . . . The landing was quite speedy but there was some congestion on the beach. Troops were in action in minimum of time."

By the time the guns had deployed on the beach, the follow-up battalion, 7th Green Howards, had landed on King Green. They moved through 6th Green Howards and towards the village of Crépon, capturing the Ver-sur-Mer battery on the way with little difficulty. Captain Perry, with the leading company, was able to bring down the first troop target on a platoon of infantry crossing open ground. By mid-day, a 'flying column' consisting of C Company, 7th Green Howards and A Squadron, 4th/7th Dragoon Guards with Captain Perry, now mounted in a carrier which had made its way up from the beach, in direct support, had been assembled to by-pass Crépon and seize the bridge at Creully, the battalion's first objective. Meanwhile,  the second wave of guns (B, D and F Troops) had landed at about 10.00 and eventually managed to make their way off the beach to come into action close to the Mont Fleury battery. Here they were able to cast off their porpoises, the contents of which were used to form a regimental reserve of ammunition and fuel which would help to keep the guns going until the normal system of replenishment was set up. (There is some evidence that not all the Nos. 1 were prepared to drag these extraordinary encumbrances all the way up to the Mont Fleury battery and so took the opportunity of the delay caused by congestion on the beach to unpack the contents and stow them in every possible nook and cranny of their Sextons.) As soon as B, D and F Troops had reported 'Ready', A, C and E Troops were ordered to leave the beach and join them to establish the first regimental position. There was little, possibly no, firing from Mont Fleury and around mid-day the batteries moved forward to a new position just north of Ver-sur-Mer. From here 341 Battery gave fire support to the flying column, which seized the bridge but found itself in an exposed salient until Crépon was secured and 6th Green Howards, on the right, moved up to occupy the high ground in the area of Villiers-le-Sec. The brigade was then poised to advance on the final objective for the day – the Bayeux–Caen road either side of the hamlet of St.-Léger.

While 7th Green Howards continued to hold Creully, 5th East Yorkshires on their immediate right and 6th Green Howards, further west, began a right hook. Now reduced to three companies, 5th East Yorkshires fought their way down from Villiers-le-Sec, across the River Seulles and into St.-Gabriel-Brécy, most of the time under heavy mortar-fire. They were held up by heavy automatic fire from the hamlet of Brécy, about a mile further south but a battalion attack across their front by 6th Green Howards with fire support – the first regimental fire plan – from 86th Field Regiment and a company of 2nd Cheshires, the divisional medium machine-gun battalion, secured Brécy and the villages of Rucqeville and Martragny, pushing the front to within about one thousand yards of the Bayeux–Caen road. Here the brigade commander called a halt.

Analysing the events of the day long afterwards, the *Official History* concludes that the D-Day objectives, which included the capture of Bayeux and Caen, were over-ambitious but goes on:

> "Yet it must be remembered that the troops had had little time for rest and no relaxation of strain since they left England on the previous day. Their attack had been launched not from a firm base but from unstable waters breaking on an enemy-held coast. Starting under such conditions, to have swept away all but a few isolated fragments of Hitler's Atlantic Wall and to have fought their way inland for an average depth of four to six miles on most of a twenty-four mile front, was surely a notable feat of arms."

Plate 102 *Soldiers of 50th Division wounded and evacuated on D-Day reach Southampton, 7th June 1944. Lance-Bombardier F.B. Adshead* (Right) *of 462 Battery recovered from his wound and returned to 86th Field Regiment, but was killed in action in Holland in September 1944.* (I.W.M. – H 39209)

The regiment had played a key part in this "notable feat" by devising the methods for the run-in shoot and in direct support of 69 Brigade once ashore. Their casualties had been remarkably light; at least one of the L.C.Ts. carrying the guns was damaged by shell-fire or by the beach obstacles but all the guns were safely landed and fire support was immediately available. For his coolness and skill in leading the 'gun end' throughout D-Day, the second-in-command, Major J.B. Morgan Smith, upon whom had fallen the burden of reconnaissance under fire and with the ever-present threat of mines, subsequently received the Distinguished Service Order – the regiment's first award for services in action.

During the night 6th–7th June it was found that Major Loveday had not returned to his O.P. from an O-group held late the previous evening at St.-Gabriel-Brécy. Travelling alone on a motor-cycle, he had been waylaid by a group of the enemy and shot through the chest. He was discovered at dawn on 7th June, taken to the regimental aid post of 7th Green Howards and from there evacuated without delay to England. Captain Kiln was called forward from his position on the landing craft that was controlling the approaches to King Red to take command of 341 Battery. The day was spent mopping up pockets of German resistance and pushing forward to the Bayeux–Caen road. The radar station at Coulombs was captured by 7th Green Howards after a stiff fight and Crépon, which had been by-passed and contained the previous day, was secured early in the morning, allowing the regiment to move forward to new gun areas near St.-Gabriel. Before leaving their overnight position, F Troop, who had met some opposition from a nearby wood the previous day, provided a dismounted party under Lieutenant Carpenter to take part, with two Shermans and two Churchill 'Crocodiles' (flame-throwing tanks), in an operation to clear the wood. The combined force captured one 88-mm. gun, four 75-mms. and some sixty Germans, including three officers. The rest of the day was quiet, with the O.Ps. still in support of 69 Brigade's battalions on the high ground south of St.-Léger and between the main Bayeux–Caen road and the railway.

For the next two days 8 Armoured Brigade attempted to fight their way from the Bayeux–Caen road south-westwards, through Tilly-sur-Seulles to the key road junction at Villers-Bocage. The brigade was reinforced by two infantry battalions and 50th Division's reconnaissance regiment, and had fire support from 86th and 147th Field Regiments, a medium regiment and part of the naval bombardment force. By the evening of 9th June the attack had only succeeded in securing the high ground around Point 103, about one mile north-east of Tilly-sur-Seulles, which was then precariously held under constant gun- and mortar-fire. It was apparent that both 12th S.S. Panzer Division and 130th Panzer Lehr Division had been committed to the battle and that the enemy was now better organised and more determined in his resistance than he had been on D-Day and D+1. In retrospect, it was perhaps unrealistic to have attempted such a swift armoured thrust on Tilly; nevertheless the capture of Point 103 and 50th Division's subsequent success in holding the feature, which was to dominate the battlefield for some time to come, was significant. The newly-arrived 7th Armoured Division was ordered to attack through 50th Division's front along the general line Tilly-sur-Seulles–

Plate 103 *A Troop Commander's carrier, RA, held up on the road towards Tilly-sur-Seules, 7th or 8th June 1944. Captain E.W.C. Hall* (standing) *was killed in action a few days later.* (I.W.M. – B 5453)

Juvigny–Noyers the following day (10th June) and for this operation 56 Brigade, previously in 50th Division, was placed under command of 7th Armoured Division with 86th Field Regiment in direct support.

The attack began at 06.30 on 10th June. A brief description of the division's progress is given by Clay (see Bibliography):

> "... All through the day their [*7th Armoured Division's*] tanks and infantry advanced slowly in the face of constant interference by small parties of enemy armed with anti-tank weapons. Each had to be neutralised in turn by infantry, and the close nature of the bocage set a limit to the speed of the tanks. These small groups of enemy were reinforced by a few armoured fighting vehicles, chiefly half-tracked vehicles, and later by tanks. Two days of hard fighting ... yielded small dividends."

Having secured Juaye-Mondaye, on the right of their advance, and Bucéels, on the left, by the evening of 10th June, the division halted for the night. Overnight, the armour-infantry mix was changed to improve the troops' capability for dealing with the enemy's defences in the close bocage country. The following day the attack was resumed, with 56 Brigade responsible for the left-hand thrust, the immediate objective of which was Tilly-sur-Seulles, and 22 Armoured Brigade attacking towards Lingèvres, about two miles west. For the second-day running, 2nd Glosters led the advance into Tilly, with 341 Battery in direct support. They had managed to fight their way into the northern part of the town by evening, against determined opposition and almost continuous mortar-fire, but they had little hope of holding their gains overnight and were withdrawn to overlook the town from the north. Lieutenant G.D. Greig, attached to 341 Battery from 124th Field Regiment was awarded the Military Cross for his gallantry as an F.O.O. with 2nd Glosters. When all the platoon commanders of the company he was supporting had become casualties, he took command of a party which had become detached from the main body and reorganised them in a defensive position, eventually regaining contact with the rest of the company. Lance-Bombardier S.M. Mitchley, Captain Hall's O.P. assistant in A Troop, also displayed great gallantry while supporting 2nd Glosters and subsequently received the Military Medal. Meanwhile, on the right, 462 Battery were supporting 2nd Essex with 22 Armoured Brigade. They had secured the wooded country around Verrières by the evening, when the armour withdrew. The *Official History* describes the night of 10th–11th June thus:

> "Shortly afterwards enemy tanks broke into the infantry positions among the woods. They were eventually driven away but about midnight, after a bombardment by guns and mortars, the enemy launched a stronger attack with tanks, infantry and a self-propelled flamethrower. The 2nd Essex had about a hundred and fifty casualties in the grim night-fighting that ensued but they lost no ground and, by calling down artillery fire 'almost on top of themselves', they beat the Germans off."

Major Scammell had indeed reported the position as "desperate" just before midnight and he and his O.Ps. had shared fully in the "grim night-fighting." Although the citation for Major Scammell's Military Cross dates his actions as 13th June, there seems to be no doubt that it was for his "courage and steady determination to give the infantry the support they needed" on 11th June that he received his award. The fire he brought down is said to have "saved the situation" and been "instrumental in enabling the depleted battalion to hold its position." Captain R.D. Turnbull, E Troop Commander played a full part by rallying troops who had lost their officers and even seized a bicycle in order to make his way through the enemy surrounding his position and summon reinforcements. The following day, 12th June, 56 Brigade was replaced by 7th Armoured Division's own infantry brigade, 131 Brigade, and reverted to command of 50th Division. B.Cs. and O.Ps. of 341 and 462 Batteries returned to the gun position, now at Jerusalem Crossroads, and were able to rest for some hours but 342 Battery's O.Ps. joined 231 Brigade and accompanied them in their push southwards to secure the crossroads at La Belle Épine. The battery command post log of 341 Battery (later edited by Lieutenant S.J. Beck to form ' 341 Battery's history') recorded " a warm sunny day, much quieter than yesterday, with everyone re-forming and regrouping." Captain J.G. Corke, who had been operating with the regiment as a forward observer bombardment, was posted in and promoted to command 341 Battery.

The 50th Division had been ordered to hold the line from La Belle Épine on the right (west) to Point 103 on the left, making such southward gains as they could against the Panzer Lehr Division, while 7th Armoured Division delivered a right hook to approach its objective, Villers-Bocage, from the west. The regiment was placed in direct support of 151 Brigade (6th, 8th and 9th D.L.I.) and on 13th June B.Cs. and O.Ps. joined their battalions for an advance southwards towards Verrières and Lingèvres during the afternoon, prior to a 'set-piece' divisional attack the following day. With direct support from 341 Battery, 6th D.L.I. made for the high ground east of Verrières. After they had experienced some early hold-ups, and, according to Captain Perry, calmly advanced through withering Spandau- and mortar- fire, the leading companies were pulled back while the opposition was 'stonked' for fifteen minutes by fire from two field regiments, one medium regiment and a heavy battery. They were then able to get on to their objective and "dig for dear life", only to be withdrawn during the evening in preparation for an early start on 14th June, a day which is well summarised in the *Official History*:

> "Next day (the 14th) the 50th Division continued the battle for Tilly-sur-Seulles and the road westwards through Lingèvres and La Sanaudière, on which the German hold had in fact been strengthened. First the Royal Air Force attacked all three places with bombs, rockets and cannon from eleven squadrons . . . Then two brigades attacked on a four thousand yard front, supported by the divisional and corps artillery and by guns of the Royal Navy and of the American V Corps on their right. Fighting continued all day. 151 Brigade captured about half of Lingèvres village and on their right 231 Brigade captured La Sanaudière. But nowhere could they break the German front."

On 151 Brigade's left, 6th D.L.I., with a squadron of 4th/7th Dragoon Guards and F.O.Os. from 341 Battery, had Verrières as their objective. After more than five hours of heavy fighting against an enemy well dug in and with several 75-mm. guns, 6th D.L.I. succeeded in occupying Lingèvres but at such cost that the battalion had to reorganise that evening with only two, rather than four, rifle companies. Captain E.W.C. Hall, A Troop Commander was killed and his assistant, Lance-Bombardier Mitchley was severely wounded in the thigh. According to the citation for his Military Medal, Mitchley, "in spite of the enemy fire, the loss of his officer and his own wound, which was causing great pain . . . insisted on remaining at his post and continued to pass back fire orders and information of the greatest value until he was no longer able to speak and was evacuated". Lance-Bombardier J. Meyer, Captain Perry's assistant in B Troop also received the Military Medal for his conduct during the attack on Verrières, which included braving mortar- and machine-gun fire to rescue Mitchley. Meanwhile, on the right of 151 Brigade's front, 9th D.L.I., supported by 4th/7th Dragoon Guards and 342 Battery, were successful in driving the enemy out of Lingèvres. Two counter-attacks were repulsed thanks to Major Swann's defensive fire planning and observation of fire, all carried out under heavy enemy fire. Major Swann was awarded the Military Cross for his "cool and skilful handling of his battery and his complete disregard of personal danger in securing observation [*which*] played a large part in holding the important gains made by the infantry he was supporting". No further attempt was made to push forward but 151 Brigade remained in the line until 16th June, when 69 Brigade attacked southwards through them and towards Hottot. The regiment was not involved in this attack but the guns joined the barrage in support of the newly-arrived 49th Division, who were attacking Cristot, three miles north-east of Tilly. After two more relatively quiet days, 86th Field Regiment was transferred to support of 50th Division's 231 Brigade, who were due to make yet another attempt to reach Hottot. The regiment was temporarily under the command of Major Morgan Smith, since Colonel Fanshawe had been wounded by mortar-fire on 18th June. (Despite splinters lodged in his head, Colonel Fanshawe managed to avoid staying in the field hospital, to which he had been evacuated, for more than about three days and according to Kiln – see Bibliography – in less than a fortnight was "snapping around us again, as nasal as ever".)

Tilly-sur-Seulles fell to 56 Brigade – helped by 6th D.L.I. of 151 Brigade on their right – on the morning of 19th June. The same afternoon, 231 Brigade attacked Hottot in the face of determined opposition. An impression of these two difficult days, which have not been described in detail in other sources, is given in 341 Battery's history:

> *"19th June*
>
> Rain and wind all day make conditions for our infantry and O.Ps. simply terrible. Another

> attack was made against Hottot and we were called upon to fire stonk after stonk. Major Swann, commanding 342 Battery, was killed in action during this attack. By tea-time we had fired 1,050 rounds. A fierce counter-attack developed before dark and we fired a further 600 rounds before the enemy gave up the struggle.
>
> *20th June*
>
> The struggle for Tilly and Hottot became more fierce. We fired 1,350 rounds during the day in support of the attacking infantry. Tilly changed hands several times during the day but by nightfall our troops were at last in full possession."

The few words accorded to these two days by the *Official History* – ". . . by the 19th, 50th Division finally drove the enemy out of Tilly-sur-Seulles and pushed south to the outskirts of Hottot" are an indicator of how, during the period mid-June–mid-July 1944, fierce fighting continued at intervals across the whole of Second Army's front, and not just the well publicised and recorded major armoured thrusts, as General Montgomery's tactics attracted German reserves to the Caen sector.

Clay describes the days immediately following 19th–20th June in a few telling sentences:

> "After the failure of this attack on Hottot the division passed through a period in which there was nothing spectacular to record – nothing to make the headlines in the newspapers at home; but it was an unpleasant period of close contact with the enemy, and of continuous attempts to gain ground at his expense. And the division, it must be remembered, was still in that sniper's paradise constituted by the Norman bocage. We were disposed with, right, 69 Brigade south of La Belle Épine and La Sanaudière, centre 231 Brigade north of Hottot, and, left, 151 Brigade in the general area of Tilly."

The regiment spent the period 21st June–6th July with the O.Ps. deployed with 231 Brigade and the guns near Chouain. The relative lull on XXX Corps's front was caused in part by the huge storm which had wrecked a large part of the 'Mulberry' artificial harbour at Arromanches, and in part by preparations for a major attack by VIII Corps on the left of XXX Corps. The storm had a big effect on the supply of ammunition and for several days the regiment was limited to thirty rounds per gun per day for targets called by its own O.Ps.; ammunition for major operations was subject to separate allocation. The delayed operation 'Epsom', an attempt to outflank Caen from the west, began on 26th June. On its right flank, 49th Division, of XXX Corps, attacked in support, gaining considerable ground, and the regiment was committed to 49th Division for two days, reverting to 231 Brigade on 28th June. The opportunity was of course taken to rest both the 'sharp end' and the 'gun end' as much as possible and steps were taken as early as 21st June to replace the officer casualties of the battles for Lingèvres, Tilly and Hottot. Captain R.J. Kiln was posted from 341 Battery and promoted to command 342 and Captain J.M.M. Wood, previously Intelligence Officer, took over A Troop.

On 7th July the guns moved to positions west of La Belle Épine and the O.Ps. joined the battalions of 56 Brigade, once more under command of 50th Division, for an operation the following day which was designed to cut the road leading south-west from Hottot to Caumont, between Crauville and La Croix-des-Landes, thus putting further pressure on the enemy who still held Hottot. The following extracts from 341 Battery's history give an impression of three days' fighting which has not even attracted a single line in the *Official History*:

> "8th July
>
> The night staffs of all the command posts worked all night preparing fire plan 'Maori'. There was a long list of targets which were on call to code-names of animals. At dawn 2 S.W.B. on the right and 2 Essex on the left started their push to cut the Hottot road. All morning progress was very slow, the enemy making much use of minefields and well concealed Spandaus. In the early afternoon enemy tanks and infantry moved up to counter-attack. Our leading troops ran into a minefield in an orchard and Captain Pamphilon, F Troop Commander was killed and his O.P. ack badly wounded on a mine. [*Gunner Heard subsequently died of his wounds.*] By 15.30 a gap was made in the minefield but the enemy threw in another counter-attack. Fighting continued until dusk with the enemy staging many attacks which were all broken up by our concentrated artillery fire. At the end of the day we had advanced about one thousand yards with heavy casualties to the S.W.B. During

Plate 104
*Command post tank of 86th Field Regiment at speed in the Odon Valley, 16th July 1944. To the annoyance of many infantrymen with whom 86th Field Regiment's O.Ps. came in contact, the gun on a Sherman O.P./C.P. tank was a dummy. The space that would have been occupied by the breech and recoil system of a real gun was devoted to extra wireless sets and a plotting board.*
(I.W.M. – B 7422)

the day Captain Wood and A Troop O.P. crew had narrow escapes. A 105-mm. shell burst just in front of their carrier without causing any casualties or damage. Later they were nearly crushed by our own tanks advancing over the ditch they were occupying. A hard day at the gun end, which was now well established . . .

*9th July*

Enemy counter-attacks threatened throughout the day but exchanges of artillery fire seemed to deter the enemy . . .

*10th July*

At dawn the S.W.B. and the Essex were again counter-attacked by the enemy at Crauville. The enemy used mortars and H.E. on our forward troops all through the attacks and Lieutenant Jones at 462's O.P. was fatally wounded by a direct hit on his carrier by a 105-mm. shell. [*Another member of the crew, Gunner Hill, died of wounds.*] After ninety minutes the attacks were broken up and the remainder of the day was relatively quiet . . . Once again the night duty staffs in the command posts had a busy time preparing a fire plan for tomorrow."

The fire plan was in support of yet another attack on Hottot, this time by 231 Brigade."Opposition", according to Clay, "was in the Hottot tradition, and a bitter battle was fought throughout the day". The regiment fired a prolonged smoke-screen on the flank of the main barrage, stopping and restarting several times, but the attack was halted just north of Hottot. After two quiet days the regiment came out of the line on 14th July, the day on which the 'Final Residue' arrived from England, bringing "tales of narrow escapes from V1s and exciting times in the Channel".

A huge operation code-named 'Goodwood' and designed to draw German armour to the Caen sector prior to an American break-out in the west, was due to start on 18th July. According to the *Official History*:

"Preliminary operations began on the night of the 15th with attacks which extended across
[104] the whole front between the west of Caen and Tilly-sur-Seulles . . . XXX Corps . . . was to

Plate 105 *The commanding officer's tank, Z/1147, with tanks of Headquarters 33 Armoured Brigade during 59th Infantry Division's attack on Noyers-Bocage, overlooking the Odon Valley, south-west of Caen, 16th July 1944.* (I.W.M. – B 7420)

secure the Noyers area and be prepared to exploit to the high ground north-east of Villers-Bocage."

The regiment was placed in direct support of 33 Armoured Brigade, which was under command of 59th Division, due to play the major role in XXX Corps' attack, with 49th Division making a limited advance on their right. A long move on 15th July positioned the guns south-east of Fontenay-le-Pesnel and the O.Ps. with 1st Northants Yeomanry and 144th Regiment, R.A.C. (The third armoured regiment of the brigade was deployed elsewhere.) The guns were less than 2,500 yards from the enemy's forward positions, which encouraged everybody to dig slit trenches but also necessitated the digging-in of the five hundred rounds of ammunition that had been dumped for each gun for the following day's fire plan. It turned out to be "a very hot tiring day, not relieved by any good news" (341 Battery's history). Ammunition expenditure was huge – 341 Battery fired 1,500 rounds in the two-hour barrage which started at 05.30, reached 2,000 rounds by tea-time and by midnight had fired nearly 3,400. The forward brigades failed to reach their objectives and the attack was resumed at 05.00 on 17th July but "owing to heavy and effective enemy D.F. on our forming-up areas . . . did not really get going until mid-day" (341 Battery's history). Some progress was made during the afternoon after considerable artillery effort – "We had five O.Ps. out and Mike and Uncle targets rained upon the command posts". The guns had another hectic night, made no easier by heavy and accurate enemy air attacks on the gun position during a two-hour H.F. programme. Regimental Headquarters vehicles were damaged by splinters, all communications to 462 Battery were cut and one gun had its picket light blown out three times but the fire plan was completed and fortunately there were no casualties. The regiment took little part in the efforts to get into Noyers, which went on throughout 18th July and continued until the morning of 19th July, when XXX Corps called off the attack. Though territorial gains were small, these operations prior to the start of 'Goodwood' were reckoned to have been successful in keeping German armoured formations engaged west of Caen, in persuading the enemy to commit his armoured reserves, and in drawing attention away from the area east of the River Orne, where three British armoured divisions would spearhead the 'Goodwood' advance.

On 20th July (D+44) 86th Field Regiment was at last relieved of all commitments in the line and moved to a rest and maintenance area at St.-André, five miles south of Bayeux. After six weeks' hard fighting there was a great deal to be done before recreation was able to take priority. All logs and diaries record how the commanding officer insisted that guns and vehicles should be cleaned thoroughly on the first day, even though it was raining hard, but later in the week the emphasis shifted to football and hockey matches, and E.N.S.A. shows. The opportunity for hot showers – both in the public baths at Bayeux and at one of the mobile laundry and bath units – was greatly welcomed. By now it had been realised that the half-tracks issued as section ammunition vehicles would be better employed as troop command posts; there were very few places that a 3-ton truck could not reach, even when loaded with ammunition. Accordingly:

"L.A.D. worked overtime in cutting back-doors and welding gadgets inside, and undoubt-

Plate 106 *Mail reaches B Troop command post, July 1944.* (Regimental Collection)

> edly the efficiency of the regiment was greatly increased by this changeover. It was in fact quite a hard time for all fitters and we were to see the value of their work later, in the great dash to Antwerp." (341 Battery's history)

Further officer reinforcements had by now arrived – Captain P.H. Cherry and Captain D. Benson to command E and F Troops, respectively; Captain J.B. Irvine as Battery Captain, 341 Battery; Captain R. Marshall, M.M., who took over C Troop following Captain Street's evacuation to hospital; and Captain J.D. Carr, who became Intelligence Officer. Captain Cherry's arrival was particularly opportune; his brother, Captain D.W. Cherry, was a pre-war Territorial officer in 86th Field Brigade and had gone to the Far East with 135th Field Regiment, where he was captured on the fall of Singapore.

The maintenance and rest period ended on 28th July when the regiment moved into the line in support of 56 Brigade, still under command of 50th Division, with the guns once more at La Belle Épine. The following day the guns moved again, to a position north-east of Caumont, and it became clear that the whole of Twenty-First Army Group was shaking out along the northern edge of what was to be known as the 'Falaise Pocket'. The southward offensive started on 30th July. The regiment began firing at 06.00 in support of 50th Division's advance and then switched at 08.00 to support of 43rd Division's thrust southwards towards Cahagnes. Although 43rd Division made rather more progress than 50th, both divisions were seriously held up, in part by minefields, some of which had been sown by the Americans. At the gun end, 341 Battery noted that targets became "spasmodic" as the attack slowed down. The *Official History* states bluntly that it was "an unrewarding and rather baffling day for XXX Corps". The next day (31st July), the regiment was committed to support of 43rd Division, who managed to make rather better progress, entering Cahagnes in the early evening and securing St.-Pierre-du-Fresne before midnight. Overnight the guns moved forward and occupied an area a mile south-west of Cahagnes early on 1st August. During 1st and 2nd August 43rd Division made slow but steady progress southwards, capturing Jurques and Hill 301, two miles to the south. Between 08.00–09.00 on the morning of 3rd August the guns moved to a position near Jurques, arriving in a partial mist, which obscured the view to the front. Then, according to 341 Battery's history:

> "As the mist cleared we saw we were on the forward slope of a hill and were overlooked by a high crest due south of us. The position of the enemy was obscure and we were a little apprehensive as we watched our own infantry clearing the woods up to the skyline to our right front . . . Approximately at 15.00 some H.E. shells landed in B Troop's field and some near A Troop command post. Sergeant Fielding of E Sub was wounded by a shell splinter and was being attended to in the lane behind B Troop when more shells landed. A.P. shells hit B Troop's No. 3 gun and ricochetted over the battery command post behind. One shell pierced the barrel of G Sub and killed Gunner Cox sitting in the layer's seat, wounding Lance-Sergeant Smith and Gunners McIntosh and Howarth. Captain Perry, B Troop Commander, spotted the tank causing the trouble, which was firing from the top of the crest in front. With Bombardier Tulloch, Collinge and Stockton of E Sub, he engaged the tank at two thousand yards with A.P. and H.E., scoring at least three direct hits. The enemy
> [106] tank caught fire and withdrew as the regiment put down a concentration."

Plate 107 *Sextons of 342 Battery firing in support of 43rd Infantry Division's attack towards Cahagnes, prior to the advance on Mount Pinçon, 30th July 1944. During 86th Field Regiment's week out of the line, 20th–26th July, the Light Aid Detachment, R.E.M.E. welded steel tubes to the front plates each side of the barrel to carry spare bogies. It is thought that no other unit adopted exactly this method of carrying bogies, so it provides an important means of identification of the regiment's guns in photographs when the unit serial number cannot be seen.* (I.W.M. – B 8236)

The tank, a Tiger, and theoretically very much the master in a duel against a Sexton, "waddled off pouring forth smoke from his turret – damaged but not dead", according to Captain Perry's account of the incident. Captain Perry was awarded the Military Cross for his "coolness and devotion to duty under heavy and accurate fire" and the incident at Jurques, in which, "in spite of accurate high-explosive fire from the Tiger, he went, without cover and quite fearlessly, from gun to gun tending the wounded and cheering them with infectious good humour" features in the citation for the Military Medal awarded to Gunner W.L. Cornell, 341 Battery's medical orderly, which was announced in the Cease-Fire List published in 1946. Some two hundred yards away, 462 Battery had their own encounter with a different Tiger, which stretcher bearers were later seen to approach. Late in the afternoon 341 Battery were at last authorised to move to an alternative position on a reverse slope. Throughout the night of 3rd–4th August the regiment fired a complicated harassing fire plan on likely enemy withdrawal routes, with high-explosive groundburst and airburst and smoke being fired simultaneously.

On 4th August 86th Field Regiment was placed in direct support of 13th/18th Hussars, who would be under command of 129 Brigade of 43rd Division for the attack on Mont Pinçon, at 1,200 feet the dominating feature of the region. The regiment moved during the night of 4th–5th August. Unusually, the move was interrupted by orders to deploy from the line of march, but before first light they had occupied positions at Les Moeux, a few miles west of Mont Pinçon. The attack began at 14.30 on 6th August. At the gun end, 341 Battery recorded that it "began badly, the infantry meeting heavier resistance than expected. We fired several Victor targets on enemy concentrations". The log then goes on to ascribe the capture of Mont Pinçon to the "sheer determination" of the infantry (a description of which is given by Essame – see Bibliography). The *Official History* gives the wider view: [107]

"... It was a very hot afternoon. The leading troops came under heavy fire as they approached the stream. [*The stream was about one mile, measured horizontally, to the west of the summit.*] One battalion, already weakened by losses on the previous day, was soon reduced to an effective strength of only sixty rifles. But while a reserve battalion was moving to pass through, the Hussars got some tanks across the stream and sent two troops on ahead to try to reach the crest. One tank overturned in a quarry and another had its tracks blown off but, with great determination and using the cover of a smoke-screen, seven climbed to the top and by eight o'clock the rest of the squadron had joined them. Shortly afterwards thick fog came down and two infantry battalions of 129 Brigade reached the hill. They dug in amongst the bracken and scrub and shared the flat hill-top with the Germans for the rest of the night. When the fog cleared in the early morning the garrison was eliminated and two hundred prisoners were taken".

Artillery support for 13th/18th Hussars was assured by Captain Ash, D Troop Commander, whose Sherman driver managed "very gingerly" to get him to the summit (see Kiln).

For the next two days, 7th–8th August, 8 Armoured Brigade, with 86th Field Regiment in direct support, remained under command of 43rd Division. There was little activity, though the guns moved twice – to Ondefontaine on 7th August and, improbable though it seems, to the upper slopes of Mont Pinçon, with 341 Battery almost on the summit, on 8th August. Then, on 9th August, 8 Armoured Brigade moved to under command 50th Division, with the regiment still in direct support. The O.Ps. all joined 13th/18th Hussars, who were due to advance southwards off Mont Pinçon with 151 Brigade, through Le Plessis-Grimoult and St.-Pierre-la-Vieille towards Condé-sur-Noireau. By early afternoon 151 Brigade had attained their objectives and, in the face of artillery-, mortar- and machine-gun fire, were astride the main road about two-and-a-half miles from St.-Pierre. The squadron that Captain Perry was supporting lost eight tanks out of fourteen. The lead was then taken by 69 Brigade and later 231 Brigade. After two days attempting to dislodge the enemy from Point 229, the high ground overlooking St.-Pierre from the west, and from the village itself, the decision was taken to by-pass St.-Pierre, which did not fall until the night of 12th–13th August, and continue the advance on Condé. On the morning of 12th August 151 Brigade re-entered the battle on the left of 231 Brigade, with Point 249 and Point 262, high ground to the south-east of St.-Pierre, as their objective. The attack went well and the heights were secured during the afternoon. While he was supporting the squadron attacking Point 262, Captain Cherry's tank was hit by an 88-mm. which killed the wireless operator, Bombardier Ingram, wounded Captain Cherry and started a fire. In full view of the enemy and under heavy shelling and small-arms fire, the tank driver, Lance-Bombardier L.J. Burrows climbed up to the turret and succeeded in putting out the fire. He then applied a tourniquet to Captain Cherry's arm, got him out of the turret and took him back under cover. Still under heavy fire, he returned to the tank, confirmed that the wireless operator was dead, and drove the tank away from the scene. For this extraordinary bravery he was awarded the Military Medal. The four days 9th–12th August were difficult at the gun end too. There was not a great deal of firing – from an area near Le Plessis-Grimoult which they had occupied on 9th August – but there were several casualties, though none fatal, from counter-battery fire.

On 13th August, 86th Field Regiment was placed under command of 43rd Division and in direct support of 130 Brigade, who were to lead the advance southwards through Proussy and St.-Denis-de-Méré, with the aim of forcing a crossing of the Noireau east of Condé. The guns moved to a position just north of St.-Pierre, where 4,000 rounds of smoke had been dumped but, since 130 Brigade had not yet been able to take over the lead from 129 Brigade, they did not fire. During the afternoon Gunner Roberts of 341 Battery was killed when B Troop's position was shelled, apparently at random, rather than as part of organised counter-battery fire. Patrols from 5th Dorsets of 130 Brigade had located the enemy immediately north of Proussy during the night and at 07.30 on 14th August the battalion attacked, successfully overcoming early resistance after which they "surged forward behind a rolling barrage towards the village ..." (Essame). With Proussy in the hands of 5th Dorsets, 7th Hampshires secured St.-Denis-de-Méré, thus opening the way for 4th Dorsets to move on the final objective north of the Noireau, Point 201, which dominated the intended crossing point. By nightfall the battalion had succeeded in this "most difficult advance" and patrols had reached the river bank. Preparations for an assault crossing by 214 Brigade lasted throughout 15th August; they included a move of the guns to an

Plate 108 *Guns of 342 Battery, Sergeant J. Burgess's sub-section leading, between positions during the advance south of Mont Pinçon, 11th August 1944.* (I.W.M. – FLM 1081)

area south of Proussy. On the morning of 16th August "the crossing of the Noireau was completed successfully under cover of our heavy artillery fire . . . We were not called upon to fire the smoke screen" (341 Battery's history). Resistance within the Falaise pocket was now collapsing fast as the enemy made for the 'Falaise Gap', between Falaise and Argentan, which the Canadians and Poles in the north and the Americans in the south were struggling to close.

The 11th Armoured Division was ordered to pursue the enemy as he fled eastwards through the narrowing pocket and 86th Field Regiment was placed under command of the division, which it joined near Flers on 17th August. Recce parties, which set off early in the morning, made a huge detour to the west, entering Flers during the afternoon only to be held up by the Military Police so that the regiment's guns could roar through the town. The guns had left much later but had been able to cross the Noireau on the newly-constructed bridge, which enabled them to avoid the detour and reach the gun area, just east of Flers, well ahead of the recce parties. Here the troop leaders laid out the gun positions and the guns had to be put 'on line' by magnetic compass, pending arrival of directors much later on. During the day a vehicle carrying both the commanding officer and the second-in-command ran over a mine. Colonel Fanshawe escaped unhurt but Major Morgan Smith was seriously wounded in one foot. He was evacuated at once and Major Scammell took over as second-in-command, with Captain Perry moving from B Troop, 341 Battery to command 462 Battery and Captain Benson, Intelligence Officer, taking over B Troop.

As the enemy increased the pace of his withdrawal – into what was almost a headlong rush through the ever-shrinking gap and across the Seine – it proved difficult for 11th Armoured Division to do more than follow up. On 18th August, for instance, the regimental war diary noted that at around mid-day the guns moved from their overnight position immediately east of Flers to an area very close to Briouze but from here "the guns did not fire as the enemy are

Plate 109 *GD at the head of D Troop, 342 Battery moving through the ruined town centre of Écouché while in support of 11th Armoured Division during the battle to close the 'Falaise Gap', August 1944.* (I.W.M. – B 9461)

retreating at such speed that our forward elements keep losing contact". Once through Briouze, however, routes which the British XXX Corps deemed theirs were being crossed by the United States XIX Corps, which continued to press north, rather than north-east, or even east. This dispute over access to roads was resolved during the afternoon of 18th August but the regiment did not move again, this time into the southern outskirts of Écouché, until the afternoon of the following day. On 20th August the Germans occupying the Gouffern Forest, which extended north and east of Argentan, were more inclined to resist but even so the forest was cleared before mid-morning. The day's 'bag' of prisoners totalled nearly one thousand on 11th Armoured Division's front alone, including the commander of the German 276th Infantry Division and his complete staff. Argentan was captured early in the evening of 20th August and during the next two days there were fast moves, apparently with no opposition, through Exmes, Croisilles and Le Merlerault to Aube-sur-Risle. The regiment's O.Ps. were with the leading elements throughout.

*The dash for Antwerp, August–September 1944*

On 23rd August 11th Armoured Division was withdrawn to harbour areas while the infantry divisions of XXX Corps moved up to the Seine to secure the west bank for the planned crossing, which 43rd Division was to make, at Vernon. Once the bridgehead over the Seine was established, Twenty-First Army Group's intention was "to destroy all enemy forces in the Pas-de-Calais and Flanders, and to capture Antwerp". In pursuance of this aim First Allied Airborne Army and First Canadian Army would deal with the Pas de Calais (the left flank of the advance), while:

> "Second Army was to cross the Seine with all speed and, quite irrespective of the progress by other armies on its flanks, secure the area Amiens–St.-Pol–Arras, with a strong force of armour making a dash for Amiens. Swift and relentless action by Second Army would thus

Plate 110 *A Sexton of 462 Battery at speed between positions, 18th August 1944.* (I.W.M. – B 9354)

> cut across the communications of the enemy opposing the Canadians. When these objectives had been gained Second Army [*was to be*] prepared to drive forward through north-eastern France and into Belgium . . ." (*Official History*).

As the crow flies, Antwerp is about two hundred miles from XXX Corps' crossing over the Seine at Vernon. Their "swift and relentless action" would be headed, once the bridgehead had been secured and break-out made possible, by 11th Armoured Division on the left of the corps axis and the Guards Armoured Division on the right. The regiment would remain under command of 11th Armoured Division for this thrust north-eastwards and so was able to benefit from five days' rest in harbour. "For a few days we remained in this quiet backwater while the tide of war still surged on", 341 Battery's history records, with details of visits to neighbouring L'Aigle, where "wine was freely distributed". The locals had hidden stocks of wine in the river and "feeling quite certain that the enemy would never return, they hauled the casks and bottles out and celebrated in traditional style" on 25th August.

Even as the inhabitants of L'Aigle and their guests were celebrating, troops of 43rd Division were crossing the Seine at Vernon under cover of a smoke-screen. By the afternoon of 26th August a bridge capable of carrying armoured cars, carriers and anti-tank guns had been constructed. Tanks began crossing on 27th August and by the following day 43rd Division had established a secure perimeter some four miles east of the Seine. Final orders for what 11th Armoured Division regarded as a "most promising operation" (*Taurus Pursuant*) were received on 27th August and the move of some ninety miles from Aube-sur-Risle to an assembly area at La Chapelle, three miles west of Vernon, was ordered for 28th August. Owing to limited road space, the main body of 86th Field Regiment did not leave Aube-sur-Risle until 17.00, arriving at La Chapelle well after midnight. It was, according to 341 Battery's history, "very, very dusty on the roads after the long column of tanks had passed through and many of us suffered from eye-strain and swollen lids".

At first light on 29th August the main body of 11th Armoured Division began to cross the Seine. Small parties, including some of 86th Field Regiment's O.Ps., had crossed earlier, but now two armoured brigades had priority, to be followed by the infantry brigade of 11th Armoured Division and then troops of 50th Division who would take over and hold the ground liberated by the armoured spearhead. On the right of the break-out from the bridgehead, and with their right flank on the boundary between Second Army and the United States First Army, 8 Armoured Brigade, for the time being under command of 11th Armoured Division, would advance along the axis planned for the Guards Armoured Division, who would cross a little later and take over from 8 Armoured Brigade. To the left of 8 Armoured

Brigade were 29 Armoured Brigade of 11th Armoured Division, with an exposed left flank, for the neighbouring XII Corps was some distance away and inclined to veer further left. The task of guarding this exposed left flank as 11th Armoured Division moved swiftly north-east was given to the Divisional Regiment, R.A.C., 15th/19th Hussars, who were to be supported by 86th Field Regiment. A flavour of the three days following the crossing of the Seine is given in 341 Battery's history:

> *"29th August*
>
> Bleary eyed we awoke before dawn and made a hasty breakfast. In the early morning light we journeyed into Vernon and, after a short wait, rumbled across the famous pontoon bridge alongside the iron bridge destroyed by our bombers . . . The approaches and exits from the bridge had been shelled early on but we crossed without incident and roared up the steep winding road . . . At the top of the hill, with the Seine behind us, we went into action on some open ground, now muddy from the steady rain . . . We did not remain long here. At 11.00 the C.O. ordered 'Move independently' and again we charged across flat open fields to our new R.V. On the way we passed Captain Perry and RB waiting in a lane with the reserve squadron of 15th/19th Hussars. Ahead of them we had a fine view of the other squadrons in extended order, advancing cautiously across open country . . . At 14.30 came another quick cross-country move. The going was becoming more sticky. The wheeled vehicles were frequently in difficulties and the motor-cyclists had a tiring time. We were now at the village of Cantiers but only remained for an hour before another quick advance to Gamaches-en-Vexin . . . We just had time to eat a hastily prepared meal before making another dash forward. We passed through the town of Étrépagny, whose inhabitants gave us a great welcome . . . Our gun area for the night was north of the town, in a small hollow . . . Despite the tiring day and the miserable rain, everyone was elated with the advance and the hearty welcome everywhere.
>
> *30th August*
>
> The advance continued at dawn in the pouring rain . . . [*We*] occupied an open position north of Sancourt. We were not called upon to fire and very soon made another dash forward. In the late afternoon there were rumours of harbour parties and we actually set off to our new area. The roads became very congested and the regiment was ordered off the road to allow more tanks of 11th Armoured Division to move up. Here we waited an hour or so, cheered by the sight of long columns of prisoners marching back down our column. Then came a surprise. At 20.00 we were told that we were moving immediately to Amiens, more than seventy miles away [*An exaggeration – the distance was in fact about 35 miles but by now many vehicles were very short of petrol.*] It got dark early because of the heavy rain and no lights were allowed except tail lights. Stealthily we journeyed through the night, passing through sleeping villages whose inhabitants peered anxiously at us from behind curtained windows. It was a great strain on our drivers and operators to keep awake but they did and we arrived safely.
>
> *31st August*
>
> Dawn found us on the outskirts of Amiens and we were immediately ordered into action just off the main axis. As we dashed out to our gun platforms, the tanks and mobile Bofors guns engaged some enemy M.T. and S.P. guns in the valley to the left of us. Ammunition exploded intermittently as the enemy vehicles 'brewed up'. We heard over the air that our leading tanks had entered Amiens. We had two more moves before lunch-time, finishing up at the village of Dury, two miles from Amiens . . . We managed a hot meal [*and*] the sun came out . . . In the late afternoon we packed up and had our triumphal entry into Amiens . . . All too swiftly we were out of the city and into action north of it. As we came into action the leading tanks were only a thousand yards ahead and were being engaged by enemy guns. The tanks consolidated for the night and we spent that night as the most forward artillery of the spearhead, supporting 3rd R.T.R. and 23rd Hussars . . ."

This bold night march resulted in the capture of a number of important bridges across the River Somme before the Germans were able to destroy them and forestalled any plans they may have had for forming a defensive line on the river. Reviewing the progress of 11th Armoured Division up to this point, *Taurus Pursuant* concludes that:

Plate 111 *Major R.J. Kiln and the crew of X/342 pause to meet the recently liberated inhabitants of Billy-Montigny, near Lille, 2nd September 1944.* (Regimental Collection)

"It was by now appreciated that the Germans, having lost the Somme position, could not form a defensive line this side of the canal systems in the Low Countries, and the division rejoiced at the prospect of continuing an advance which had come to resemble a triumphant progress as each liberated village prepared a warmer welcome and a thicker barrage of fruit."

The enemy's withdrawal now developed into something closer to headlong flight, with only token resistance, which barely slowed down the advance of 11th Armoured Division or the Guards on their right. During 1st September 29 Armoured Brigade pushed steadily on, by-passing resistance, which was left to the follow-up infantry. By nightfall the guns had travelled about 45 miles and joined the forward elements of the division near Aubigny-en-Artois, just north of the main Arras–St.-Pol road, north-west of Arras. The next day, 2nd September, turned out to be "another great day of liberation" (341 Battery's history). The axis of advance shifted a little to the east, across Vimy Ridge, through the easterly suburbs of Lens, to finish with 29 Armoured Brigade concentrated north-east of the town and the regiment's guns in action on the outskirts. An airborne operation in the area Courtrai–Lille–Ypres planned for 2nd September was cancelled owing to unsuitable weather and late that evening XXX Corps was ordered to advance on Brussels and Antwerp starting as early as possible (*Official History*).

Curiously, 341 Battery's history records 3rd September 1944 as "the most tiring and exciting day of the war". Distance and success had evidently lent enchantment to the view of D-Day and the grinding days fighting for Tilly-sur-Seulles and Villers-Bocage. Nevertheless, in contrast to the previous few days, there was plenty of contact with the enemy and the *Official History* confirms that 11th Armoured Division "had to overcome strong opposition at several places, especially approaching Lille . . ." The division began their advance early on 3rd September pushing from Lens towards Lille on two roads about four miles apart. By 10.00 the 23rd Hussars, leading the right-hand column, had reached Frétin when the enemy attacked in the area of Attiche, a village about three miles back. A self-propelled 88-mm., or possibly a tank, shooting from a wood on the right of the road, quickly hit six or seven 3-tonners carrying ammunition and petrol. Major Corke, commanding 341 Battery, travelling in his Jeep with a driver and signaller, turned round and sped down the column to investigate. As the Jeep passed a burning truck, the cargo exploded, killing Major Corke instantly and seriously wounding his driver. Forward of the ambush, in the village of Avelin, 341 Battery went to 'tank alert' in the streets and Sergeant Couzins of E Sub, B Troop was ordered to take his gun forward and establish an outpost on the northern edge of the village. Turning a corner he saw an enemy six-gun battery in action in a shallow valley less than two thousand yards away. He immediately engaged the nearest gun over open sights, knocking it out with his third round.

"Five rounds gun-fire", Sergeant Couzins later recalled, "scattered the remaining crews, who ran away from us towards the head of the column, where they were captured. I would have liked our commanding officer to have seen our third round on the target; he once gave me the rough edge of his tongue during a practice anti-tank shoot and he would have been pleased to see the result of it." For this action Sergeant Couzins was mentioned in despatches. Meanwhile, another pocket of enemy resistance was located at a chateau bordered by woods on the southern edge of Avelin. No tanks were available, so Major Scammell in his X tank (which had no main armament) took Sergeant Burgess of D Troop, 342 Battery forward with his gun to deal with the enemy, who by now were firing at the vehicles of Headquarters 159 Brigade on the road a short distance away. After a recce on foot with Major Scammell, Sergeant Burgess took his gun across the open, where it was subjected to a hail of enemy fire, and halted less than one hundred yards from the chateau, where he fired several rounds through the windows. The enemy then showed a white flag and four officers and ninety other ranks surrendered. Further prisoners were taken as the dismounted gun detachment and B.C.'s party mopped up the surrounding buildings and woods. Sergeant Burgess received the Military Medal for his coolness, courage and initiative in this action, which cleared remaining resistance at the rear of the column and enabled the advance to continue. No sooner had the guns got back on the road, however, than some German tanks which had remained silent and hidden on the opposite side of the road began to fire on passing vehicles. At once, 342 Battery were ordered to deploy from the line of march and they put down a smoke-screen, under the cover of which vehicles that could not leave the road were able to dash past. By 14.00 the situation was again fully under control and 23rd Hussars had crossed the Franco–Belgian border and reached Tournai, followed by the regiment's guns an hour or so later. It had, according to *Taurus Pursuant*, been decided not to enter Antwerp that night but:

> "No further organised resistance was met, and considerable progress was achieved. After eliminating a small enemy pocket at Ninove, 23rd Hussars pushed on to cut the Ghent–Brussels road at Asse by 21.00, and a further hour's journey saw them astride the Brussels–Antwerp highway at Wolvertem . . . The greater part of the division concentrated for the night in the area south-east of Alost and 29 Armoured Brigade prepared to move on at first light the next day."

The regiment, which had harboured overnight near Asse, was back on the road at dawn on 4th September with orders to support 15th/19th Hussars, who were to cover the crossing of the Scheldt at Dendermonde and then protect the left flank of 11th Armoured Division as it moved towards, and eventually entered, Antwerp. Mid-morning saw the guns in action at Lebbecke, just south of Antwerp, with their local defences sited facing west, and leading elements of 11th Armoured Division in Antwerp having secured, undamaged, the docks on the north bank of the Scheldt with considerable help from the Belgian Resistance – the *'Armée Blanche'*.

Plans were now being drawn up for Second Army to continue its swift advance in order to seize bridges over the River Rhine (in Dutch, the Waal) between Wesel and Arnhem (Operation 'Comet'). On 6th September, XXX Corps attempted to move forward on a wide front, but whereas the Guards Armoured Division and 50th Division made useful progress on the right, crossing the Albert Canal and eventually reaching the Meuse–Escaut Canal, 159 Infantry Brigade of 11th Armoured Division were unsuccessful in breaking out of Antwerp and advancing north-eastwards towards Breda. The situation in Antwerp is described by Major Kiln in detail which is not apparent from the *Official History*. The regiment's guns had moved to Willibroek, immediately south of Antwerp, on 5th September and had fired on the following day in support of 159 Brigade's efforts to cross the Albert Canal and force a way through the industrialised north-east corner of the city. Then:

> "On the afternoon of 7th September I was withdrawn and returned to the gun end. Orders from the Colonel that night were dramatic. The whole of 11th Armoured Division were to withdraw from Antwerp and proceed . . . to reinforce the Guards Armoured Division, who had established a bridgehead [*over the Albert Canal*] at Beeringen, some thirty or so miles . . . to the south-east. The 50th Division also were to move south-east along the Albert Canal. Antwerp was to be evacuated until the 51st (Highland) Division arrived. This division was moving up the coast on our left and they were not expected to get to Antwerp until first

light on 9th September, although armoured cars might make it late on the 8th. The 86th Field Regiment were to hold Antwerp for a day and a night until the 51st Division arrived.

That night 11th Armoured Division, without us, moved completely out of Antwerp. George Fanshawe's orders were that 341 Battery and 462 Battery were to guard the north of the city, that is the docks and the Albert Canal. With 342 Battery, I was given the task of guarding the tunnel under the Scheldt on the west side of the city centre, and at all costs preventing the Germans on the other side coming through it. We were also to protect the east side of the town, particularly the crossing of the Albert Canal at Wijnegem, from which a main road led into Antwerp from the east. The regiment's guns were to remain in their position on the southern outskirts of the city, so that they could cover the whole city area and its approaches from west, north and east. We were instructed to take any spare men, tanks and carriers forward with our O.Ps. as required, to provide 'infantry' support.

We were to make as much noise and vehicle movement as possible – for example, we should fire at the smallest enemy movement – to persuade the Germans that they had a division against them! In addition, we were to liaise with and arm the 'White Army' and use them to help us where possible."

The next day, 8th September, is described in 341 Battery's history as "for the most part a quiet day with a few targets across the river". All regimental sources agree that the troop commanders were in a curious position. To reach their O.Ps. they drove through Antwerp in their Shermans or carriers, stopping as necessary to do shopping and would then "drive up to a building, catch the lift to the roof and spend the rest of the day observing the enemy in the factory areas" (341 Battery's history). Wireless communication from O.Ps. to the guns was not always clear, owing to electrical interference said to be caused by the city's tram network. In an effort to overcome this problem the commanding officer delivered a 'high-powered' No. 19 set to Captain Ash's O.P. overlooking the area west of the River Scheldt. The set helped – but at the cost of huge effort, remembered years later, in manhandling the set and the batteries up several floors, then up a narrow spiral staircase, and then, of course, down again when the O.P. moved.

During the afternoon of 8th September Major Kiln was seriously wounded while working with the White Army to prevent parties of German infantry crossing the Albert Canal on a bridge that had not been fully demolished. In the same action Lance-Bombardier Beavis fired RB's main armament for the first time, hitting the offending Spandau position with his second round. (A replacement RB with 75-mm. gun had evidently been supplied in lieu of the O.P./C.P. version with dummy gun authorised by the establishment.) Two armoured cars on reconnaissance ahead of 51st Division had arrived at Major Kiln's position, enabling him to hand over the situation at Wijnegem to them before he lost consciousness; the main body of the division must have arrived overnight. The regiment left Antwerp the following day, making a long road-move to cross the Albert Canal at Beeringen early on 10th September and come into action near the village of Kursaal, within the XXX Corps bridgehead, initially under command of 100 Anti-Aircraft Brigade, who had been given control of the corps anti-tank defences. These defences were never put to the test and for the batteries Kursaal became "quite a rest area" from 11th to 14th September. The pit-head baths at Beeringen were welcome; football was played against the local inhabitants; and the contents of a German supply train captured earlier at Antwerp were distributed by 11th Armoured Division, in the form of a dozen bottles of wine and liqueurs, about 1,500 cigarettes, fifty packets of tobacco and some cigars to each troop.

### *With the United States Army – Operations 'Market Garden' and 'Clipper', September–December 1944*

On 14th September Field-Marshal Montgomery issued a new directive which made clear that the British Twenty-First Army Group and the United States Twelfth Army Group, to the south, had a joint objective – the encirclement and isolation of the Ruhr, Germany's major industrial area. Within the overall plan, Second Army's task was "to operate northwards and secure the crossings over the Rhine and Meuse in the general area Arnhem–Nijmegen–Grave". An airborne corps of three divisions would be placed under command of Second Army for these operations, which were to be "rapid and violent without regard to what is happening on the flanks" (*Official History*). Orders which Lieutenant-General Horrocks gave to XXX Corps on 16th September clarified the key role that the corps would play in Operation 'Market Garden'. In the airborne part of the operation ('Market') 101st U.S. Airborne Division were to seize and hold the bridges at Eindhoven, Zon, St.-Oedenrode and Veghel and keep open the road from Eindhoven to Grave; 82nd U.S. Airborne Division were to seize and hold the bridge at Grave, the bridges over the Maas–Waal Canal and the rail and road bridges at Nijmegen, secure the high ground around Groesbeek, south-east of Nijmegen, and keep open the road from Grave through Nijmegen; 1st British Airborne Division with 1 Polish Parachute Brigade under command were to seize and hold the bridge at Arnhem and establish a bridgehead north of the Lower Rhine from which further ground operations could be mounted. The Guards Armoured Division would lead the advance over the 'airborne carpet' (Operation 'Garden'), which would be along a single road – the only major road available. The flanks exposed by the advance would be secured by 50th Division until the neighbouring corps (VIII on the right and XII on the left) caught up. General Horrocks emphasised that speed was absolutely vital; it was important to link up with 1st Airborne Division at Arnhem within 48 hours of the start of the operation, which was timed for the early afternoon of 17th September.

Meanwhile, 86th Field Regiment had been released from the anti-tank screen on 15th September and moved to a gun area immediately south of the Meuse–Escaut Canal, with "the guns and command posts . . . in the back gardens of houses in the village of Lommel" (341 Battery's history). There they spent the next day preparing the fire plan and received orders for their part in Operation 'Garden', which is summarised as follows in 341 Battery's history:

> "Advancing, as we would be, through enemy territory on a single road, our supply lines would be particularly vulnerable. Speed was essential to the whole operation and we could not succeed if the supplies were cut. To defend the route, three squadrons of the 15th/19th Hussars, each with a battery of the regiment attached, were to form small strong-points along the route. Working in conjunction with the American troops, we were to keep the supply route open at all costs. 341 Battery were to be the first across the canal. Our squadron of the 15th/19th Hussars were to link up with the U.S. paratroops at Zon and we would defend the bridge there. 342 Battery would pass through and help defend the bridges at Veghel. 462 Battery would pass through them and go to Grave . . ."

H-hour was dependent on the commanders of Operation 'Garden' knowing that 'Market' was 'on' and was declared for 14.35. The part played by the artillery (some 350 guns in all) in the opening stages is described in the *Official History*:

> "At two o'clock the artillery started heavy counter-battery fire and concentrations on selected targets. At half past two 50th Division's heavy mortars opened up and two minutes later a field artillery barrage was brought down, four hundred yards ahead of the front line extending a thousand yards on either side of the road. Three minutes later, as the barrage began to move slowly forward, the Guards Armoured Division drove out of the bridgehead . . ."

A recognisably similar scene is described in 341 Battery's history:

> "Then in the distance to the north-west we could dimly make out the long trail of gliders making their way to Zon, Grave and Arnhem. The 'milk round' began almost at once and a terrific concentration of shells was poured into the enemy gun positions surrounding the bridgehead. After this we fired a rolling barrage to saturate both sides of the main road as the leading tanks edged their way forward towards the Dutch border. Immediately the barrage was over, our battery ceased fire and moved over the canal by the Bailey bridge. We went into action again about one thousand yards or so from the bridge . . . In this open space just north of the canal were packed many hundreds of tanks and vehicles and guns. Shells from our own guns on the other side of the canal were whistling overhead as the 'milk round' went on and another barrage was fired. Our leading tanks were meeting stiff opposition. The first nine were knocked out in the space of two hundred yards.
>
> We dug in. At dusk the bridgehead area was subjected to heavy enemy shelling for nearly 45 minutes but although many shells fell close, no-one in the battery was injured . . . During the night the enemy staged a counter-attack on the bridge, attacking the factory area to the east of Lommel. After some sharp fighting they were beaten off."

Plate 112 *RD on the crowded road from the Escaut Canal towards Nijmegen at the start of Operation 'Market Garden', 17th September 1944.* (I.W.M. – FLM 1085)

At the 'sharp end' the leading tanks had reached Valkenswaard by 19.30 and had taken up positions for the night. The airborne divisions had had "an impressive day" (*Official History*) and had captured the greater part of their objectives. However, and importantly, the bridge over the Wilhelmina Canal at Zon was blown as the Americans approached.

The advance was resumed on the morning of 18th September and the leading elements of Guards Armoured Division reached Eindhoven, now in American hands, during the afternoon. The way was then secure to the blown bridge at Zon and bridging materials, stockpiled well forward in the bridgehead, were being called forward. By now all the regiment's batteries had 'run out of range'. The fact that 341 Battery, the furthest forward, had "another long day of firing" indicates that for much of the time they must have been supporting the defence of the exposed flanks rather than helping the Guards move forward. The bridgehead area was severely bombed after dark on 18th September. Personnel of 341 Battery had lucky escapes and three of their 3-ton vehicles were "riddled with A.P. splinters and were immovable". It was, according to their history, "a very trying time for all concerned . . . our first experience of deliberate air attack on our own position and it was not pleasant". The other two batteries escaped this raid but Lieutenant Dovey, C.P.O. of 342 Battery, was killed as he moved across the Bailey bridge on the way to recce a new gun area.

The 19th September had all the makings of a more promising day. At 06.15 XXX Corps engineers finished work on the replacement bridge at Zon. The Guards Armoured Division crossed at once and by 08.30, after a fourteen-mile dash along roads that were not yet properly secured, their leading elements joined up with the U.S. 82nd Airborne Division at Grave and moved on immediately to Nijmegen. The orders for reinforcing the Americans were changed. Instead of the pre-arranged three squadrons of 15th/19th Hussars, each with a battery of 86th Field Regiment in direct support, the layout was now – 15th/19th Hussars complete, with a squadron of the Royal Dragoons (armoured cars) under command and 341 Battery in direct support, at Zon; 44th R.T.R. with a squadron of the Royal Dragoons under command and 342 Battery in direct support, at St.-Oedenrode; 462 Battery to wait south of the 

Meuse–Escaut Canal for eventual deployment in support of infantry of 50th Division providing flank protection in the Nijmegen area. During the morning 341 Battery moved up and went into action just to the north-west of Zon. Their first engagement, late that afternoon, was with six Panther tanks firing on the village from the south-east – an indicator that for several days the 'zero line' in which the guns had been deployed was nominal and targets could be expected anywhere within 360 degrees! Lieutenant Craston manned an O.P. in the church tower and despite attempts to dislodge him was successful in forcing the tanks to withdraw. That night "passed off quietly" but the enemy returned to the attack on the morning of 20th September. He was repulsed by 15th/19th Hussars, supported by fire from 341 Battery and the agreed 'bag' was six tanks ("we got two and 15th/19th got four"). There were no further attacks on Zon and the rest of the day was taken up with a reinforcement wave of 101st Airborne Division landing by parachute and by glider – an event for which 341 Battery had a grandstand view. During the evening there were reports of tanks approaching Zon and the battery spent several hours at 'Stand-to'. Meanwhile, 462 Battery, still in their original gun area behind the Meuse–Escaut Canal, received orders to deploy beyond the Rhine, north-east of Arnhem as part of the flank guard to "the expanding British airborne bridgehead". Such was the state of knowledge of affairs at Arnhem! The very good news, which probably did not reach the batteries until the following day, was that 82nd Airborne Division's supremely gallant attack across the Waal had resulted in the capture of the Nijmegen railway bridge, and that at about the same time, after fighting all day through the town to reach the southern approaches to the road bridge, 2nd Armoured Battalion Grenadier Guards had made their brilliant dash across under fire of all kinds, expecting the bridge to be blown any second. The Nijmegen bridges were at last in our hands, although fighting continued close by, especially in the eastern suburbs of the town. Allied air superiority was fortunately almost complete, for at mid-day on 20th September there were about one thousand vehicles, mainly of Guards Armoured Division, between Zon and Grave and some twenty thousand stretching over thirty miles southwards from Zon.

On the morning of 21st September the 44th R.T.R/342 Battery group were able to move up to St.-Oedenrode and join the battle to keep the road open. (Although they were ready to move at 10.15, 462 Battery were 'left out of battle' all day, being unable to obtain the degree of priority that would allow them to join the column of vehicles making their way northwards across the Meuse–Escaut Canal. They finally got on the road at 22.45, behind the administrative 'tail' of 1st Airborne Division, who were struggling forward to join the parachuted and airlanded elements of the division at Arnhem.) While 341 Battery, in the relative quiet of Zon, spent the day combing the nearby woods for abandoned American equipment, things began to warm up during the afternoon for 342 at St.-Oedenrode. Major Neville Whitmee had been posted in to command 342 on 19th September. He left a graphic account of the actions on the St.-Oedenrode–Veghel–Uden road between 21st–26th September in the form of a typescript entitled 'Veghel – Three Zero's Version' (a reference to his wireless call-sign as B.C. 342), extracts from which appear below:

> "As far as 342 were concerned, the battle of Veghel really started with the shelling of the market square in St.-Oedenrode during the afternoon of 21st September. The battery had gone into action south of St.-Oedenrode, not far from the brickworks, with a zero line of 360 degrees and the usual requirement of being able to fire at least ninety degrees either side. B.C. 342 and D Troop Commander [*Captain Ash*] were in the square alongside Tactical Headquarters of 44th R.T.R., whom 342 were supporting, they in their turn being under command of 101st U.S. Airborne Division, to help them hold their portion of the centre-line. C Troop Commander [*Captain Marshall*] was with A Squadron south of the town, in reserve but looking out to the east.
>
> The report that two thousand enemy with one hundred '88s' were coming down from S'Hertogenbosch with the order to capture St.-Oedenrode and cut the centre line at all costs was a little disturbing to all concerned, especially as this information was followed by a further report that enemy armour in some strength was also advancing from the north and west. C Squadron took up a holding position north of St.-Oedenrode and B Squadron motored to Veghel to reinforce that part of the 101st holding Veghel's two bridges. [*Note: The intelligence about the threat to the road was substantially correct. Powell – see Bibliography – includes excellent diagrams of the attempts by the German battlegroups commanded by Huber and*

*Walther to cut the road from west and east respectively.*]

That enemy guns were in the area was confirmed by the shells that began to fall in the centre of, and around, St.-Oedenrode, with far too many bursting in the trees which surrounded the square. B.C. 342 and Captain Ash went to ground in their Shermans pretty quickly. It is wonderful what a feeling of security you get inside a tank with shells bursting in the area, especially when shell splinters and bits of tree come pitter-pattering on the outside. Shelling occurred pretty regularly about every half-hour, lasting for five minutes or so. Unfortunately the commanding officer always seemed to arrive at the beginning of one of these shelling periods and B.C. 342 very reluctantly got out of his tank to talk to him.

This was B.C. 342's introduction to battle, having only recently joined the regiment and taken over 342 Battery (which he had not yet seen) some eighteen hours before. Having been presented with a Sherman (into which he had never been) in the middle of Eindhoven and told that he had a self-propelled battery (never having seen a Sexton) in action somewhere up the centre-line and that he was supporting a tank regiment (an entirely new game to him) left him a pretty bewildered officer. Within the next few hours, under shell-fire in a built-up area, he wondered if it was the usual thing that happened, tried to look as if he thought it was, and on the whole was a very frightened fellow.

Captain Ash managed to get a rough bearing on one of the guns firing into the square, which was confirmed by Captain Marshall, who could see the others. B.C. 342 then fired his first rounds in anger – a Mike target at the estimated map reference. Whether effective or not, this certainly quietened down the enemy shelling for a time. Captain Ash pushed off to Veghel to act as F.O.O. to B Squadron but met them coming back over the canal on their way to join some of the 101st Division at Eerde [*south-west of Veghel*]. Reports were now coming in of the enemy attacking St.-Oedenrode from Schijndel [*to the west*] and it was as a result of these that B Squadron went to Eerde and A Squadron, with Captain Marshall as F.O.O., went through C Squadron to attack north towards Schijndel. They did not make contact that evening, however, and bedded down for the night some two thousand yards north of St.-Oedenrode. [*'Did not make contact' hardly describes the situation. Captain Marshall had the fascinating experience of seeing a Tiger moving slowly across his front at a distance of about one hundred yards. He was unable to do anything, though, since RC was an orthodox O.P. tank with dummy gun.*]

Captain Ash fired battery targets throughout the night and had the satisfaction of brewing up some ammunition vehicles on the road south of Schijndel. The commanding officer arranged with General Maxwell D. Taylor, commanding 101st Airborne Division, for a fire plan to be fired at first light and for harassing fire during the night. Altogether, 342 fired close on 150 rounds per gun between 18.00 and 06.00."

As 22nd September dawned, 342 Battery fired their fire plan and A and B Squadrons of 44th R.T.R. began counter-attacking against the Huber battle group's thrusts towards Veghel from the west. Their action lasted most of the day, with Captain Marshall firing at least a dozen targets, with which, among other things, he brewed up some more ammunition lorries. At daylight, too, 462 Battery was in the centre of Eindhoven, where all traffic was halted until 08.00. The gun group was then ordered to overtake the 1st Airborne Division's echelon vehicles. They did so, driving almost in the roadside ditches at times, until, some ten miles north of Eindhoven, the traffic thinned and the guns could work up to best possible speed. By 11.30, 462 Battery had reached Grave and received orders to go into action south-east of Nijmegen. They had thus escaped by a matter of minutes the Walther battle group's thrust from the east against the road between Veghel and Uden, and the excitements and difficulties which befell 341 and 342 a few miles to the south. Here, but for a stroke of luck, 342 Battery would have been seriously short of ammunition. Major Whitmee happened to overhear a conversation at a traffic control-post to the effect that a lorry-load of ammunition destined for the Guards Armoured Division had been abandoned only three hundred yards away. While the Military Police were arranging for the truck to be moved, Major Whitmee made private, and very swift, arrangements to move the contents. All went well, he recorded, "and 342 were the richer by nearly sixty rounds per gun". Major Whitmee's account of events on 22nd September continues:

"Soon after 462 Battery had gone through St.-Oedenrode the traffic was stopped by the commanding officer of 44th R.T.R. owing to the shelling of the road and a new threat to the

Plate 113 *'Sign, directional' on the road to Nijmegen, September 1944.* (I.W.M. – FLM 1083)

centre-line north of Veghel. As 341 Battery were getting a little long in the range, it was decided to move them up to a position a couple of thousand yards short of Veghel. As the traffic had been stopped, B.C. 342 arranged with a traffic control captain to have 341 Battery specially brought through St.-Oedenrode but he brought into the square two batteries of 124th Field Regiment instead. Here, then, we had an awful conglomeration of vehicles huddled together in the centre of St.-Oedenrode and about to be shelled at any moment. Captain Marshall found a battery commander of 124th Field Regiment and suggested that he should join our battle as he could not go forward. He was quite willing to do so but all their recce parties, with directors, etc. had got through before the road was cut. To get over this, Captain Marshall arranged for one battery to go into action alongside 341 Battery and the other alongside 342 Battery and for us to pass the line to them. While this was being done Major Roncorani, commanding 27/28 Battery, the 4.5-in. battery of 7th Medium Regiment, bowled into the square. B.C. 342 knew him well (in fact, used to play rugger with him for Hertfordshire and for West Herts until he got too good and played for England). He was invited to joint the battle as well, agreed at once, and deployed his battery behind 342. Quite a nice little artillery group was being built up. Now the centre line was definitely cut just north of Veghel and C Squadron, 44th R.T.R. was sent up [*from St.-Oedenrode*] to hold the canal bridge [*immediately south-west of Veghel*]. Meanwhile, Captain Marshall with B Squadron, after leaving a troop in Eerde, had come flat out through country which they feared might contain enemy, to a position north of Veghel. At last light Headquarters 101st Airborne Division and Headquarters 44th R.T.R., with B.C. 342 in tow, moved to the centre of Veghel; the troop of B Squadron came in from Eerde and C Troop Commander with A Squadron again harboured north of St.-Oedenrode."

The two batteries at Veghel spent a rather jumpy, though in fact quiet, night and the road remained closed.

At first light on 23rd September, 44th R.T.R. mounted an operation to clear the road between Veghel and Uden. Leaving A Squadron, with Captain Marshall as F.O.O., to maintain the close-in defence of the canal bridge at Veghel, B and C Squadrons, with Captain Ash and Captain Wood [*A Troop Commander*], respectively, as F.O.Os. supported troops of 101st Division fighting their way northwards and eastwards. It was:

"a very, very exciting morning for our O.Ps. and hard work for the gun end and command post staffs . . . Our O.Ps., under constant shellfire, did great work in bringing down fire from our guns on to enemy concentrations. Many attacks were broken up before they got moving. Others were stopped by our shellfire just when the Americans were in a dangerous situation. The gun end were kept constantly on the alert, answering many calls for fire. The battery command post was now a miniature H.Q.R.A. A battery of 25-pdrs., a battery of mediums and a battery of 3.7-in. H.A.A. guns had been surveyed on to our grid. Telephones were laid to them and all orders for fire were passed on, so that the O.Ps. had quite a useful concentration of artillery to call on. The H.A.A. guns put down airburst over the enemy, which proved particularly effective. By tea-time the excitement died down and the enemy withdrew defeated. The route was saved – for a time, anyway. Our O.Ps. had a very difficult time. Captain Perry, our acting B.C. was wounded in the legs by shell splinters but insisted on carrying on. He was later evacuated . . . Convoys again started moving up the main axis . . ." (341 Battery's history).

A battle group from 101st Division, supported by B Squadron, 44th R.T.R. and F.O.Os. from 86th Field Regiment had indeed succeeded in pushing up the road to Uden, clearing it as they went, and had linked up with armour from the Guards Armoured Division who had come down from Grave. This was more than Walther's battle group could manage and the road north-east of Veghel was not attacked again. Much earlier in the day, 462 Battery's mission to deploy north of the Lower Rhine was cancelled and they were ordered to stay in their position south-east of Nijmegen and were placed formally in support of 82nd Airborne Division. Such was the area that they might be called upon to defend, that E Troop's zero line was 10 degrees and F Troop's 110 degrees.

The next day dawned finer, with the road still open and everything on the move. The artillery group that had assembled around 341 and 342 Batteries broke up, 124th Field Regiment and 27/28 Medium Battery returning to their original deployments further north. They were followed by 341 Battery, who moved up to the woods near Groesbeek to join 462 Battery in a regimental position. There, after adopting a common zero line of 90 degrees, the two batteries spent an uneventful day. Back at Veghel, 44th R.T.R. spread their squadrons out – B Squadron with Captain Ash to Uden, on the northern edge of 101st Division's area, C Squadron to Erp, south-east of Veghel and A Squadron with Captain Marshall to Eerde, south-west of the town. To remove them from their isolated position south of St.-Oedenrode, 342 Battery were moved up to a position about one thousand yards due south of Veghel. Major Whitmee recorded:

> "The road Veghel–St.-Oedenrode was shelled consistently throughout the latter part of the morning with Captain Marshall [*at Eerde*] firing many battery targets back. The day did not now seem as fine as it had dawned. A large number of our ammunition and petrol lorries were brewed up and the traffic stopped again.
>
> At mid-day, 342's position was heavily shelled by 105s and Sergeant Mackillican, No. 1 of F Sub was killed. At 13.00 it was shelled again and Sergeant Ilott and Gunner Lazenby were wounded and a gun put out of action by a large shell splinter denting the barrel. The position was shelled again at half-hourly intervals until the troops were stepped back to alternative positions at about 15.30. All this time the battery was answering calls for fire from Captain Marshall and the infantry of 101st Division.
>
> About this time the battery reported the presence of a self-propelled 88-mm. on or near the road north-west of their position . . ."

A troop of C Squadron was sent southwards from Veghel to clear the road but unfortunately only confirmed the truth of the report – three Shermans were knocked out in quick succession. The alarming discovery was then made, as it began to get dark, that 231 Infantry Brigade, in whose area 342 Battery were deployed, had moved, leaving the battery "out on its own in Panther-infested country with no infantry support whatsoever". Arrangements were made to bring 342 Battery inside what was, in effect, 'Veghel garrison' but guides sent to meet the battery failed to find them – they had moved to alternative positions and it was extremely dark. Thereafter:

> "The night of 24th–25th September was a black night in the history of 342 Battery. No-one got a wink of sleep; everyone was super-keyed-up, expecting to be attacked at any moment. B.C. 342, Captain Marshall and Captain Ash all sat in their Shermans with ears glued to the wireless, fearing to hear that the battery had been 'put in the bag'. Their position could hardly have failed to be located, as they had been firing from it all afternoon and evening . . .
>
> At 05.15 the battery began to pack up ready to move. At 05.25 they started off as quietly as possible down the back tracks [*recced in the dark by the C.P.O.*], which would bring them on to the centre-line only just before the canal bridge. At 05.50 the drawbridge of Veghel was lowered and the portcullis raised and with a roar of Sextons 342 thundered into the garrison to be welcomed by a hearty shelling of the whole village. To say that the whole military set-up in Veghel was relieved to hear that 342 were safely in would be putting it mildly. Everyone seemed to know of their plight, and the betting for and against them getting back without loss was very brisk. Not a vehicle was lost, nor were there any casualties."

The battery moved north-east out of Veghel and came into action alongside 90th Field Regiment (the self-propelled regiment of 50th Divisional Artillery) at Havelt, forming an ad-hoc fourth battery. Efforts were made to clear the road from Veghel to St.-Oedenrode by sending B Squadron, 44th R.T.R. along the 'back tracks' used early in the morning by 342 Battery and running roughly parallel with the centre-line. The squadron suffered casualties and although isolated armoured vehicles did succeed in making the dash from St.-Oedenrode and linking up with B Squadron early in the afternoon, the area was not cleared until a troop of B Squadron supported a battalion of 101st Division moving south and south-west to meet tanks of 7th Armoured Division fighting their way north-eastwards. Even then, a handful of enemy armoured vehicles were clinging to the road junction half-way between St.-Oedenrode and Veghel. It was not until early in the morning of 26th September that a combined effort by B Squadron, with Captain Ash as F.O.O., and troops of 101st Airborne Division, together with the leading elements of 7th Armoured Division, dislodged these remnants of Huber's battle group and reopened the road. Major Whitmee ended his account:

> "The traffic flowed freely, a truly welcome sight to the people in Veghel, and it has not stopped since.
>
> Although Veghel was shelled, mortared and threatened from the woods to the north-west, and although 342 stayed in the same position for a further seven days, shooting several times a day, that finished the 'Battle of Veghel'. The last few days were no Gunner's battle. The area became so confused with patrols of both sides that you could not fire at all without making exhaustive checks with maps and telephones to make sure that there were no 'own troops' in the target area."

Meanwhile, on the night of 25th–26th September the first efforts were made to evacuate the remaining troops of 1st Airborne Division from north of the Lower Rhine. Arnhem had indeed proved 'a bridge too far'.

Perhaps understandably, the part played by the United States 101st Airborne Division and the British 'independent armoured group' under its command in maintaining the single supply line to the forward troops of XXX Corps has received relatively little attention compared with the saga of 1st Airborne Division north of the Lower Rhine, or the heroic capture of the rail and road bridges at Nijmegen. (Powell – see Bibliography – is unusual in examining closely the German attempts to cut the road.) It will be clear from the foregoing account, however, that 86th Field Regiment, and especially 342 Battery, played a crucial role in providing artillery support, not only for the British armoured units to which they were affiliated, but more generally for the Americans, whose airlanded artillery resources were inadequate to deal with the unexpectedly heavy German armoured attacks. Formal recognition, signified first by letters from General Maxwell D. Taylor, commanding 101st Airborne Division and General Dempsey, commanding Second Army, and then by Colonel Fanshawe's 'immediate' appointment to the Distinguished Service Order, concentrates on the first occasion on which the road was cut – north of Veghel on 22nd–23rd September. But it is clear that the "timely and invaluable assistance they rendered this division in the repulse of enemy attacks . . ." (Letter from General Maxwell D. Taylor to General Dempsey dated 3rd October 1944) continued under Major Whitmee for the next three days. The week's fighting was without doubt an achievement comparable to D-Day in 86th Field Regiment's eleven months of war in North-West Europe.

As recorded briefly above, 341 Battery had moved up to join 462 Battery in support of 82nd U.S. Airborne Division from a regimental position in the woods near Groesbeek, south-east of Nijmegen, on 24th September. The division were occupying the high ground between the rivers Maas and Waal, looking east across the Dutch–German frontier and into the Reichswald Forest. Here, as further south, there was the ever-present danger of counter-attack. During one action on the afternoon of 25th September, E Troop's O.P. received a direct hit and Lance-Bombardier Adshead and Gunner Sharp were both killed. (Adshead's death was perhaps particularly unfortunate; he had been wounded and evacuated from King Red on D-Day but had returned to 462 Battery in time to be one of the survivors when Captain Cherry's tank was hit near Mont Pinçon on 12th August.) Another counter-attack, which took place on the night of 30th September–1st October, is described in 341 Battery's history:

> "At night the enemy put in a desperate counter-attack from the direction of Beek towards Nijmegen. The woods echoed and re-echoed to the sound of guns and mortars all night.

Many enemy shells landed around our gun positions. As we fired, the range gradually dropped – 4,000 – 3,000 – 2,000 – 1,500 – and we were beginning to wonder. Our forward O.P. was over-run and had to evacuate hurriedly in the dark. Our fire became so concentrated, however, that the enemy could not consolidate, and slowly the range crept up until we breathed a sigh and relaxed when firing stopped with the range back at 4,000 odd. But it had been a nerve-shattering night and no-one got much sleep until dawn."

During the first few days of October, 82nd Airborne division was, according to the *Official History*, "subjected to several hard though disjointed attacks . . . fighting then died down somewhat . . .". Waves of heavy shelling of the gun positions encouraged everybody to chop down trees, which fortunately were plentiful, and construct dug-outs with substantial over-head cover. On 3rd October permission was obtained for one battery at a time to rest out of the line and 341 started the rota by moving into a barracks in Nijmegen for 48 hours of rest, cleaning and maintenance. The regiment ceased to support 82nd United States Airborne Division on 12th October. A few days later a generously worded 'Letter of Commendation' from Brigadier-General James M. Gavin, commanding the division, reached Headquarters XXX Corps. It referred to the role that Lieutenant-Colonel Fanshawe had undertaken as, in effect, C.R.A. of the "constantly changing organisation of [*British*] artillery units available to give fire support" between 24th September and 12th October and expressed appreciation of the "exceptionally fine job" that he had done in "successfully working out the complicated co-ordination of the employment of the British artillery units in support of the division".

On leaving the Americans, 86th Field Regiment came under command of Guards Armoured Division and moved with the division into a rest and maintenance area centred on Grave. The regiment were due to remain out of the line for at least a fortnight but according to 341 Battery's history:

Plate 114 *Panoramic view from A Troop's O.P. near Groesbeek, late September 1944. Captain J.M.M. Wood and his signaller can be seen in the foreground.* (Drawing by Bryan de Grineau) (Illustrated London News)

Plate 115 *342 Battery resting 'out of the line', autumn 1944.* Left – *Gunner Palmer smartens up Gunner Farr.* Right – *Ammunitioning X tank. X/342 had recently been replaced by a 'real' Sherman, rather than an O.P./C.P. tank with dummy gun.*

(Regimental Collection)

"From the start it never looked like being a rest. New men had arrived to replace our casualties and they had to be trained and fitted into our teams. New detachments had been formed and young N.C.Os. promoted to more important posts who had not had much experience in handling their new men. So from the start we got down to some intensive training . . . [*Details of the programme follow, with Reveille at 06.30 and Tea at 17.30.*] After that there was little to do except go to bed as it got dark early and the electricity was not on . . .

P.T. probably came in for more abusive language than any other item on the programme. The Dutch villagers stared to see us at crack of dawn, officers and men alike, running up and down the lanes . . .

Marching and rifle drill came in for its full share of abuse too. Why seasoned soldiers who had fought all the way from the beaches should have to shoulder arms again could not be swallowed. The presence of a drill-sergeant from the Scots Guards, however, showed the importance attached to this discipline and we found we were still soldiers after all, and not heroes . . ."

In a letter to Major Morgan Smith dated 16th October, Colonel Fanshawe put things from his point-of-view:

"Now we've pulled out and are overhauling ourselves and doing individual training. Doing miniature range, too, and don't we need it! Vehicles are being sent all over Europe to find battledress, rum, Sherman engines and PAINT! I don't know what they'll come back with. The furthest have gone to Caen from where I suppose they will return one day."

The billets, it must be said, were extremely poor, with some soldiers sharing their barns with cows or pigs. As usual, though, some were allocated leave in Antwerp, some were invited to local farms for meals and everyone was able to enjoy the baths and the canteen in Nijmegen. It was while waiting to return from a trip to the baths and canteen on 4th November that a party from 341 Battery fell victim to a single bomb dropped by a German sneak raider. Bombardier Sharp was killed and eleven other ranks wounded, fortunately none of them very seriously.

On the following day, 5th November, the regiment received sudden orders to move. Batteries had less than two hours notice, as always just as a meal was being served. There ensued "a most unholy scramble and many had indigestion but we moved punctually at 14.00". Orders were to relieve 13th R.H.A. in support of 29 Armoured Brigade of 11th Armoured Division, who were in the line facing the River Maas near Venray. After harbouring for the night near Oploo, batteries occupied positions vacated by 13th R.H.A. during the morning of 6th November in absolutely appalling weather – half a gale, sleet, rain and snow". The front was relatively quiet. Several regimental targets, mainly counter-battery tasks, were fired during the first two days. On 8th and 9th November the only firing was to test the new 222 fuze. Then, on 10th November, recce parties left suddenly and 13th R.H.A. arrived to take over their old positions. The guns moved overnight through Eindhoven, Diest, Beeringen and Leopoldsburg, then eastwards to cross the Maas and the Juliana Canal and come into action the following afternoon in the three villages of Born, Guttekoven and Einighausen, north-west of Sittard, only a couple of miles from the Dutch–German border. United States troops had captured the area a few days earlier. O.Ps. were deployed at once in and near Nieuwstad. Captain Ash later recalled that it was from here that he carried out the only 'registration' shoots that he remembered firing throughout the campaign. (Registration shoots are fired when time permits to confirm the position of reference points or potential targets and to enable the firing data thus obtained to be held in the command post for ready re-use.) The few rounds Captain Ash fired seemed to upset the Germans and his O.P. in the church tower at Nieuwstad was subjected to heavy return fire during the evening service. The only casualty was Captain Ash's carrier driver, who was wounded and evacuated. The next morning the tower was engaged by direct fire and had to be abandoned.

Field-Marshal Montgomery had issued a new directive to Twenty-First Army Group on 2nd November. Once the operations to open the approaches to the port of Antwerp and drive the enemy north of the Lower Maas had been completed, Second Army were to drive the enemy east of the Meuse in the Venray–Roermond sector, starting on 12th November. As soon as possible thereafter the right flank was to be extended southwards to Geilenkirchen, taking over part of the United States Twelfth Army Group front (*Official History*). While the clearance of the 'Venlo Pocket' fell to VIII Corps and XII Corps, XXX Corps moved south to take over ground recently won by the United States Ninth Army and line up on an axis running through Sittard to Geilenkirchen. The United States 84th Infantry Division, which had only just arrived in theatre and had no combat experience, was placed under command of XXX Corps for the advance on Geilenkirchen, code-named Operation 'Clipper'. The Americans were ordered to advance on the right of the corps front, with 43rd Division on their left. The Guards Armoured Division would start the battle in corps reserve but units of 8 Armoured Brigade, the only other formation then under command of XXX Corps, were placed in support of the attacking divisions. Although 86th Field Regiment had expected to be under command of the Guards Armoured Division, they were at an early stage moved to under command 84th United States Infantry Division and in direct support of the Sherwood Rangers, the regiment from 8 Armoured Brigade that was also under command of the division. Colonel Fanshawe and his tactical headquarters placed themselves alongside the 84th Divisional Artillery headquarters to repeat the processes of liaison and provision of supporting fire from neighbouring British artillery that they had learned, and so successfully applied, in the Nijmegen salient some weeks before.

Recce and ammunition parties, for there was to be considerable dumping in preparation for the barrage that would precede the attack, moved across the Dutch–German border on 14th November to prepare positions around the village of Grothenrath, a few miles south-west of Geilenkirchen. The bad weather continued, making the task of dumping ammunition and preparing the gun positions very difficult. Ammunition lorries stuck in the treacherously soft ground and most of the ammunition had to be dumped some distance from the gun platforms and then man-handled. The guns moved on 16th November, the same day that Major Loveday, wounded and evacuated on 6th–7th June, returned to the regiment and resumed command of 341 Battery. Barrage traces had been issued the previous afternoon and command post staffs were busy with calculations; the inevitable amendments arrived the next day. On 17th November:

> "All civilians left the village and we had full possession of the houses. We had the responsibility for feeding the animals. B Troop alone had eight cows, two horses, two sheep, four pigs, several dogs and various rabbits. The gunners enjoyed milking the cows.
>
> The operation orders for 'Clipper' were studied in more detail. The fire plan was in four phases:
>
> *Phase 1* The U.S. 84th Division with the Sherwood Rangers in support were to put in a right hook around Geilenkirchen to capture Prummern.

*Phase 2* The British 43rd Division were to left hook and capture Bauchen, Suggerath and the high ground to the north-east of the town. By the end of Phase 2, Geilenkirchen would be dominated by our troops on the high ground either side.

*Phase 3* A thrust through the centre, expected to be an easy clearing-up operation in the town itself.

*Phase 4* The 43rd Division would advance to capture the villages north of Geilenkirchen and consolidate the gains.

Our O.Ps. were to go with the Sherwood Rangers. Towards evening the weather became worse and rain began to fall steadily" (341 Battery's history).

An unidentified officer of 342 Battery has left an account of the battle, the fire plan for which began at 04.45:

"The barrage with which the battle opened was one of the most intense of the whole campaign. We fired about 400 rounds per gun of high-explosive in the initial stages alone, that is to say on 18th November, the first day of the attack. That day everything went according to plan and all objectives were captured. The intensity of the artillery fire had stunned the outer defences and there was little serious opposition. By the following morning, however, the position had changed. As so often happened, the Germans had rushed up their reserve of first class fighting troops from their panzer and parachute divisions. They brought up Tiger tanks and 88-mm. S.P. guns, so the momentum of the attack was lessened. Not only that, but the attackers were now into the concrete defences of the Siegfried Line. Here, each farm-house concealed a pill-box and German tanks fired from prepared hull-down positions, picking off our Shermans as they advanced over the open ground. The muddy fields, torn up by our own artillery fire and soaked by torrential rain, made going for tanks and infantry alike very difficult by day and almost impossible by night. Time and again our O.Ps. had to call for smoke from the guns to screen our advancing tanks or blind the area from which some unseen 88-mm. was picking them off one by one.

During the afternoon of 19th November the regiment moved to a new area at Gillrath. This was an open, muddy position, where for four days there was almost continuous firing and equally continuous rain. Bivvies and ammunition were dug in on our arrival but it was not long before all were flooded out and nearly everyone soaked through. The guns became bogged after they had switched a few times and platforms had to be altered often. The surrounding area became a mud-heap. The damp and blast combined to make the Tannoys very unreliable. On top of all this, a big ammunition dumping programme was needed to keep pace with the demands of the O.Ps. The ground was far too soft to bear the weight of a 3-tonner and the verges of the road through the gun position developed into a dumping area. This was too far from some troops, so 3-tonners were towed up to these positions behind tanks, but not without incidents. At one time Lieutenant Smallman, C Troop G.P.O., was in the unenviable position of having four 3-tonners and two half-tracks bogged on his position at once, and in the middle of firing a smoke-screen. Needless to say, to complete the picture the vehicles had cut all the Tannoy cables.

Some of the smoke-screens lasted for several hours and more than once they had to be fired by batteries in turn, the next taking over when the previous one had run out of smoke. Ammunition parties were collecting all available smoke from 43rd Divisional Artillery and from the Essex Yeomanry [*147th Field Regiment – in direct support of 8 Armoured Brigade*]. It seemed to those on the dump that the flow would never end, and at times they were convinced that the same rounds were merely being taken from 341 to give to 342 to replace a load just sent to 462, and so on. However, the screens were always kept going. The gunners worked like Trojans, fetching the rounds from the dumps across the ever-deepening mud to the guns, setting the fuzes and firing the rounds almost as soon as they had arrived. There was no hope of using half-detachments only and resting the others. Everyone had to be on the job all the time, soaked through as they were. Improvised drying rooms were made, where a few at a time could get a fresh start against the rain. The rum ration did not fail to arrive and lent its not inconsiderable strength to the work."

While 341 Battery's history tells recognisably the same story, sometimes in greater detail, the

*Official History* devotes less than half a page to the struggle for Geilenkirchen and the surrounding villages and implies that it was the weather, and consequent appalling 'going', that brought the advance to a halt, rather than objectives successfully gained. The short account concludes, "For the time being XXX Corps was not required to go further in the waterlogged country between the Meuse and the Roer and the United States 84th Division returned to the American Ninth Army". As far as 86th Field Regiment were concerned:

> "Towards dusk [*on 23rd November*] the downpour settled into steady rain, sank to a drizzle and finally ceased. As we sighed with relief news came that we were to come out of action in the morning . . . No more welcome news could have been given to the tired and miserably wet gunners."

As a result of a recommendation from the commanding officer of the Sherwood Rangers, Captain Marshall received the Military Cross for his gallantry as F.O.O. with B Squadron throughout the six-day operation. The Americans were quick to recognise both their own inexperience and Colonel Fanshawe's "outstanding services" as senior representative of the Royal Artillery at Headquarters 84th Infantry Division and appointed him to the Legion of Merit. Captain Wood, Troop Commander of A Troop and his O.P. signaller Lance-Bombardier Stevenson were awarded the United States Silver Star and Bronze Star, respectively, both citations mentioning the intense fire under which they operated.

The regiment returned on 24th November to the positions at Born, Guttekoven and Einighausen that they had occupied a fortnight previously; O.Ps. were again manned on the German border. The first two days were spent 'out of the line', attempting to remove the mud and to catch up on sleep. They then assumed a defensive routine in support of Guards Armoured Division which lasted, with very little firing, until 5th December. Here, according to 341 Battery's history:

> "We had our issue of winter clothing. Besides the usual gloves, woollens and leather waistcoats there were some rubber boots and, most welcome of all, brand new 'tank suits', waterproof with zip-fasteners and hoods. They were issued to tank and gun crews only but not every member was lucky enough to have one. If only we had had them at Geilenkirchen we might not have been so miserable."

From 6th to 17th December the regiment were again out of the line in the area of Grootdoenrade, just south-east of Sittard but short of the German border, for much-needed maintenance. It was expected that XXX Corps would soon attack north-eastwards from Sittard towards Heinsberg, bringing the front-line up to the River Roer. This involved crossing open, ploughed land, which in the prevailing weather conditions could be treacherous to tanks, so the tank crews busied themselves with fitting special shoes to the Sherman tracks in order to give a better grip in the soft, muddy ground. Gun positions were prepared just west of Gangelt, inside the German border. On the morning of 17th December it was learned that the impending attack had been postponed indefinitely and batteries began planning their training programmes. Then, suddenly, during the afternoon orders were received for gun positions to be ready on the edge of Grootdoenrade village and for the regiment to be ready to occupy them at a moment's notice.

### *In the Ardennes, December 1944–January 1945*

The cause of these 'alarms and excursions' was the opening the previous day of the Germans' last desperate bid to cut the Allied armies in two by a massive armoured thrust to recapture Antwerp – the 'Ardennes Counter-offensive' or, in American terms, the 'Battle of the Bulge'. Initially, the counter-measures were left entirely in American hands, since the breakthrough was well inside the United States Twelfth Army Group's area of operations. Accordingly, while making plans for immediate defence in case their own front were threatened, XXX Corps continued to prepare for withdrawal from the Sittard area and redeployment for operations further north under First Canadian Army. The Guards Armoured Division, with 86th Field Regiment still under command, had been allocated an area around Louvain for maintenance, training and rest before moving north. Billeting parties left the regiment on 19th December and 341 Battery's history records that "prospects of Christmas out of action in Belgium were tempting". During the afternoon of 20th December the guns joined the Guards Armoured Division column, expecting to move into billets in the village of Rhode-St.-Pierre, north-east of Louvain, but an order to divert southwards was received during the night. The long and tiring night move was brought to an end by a very unpopular staff officer, who directed the column to turn off the route. By the morning of 21st December the regiment was concentrated in the village of Hakendover, near Tirlemont. On 20th December command of all forces to the north of the German penetration was vested in Field-Marshal Montgomery, who ordered XXX Corps to defend a 'stop-line' on the rivers Meuse and Sambre, from Liège in the east to Charleroi in the west. The Guards Armoured Division were to hold the centre of this line, between Huy and Namur, with the tasks of preventing any crossings of the Meuse between those two points and being prepared to counter-attack across the river. On 22nd December 341 Battery was placed in direct support of 2nd Armoured Battalion Welsh Guards, the divisional reconnaissance regiment, who were due to operate south of the Meuse. The battery accordingly moved to join the Welsh Guards at Jodoigne, eight miles south of Tirlemont, and while recce parties picked out possible gun positions around Namur, the rest of the battery, having judged that they would spend Christmas at Jodoigne, began to prepare for the festivities at their billet in a girls' convent school.

As things turned out, none of the batteries ate their Christmas dinner on Christmas Day. Another stop-line had been created by deploying 29 Armoured Brigade southwards along the River Meuse from Namur to Givet. The brigade, which had been snatched from its re-equipment programme at Ypres – it was converting from Sherman to Comet tanks – had moved without its armour, leaving parties to reclaim their tanks from the depots they had handed them over to and catch up with all speed. This they had done, but no artillery had come with them (from 11th Armoured Division) and on 23rd December 86th Field Regiment was placed in support of the brigade. On Christmas Eve, therefore, 342 and 462 Batteries left Hakendover (and their preparations for Christmas) and joined, respectively, 23rd Hussars at Givet and 3rd R.T.R. at Dinant. The following day (25th December), 341 Battery, still with the Welsh Guards, moved to Namur, but here they transferred affiliation to the 2nd Fife and Forfar Yeomanry, while maintaining contact with the Welsh Guards, on their roving commission south and east of the river, for a further day.

The time 86th Field Regiment spent in action in the Ardennes divides into two sections – first the period of continuing defence, which lasted until 1st January, and second the counter-attack, designed to put pressure on the tip of the German thrust while the Americans attacked strongly from north and south, which began on 3rd January. In the early stages 29 Armoured Brigade adopted a forward defence. The brigade came under command of 6th Airborne Division, which had been rushed out from Britain to assist in containing, and then reversing, the German attack, on 28th December. An unidentified officer, probably of 342 Battery, has left an account of the regiment's time in the Ardennes, extracts from which follow:

> "On Christmas morning both batteries [*341 Battery was still with Guards Armoured Division*] crossed the Meuse. The 23rd Hussars, with 342, [*crossed at Givet and*] went about ten miles east to Beauraing, where a defensive position was formed, and saw nothing of the enemy for some days. However, 3rd Royal Tanks had gone only a few miles east from Dinant when they met a German armoured column moving up past Ciney. Some sharp fighting ensued in which 462 did a good deal of effective firing and the enemy advance was halted.
>
> Without infantry, 29 Armoured Brigade were in no position to attack, especially as the snow which fell after Christmas made the roads impassable to tanks. The cold at this time was extreme. All day the temperature never rose above freezing point and at night there was as much as twenty degrees of frost, so naturally tank activities were reduced to a minimum. C Troop of 342 Battery took part in a fine offensive action on 30th December, when they went fifteen miles across country in front of the forward defended localities to support a forward patrol of 61st Reconnaissance Regiment pushing towards Bure."

Meanwhile, 2nd Fife and Forfar Yeomanry and 341 Battery had moved south from Namur, through Dinant, and deployed on high ground beyond Falmignoul, east of the Meuse, and some three miles south of Dinant, with the battery in the village itself. Here, according to 341 Battery's history:

> "We decided to trust to luck and eat our Christmas dinner tomorrow (28th December). The morning was spent in preparing the dinner. A small school was located near the battery command post, where the dinner could be cooked and two class-rooms would do for seat-

> ing both gun troops. The H.Q. Troop men were to be seated in the café used by the battery as a command post. Each troop vied with the others in improvising decorations for its room and they were quickly made, and colourful and seasonal greetings chalked on the blackboards. Chairs and tables were collected from four nearby cafés, the owners gladly co-operating . . . Roast potatoes, tinned turkey, pork, peas, greens, bread sauce and apple sauce were followed by Christmas pudding and sauce. Each man also had two bottles of beer, a few sweets, an apple or orange, cigarettes and a cigar. The officers and sergeants assisted in the serving and afterwards joined in the community singing and the cheers for the cooking staff under Lance-Sergeant Welch. The celebrations were continued in the evening in the many cafés in that small village. The officers had their Christmas dinner in one of them . . ."

A laconic entry in 342 Battery's command post log for 27th December "Christmas fare eaten" suggests that the other two batteries, already in action in support of their affiliated units, may not have had quite such a celebration.

Early on 1st January 1945 Headquarters 29 Armoured Brigade received their first operation order from 6th Airborne Division. The armoured brigade was to be used "in support of the parachute and airlanding brigades, their combined task being the exertion of maximum pressure on the enemy during his withdrawal eastwards" (*Taurus Pursuant*). By now all three regiments of the brigade were concentrated east of the Meuse, astride the road Givet–Beauraing, the easterly extension of which would form the axis of advance. The guns were moved forward on 2nd January. The extraordinarily difficult road conditions are described in 341 Battery's history:

> "We made a very difficult and slow advance over the now icy roads to occupy a position at Wellin, only to learn we were out of range and had to push on again to Resteigne. It snowed again during the day and towards evening froze again. The last few miles of the journey were some of the most difficult hours of driving our tank and gun drivers had to endure. The cold was intense and the roads just sheets of ice. The journey took us up and down steep hills – the upward journey negotiated painfully and slowly, hugging the bank; the downward journey covered by a series of slides and rushes, often finishing up against the parapet of a bridge over a deep gorge. Often our hearts beat fast as we wondered whether the parapets would hold the weight of thirty or forty tons of steel sliding towards them. One S.P. slid against the side of a house on a downward slope and was quite unable to move any further, the crew having to spend the night by the roadside. It was long past dark before the guns reached their area and almost midnight before we could report the battery ready for action."

For the advance the following day Headquarters 29 Armoured Brigade had under command 2nd Fife and Forfar Yeomanry and 7th and 13th Parachute Battalions, with 86th Field Regiment in direct support. The intention was "to seize the villages of Bure and Wavreille, subsequently exploiting eastwards to Grupont and Forrières". The unidentified officer quoted above described the action that followed:

> "No real opposition was met until 3rd January when the villages of Bure and Wavreille and surrounding high ground were attacked. The assault on Bure was the job of 13th Parachute Battalion, supported by 342 Battery and a squadron of 2nd F.F. Yeo. The fighting in the village was extremely fierce, for the German infantry were of the very best quality and well supported by Tiger tanks. In the four days of the battle both sides suffered heavy casualties. The road up to Bure from Tellin was under observation from the high ground to the east, so supplies could only be brought up and wounded evacuated under cover of darkness. There was hand-to-hand fighting in the houses, and constant attack and counter-attack. Parties of troops would infiltrate behind enemy lines and hold out, isolated, either to be relieved, captured or killed. All the time the guns, in sharp bursts of activity, would lay down concentrations of defensive fire. The village was cleared and held against counter-attack during the 4th and 5th, but our troops were eventually ordered to withdraw. At 00.10 on 6th January the remainder of 13th Parachute Battalion retired to Tellin, covered by a short artillery programme.
>
> On the same day that Bure was attacked, Wavreille was cleared and a hill south of Wavreille and north-west of Bure was also captured. This hill, known as Chapel Hill

Plate 116 *View from the turret of X/342 in the Ardennes, early January 1945.* (Regimental Collection)

because of the small chapel in a clearing in the woods on it, was important since it overlooked all the country to its north, east and south. Captain Benson was the F.O.O. supporting 2nd F.F. Yeo. in this attack. As they came over the southern part of the ridge a Tiger opened up on them from a position fairly close behind. Fortunately for Captain Benson, the Tiger chose a Sherman Firefly for its first target and he was able to get under cover without damage. The hill was cleared soon afterwards and remained in our hands without being counter-attacked.

Chapel Hill will always be remembered by those who occupied it. By day it was held by one squadron with a F.O.O. in an O.P., but no infantry. At night the squadron harboured round the chapel clearing, while a company of infantry stood guard. The cold was intense, the snow thick and continually increasing. The O.P. was in a Sherman parked on the forward slope in a young pine plantation. It was fairly well camouflaged by the trees but too much movement would have given away its position. For the whole day the crew lived inside, cooking in the turret to get what warmth they could from the stove. There was no chance of making a bivvy, so they slept inside. This was also advisable, as the area was stonked from time to time. Very little was seen of the enemy and it developed into a fight against the weather. Suffice it to say that each squadron had to be relieved after 48 hours to get some comparative rest in either Tellin or Wavreille."

This account understates the desperate nature of the fighting in Bure (which is described in gruelling detail by one of the company commanders of 13th Parachute Battalion in an account quoted by Harcelrode – see Bibliography). The battalion's casualties during the period 3rd–5th January totalled seven officers and 182 other ranks, of whom nearly seventy were killed. A recommendation initiated by the commanding officer of 13th Parachute Battalion, which resulted in the award of the Military Cross to Major Whitmee, B.C. of 342 Battery, included the assessment that "from the beginning to the end of the action the support given by the guns under his control was quite exceptional. Repeatedly during periods of almost continuous enemy counter-attacks their quick and accurate fire broke up the attack, often right on top of our positions, and was of incalculable value to the morale and confidence of our troops".

The unidentified officer's account now takes up the story after the withdrawal from Bure:

"Pressure from the flanks soon caused the enemy to withdraw and by 9th January the regiment was in action at Wavreille. The ground west of the River Lomme between Forrières and Grupont was clear of the enemy. There was little firing on 10th January and on the 11th a regimental position was surveyed to the east of Forrières. That position, however, was never occupied. The enemy were retreating fast, and as we were on the point of the salient, we were 'nipped out' by the flanking divisions. Our part in the Ardennes Campaign was over.

After two days [*between 16th and 18th January*] the regiment moved north to the area of Montaigu, west of Diest, for rest, maintenance and training. The regiment moved in two parts, first the 'soft' vehicles, then the tracked. It was an achievement that the tanks made the journey in less than three days. So ice-bound were the roads that tank tracks would not grip and as far as possible the route had to be across country. Where the road was used, all hills had to be sanded, or battens placed beneath the tracks, to enable the tanks to move at all. The ending was typical of the whole battle, which was as much against the elements as against the enemy."

Among reinforcements who had reached the regiment during this period were Captain P.A. Turner and Lieutenant A.E. Warren, who had both been posted from 86th Field Regiment to 191st Field Regiment when that regiment was formed in December 1942. On hearing of the imminent disbandment of 191st Field Regiment in December 1944, Captain Turner had somehow managed to contact Colonel Fanshawe and had been told in no uncertain terms to rejoin 86th at once, leaving the paperwork to be sorted out later. This he had done, but on arriving found that Colonel Fanshawe had left 86th Field Regiment on promotion to brigadier and appointment as C.R.A. 3rd Infantry Division on 27th December, just as the campaign in the Ardennes was gaining momentum. Command of 86th Field Regiment had then passed to Major R.G. Gordon-Finlayson, who had been posted in as second-in-command early in September, in replacement of Major Morgan Smith. Major Gordon-Finlayson's temporary command covered the greater part of the Ardennes campaign and would last until early April 1945.

### *The battle for the Rhineland, February–March 1945*

On 15th January XXX Corps had indeed been released from its commitments in the Ardennes and returned to First Canadian Army for the operations to move the Allied front from the line of the Rivers Maas and Roer up to the west bank of the Rhine, preparatory to a crossing of the Rhine and advance into Germany, specifically to occupy the Ruhr. Two associated operations were planned. In the northern area First Canadian Army's Operation 'Veritable', would begin on 8th February, advancing south-eastwards from the area of Nijmegen and clearing the flat, low-lying land to the line Venlo–Xanten. Ninth United States Army would use the line Venlo–Xanten as its left-hand boundary and in Operation 'Grenade', starting on 10th February, would advance north-eastwards to occupy the left bank of the Rhine between Xanten and Düsseldorf.

Some time for regrouping, resting and reinforcement of XXX Corps was necessary after the Ardennes battles and the corps returned to the area around Louvain which it had left in such a hurry before Christmas. An area a few miles to the west of Diest was allocated to 86th Field Regiment and between 16th and 18th January they moved in – R.H.Q. to Montaigu, 341 Battery to Schoenderbueken and 342 and 462 Batteries to Sichem. Here, according to 341 Battery's history, the billets were comfortable and the local inhabitants friendly, though very short of food. Maintenance and painting were put in hand at once and courses organised. The leave roster planned for the end of December but interrupted by the German offensive was reinstituted and a few lucky officers and men were granted ten days' home leave.

For Operation 'Veritable' 86th Field Regiment was placed under command of 15th (Scottish) Division and in direct support of 6 Guards Armoured Brigade, who were also under command of the division, together with an armoured car regiment, a regiment each of flail and flamethrowing tanks, armoured engineer squadrons and two regiments of armoured personnel carriers. The early part of the operation – the break-in – was planned in four phases, beginning at 10.30 on 8th February. Initially 46 Brigade Group (right) and 227 Brigade Group (left) would secure the general line Frasselt–Kranenburg. In Phase 2, starting under 'artificial moonlight' at 21.00, 44 Brigade Group would pass through 46 Brigade, breach the Siegfried Line north of the Reichswald Forest and secure Nutterden. Phase 3, starting at 01.00 on 9th February under continuing artificial moonlight would see 46 Brigade Group secure the high ground overlooking Cleve before daybreak, while 227 Brigade Group would open the northern axis Kranenburg–Cleve and clear the wooded area north-east of Cleve. Finally, these two leading brigade groups would clear the greater part of Cleve. Thereafter exploitation south-eastwards would follow.

In his *History of the 15th (Scottish) Division*, published in 1948, H.G. Martin uses 'Veritable' to illustrate the complexity and sheer hard work facing the artillery in preparing and firing the counter-battery and barrage programme associated with a large-scale attack. This account, which stands as a tribute to the Gunners, especially in North-West Europe, bears repeating in full, even fifty years after it was published:

"The artillery support for this operation calls for special mention, for it was to be on an unprecedented scale, greater even than that at El Alamein. Here in the Nijmegen bridgehead no less than 1,334 guns had been concentrated, ranging from super-heavies to field guns. Till 05.00 on 8th February, however, no artillery activity was to be permitted other than the normal activity of the two Canadian divisional artilleries which had been holding the line. Thereafter the fire plan was to be as follows:

| | | |
|---|---|---|
| 1. | 05.00–07.30 | Destructive fire on enemy defences. |
| 2. | 07.30–07.40 | Smoke-screens designed to draw enemy defensive fire and so reveal his gun positions. |
| 3. | 07.40–07.50 | Pause – to permit sound-ranging and flash-spotting on gun positions revealed by Serial 2. |
| 4. | 07.50–09.20 | Renewed destructive fire. |
| 5. | 09.20–10.00 | Intensive counter-battery fire; and opening line of barrage, consisting of mixed H.E. and smoke. |
| 6. | 10.00–10.30 | Opening line of barrage, thickened up in depth as infantry close. |
| 7. | 10.30 (H-hour) | First lift of barrage. |
| 8. | 16.00 | Last lift of barrage – 6,000 yards from first lift. Artillery then to switch to front of 3rd Canadian Division. |
| 9. | 17.00–21.00 | Support of 3rd Canadian Division. |
| 10. | 21.00–01.00 | Support of second phase of 15th (Scottish) Division's and 53rd (Welsh) Division's attack. |
| 11. | 01.00–Daylight | Support of third phase of 15th (Scottish) Division's attack. |
| 12. | Daylight | Prepare to support fourth phase of 15th (Scottish) Division's attack. |

The barrage, which was to cover the front of the three centre divisions only, was to move by a series of three-hundred-yard lifts at intervals of twelve minutes [*see Plate 33*]. The end of each twelve minute period was to be notified to the infantry by the firing of yellow smoke by one 25-pdr. per troop.

For the artillery this programme was only the beginning of a fortnight of almost unceasing battle. The programme may serve, therefore, to convey some idea of the exacting nature of the Gunners' task. When a division is attacking, its C.R.A. becomes for the time being the senior partner and director of the artillery 'combine', and he directs the fire not only of his own divisional artillery but also of all other guns within range. In consequence, the man behind the gun – even when the infantry of his own division is standing by – seldom gets any rest. And when his own division is attacking, then of course the Gunner gives each infantry brigade in turn the benefit of the full weight of all the guns of the division. Repeated brigade attacks such as were to occur throughout Operation 'Veritable' mean repeated moves for the guns, with more positions to be reconnoitred, more ammunition to be brought up, more survey to be done, more gun-pits to be dug, more calculations to be worked out and task-tables to be prepared – and prepared with an accuracy which, even in the uttermost depths of exhaustion, can yet admit of no error, for the lives of our own infantry are at stake. On one occasion during 'Veritable' no less than seven hundred guns answered a Victor call for all available guns.

The artillery had changed a lot since those early days in May 1940 when the division first deployed its gimcrack armoury in Essex. In the campaign in North-West Europe the artillery concentration was Britain's secret weapon – and it was never used better than in Operation 'Veritable'."

The guns and armoured vehicles of 86th Field Regiment moved up to Nijmegen to join the huge concentration of artillery behind the XXX Corps front on 1st February and harboured in the eastern fringes of the Groesbeek Forest, short of their eventual deployment area. Here, all vehicles and tents were heavily camouflaged, movement kept to an absolute minimum and fires kept severely under control. In the bleak February weather, with little to do except wait, "life was rather miserable". On 6th February the 'soft' vehicles left Montaigu and after a "long and very devious route" reached the harbour area in the early hours of 7th February. Work on the fire plan went on throughout 7th February, based on troop centres which had already been surveyed but not yet occupied – no forward movement of the guns was allowed until 10.00 on 7th February. Sharp at 16.00, the guns "came out of hiding and moved on to their platforms". Then began the task of digging slit trenches and new bivouacs, digging in command posts and preparing the 4,800 rounds which had been dumped on each battery position. D-day for Operation 'Veritable' – 8th February 1945 – is recorded as follows in 341 Battery's history:

> "Reveille was at 04.00. A light mist blanketed any noise and the silence was quite eerie as we picked our way in the darkness to our guns and ammunition stacks. All around in the woods one could imagine hundreds of sleepy gunners preparing hundreds of guns and thousands of shells for the great offensive. Then at 04.30 it began. The 'Milk Round' came first – General Horrocks's term for our counter-battery tasks. All the guns in the world seemed to be firing at once and the roar was terrifying. The trees doubled every sound as the leaves and branches threw back echoes. All around us A.A. Bofors guns were firing tracer shells and the sky seemed filled with tiny balls of red and pink sliding through the air over the tree tops. Every now and again a roar like an express train sounded above the gunfire as the rocket batteries in the valley behind opened up. The firing and banging went on without pause until 09.45 and at 10.00 the big barrage started. More than 1,200 guns were engaged in this barrage and the noise beggars description. Some enemy shells landed in front of our guns, less than two hundred yards away, but the explosions were not heard above the general din. Fortunately there were no casualties although some members of the Echelon had narrow escapes. [*Although there were no casualties in 341 Battery, 342 were not so lucky. Bombardier Stanton of C Troop died of wounds received while serving his gun.*] At 15.00 we ceased firing, although the barrage was still continuing, and moved forward about three miles over muddy and shell-torn ground to establish a position in some open fields east of Groesbeek. Our recce parties then went ahead to prepare new positions in Kranenburg and had to remain there all night. All routes were track-deep in mud and the congestion was terrible. There was no hope of moving the regiment any further that night. We resumed firing and kept it up until dusk. At 18.45 there was a sudden silence and for precisely two minutes not a sound of a gun or shell was heard. Then at 18.47 the noise began again and continued without pause all through the night . . ."

The B.Cs. and O.Ps. had taken over Churchill tanks in order to match the Guards armoured battalions they were supporting, one of which had been placed under command of each of the infantry brigades, forming a ' brigade group'. The War Diary for this period has not survived and it is accordingly very difficult to account for their movements with the attacking troops. It is clear from the *Official History* that:

> ". . . the opening phase went well, 46 Brigade on the right and 227 Brigade on the left having more trouble with mines and mud than with the enemy . . . Flails succeeded in opening one gap on the right but elsewhere were bogged soon after the start and the infantry had casualties in the uncleared minefield. With close support from artillery and flamethrowers 46 Brigade had cleared the long straggling village of Frasselt by dark and 227 Brigade captured Kranenburg. 44 Brigade, which was to force the Siegfried defence line [*Phase 2*], had been delayed when its Special Breaching Force of nearly three hundred heavy armoured vehicles was virtually brought to a standstill along the rough track which had been carrying traffic of the two leading brigades for most of the day. Eventually a detour was made with the aid of bulldozers, but it was four in the morning [*rather than 21.00 the previous evening, as planned*] before a start could be made on the Siegfried Line."

Optimistically, as it turned out, General Horrocks put his follow-up formations, Guards Armoured Division and 43rd Division on stand-by to move forward during 9th February but low cloud and heavy rain went on well into the afternoon, curtailing air support and making movement even more difficult. In the 15th (Scottish) Division's area the traffic problem got worse as the day went on. The secondary routes, all unpaved tracks, were by now virtually impassable and the main Nijmegen–Cleve road was largely under water, sometimes to the extent of nearly two feet. In the morning the guns moved up to a position in the south-western outskirts of Kranenburg which 341 Battery found "almost impossible to occupy – mud and water surrounded everything". In the same area 342 Battery were obliged to abandon the positions they had been allocated and come into action on the railway, which provided platforms that were not actually thigh-deep in water. Despite the difficult going, though now well behind the planned schedule, 44 Brigade Group had succeed in breaching the Siegfried Line north-east of Frasselt and capturing Nutterden. The brigade then pushed eastwards and "as darkness fell, gained a sound footing on the Bresserberg ridge, just off the western outskirts of Cleve and barely a mile from Materborn village" (*Official History*). The 15th Division was now ordered to hold the high ground overlooking Cleve and, on the morning of 10th February to clear the town. 'Flying columns', each supported by a battery of 86th Field Regiment, were to get ready to exploit towards Calcar, some seven miles along the road to the south-east, and to seize the Emmerich ferry, on the Rhine about six miles across the flooded area north-east of Cleve. Meanwhile, the 43rd Division had been called forward to attack southwards from Cleve towards Goch. The *Official History* is gently critical of General Horrocks's "attempt to move two divisions [*15th and 43rd*] along the same axis, stretches of which were under two or three feet of water" and describes the crowded confusion on the western and southern flanks of Cleve, which resulted in the operation by 15th Division to clear the town lasting well into the following day. The regiment had had a quiet day on 10th February, then on the morning of the next day moved further east (but not yet within gun range of Calcar or Emmerich). Batteries found it necessary to recce carefully routes out of their positions and towards the main road, and to use aiming posts both as signposts and to mark the depth of water. As 341 Battery left Kranenburg they observed that the column "looked like a water carnival, rather than a regiment of artillery". Once in action, targets were in the centre and northern suburbs of Cleve as the Scotsmen "fought their way into Cleve against determined opposition" (*Official History*).

The planned break-out from Cleve by a mobile column of all arms towards Calcar was mounted on 12th February, with 341 Battery assigned to direct support. Opposition was encountered at once and the battery hurriedly occupied a position on the western outskirts of Cleve from which they "fired over the housetops at the enemy guns and mortars shelling our leading troops". It proved impossible to treat the advance on Calcar as a 'coup-de-main', indeed "the enemy had reacted strongly to 15th and 43rd Division's threats to Calcar and Goch . . . areas of vital importance for the retention of the more open country west of Wesel and . . . [*they*] . . . had managed to improvise a new check-line between Moyland and the Cleve Forest to connect with the entrenchments that already existed between Cleve and Goch" (*Official History*). In the face of this resistance, attempts to move south-eastwards towards Calcar and Xanten were postponed and 15th Division joined the rest of XXX Corps moving on Goch. Importantly, too, the congestion on the few available roads had been eased by successes on the corps' southern flank. In response to the change of axis, 86th Field Regiment moved on

Plate 117 *Bedford 15-cwt. of 86th Field Regiment Signal Section, recognisable by its red unit serial number on white-above-blue ground, followed by Fordson 3-ton Q2 of R.H.Q., in the floods at Kranenburg, February 1945.* (I.W.M. – FLM 1086)

14th February and again on the 15th, from Cleve into the edge of the Reichswald Forest, and then into positions around the village of Bedburg – the latter uncomfortably close to the enemy's improvised Moyland–Cleve Forest line. Counter-battery fire and mortaring caused a great deal of difficulty, but fortunately no serious casualties, throughout 15th February. On 16th February the Canadians began to push down the flooded area between the Cleve–Calcar road and the Rhine and much of the regiment's effort that day was in their support – almost 180 degrees opposed to their original deployment for the advance on Goch. D Troop of 342 Battery found that the Canadian start-line was behind their position and the axis of advance through the position. The 'Kangaroo' armoured personnel carriers played havoc with the Tannoy cables between the command post and guns.

The next day 43rd Division made considerable progress towards Goch and the regiment moved to a position half-way between Cleve and Goch in order to support 15th Division's move through 43rd Division to attack Goch itself on 18th February. By midnight, troops of the division were fighting on the outskirts of Goch. The garrison formally surrendered on 19th February but pockets of resistance remained and it was not until 21st February that the town could be declared free of German troops. Meanwhile, the guns had had a difficult night on 18th February when the Canadians on the Goch–Calcar road were over-run by a German counter-attack and enemy tanks and infantry were reported some 1,500 yards behind the gun area. For some hours the regiment was at 'Stand-to' with the guns laid on S.O.S. tasks almost in exactly the opposite direction to the zero line, but the Canadians restored the situation in the very early hours of 19th February and tension on the gun positions was considerably eased.

First Canadian Army was now well into the exploitation phase of Operation 'Veritable'. The advance south-eastwards was resumed on the XXX Corps front on 22nd February and the regiment, which had moved close to Goch on 21st February had two very active days supporting the two leading divisions – 15th (Scottish) and 53rd (Welsh) – as they made for Weeze, four miles south-east of Goch. They encountered heavy opposition. Calls on the regiment were "almost continuous" on the 22nd and 341 Battery recorded "more heavy work with plenty of fire plans and targets" on 23rd. A set-piece attack by 53rd Division down the Goch–Weeze road on 24th February was preceded by a four-hour bombardment beginning at 01.30 and involving a change of target every three minutes. With some pride, 341 Battery recorded that "it says much for the high standard of training that, despite the weariness of the gunners after previous long days of firing, not a single serial was missed . . ." Fire support for 53rd Division continued throughout the day.

During the two days 24th–25th February 3rd Infantry Division took over the line from 15th Division and 6 Guards Armoured Brigade was transferred to under command 3rd Division. The second part of the operations to clear the area between the Maas and the Rhine was due to begin on 26th February. On the left, II Canadian Corps was reinforced by 11th Armoured and 43rd Infantry Divisions, previously under command of XXX Corps, which now consisted of 3rd, 51st, 52nd and 53rd Infantry Divisions and the Guards Armoured Division. The inter-corps boundary ran approximately along the line of the Cleve–Sonsbeck road. H-hour for what Scarfe (see Bibliography) claims turned out to be "the last full-scale pitched battle of the war" was 07.00 on 27th February. The Canadian attack on XXX Corps' left had begun during the afternoon of the previous day, while 3rd Division was preparing and patrolling. From their position near the road, halfway between Cleve and Goch, 86th Field Regiment spent the day in support of the Canadians.

The 3rd Division's advance began with 9 Brigade on the left and 8 Brigade on the right. From a start-line on the Goch–Calcar road, the two brigades moved south-eastwards through thick woods, close behind the barrage and supported by the Churchill tanks of 6 Guards Armoured Brigade. By 11.00 the leading troops of 9 Brigade had reached their first objective, the Udem–Weeze road, against resistance that was at times stubborn and proved costly in casualties. On the extreme right of the Phase I objective was an important bridge carrying the Udem–Weeze road over a small river. If secured intact, it would enable 53rd Division, on the right, to approach Weeze, their objective for the following day, from the flank as well as head-on. The leading elements of 8 Brigade reached the road by 13.30 and C Company of 2nd East Yorkshires were despatched to seize the bridge, which was secured by 14.00; fortunately the demolition charges had failed to detonate. The German attempt to recapture the bridge began at about 19.00. C Company, reinforced by B Company just before midnight, and with massive

D.F. support from all guns within range, conducted an epic defence against counter-attacks which lasted until daylight. At about 09.00 on 28th February the bridge was handed over to 53rd Division. In the first 24 hours of the advance, 2nd East Yorkshires had lost eight officers and 150 other ranks killed or wounded.

Phase 2 of 3rd Division's attack – the capture of Kervenheim, a village about two miles beyond the first objective – was led by 185 Brigade, who advanced across difficult country – 'woods, waterlogged clay fields, scattered houses, no roads to speak of' (Scarfe) against increasing resistance. By nightfall, at about 18.00, they were close to their objective and during the night patrols penetrated right up to the outskirts of the village. It took all the following day (1st March) for the brigade to clear the enemy from Kervenheim. By now, the guns were at extreme range, possibly out of range of Kervenheim, but the O.Ps. remained with the armoured battalions they were supporting. Just as Kervenheim was falling to 185 Brigade, supported by 4th Armoured Battalion Coldstream Guards, Captain Wood, A Troop Commander, was killed in action by a mortar bomb which landed on his tank. The next day the guns were ordered forward to Bucholt, while 185 Brigade continued southwards towards Winnekendonk, a distance of about four miles. During the day, however, 86th Field Regiment's short contact with 3rd Infantry Division ceased. "We received sudden orders to join an armoured thrust by the Guards Armoured Division from Goch" (341 Battery's history). The regiment accordingly moved back to a harbour area on the outskirts of Goch, where they just managed to get tents pitched "before sleet and rain arrived to make conditions unpleasant".

The push south-eastwards by XXX Corps had now reached the left-hand boundary of the United States Operation 'Grenade' – the Venlo–Geldern–Wesel road – and 53rd Division, on the right of XXX Corps' front, was ordered to wheel to the left and fight towards the Rhine with the Americans on their right. It was originally planned that 3rd Division would halt between Winnekendonk and Kapellen, allowing the Guards Armoured Division to move through their lines and advance as quickly as possible "with the object of pushing the remaining Germans still west of the Rhine across the river at Wesel" (Rosse – see Bibliography). The first objective on the way towards Wesel would be the village of Kapellen, after which the division would occupy the wooded high ground known as the Bonninghardt Ridge. However, as they advanced eastwards from Kevelaer the Guards were held up by obstacles that their bridge-layers could not span and 3rd Division received sudden orders to capture Kapellen during the night of 4th–5th March. They succeeded to the extent that the Guards' attack on the Bonninghardt feature could begin on the morning of 5th March. Meanwhile, 86th Field Regiment's guns, which had moved during 4th March to a position just west of Kapellen, moved again during the night and fired in support of the Guards as they beat their way through thick woods towards Bonninghardt village against pockets of strong resistance. The defence of the village itself, by German paratroops, was particularly difficult to overcome and it was well into the night of 6th–7th March before the ridge was entirely clear of enemy. From the ridge the ground sloped gently north-eastwards and then flattened towards the left bank of the Rhine opposite Wesel, about eight miles distant. The enemy west of the Rhine were now squeezed in a 'pocket' and were being pressed from the north-west by the Canadians, from the south-west by the Guards Armoured Division and 53rd Division and from the south-east by the Americans. They were conducting a fighting retreat on the two bridges which still stood across the Rhine at Wesel. The Guards Armoured Division resumed their advance during the afternoon of 7th March with 2nd Battalion Scots Guards leading, supported by tanks of 2nd Armoured Battalion Welsh Guards with O.Ps. from 86th Field Regiment. Their first objective, about two miles ahead, was the point where the railway from Xanten to Rheinberg crosses that from Geldern to Wesel. The advance was recorded in 341 Battery's history:

> "The Scots Guards put in an attack in the centre of the pocket, pushing north-east from Bonninghardt. The Welsh Guards formed a strong left flank protection. The battle was quite a noisy affair, although most of the firing came from our own guns and tanks. The Welsh Guards' tanks established themselves on some high ground and, firing over the heads of the infantry, emptied their guns into farmhouses and buildings and likely pockets of resistance. Our O.Ps. with the Welsh Guards had little firing to do, although they had quite a hot time when a German anti-tank gun began picking off the Guards' tanks. After two had been

brewed up, the others had to withdraw. The regiment was kept busy answering calls for fire from the Scots Guards and there was some effective shooting at tanks and guns in the region of Alpen. By nightfall all the objectives had been taken and the battlefield was glowing with the fires of many burning farm buildings. During the night the Royal Engineers built a bridge over a stream under some deadly harassing fire from German guns."

Rosse captures the atmosphere of the night of 7th–8th March and the following day, recording the huge efforts made to build a new Bailey bridge and free a 'scissors' bridge laid earlier which had been blocked by a broken-down tank. Both bridges, he states, "were necessary in the morning, as it became increasingly obvious that a great last effort must be made finally to eliminate the bridgehead."

The task now was to get a foothold on the Xanten–Rheinberg road and then capture the last remaining village before the river bank – Menzelen. On the morning of 8th March the Scots Guards resumed their advance and progressed about one thousand yards against very stiff opposition and heavy shelling and mortaring. The extent of their advance was limited, however, by difficulties which the formations on their flanks were experiencing. Next day, 9th March, after a further delay and eventual decision to attempt to press on despite the lack of flanking support:

"In the afternoon, the Coldstream Guards [*5th Battalion supported by tanks of 1st Armoured Battalion*] having relieved the Scots Guards during the night, put in a strong frontal attack on the town of Menzelen. The regiment fired a long smoke-screen on the flank of the attack to prevent observation from the high ground at Xanten. As the Guards crossed the railway embankment and made for the main road they ran into withering D.F. fire from all arms. The regiment engaged many Mike and Uncle targets and the Coldstream, pressing home the attack, got astride the main road and entered Menzelen. That night, just before and after dusk, saw a great increase in enemy mortaring. Nebelwerfers seemed to be firing from many points in the remnants of the pocket. All targets were quite haphazard and it was guessed that the enemy were having a last fling before withdrawing across the Rhine. The whole divisional artillery kept up a steady bombardment of the suspected mortar areas and the approaches to the Rhine crossing for over two hours." (341 Battery's history)

The next morning at about 09.00 the regiment's O.Ps. saw two huge explosions in the mist from the direction of the bridges and it was soon confirmed that both had been blown. The battle for Germany west of the Rhine was over.

It had been a month of bitter fighting against an enemy who had put up a fanatical, at times suicidal, defence. The historians of the various formations and units engaged all emphasise the rigour of the struggle, not only against the enemy, but also against the elements, and especially the resulting mud. In his history of the 15th Division, Martin records that the division had very nearly reached the limit of human endurance and quotes an apparently unpublished history of 46 Infantry Brigade, "We had been ordered to fight ourselves to a standstill and we had done so". Rosse states that Operation 'Veritable' was responsible for some of the toughest and most sustained fighting in which the Guards Armoured Division were ever engaged, while the *Official History* describes the battle for the Rhineland simply as "a grim struggle". It was a struggle in which 86th Field Regiment played a full part with, perhaps, less recognition than was deserved, though C.R.A. 15th Division paid the regiment a handsome tribute in passing on congratulations he had received, by pointing out that he had four regiments under command, rather than the usual three, and that "25 per cent of the credit goes to your regiment with the grateful thanks of 15th (Scottish) Division". The only award that can be traced to 'Veritable' is Lieutenant Burlton's Mention-in-Despatches, which resulted from a recommendation by the commanding officer of 4th Armoured Battalion Grenadier Guards, the unit he supported throughout the operation.

### *Across the Rhine and beyond, March–May 1945*

Field-Marshal Montgomery's final directive for the crossing of the Rhine was issued on 9th March 1945. The 'intention' was summarised as "to cross the Rhine north of the Ruhr and secure a firm bridgehead, with a view to developing operations to isolate the Ruhr and to penetrate deeper into Germany" (*Official History*). The crossing was to take place on a front of two armies (Second Army and Ninth United States Army) between Rees in the north (left boundary of Second Army) and Rheinberg in the south. Within Second Army, two corps would take part in the assault crossing – XXX Corps, now returned to Second Army, on the left, with objectives in the general area of Rees, and XII Corps on the right, at Wesel. Two airborne divisions would drop east of the Rhine on XII Corps' front. The 51st Division would lead the assault at Rees and infantry, ferried across the river in a variety of craft, would be responsible for expanding the bridgehead until Bailey bridges could be built, allowing significant numbers of tanks to cross and armoured divisions to assemble ready to break out.

The regiment came out of action on the morning of 11th March, remaining in harbour in the woods near Bonninghardt until 14th March, when they moved into billets in Nijmegen. Here, 341 Battery's history records, they "settled down for the usual bout of administrative work and maintenance, with painting as the usual side-line". The record continues:

"During this time the most intensive preparations for the assault crossing of the Rhine were being made. We learned that the regiment's guns were to cross the Rhine on specially constructed rafts. These rafts were sections of Bailey bridges on four pontoons and the whole contraption was winched across by special winches operated by the Royal Engineers. Our officers witnessed a demonstration of these rafts on the canal at Nijmegen.

The area on the west bank of the Rhine which was to be the scene of the assault crossing was one vast camp of vehicles and artillery. It was labelled 'The Pig Hotel' [*probably a reference to XXX Corps' formation sign – a boar*] and was protected from enemy view by a smoke-screen stretching several miles. An ammunition party was sent on 19th March to our allotted gun area to assist in the dumping of ammunition. All movement and work was carried out at night.

On 20th March the regiment moved into a concentration area on the south-eastern corner of the Reichswald Forest. The weather was warm and spring-like and we might have been on one of the many exercises in England that we had practised for D-Day itself. The organisation for the Rhine crossing followed that of D-Day almost to the letter. On 21st March we were split up into our various groups according to bridge classification, rafts or Buffaloes and general priority. The S.Ps. were to cross by rafts, the carriers by Buffaloes and the half-tracks and soft vehicles by the bridges, once they had been constructed. We were to be reassembled as a regiment in a marshalling area on the east of the Rhine and everyone was briefed with the routes, signs and code names.

But first we were to join in the preliminary bombardment and barrage to support the assaulting infantry. On the night of 21st–22nd March we moved up to our allotted gun position at Gesthuysen, about five thousand yards due south of Rees. We were obliged to take a very circuitous route via Goch, Weeze and Udem, through the Hochwald Forest and then across country to Gesthuysen. The journey from Weeze through much-bombed Udem and through the woods was made without any lights and it says much for the skill of our drivers that everything went smoothly and all vehicles parked at their appointed places. We arrived about 04.00 on 22nd March and by first light every man and vehicle was out of sight and camouflaged around farm buildings. The fine weather and the smoke-screen enabled us to get a certain amount of necessary digging and preparation done during the day."

For the assault phase of the Rhine crossing 86th Field Regiment was placed under command of 51st (Highland) Division, who were due to attack on a two-brigade front. On the left, 154 Brigade would cross from the village of Honnepel and advance north-eastwards through Klein Esserden, Speldrop and Bienen, while on the right 153 Brigade would land a battalion either side of Rees and, after securing the town, move northwards along the Rees–Isselburg road. The follow-up brigade would expand the bridgehead, after which 43rd Division would cross and move through 51st. The two assault brigades were to cross in Buffaloes (amphibious tracked vehicles), accompanied by D.D. tanks. The regiment received the orders and the fire plan for the operation, code-named 'Plunder' during the morning of 23rd March. H-hour for the assault crossing at Rees was 21.00 that evening, the time at which the first landing vehicles would enter the water on the Allied side. The event is recorded in 341 Battery's history:

"Our guns went into position at 15.00 ... There was no preliminary bombardment; the operation began with the roar of massed guns at zero hour and the firing continued all night. Bofors, mortars and rockets all joined in and the air was alive with tracer shells being pumped into the defences on the opposite bank. Soon after midnight an unfortunate accident occurred on D Sub of A Troop. No one will ever know what happened but it would seem that in loading the gun in the dark the loader accidentally hit the shell fuze against the breech. Normally this would not cause an accident but the fuze must have been faulty. The shell exploded, killing instantly the occupants of the compartment, Bombardier Hawkesworth and Gunners Rawlinson and Unwin . . ."

At first the assaulting brigades encountered little opposition and by dawn 154 Brigade had reached Speldrop, a mile from the bank, and 153 Brigade had occupied part of Rees. The enemy fought back hard, though, and Rees was not finally cleared until the afternoon of 25th March, by which time 154 Brigade had reached the general line of the Emmerich–Wesel railway. With the right bank of the Rhine now secure, bridging operations could begin. Throughout 25th March the regiment's recce parties were on stand-by to cross the Rhine and the guns to move to a position very close to the bridging sites on the left bank, immediately opposite Rees. The guns were the first to move, on the afternoon of 26th March, by which time 'Lambeth Bridge', which was not capable of carrying tanks, was already in use. The gun area allotted turned out to be subject to a good deal of harassing fire, probably more with a view to interrupting bridging operations than counter-battery, and after dark there was some movement to alternative positions about one thousand yards away and immediately south of 'London Bridge', on which the Royal Engineers worked all night under shell-fire. Meanwhile, recce parties had left for the opposite bank by 'Lambeth Bridge'. As the reconnaissance of the first gun area on the other side of the Rhine proceeded, Gunner Southgate, A Troop's G.P.O. ack was killed by a shell.

By now, the bridgehead was expanding well, though at times opposition was fierce. The 43rd Division had crossed the Rhine and entered the battle on the left of 51st Division, while part of 3rd Canadian Division had also crossed and were occupying the left of the line, between the Rhine and 43rd Division. In the early hours of 27th March 'London Bridge' was completed, as recorded in 341 Battery's history:

*"27th March*

We ceased fire at 04.30 and prepared to cross the Rhine. The Class 40 'London Bridge' had been completed during the night by magnificent work on the part of the Royal Engineers. All our previous plans for crossing were cancelled, as it was now possible to cross as a complete regiment. At 06.00 we began our crossing and it was a proud moment when we roared up the bank on the opposite side and entered the rubble-strewn streets of Rees . . . We stayed at Speldrop for a few hours only, moving on through Millingen. Our route was changed while on the move, as the dispersal point was under small-arms fire. We went into action alongside the railway running south from Millingen and about 2,500 yards from the autobahn, which was still in enemy hands. We had to share the area with a 25-pdr. regiment from 43rd Division . . . Ruined farm-houses made comfortable command posts.

*28th–29th March*

We remained near Millingen for two days. Opposition was still very strong . . . However, after some grim fighting Anholt and Isselburg were captured . . . and also Emmerich, so the bridgehead was now secure. As previously ordered, we were to join the Guards Armoured Division and break out of the bridgehead. Our objective was . . . Bremen.

*30th March*

The Guards started to pass through . . . We waited to join in the column and at 18.00 were on the move. However, we did not get very far and the whole regiment harboured beside the road between Anholt and Dinxperloo."

The Guards Armoured Division had crossed the Rhine on 30th March with orders to advance towards Bremen and Hamburg. As soon after leaving the bridgehead as space permitted, the division was to broaden its front to allow it to advance with both brigades 'up' on parallel 'centre-lines'. The brigades had been reorganised to give an equal balance of armour and infantry in each and, in anticipation of swift movement, a self-propelled field regiment was placed in direct support of each brigade – the Guards Armoured Division's own 153rd Field Regiment with 5 Guards Armoured Brigade (2nd Armoured and 1st Motor Battalions Grenadier Guards; 2nd Armoured and 3rd Battalions Irish Guards) and 86th Field Regiment with 32 Guards Brigade (1st Armoured and 5th Battalions Coldstream Guards; 2nd Armoured Battalion Welsh Guards and 2nd Battalion Scots Guards). The advance would be led by 5 Brigade until such time as 32 Brigade had room to deploy along a new centre-line to the left of 5 Brigade. The opportunity did not arise until early in the afternoon of 31st March – "So heavily were the Grenadiers and Irish Guards engaged that not until half-past two that afternoon could the Coldstream get clear of their tail and break out into open country. Then the column began to move fast . . ." (Howard – see Bibliography). The regiment's experience reflected that of the units they were supporting, as 341 Battery's history shows:

*"31st March*

. . . We joined the Welsh/Scots Guards group and were given the left centre-line. We passed through Dinxperloo soon after breakfast and entered Holland once again. Between there and Aalten we went into action quickly alongside the road but were not called upon to fire. The Germans were apparently relying mainly on demolitions to hold up our advance. The demolitions would be covered by small parties with panzerfausts [*anti-tank rocket-launchers*] and Spandaus, who withdrew as soon as an organised attack had been arranged. We were forced by the demolitions to journey across country and along narrow tracks, rather than on the main roads. We by-passed Aalten, passing through Lichtenvoorde and Zieuwent. On one occasion we had to cross a canal by a very flimsy wooden structure not worth calling a bridge. A sigh of relief went up as each tank or Sexton edged safely across. We kept to the west of Groenlo and occupied a position near the village of Beltrum.

*1st April*

The advance continued in the morning [*with the Coldstream Group in the lead*]. We struck the main road again at Eibergen and made good progress through Haaksbergen. Some opposition was met on the approaches to Enschede and we occupied a position in the village of Boekelo, some two to three miles west of the town . . . At Boekelo R.H.Q. established itself in a house where the owner spoke English. He had a telephone which was still working and he obtained information about the situation in Enschede by ringing various numbers. Some valuable information about enemy locations was thus obtained and passed back. Attempts were made to enter Enschede from the north-west but the canal bridges were blown before our tanks could get across. At one bridge two of our tanks did succeed in getting across before it was blown and the crews did some fine work mopping up the retreating demolition party. Our tanks succeeded in getting into Enschede that night but were held up by S.S. troops resisting strongly in the area of the airfield on the north-eastern outskirts."

It was, in fact, the Scots-Welsh Group who had met resistance at the airfield while trying to reach Oldenzaal before dark, but as the light was rapidly failing they were ordered to harbour and attack the airfield at first light. At dawn on 2nd April, 341 Battery, whose O.Ps. were with the Scots-Welsh Group, moved into the outskirts of Enschede and prepared a fire plan for the attack on the airfield. The attack duly went in but the airfield was "unoccupied, with the three 88-mm. guns which had been so troublesome the previous evening abandoned in perfect order" (Rosse). The brigade then moved through Oldenzaal and changed direction from north to north-east with Nordhorn as their next objective. According to 341 Battery's history:

"We pushed on towards the German border, passed through Oldenzaal and were then held up at a canal bridge outside Nordhorn. The Royal Engineers built a new bridge in a few hours. The battery went into action alongside the bridge as the leading tanks dashed into Nordhorn . . . The first bridge in Nordhorn had been blown but not completely demolished and it was possible to get across. The second bridge, however, was completely destroyed. A third, further north, was only partly damaged and it was decided to repair it as soon as possible . . . By 23.00 the bridge was ready. It was decided to push on with the aim of capturing, intact if possible, the bridge over the Dortmund–Ems Canal at Lingen, some twenty miles away. Two squadrons of the Welsh Guards' tanks with our O.Ps., Captain Anderson in RA and Lieutenant Beck in RB, and Scots Guards infantry riding on the back of the Welsh Guards' tanks got across the second bridge in Nordhorn before it collapsed. It was impossible to repair it for eight hours at least. The leading squadron commander decided to push on and trust to luck. Headlights which had been used to negotiate the bridges were switched off and then the tanks raced out into the darkness. The remainder of the column,

Plate 118 *Crossing the Rhine at Rees, 26th–27th March 1945.* Left – *The crew of X/342 wait for the Class 40 'London Bridge' to be completed.* Right – *View from the turret as X/342 crosses London Bridge.* (Regimental Collection)

including the battery's guns, were stuck in the streets of Nordhorn and on the outskirts and had to remain there all night. The leading tanks ran into a German 88-mm. gun being towed by a captured Sherman. Before they could man the gun it was knocked out. It blocked the road, however, and a detour had to be made in the darkness across country – very tricky work. Small-arms fire was met from certain farm-houses which were brewed up by the tank guns and soon the trail was marked by burning buildings. After an exciting dash through woods, the leading tanks entered the town of Lingen, only to be held up by a road block in front of the all-important bridge. The infantry were now dismounted, some to clear the obstacle, some to dash across the bridge. As the leading tank was passing the obstacle and about the cross the bridge it was blown . . ."

Although no armour could cross the Ems, two companies of the Scots Guards crossed in assault boats and established themselves on the eastern bank. However, enemy opposition became stronger with daylight and it was clear that Lingen was quite strongly held. Orders were accordingly given for the Scots Guards to regroup west of the river and the 3rd Infantry Division was brought up for a set-piece crossing of the River Ems and the Dortmand–Ems Canal, about one mile further east. Meanwhile, however, armoured cars of the Household Cavalry had reconnoitred northwards and found a bridge across the Ems some three miles north of Lingen. To quote Rosse, "It was fully prepared for demolition and moreover was covered by enemy infantry, together with 88-mm. guns; but so long as it remained standing a chance existed of capturing it and Brigadier Johnson told the Coldstream Group to try its hand at the venture". Further reconnaissance demonstrated that there was a formidable road-block on the west side of the bridge, making any question of a dash across by tanks impossible, and that there were three 88-mm. guns, well dug-in and sandbagged. Six 500-pound bombs had been rigged as demolition charges. Under cover of a regimental concentration brought down on the immediate area of the bridge without preliminary ranging, tanks of 3 Squadron, 1st Armoured Battalion moved up to firing positions overlooking the river from a wooded ridge. The fire then lifted on to woods behind the bridge, the tanks opened fire with their 75-mm. guns, machine-guns and aerial rockets fired from rails attached to the tank turrets, and infantry of 3 Company, 5th Battalion moved to firing positions on the river bank and joined in. Captain I.O. Liddell, commanding 3 Company then climbed over the obstacle and, with extraordinary gallantry that later resulted in the award of the Victoria Cross, ran on to the bridge in full view of the enemy and succeeded in cutting the wires to all six bombs. He was swiftly followed by one of his platoons and a troop from 3 Squadron, which battered down the road-block and joined in the mopping-up. With the bridge firmly in our hands, troops of 3rd Division were at once diverted to cross it, although it was by now after 19.00, and they succeeded in putting a battalion across the canal in assault boats during the night and following up with a second battalion early in the morning of 4th April. During the day, the Coldstream Group, working southwards from the bridge on the narrow finger of land between the River Ems and the canal, and the 3rd Division, moving along the far bank of the canal, gradually forced the enemy out of Lingen. With some help from Guards Armoured Divisional Artillery, including 86th Field Regiment, who fired in support of 3rd Division as well as their own, the Coldstream drew level with the Scots-Welsh Group, across the river, by

Plate 119 RD (Top) *crosses the River Ems at Lingen in support of the Guards Armoured Division's advance, followed by one of the batteries' H tanks* (Bottom), *6th April 1945.*
(I.W.M. – BU 3168–9)

nightfall and soon afterwards the town was secured, though the *Official History* records that it was not finally cleared of the enemy until the morning of 6th April. The regimental gun area was strafed by low-flying enemy aircraft during the afternoon. According to 341 Battery's history, Bofors guns assigned to the protection of the divisional artillery "had a field day, and all the gunners enjoyed themselves firing off their Brens and rifles whenever a German fighter appeared". There were no casualties from enemy action but Gunner Ager of 342 Battery died of wounds caused by a wandering 40-mm. shell.

The 5th April was an inactive day as far as Guards Armoured Division were concerned; 86th Field Regiment fired a few targets in support of 3rd Division as they cleared pockets of resistance and consolidated the bridgehead. On the following day the division began the break-out north-eastwards, this time on a single centre-line with 32 Brigade in the lead. Their next large-scale objective was a crossing of the River Weser, south-east of Bremen, some eighty miles distant. The advance was headed by the Scots-Welsh Group, as 341 Battery's history records:

> "The Scots-Welsh Group were ordered to break out of the bridgehead and push on. Objective for the night . . . was Bremen . . . but we had reckoned without the enemy . . . As the road entered a thick forest [*near Ramsel*] it was blocked and mined. The leading tank went up on a mine and a bulldozer brought up to push the obstacle away was knocked out by an 88-mm. gun firing directly down the road from the other end of the forest. The road-block was covered by Spandaus and panzerfausts and a company commander of the Scots Guards was killed while leading his men through the woods to clean up the pocket."

By the early afternoon the brigade had only moved about three miles from the perimeter of
 the Lingen bridgehead but here the road forked and the Coldstream Group were ordered to

Plate 120 *F Troop, 462 Battery cross the River Ems at Lingen, 6th April 1945.* Top – *A Sherman C.P. tank at the head of the column.* Centre – *F Sub-Section (Sergeant F. Whybrow).* Bottom – *Close-up of G Sub-Section (Sergeant G. Colt).* (I.W.M. – FLM 1236–8)

establish a second centre-line on the right fork, towards Freren and Fürstenau, while the Scots-Welsh Group continued towards Lengerich. Both routes were stubbornly defended and the Scots-Welsh spent the afternoon stalking 88-mm. guns with help from 341 Battery:

> "This time we were held up by four 88-mm. guns which put down an effective air-burst barrage over the leading tanks. Here there was some effective co-operation between the Air O.P., the artillery and the ground forces. Through our B.C. the Air O.P. directed the fire of our guns on to the enemy and kept it there while our tanks and infantry deployed. This kept the German gunners down in their shelters. When our tanks and infantry were about two hundred yards from the enemy guns the Air O.P. stopped the shelling and before the enemy gunners had time to recover all four guns were overpowered and captured."

The Scots-Welsh Group harboured for the night just short of Nordholten, two-thirds of the way to Lengerich. Meanwhile the Coldstream, equally troubled by fierce resistance, had secured the villages of Ramsel and Backum.

Orders for 7th April were for the Scots-Welsh Group to capture Lengerich and for the Coldstream, after seizing Thuine, to rejoin the Scots-Welsh at Lengerich, handing over the Freren–Fürstenau centre-line to 5 Brigade. On the Scots-Welsh road:

> "The advance was resumed . . . but after about three miles a road-block was encountered covering the entrance to Lengerich. An enemy S.P. gun on our left flank opened up and knocked out the two leading tanks as they tried to make their way round the road-block. It was decided to put in a full-scale attack on Lengerich. The battery, which was on the move, went into action just past Nordholten and a fire plan was prepared. Typhoon bombers were called up [*their targets indicated by red smoke fired by the battery*] and before the attack went in they put in some effective rockets on the town and enemy positions. After a preliminary bombardment of wooded areas around the town the attack went in. Advancing behind the tanks, the infantry entered the town to find it deserted except for a few women and old men. Not a shot was fired . . . The leading squadron of the Welsh Guards pushed on to the village of Handrup and linked up with the Coldstream Group, who, advancing on our right flank, had made slightly better progress. They had caught the enemy retreating from Lengerich unawares and inflicted quite a few casualties. The battery remained in action just east of Nordholten." (341 Battery's history)

The Coldstream had, indeed, successfully occupied Thuine during the morning and, hearing that the Scots-Welsh Group were more heavily engaged at Lengerich, had pushed the 1st Armoured Battalion ahead to see if they could help. Their reconnaissance troop found a way through the pine forests and bogs and succeeded in reaching the main road out of Lengerich to the east. Tanks moved up and by 18.00 the whole group were firmly astride the road, leaving only the northern exit from the town, which the Germans had quickly taken.

The next day, 8th April, the Scots-Welsh Group rested in Lengerich while the Coldstream advanced on Berge, about twelve miles further on. The day was marked not only by road-blocks but by heavy and accurate shelling of the brigade column by roving 88-mm. S.P. guns. During one such attack the commanding officer's Jeep driver, Gunner McKay, was killed; in another a Jeep belonging to the regimental signals section was hit and Corporal Hucknall killed and Driver Gibb so seriously wounded that he died later the same day. During the afternoon, in an action similar to that at Lengerich, the Coldstream Group cut the escape routes from Berge and entered the town after a heavy bombardment. This time the enemy made a stand but by nightfall resistance had ended and the two battalions consolidated their hold on the burning ruins of the town. The guns had moved twice to keep up with the advance.

Rosse states that 32 Brigade found progress beyond Berge "exceedingly difficult", pointing out that "the country was traversed by water obstacles in every direction and the bridges along the few passable roads were all either destroyed or held and prepared for demolition". The Scots-Welsh Group took the lead on 9th April and by evening, in the face of blown bridges over two canals, were poised to attack Menslage the following day, provided that the canals had been bridged. After working all night, the Sappers completed two bridges and the advance was resumed on 10th April, as recorded in 341 Battery's history:

> ". . . To enter Menslage it was necessary first to capture the village of Herbergen, which lay to the north-west . . . The leading squadron crossed the Hase Canal under cover of a morn-

Plate 121 *The last photograph of the guns in action – 341 Battery firing in support of the Guards Armoured Division from a position near Menslage, 9th April 1945. The Sexton self-propelled gun was not issued with any form of canopy but steel tube frameworks were made and fitted by the Light Aid Detachment, R.E.M.E. during the autumn of 1944 and tarpaulins or tents used as a protection against rain and wind.* (I.W.M. – BU 3576)

ing mist but failed to enter Herbergen, which was defended by a well-concealed and determined enemy. The battery was moved up to give better fire support and occupied a position between the two canals, directly opposite Menslage and less than a mile from its buildings, which could be seen quite clearly. A company/squadron attack on Herbergen took place, the Welsh and Scots Guards and artillery co-operating very well, and many prisoners were taken. The enemy withdrew into Menslage itself, the woods immediately behind the church, and some farm buildings and woods to the north of the town. The latter were very effectively shelled by the regiment in a most accurate shoot, the first rounds bursting on the roofs of the farms. In ranging on the enemy in the woods behind the church, the first ranging round passed straight through the church steeple and the second grazed its slated sides.

Another company/squadron attack was launched on Menslage itself, accompanied by a bombardment of the town by the regiment's guns. From their gun positions the battery could clearly see their own shells hitting the targets, destroying the church steeple, which eventually caught fire and was burned down. Its fall caused consternation as it had been used by everyone, including the survey regiment, as a G.A.P. [*gun aiming point*] or R.O. [*reference object*]. In a very short time the town was in our hands. The enemy had used his mortars and air-burst 88s to good effect in the early stages of the attack, timing his defensive fire to coincide with our barrage and giving the appearance of short rounds from our own guns. His mortaring caused several casualties and mines proved difficult. The enemy, however, suffered very heavily. Many of the prisoners looked very young – some little more than boys of fourteen . . ."

The Coldstream Group took over the lead next day, with orders to force a crossing of the River Hase, just beyond Menslage, and to capture the village of Boen, about half a mile beyond the river but dominating the proposed bridging site. With Boen in 32 Brigade's hands, 5 Brigade would move through to take over the lead. Howard described the ensuing action:

"On the night of 10th April the 5th Battalion made all its preparations and at dawn next day, with 1 Squadron in support . . . set out towards the river, one thousand yards ahead. 2 Company was leading; the morning mist hid its platoons as they approached the Hase, and only mines delayed their progress over the flat and open fields. But the bridge was already destroyed and as the mist lifted the battalion found itself exposed to the fire of snipers and machine-guns from the farther bank. An assault with boats and timed barrages seemed the only way to cross the river, but so flat was the ground and so sparse the cover that the commanding officer found it difficult even to reconnoitre. He managed, however, to reach the river bank by crawling through the only wood on the battalion front. At noon he was planning an assault crossing to take place that night, when news arrived that a bridge was still standing three miles up-stream – on the battalion's right. Major Hamilton at once took 4 Company to investigate, and found the bridge; it was partly blown, but a few planks still

Plate 122 *Gunner F. Kalabza, equipment repairer in 342 Battery, smiles across his work bench at news of the cease-fire, May 1945. Each battery had an equipment repairer on the establishment as part of the 'Q' team. Duties included boot repairs (as here) in addition to repairs to webbing, canvas and leather.* (Regimental Collection)

lay in position, and the guardsmen rushed across and dealt with the Germans beyond. The other companies followed. Now they had to return through thick woods along the far bank to clear the enemy from the original bridge site, and to capture the village of Boen. By 18.30 they had cleared the woods and were in position on their western edge to assault the village; then, while 2 Company dealt with the Germans who still held the river bank, 1 and 3 Companies attacked the village. The light was failing and it was a long, tough fight; 2 Company lost their C.S.M., and in Boen die-hard snipers held out long after the village had fallen; but by 20.30 all was over . . . By 06.00 next morning the bridge was complete and 5 Brigade took up the advance . . ."

Although the citation for Captain Turner's M.C. places the action on 12th April, there seems no doubt that he was acting as F.O.O. with 2 Company as they arrived at the river bank. He was ordered to establish an O.P. on the bank and suppress the opposition on the other side of the river by artillery fire. The citation states that "despite small-arms fire from very close range, which killed an officer beside him, Captain Turner crawled to a position from which he could see the enemy and, still under continuous fire, brought down most effective fire on the enemy. He remained in this exposed position directing fire which neutralised the enemy in the area until the crossing had been effected". Captain Turner's was not the only decoration awarded for this period of service in direct support of 32 Guards Brigade. On 2nd April, Lieutenant-Colonel R.C. Symonds had been posted to command of 86th Field Regiment, joining as the advance neared the River Ems. From then on, according to the citation for his D.S.O., "he was continuously and without relief with the leading troops of the armoured battalions . . . giving magnificent support to the leading tanks in the way he handled the deployment of his guns and arranged fire plans. His quick appreciation, untiring energy and coolness under fire, when first his Jeep and then his tank were hit, were an inspiration to those with whom he worked; and the soundness of his decisions undoubtedly saved a great number of casualties that might have occurred in the numerous attacks".

Resistance to the advance of the Guards Armoured Division lessened considerably as the Germans concentrated their forces for the defence of Bremen and the division made considerable progress during 12th and 13th April, so that when ordered out of the line on the morning of 14th April for a rest prior to joining XII Corps, they had reached the general area of Cloppenburg. Such actions as had taken place had been in the nature of mopping up and there had been little call for artillery support, though 86th Field Regiment remained with the division and took over the village of Westerenstek, some five miles west of Cloppenburg, as their rest area. Rosse later commented that the rest was "not undeserved", and that for nearly three weeks the Guards Armoured Division had been fighting almost ceaselessly. Although the fighting had not been particularly severe, judged by the standards of Normandy or the Reichswald, casualties in men and tanks had been serious. Officers and men of 86th Field Regiment would probably have taken much the same view and perhaps regretted leaving a 'spearhead' armoured division with which they had had a happy and successful association.

The Guards Armoured Division was replaced in XXX Corps by 52nd Infantry Division, so that for the advance on Bremen the corps consisted of 3rd, 43rd, 51st and 52nd Infantry Divisions. The only armoured formation under command was 8 Armoured Brigade but specialist armour was on call from 79th Armoured Division. After three days' rest, 86th Field Regiment came under command of 51st Division and on 18th April made a long road-move to join the division as they prepared to attack Delmenhorst. On arrival the O.Ps. joined

Plate 123 *Drivers of 342 Battery about to parade for guard mounting, May–June 1945. All four appear to have new suits of battledress, which are of 1940 'utility' pattern with the blouse buttons visible. They are wearing 1937-pattern webbing with cartridge carriers, as normally issued to units other than infantry, and have the No. 4 rifle.* (Regimental Collection)

13th/18th Hussars (under command from 8 Armoured Brigade) and 2nd Derbyshire Yeomanry (51st Divisional Regiment, R.A.C.), who were operating on the division's flanks, carrying out a reconnaissance role and meeting opposition in patches. Some small fire plans were fired to assist in the clearance of villages. The assault on Delmenhorst was planned for the morning of 20th April, but an attack by 152 Infantry Brigade on the village of Adelheide and the airfield and bridges close by during the night of 18th–19th April was to be the turning point of the battle. When the assault went in on 20th April the town fell without a shot – including the whole of the regimental fire plan – being fired. Delmenhorst turned out to be one vast hospital, full of German battle casualties and civilians injured in the air raids on Bremen. The O.Ps. established themselves in tall buildings and, while the regiment had a quiet two days on 21st–22nd April, they had a grandstand view of the R.A.F. raids on Bremen which preceded the ground forces' attack on the city.

On 23rd April 86th Field Regiment came under command of 3rd Division. Their preparations for the attack were described in 341 Battery's history:

> "We came under command of 3rd Infantry Division and had the pleasure of working under our former C.O., now Brigadier Fanshawe, as C.R.A. for the first time. We moved through Delmenhorst and Mackenstadt and occupied a position at Erichshof, a mile south of Brinkum and five or six miles from [*i.e., due south of*] Bremen. A Troop's guns were in the back gardens of suburban villas; B Troop's were some four hundred yards behind, on the edge of a small wood. We were just out of sight of the tall buildings and chimneys of Bremen. We began immediately on preparations for the fire plan for the attack. Four divisions were operating – 43rd and 52nd Divisions were advancing up the east bank of the River Weser, having forced a crossing above Verden, while 51st Division and 3rd Division were to attack Bremen from the west and south respectively. The area between 3rd Division's front and Bremen had been flooded by the enemy. It was planned to make a feint attack with 51st Division from the west and then send in 3rd Division for the main attack. The infantry were to be carried in Buffaloes and other amphibious vehicles across the flooded area and take the enemy by surprise from the rear."

The regiment took part in a huge programme of harassing fire which began on the evening of 23rd April and continued, as 'softening up' in which medium and heavy guns, Typhoon rocket-firing aircraft and medium bombers took part, throughout the following day. There is no evidence, either in the War Diary or in 341 Battery's history, that the regiment's O.Ps. played a prominent part in the battle for Bremen which began, as far as 3rd Division was concerned, just before midnight on 24th April with 9 and 185 Brigades, on left and right, respectively, moving through outlying villages and swinging north-westwards along the left bank of the Weser. By the evening of 25th April the assaulting brigades had secured all their objectives, including the main railway bridge linking the south-western suburbs to the greater part of the city on the right bank. The following day 8 Brigade moved through, clearing the left bank of enemy pockets, some of which continued to resist fiercely. By the 26th April, described by Scarfe as 3rd Division's "last day in action proper", there was nothing more that the regiment could do but take stock. It had been an easy battle for them. The only fatal casualty had been Bombardier Waterton of 341 Battery, who was killed on 25th April by a random shell from a

German gun that was still in action to the north of Bremen. The previous day news had reached the regiment that the bodies of Lieutenant Coultas, Regimental Survey Officer, and his driver, Gunner Wilson, had been discovered on Delmenhorst airfield. They had been missing for two days and it was evident that their Jeep had run over a mine. Perhaps 341 Battery's history, based, it will be remembered, on Lieutenant Beck's diary, should have the last word on Bremen:

> "26th April was noteworthy for the twenty crates of 'Beck's Beer' obtained from a brewery of that name in Bremen. How the brewery had survived the bombardment we did not know, as all the surrounding buildings were flat. Its contents, however, did not survive the 'peace' very long. What the various army lorries did not take away, the freed slave workers of all nationalities consumed in a riot of drunken happiness. This was the first beer we had tasted since Christmas and although it was weak and German it went down very well."

With Bremen secure, XXX Corps was now directed into the area between the rivers Weser (on the west) and Elbe (on the east), which included such important objectives as Bremerhaven and Cuxhaven. The regiment reverted to command of 51st Division on 27th April and followed the division along the south bank of the Weser, through Thedinghausen, to cross the Weser north of Verden and follow the main road northwards to Rotenburg. Here they turned due west and came into action near the village of Eckstever immediately after crossing the Bremen–Hamburg autobahn. The enemy's front was crumbling and there was no firing on the 28th or 29th, when the regiment was ordered forward to positions near Bevern in order to support 51st Division's attack on Bremervörde. While the usual preparatory work was going on during the evening of 1st May, 462 Battery's command post was hit, apparently by random harassing fire, Gunners Alcock and Stovold were killed and three others wounded. The attack took place during the night of 1st–2nd May. Demolitions made for a troublesome approach and long-range harassing fire was a nuisance but German infantry were only too anxious to give themselves up and the Highlanders made good progress. On 3rd May 51st Division broke out from their bridgehead over the Oste at Bremervörde, making for Bremerhaven and Cuxhaven against virtually no opposition and assisted by the occasional Mike target and some harassing fire from 86th Field Regiment. The following day the regiment occupied what was to be their last position in action, near Lintig. From their O.P. in a windmill, officers of 341 Battery watched the enemy surrendering in droves. Fire plans in support of local advances were abandoned but during the afternoon some regimental concentrations were fired on enemy gun positions that were shelling the roads out of Lintig. A cease-fire was ordered at 17.45 while surrender talks took place, and at 20.30 the news came on the B.B.C. that a general surrender of all German forces in Twenty-First Army Group's area would take effect at 08.00 the next day, 5th May. The regiment's eleven-month campaign in North-West Europe was over.

### *With the Army of Occupation, May 1945–April 1946*

The final ratification of the surrender of Germany and all her forces was not signed until just before midnight on 8th May, which became 'Victory in Europe' ('V.E.') Day and was duly celebrated. Then, on 12th May, 86th Field Regiment rejoined Guards Armoured Division and moved to the Cuxhaven area to take part in the general disarming of German forces. They stayed for a week, based in the village of Oxstedt, a few miles south of Cuxhaven, searching the surrounding area for weapons and war material of all kinds. The regiment's area of responsibility included an experimental ordnance station operated by Krupps, which proved to be full of trial V1 flying bombs, many and varied results of armour penetration tests and an immense experimental gun. On 18th May, Guards Armoured Division moved to the area of Verden and the regiment occupied the villages of Stedorf, Dörverden and Westen, a few miles south of Verden, which were to be their home for nearly another year. Here, after a thorough search of the buildings and surrounding countryside, made more difficult by the presence of large numbers of refugees from Bremen, they settled down to a period of general maintenance and cleaning up.

The warm relations between 86th Field Regiment and the Guards Armoured Division were exemplified on 31st May, when G.O.C. Guards Armoured Division, Major-General A.H.S. Adair inspected the regiment and in a farewell speech referred cordially to the "epic days" that the regiment had seen with the division. The Guards Armoured Division was due to lose

Plate 124 *86th Field Regiment Light Aid Detachment, R.E.M.E. at work on the armoured vehicles prior to hand-over, probably June 1945.*
Left – *The Quartermaster, Captain P.E. Felstead, M.B.E.,* (far right, in front of tank) *checks progress.*
Right – *Changing the engine of a Sexton.* (Regimental Collection)

its armour, absorb 6 Guards Brigade and move to occupation duties in the Ruhr as simply the 'Guards Division'. The regiment were invited to send a large representative party, as spectators, to the division's 'Farewell to Armour' parade, held on Rotenburg airfield on 9th June. Here those battalions that had been armoured drove off parade in their tanks and returned "marching in true Guards style".

With the Guards gone, 86th Field Regiment came under command of 51st (Highland) Division, as part of which they carried out the tedious round of occupation duties as an artillery regiment in name only. Captain Ash (shortly to be promoted to command of 342 Battery) recorded that, apart from inspections and searches, most of the time up to the end of July was filled with sports fixtures, both within and outside the regiment, and with numerous films and other entertainments. In a meadow beside the River Aller 342 Battery laid out a cricket pitch and constructed a 'lido', complete with slide. They also converted the local inn into an authentic English pub, which even had a skittle alley. Life cannot have been entirely devoted to sport and leisure, however, for between 9th and 11th August all the 'A' vehicles – tanks, self-propelled guns, carriers and half-tracks – and their associated stores were handed back to Ordnance. They were all "brightly painted and looking as fresh as if they had just come off the production lines" (341 Battery's history) and were the product of many hours of work by the L.A.D., and the battery fitters and mechanics, who put the engines, running gear and armament into best possible order and then handed over to anyone capable of wielding a paintbrush.

There were big changes in the personnel of the regiment, too. During July, while the war against the Japanese in the Far East continued, it was announced that officers and men (other than Regulars) of 'Age and Service Groups' 1–26 would not go to the Far East and plans were drawn up for units that would remain in Europe to consist of Groups 1–26 and those earmarked for the Far East to contain the higher groups. The regiment was selected for service in the Far East and towards the end of July all officers and men of Groups 1–26 were transferred to 147th (Essex Yeomanry) Field Regiment and 86th Field Regiment received a draft of Groups 27+ in exchange. This exchange marked the end of the regiment as an embodied Territorial unit. Only three pre-war Territorial officers remained on strength – Major Scammell, who had served continuously since mobilisation and had been selected for transfer to a Regular commission, and Captain Turner, who had been mobilised with 86th Field Regiment, transferred to 191st and then returned to 86th, both left towards the end of August, leaving only the Quartermaster, Captain Felstead, who stayed into September.

By this time, of course, the war against Japan was over. Embarkation leave, due to begin on 21st August, was cancelled at the last moment and the regiment was left with many new personnel and very little equipment. All efforts were now directed towards sorting out those due for imminent demobilisation and those who would stay on in the 'British Army of Occupation'. The ranks were gradually thinned by transfers to other units or by personnel proceeding towards release, and there was a constant coming-and-going of officers. Cricket gave way to football, both Association and Rugby, and swimming to ski-ing, for which small parties went on local leave into the Harz mountains. In February 1946 the Rivers Weser and

Plate 125 *B.C.'s party of 341 Battery relaxing with X/341, which has been serviced and smartened up ready for hand-over. The original X/341* (see Plate 94) *was of welded hull construction with pronounced vertical sides, as, apparently, were all O.P./C.P. tanks issued to 86th Field Regiment before D-Day. At least two replacement tanks had cast hulls with a much smoother outline, as here.* (Regimental Collection)

Aller threatened to flood the regimental area and sand-bagging parties were despatched to raise and strengthen their banks, especially at the confluence of the rivers at Verden.

The commanding officer, Lieutenant-Colonel R.C. Symonds, D.S.O., became a true Herts Yeoman by adoption and did everything possible to maintain the character of the regiment and to safeguard its future in the post-war Territorial Army, particularly by correspondence with the Honorary Colonel, Brigadier Sir Geoffrey Church, and with Hertfordshire Territorial Association. In letters to Sir Geoffrey dated 27th August and 19th December 1945, Colonel Symonds, who had flown to London to try to squeeze information on the future of the regiment out of the War Office, but without a great deal of success, outlined the measures he had taken to ensure that men were posted out in the largest possible groups, so that they could
[150] maintain contact and foster the old spirit. But, realistically, he pointed to the inevitable run-

Plate 126 *The officers of 86th Field Regiment at Dörverden, June 1945.* Back row (L.–R.) *Lieutenants G.L.W. Burlton, A.F. Hayward, S.J. Beck, Captain A.P. Hegarty, R.A.M.C., Lieutenants G.P. Eisen, J. Hindshaw, R. Signals, J. Prentis, C.S. Weedon, D.P.T. Deshon, A.L. Dorling, D.M. Mathers, P.R. Heaton-Ellis.* Third Row – *Lieutenant F. Fowler, Captains R.C.J. Anderson, D.J. Carr, W.A. Barton, G.M. Blackie, N.M. Pickford, R. Dorey, S.A. Revie, M.B.E., R.E.M.E., Lieutenant P.H. Cherry, Captain H. Potter, Lieutenant G.H. Jamieson.* Seated – *Captains J.G. Ash, D. Benson, R.R. Thornton, Majors E.G. Scammell, M.C., J.H. Gibbon, M.B.E., Lt.-Col. R.C. Symonds, Majors N.M. Whitmee, M.C., G.A. Loveday, Captain (Q.M.) P.E. Felstead, M.B.E., Captains R.S. Marshall, M.C., M.M., P.A. Turner, M.C.* Seated on ground – *Lieutenants W. Gear, J. Bartlett, H. Treble, A.E. Warren, E.C. Smallman, V.R.H. Yarnell.* (Regimental Collection)

Plate 127 *The warrant officers of 86th Field Regiment at Verden, May–June 1945.* Back row (L.–R.) *W.O.IIs (T.S.Ms.) Chappell (E Troop), Thompson (B Troop), Fisher (F Troop), Cooper (C Troop), Francis (A Troop), Darlow (D Troop).* Front row – *W.O.II (B.S.M.) Osborne (341), W.O. II (A.Q.M.S.) Durnford, R.E.M.E., W.O.I (R.S.M.) Lightfoot, W.O.II (R.Q.MS.) Watham, W.O.IIs (B.S.Ms.) Paufley (462), Sawyer (342).* (Regimental Collection)

down and dissolution of the regiment and regretted "the indignity when we were made to take off our black berets", a measure he had decided it was best not to resist. Colonel Symonds must have regarded the return to the regiment of Major Perry, who had now recovered from the wound he had received in Holland in September 1944 and was posted to comand 341 Battery, as a welcome influx of pre-war Territorial blood. Major Perry, and Captain Ash who had joined 86th Field Regiment on first being commissioned in March 1941 and had served since then, remained on the strength to the last.

By the time the final, or 'Cease-Fire', list of decorations for the campaign in North-West Europe was published in January 1946, many of those those whose names appeared in it had left the regiment. By tradition a cease-fire list enables commanders to look further back than the immediately-past period authorised for the campaign, and the recommendations for two of the regiment's three Military Crosses and all three Military medals paid tribute to the bravery of the recipients throughout the campaign in North-West Europe. Captain Ash, D Troop Commander, was additionally cited for gallantry as an F.O.O. on the Dutch–German border in October–November 1944 and with the Guards Armoured Division as they pressed towards Wesel at the end of Operation 'Veritable', while Captain Carr, F Troop Commander, was particularly noted for "initiative and coolness of the highest order" while working with the 82nd U.S. Airborne Division near Nijmegen in September 1944 and for his gallantry while supporting the Scots Guards, again in the drive towards Wesel. The Military Medals were awarded to Gunner Cornell, medical orderly in 341 Battery, Gunner Dennis, driver of Captain Marshall's tank, RC, and Bombardier Miles, vehicle mechanic in 342 Battery. The associated Mentions-in-Despatches, which were not published until the beginning of April 1946, included the universally respected, but nevertheless popular, R.S.M. of 86th Field Regiment, W.O. I Lightfoot. Of the very small number of foreign decorations that reached the regiment, the award of the French Croix de Guerre with Gilt Star to the adjutant, Captain Thornton, also gave great pleasure to all ranks.

Plate 128 *C.P. tank and guns of A Troop, 341 Battery lined up to await hand-over, August 1945.*
(Regimental Collection)

On 23rd March 1946, by which time the whole regiment was concentrated in barracks in Verden, Regimental Headquarters received H.Q. B.A.O.R. letter 3794/7/A Org.(2) dated 21st March, which ordered the personnel of 86th Field Regiment to be dispersed to other units and the regiment to be placed in suspended animation by 10th April. As explained in Chapter 1, all first-line Territorial units were placed in suspended animation pending decisions on the composition of the post-war Territorial Army. With very few exceptions, officers and men of 86th Field Regiment, as it existed in April 1946, neither knew of the regiment's many achievements, nor cared for its future, and, as was the case at the end of the 1914–1918 War, the pre-war Territorials, now disembodied, were far more concerned with returning to civilian life than with the continued existence of their regiment. Had they known as they left their demobilisation centres that plans for its rebirth were under active discussion, it is doubtful whether they would have taken any notice.

# Chapter 5

# *The Duplicate Unit – 135th Field Regiment, R.A., September 1939–August 1945*

*With Home Forces, September 1939–October 1941*

As recorded in Chapter 3, the 'key parties' of 86th Field Regiment were called out on 24th August 1939 and general mobilisation was ordered on 1st September. At Peterborough, Bombardier Austin, then a gunner in 336 Battery, whose extensive memoirs and correspondence with the regimental historian are in the Regimental Collection, returned from work to find that he was to report to the drill-hall at once "with everything I had, so off I went with my cap, field service, water bottle and haversack". After minimal documentation he returned home for the night with orders to parade at 10.00 next morning. Then:

> "On Saturday morning we lined up . . . At one table we received our £5 call-up money and at another our ten shillings for small cleaning gear – button stick, shoe polish, Brasso and brushes – which we had purchased ourselves. Men who lived within one mile of the drill-hall could return home. Those living more than a mile away had billets arranged, though there was some latitude in the arrangement. 'Come back at 09.00 on Sunday', we were told . . .
>
> While we were eating at home we received a meal allowance of a few extra shillings. In the meantime a door was made in the wall to gain access to the P.S.A. Hall. This was taken over as our dining-hall; all meals had to be taken there and the food allowance was stopped. The Unity Hall in Northfield Road was taken over as a lecture room and it was here that Sergeant Johnson, our signals instructor, told us that morse code on buzzer had been increased to ten words a minute and lamp to eight words a minute . . .
>
> Within a few days a motley collection of vehicles was requisitioned – from 'T for Transport', 'Read's Rapid Removals' and a local coal company. Most of these vehicles proved to be thoroughly unreliable . . . all wireless sets were called in, as were all boiler suits . . . Civilian boots were issued . . . having been bulk-purchased from the local Co-op . . .
>
> Each evening before we were dismissed Battery Sergeant-Major Griggs would read out the following day's orders. On Tuesday evenings, referring to Wednesday, he would finish by saying 'Oh, Oh! This day will be a half-holiday' . . ." (It was reportedly on one such half-holiday that Colonel Hudson visited a battery drill-hall and noticed a young gunner who failed to salute him. On being asked why he had not saluted, the soldier is said to have replied "But I've got the afternoon off"!)

A similar situation no doubt prevailed at Hitchin, where, Lieutenant Berry later recalled, embodiment was "followed by some lovely summer days which we spent in gun drill on the field opposite the drill-hall [*Bearton Camp, in Bedford Road*], or in learning the theoretical side of gunnery in the lecture room . . . We had practically no equipment or transport . . .".

Meanwhile, Regimental Headquarters of 135th Field Regiment had mobilised at Hertford, alongside Regimental Headquarters of 86th Field Regiment. Nominal independence of the duplicate regiment was achieved on 7th September but the headquarters remained at Hertford until suitable premises were found and requisitioned at 91 Bancroft, Hitchin. The

Plate 129 *Officers and N.C.Os. of D Troop, 344 Battery at Hitchin, September 1939.* Standing (L.–R.) – *Lance-Bombardier Stokes, Bombardier Williams, Lance-Bombardiers Last, Andrews, Burgess, Sharp, Taylor.* Seated – *Sergeant Ramsbottom, 2nd Lieut. Dearden, Captain Wells, Lieutenant McMullen, T.S.M. Stokes.* (Regimental Collection)

move to Hitchin was completed on 20th September. At the time that the two regiments split, Lieutenant-Colonel Hudson was in command of 135th Field Regiment, with Major Banham as Second-in-Command, Captain Halford-Thompson, Adjutant and Lieutenant Oakes, Quartermaster. Major Lutyens was commanding 336 Battery and Major Sanders 344 Battery. After inter-postings between batteries on 1st October 1939, the officer 'order of battle' was as shown in Appendix 3.

During October the first suit of battledress was issued to each man, accompanied by long woollen pants and khaki flannel shirts, woollen jersey and braces. But web equipment, including anklets, was not yet available, so short puttees were issued to secure the bottoms of the battledress trouser legs above the boots. Men without greatcoats – the majority – received a temporary issue of the single-breasted infantry pattern and all ranks were issued with the early rubberised cotton anti-gas cape. Captain McMullen later recalled that, "when battledress became 'de rigeur', we officers of 135th decided we would have our own distinctive material, which we bought and had made up by a tailor . . . It was a sort of 'elephant grey' khaki. We got away with it for some time but were eventually choked off by some inspecting brass-hat . . .". Appearing in his new battledress complete with Sam Browne belt and brown leather anklets, 2nd Lieutenant Egar was swiftly told to remove his belt, but no fault could be found with the anklets, which he continued to wear.

At the beginning of November 1939, 18th Division was moved to Norfolk as part of the 'Julius Caesar' plan, under which "a suitable proportion of such troops as would normally be at home would be disposed within easy reach of the East Coast" (*Official History*). The orders to move are recorded as having reached 135th Field Regiment with rather more sense of urgency than perhaps a routine deployment warranted. They were much on the lines of 86th Field Regiment's "sudden East Coast scare" (see Chapter 4). The regiment was concentrated in the area Kimberley (R.H.Q. and 336 Battery) and Wymondham (344 Battery) and by 11th November 344 Battery had pooled all their resources to send a 'battery' of four 4.5-in. howitzers much nearer to the coast – first to Fakenham, then two days later to the anti-aircraft practise camp at Weybourne, on the coast just west of Sheringham. Details of the intended role of these guns have not survived, though Major Sanders later commented:

Plate 130 *The black-on-khaki slip-on shoulder title worn on the shoulder straps of the battledress blouse by other ranks of the Royal Artillery until December 1941, when it was replaced by the red and blue arm of service strip worn on the upper sleeve.* (Regimental Collection)

Plate 131 *Gunner G.D. Austin, 336 Battery, early 1940. He is wearing 1937-pattern battledress, with concealed buttons, embellished with the Royal Artillery white lanyard and brass grenade collar badges. The slip-on 'R.A.' shoulder title can just be seen.* (Regimental Collection)

"The operational side of our work was a bit vague, since it appeared that with four guns we were defending twice as many miles of coast-line and, had Hitler attempted the invasion just there, we could not have offered much effective resistance. But we felt no doubts at all in our minds and every man would have welcomed the whole German army, so delighted were we to be doing a real job at last . . . We were quartered at Weybourne Camp and living with the 5th Royal Norfolks, with whom we established a firm friendship – one which was to endure through all the vicissitudes of the next two years . . ."

Back in the regimental area, meanwhile, R.H.Q. and the officers' mess had been established in Kimberley House. The quartermaster's stores occupied the extensive cellars of the house and 336 Battery were "squeezed into the stables and outhouses", with any men who could not be fitted in finding quarters in a derelict farmhouse nearby – known to everyone as 'Cold Comfort Farm'. The more fortunate 344 Battery were "at Wymondham, spread over a Methodist hall, a bathing club, a Women's Institute and a large [*disused*] garage".

At some time late in November, or perhaps early in December, according to Major Sanders:

". . . We received our new transport. It was a great day when the regimental order appeared calling for a number of drivers to travel to Colchester and collect some forty 'new' vehicles which had been allotted to us. The thrill soon passed when we saw them. Fortunately the humour of the situation overcame our disappointment. By a feat of engineering about three-quarters of them were transported to Kimberley, where many of them just died where they stood. We got a good deal of amusement but little service from these poor old crocks but they were all we had to train with for several months. The procedure was to keep one vehicle in the cookhouse overnight so that it was warm enough to start, with some effort, in the morning. Then this would tow another into life, and so on until we had a few running."

Bombardier Austin had his own memories of training without vehicles:

"While at Kimberley it was decided that we should learn deployment, so we assembled on a meadow nearby and, for instance, the six men who would ride in the H truck fell in, followed by the six in Y and then the six in M1. The drivers carried a little yellow flag on which was painted the vehicle number; and so we trotted around the meadow, with some drivers adding a little humour by pretending to steer and at the same time making a noise like a motor engine . . ."

Against this background, Lieutenant Berry's report of training with cardboard instruments can readily be believed.

Christmas 1939 was celebrated in the usual style, with the warrant officers serving tea to the troops in bed, one of the trumpeters still on strength, sounding 'No parades today' and the officers serving Christmas dinner, which, according to Bombardier Austin, consisted of turkey, Christmas pudding "and in general so much to eat that we could hardly breathe after dinner". Part of 344 Battery celebrated Christmas at Weybourne but it is not clear how long they stayed there. It seems probable that they were withdrawn early in January, no doubt on the grounds that the 'invasion season' was well past. During the whole of January 1940 snow stood four to six inches deep and there were between ten and twenty degrees of frost (Fahrenheit scale) every night. Training was hampered by an outbreak of influenza among all ranks and then some cases of measles and mumps. The regiment would have had considerable difficulty in dealing with these illnesses, had it not been for the Wymondham Centre of the Norfolk Branch, British Red Cross Society, who opened a temporary hospital in a big house known as 'Lou Ness'. As a result of the extreme cold, it was decided that 336 Battery could no longer remain in the stables and outhouses of Kimberley House. One troop, probably accommodated at 'Cold Comfort Farm', had moved into the drill-hall at Wymondham before Christmas; now the whole battery occupied Hingham Hall, about three miles south-west of Kimberley. Serious nuisance though the prolonged frost was, it did enable officers and men to relax on the ice. Lieutenant Berry later recalled how "many of us spent our leisure hours on the beautiful lake at Kimberley or on the mere at Scoulton, improving our skating and playing ice-hockey. Captain Keane and Major Banham were the experts and some of the Peterborough battery brought out their long fen skates and gave us demonstrations of their local style".

As far as 135th Field Regiment were concerned, the period February–May 1940 seems to fit in well with the idea of the 'Phoney War'. The regiment was reduced to six operational guns – four 4.5-in. howitzers in 336 Battery and two 18-pdr. Mk. II PA in 344 Battery. Even so, the War Diary describes March as a month of "intensive training". Personnel began to leave too. During March parties were sent to man anti-aircraft Lewis guns on coastal shipping. They returned some weeks later, one at least having had his ship sunk beneath him and another having attracted for good the nickname 'Sailor'. In April volunteers for the new 'Independent Companies', later to become the Commandos, were called for. Twenty men from the regiment were selected and joined the company formed from units of 18th Division, which was incorporated into No. 8 Commando. There continued to be a funny side to almost every activity. Bombardier Austin particularly remembered the preparations for an inspection:

> ". . . Now we only had one battledress each, so to smarten us up the whole battery lined up in the dining-hall, at the end of which was a door with an upper panel of frosted glass leading into the bar of the inn. Behind this door were Mrs Banham and Mrs Neal [*wives of the battery commander and battery captain*], armed with flat-irons. The first soldier approached the door, took off his trousers and gave them to a hand which protruded from the door. Then he waited in his pants, woollen, long until the hand came out with the ironed trousers. He put them on and left while the next man moved up in his pants, woollen, long, and so on . . . After all that the parade was postponed!"

The German attack through Belgium and into France led to a redeployment of units of 18th Division to immediate coast defence and the regiment joined 53 Infantry Brigade on a stretch of the Norfolk coast between Wells-next-the-Sea and Sheringham. During 10th–11th May, 336 Battery (four 4.5-in. howitzers) and 344 Battery (two 18-pdrs.), who between them, according to the *Official History*, provided exactly half the fire-power available to 18th Divisional Artillery, moved up to the coast. In 336 Battery:

> ". . . the concept of the four-gun battery fell to pieces . . . All of A Troop and C Troop and much of B.H.Q. had just had T.A.B. injections and were prostrate in their bunks in no fit state to move, so it was decided to send B Troop with the four howitzers. They could hardly dash, as ordered, for the guns still had wooden wheels [*and were thus limited to eight miles per hour*]. So they set off for the Weybourne area, where the beach was ideal for an invader to land, with guns towed by the trucks 'T for Transport', 'Read's Rapid Removals' and 'Ellis and Everard – Coal Suppliers' . . . Progress was painfully slow . . ." (Austin)

Meanwhile, the officers and men not required to man the guns on the coast remained in the Wymondham area, where they formed part of 18th Divisional Artillery Rifle Regiment, a scratch force intended primarily for the anti-parachutist role. Bombardier Austin, who had himself been laid low by the T.A.B. 'jab', recorded:

"... Those of us left behind were to proceed when fit to the drill-hall at Wymondham. Eastern Counties omnibuses were hired to move our equipment. The rear emergency doors were opened and duckboards, buckets, tents, etc. were put into the buses on top of the seats and away they went. Those of us remaining coupled up the two drill-purpose howitzers and set off for Wymondham ... There, most men were billeted in the drill-hall. Those of us overflowing were in bell tents in a field a little behind the drill-hall. It was May and the weather was quite nice ... We were now all issued with Canadian Ross rifles ... and training as skirmishing parties began in earnest. Captain Deacon was in charge and when the 344 Battery trumpeter blew the 'Alarm' on Wymondham market place we had to fall in ready to march off ... On one such occasion we marched along the main street of Wymondham with Captain Deacon heading the column on horseback. The citizens waved goodbye from their windows and from the kerb-side. We went along some country lanes behind Wymondham and eventually finished up back at the drill-hall in Pople Street. 'Look. They're back', the citizens cried out in amazement. Gunner Nicholls, E. was put in charge of Captain Deacon's horse. It was in the field with us and was made a great fuss of by the men ...

One evening we went to the little cinema at the end of Pople Street ... while the film was on a notice was flashed on the screen 'All 336 Battery personnel report back to barracks immediately' ... It was not a German invasion but we all had to go off in various parties. A large number of men went to do guard duties at divisional headquarters at Sprowston, near Norwich. The party I was with went to Arminghall, near Norwich, to guard an R.A.S.C. ration depot. Sergeant 'Splitpin' Wright was in charge. We did 24 hours on guard and 24 hours off. During our off-duty period we used to go into Norwich by Eastern Counties bus, the terminus being not far along the road ...

After a week or so we moved to Watton, manning road-blocks. There was a block on the road to Norwich near the airfield, another on the road to Dereham and our block was near a little park called Loch Neaton, with a nice little lake. We were to use the pavilion as a shelter ... All the road blocks were connected by field telephone via an omnibus circuit. We built an observation post with sandbags close to the Thetford to Swaffham branch-line railway. Too close, in fact, and as the train came by the tank-engine would catch the sandbags. One morning we arrived back from our breakfast at Merton Hall to find railwaymen throwing our dismantled sandbag enclosure down the embankment. I was the first to arrive and was met by an irate railway inspector, complete with bowler hat and watch chain ... The

Plate 132 *Gunner Austin enjoying a spell of guard duty at a road-block manned by 336 Battery near Watton, Norfolk, June 1940. He has been issued with full web equipment, including basic pouches, but is wearing puttees, rather than web anklets, which were not issued until the autumn of 1940. His No. 3 Lee-Enfield rifle is on a rest on top of the sandbag wall.* (Regimental Collection)

Plate 133 *A road-block guard from 336 Battery at tea, June 1940. L.–R. Sergeant Johnston, Gunners Bishop, Austin, Lee, Grey, Baker, Wagstaffe, Flack. The oblong mess-tins issued with 1937-pattern web equipment can be seen on the near left corner of the table. Note also the collarless khaki flannel shirt then issued for wear under the battledress blouse.* (Regimental Collection)

outcome was that a corporal from the Royal Engineers came over to show us how to construct a sandbag enclosure properly [*and the regulation three feet six inches from the track*] . . . Fifth column fever was at its height. At night we would observe coloured Very lights . . . Lieutenant Laing gave us excellent instruction on how to fix the position of the lights [*by cross-bearing*] . . . We would do this and personnel from R.H.Q. would dash off in a fast car to try to intercept . . . To my knowledge no-one was ever caught . . . My own view is that . . . they were lights being used at our airfields or by infantry on night exercises. The men on duty at the road blocks always had loaded rifles and we had a list of cars which, if they did not stop when ordered, were to be fired on immediately."

During May there was a welcome issue of a second suit of battledress and a second pair of boots. Web equipment was also issued or, as described by Bombardier Austin, "a big heap of it was deposited on the grass and we had to sort it out. Those men amongst us who had transferred from the Northamptonshire Regiment became quite important as they knew how to put it all together".

It is not possible from surviving records to reconstruct the detail of the regiment's deployment during the summer of 1940, or keep account of their gradual increase in fire-power. By 18th–19th May, 336 Battery's 4.5-in. howitzer troop was deployed at Cley-next-the-Sea and 344 Battery's two 18-pdrs. were at Catton. Forward Regimental Headquarters had deployed for a time to Holt, still in support of 53 Infantry Brigade, but had returned to Wymondham. At the end of May practise firing, presumably at seaward targets, took place, but with only two 4.5-in. howitzers and two 18-pdrs. By the end of the month Regimental Headquarters and battery echelons had been established at Merton Hall, near Watton, from where they supported the gun troops on the coast and the mobile rifle troops and static road-blocks and observation posts in the Watton area. Recording the deployment of E Troop, 344 Battery to Little Cressingham in the middle of June, the War Diary also describes the troop as having four 4.5-in. howitzers, so it looks as if more howitzers had arrived, though possibly only through D.P. guns being passed as fit to fire. Early in July, Forward Regimental Headquarters returned to Holt and it was evidently decided to reorganise the regiment on the basis of its tactical employment. All guns and personnel at the coast came under command of 344 Battery and all rifle troops inland under command of 336 Battery. This confusing arrangement was apparently 'unscrambled' five or six weeks later, as more guns became available and the tactical control of another battery headquarters was needed at the coast. Meanwhile, the situation was further confused by the detachment of a party of signallers to assist in the training, and, if necessary, operations of 57th (Newfoundland) Heavy Regiment, who established their 9.2-in. batteries behind 53 Infantry Brigade's frontage and gave a very powerful boost to defensive fire-power. In the middle of August three officers (including Captain Keane, who eventually made his way back to the regiment) and 57 other ranks were exchanged for a similar number from the 97th Field Regiment, who had had experience with the British Expeditionary Force in France and Flanders.

Plate 134 *An 18-pdr. Mk. II on Carriage Mk. II PA in service with 344 Battery at Catton, Norfolk, June 1940.*
Left – *T.S.M. Waldock strikes an informal pose and obscures much of the detail. The disc wheel, typical of the U.S.-made 'pneumatisation set' can be seen.*
Right – *An unusual combination – a Morris-Commercial Quad, with pneumatised 18-pdr. The gun is hooked directly to the Quad, presumably because 18-pdr. ammunition would not fit into the limber then being issued (Trailer, Artillery, No. 27), which was designed to carry 25-pdr. rounds. Note the 18th Division formation sign stuck inside the windscreen.*
(Regimental Collection)

On 24th August 1940 the first consignment of eight 75-mm. guns reached 135th Field Regiment and was allocated to 336 Battery, who now moved all personnel to the coast. Four guns each went to A Troop at Lowes Farm, Holt and B Troop at Aylmerton. C Troop took over the two 18-pdrs. originally manned by F Troop, 344 Battery and in addition manned two 4-in. naval guns which were incorporated in the beach defences. Bombardier Austin records that as well as the two troop positions at Lowes Farm and Aylmerton, there were further prearranged positions on the road between Salthouse and Sheringham with gun-pits already prepared and telephone and Tannoy wires laid. The 75-mm. guns had no limbers and were carried [*'porté'*] in 30-cwt. Fordson trucks. According to the book, the guns were to be loaded and off-loaded by means of the steel ramps provided for each wheel, under the control of a hand-winch mounted behind the vehicle cab. In 336 Battery it was found that coming into action (i.e., off-loading) with cable and winch was altogether too slow and the gunners perfected a method of running down the ramps with the gun and then swerving to left or right according to the direction in which 'Action' had been called. E and F Troops of 344 Battery also received 75-mm. guns. According to the War Diary, D Troop was deployed with four 18-pdrs., although it is possible that this is a mistake and in fact they had 4.5-in. howitzers, for as late as November 1940 the regiment sent 4.5-in. howitzers to workshops at Cambridge to have pneumatic-tired wheels fitted. If the substitution of two 4-in. naval guns for orthodox field guns is discounted, by the beginning of September 1940 the regiment was at last up-to-establishment in guns and organised in two batteries, each of three troops. Practise shoots were carried out on targets at sea and on the marshes in mid-September. Then, towards the end of the month, after some hurried gun drill on borrowed 18/25-pdrs., 336 Battery went by train for a short firing camp at West Down on Salisbury Plain, where they used 'pool' guns and vehicles. After a 24-hour train journey back to Holt (described in detail in Bombardier Austin's memoirs), 336 Battery resumed duty in the coast defences while 344 went to Salisbury Plain.

As a means of bringing manpower and organisation to the defence of exposed beaches, 64 'defence batteries' were formed in September 1940 to man the miscellany of direct-fire weapons being pressed into service, many from naval sources. These batteries, designated 901–964 Defence Batteries were, with five exceptions, grouped in 'defence regiments' in October 1940. Among the independent defence batteries was 901 Defence Battery, which was raised around a cadre of 64 other ranks recently arrived in 135th Field Regiment. The battery was commanded by Major J.R.O'B. Warde, who had joined 135th Field Regiment in August as the senior officer 

Plate 135 *Miscellaneous weapons on display at Catton, Norfolk, June 1940.*
Left – *Sergeant Williams demonstrates the .5-in. anti-tank rifle*
Right – *Lewis gunners. The .303-in. Lewis light machine-gun, of First World War vintage, was shortly to be replaced by the Bren gun.* (Regimental Collection)

of the party from 97th Field Regiment. No record of the history of 901 Defence Battery has survived, though it does seem that the battery continued to serve on the coast of Norfolk. There is no evidence that any attempt was made to carry on the name or traditions of the Hertfordshire Yeomanry in 901 Defence Battery, which was disbanded early in March 1941.

Early in November 1940 135th Field Regiment was placed in support of 222 Infantry Brigade, one of the brigades formed specifically for beach defence, which was then under command of 18th Division. By now, life in tents was quite unpleasant and in the middle of the month the regiment moved into billets in Holt (R.H.Q.), West Runton (336 Battery) and Sheringham (344 Battery). Bombardier Austin records that the house in which he was first billeted was "not much warmer than the tents, there was no hot water and we had to sleep on the floor", but also notes with some satisfaction that No. 11 wireless sets had now been issued and the signallers were enthusiastically training with them.

No sooner had R.H.Q. and the two batteries occupied their winter quarters, than orders arrived for the regiment to be reorganised to consist of three batteries, each of two troops. Accordingly, on 27th November, C Troop of 336 Battery and F Troop of 344 Battery were detached to form the new battery, known for the time being as 'C' Battery and under the command of Captain Daltry. The original A and B Troops had no need to change their designations; D and E Troops of 344 Battery became C and D Troops; and the original C Troop changed to E, so that 'C' Battery consisted of E and F Troops. The existence of the third battery may only have been temporary, however (see below).

Late in 1940, probably in November and before the formation of 'C' Battery, the regiment received 36 Quad gun tractors in preparation for the eventual issue of 25-pdr. guns. The eighteen Guy 'Quad-Ants' and a similar number of Morris C 8s were conveniently split on arrival so that 336 Battery had all the Guys and 344 Battery all the Morrises, but the logic lapsed almost at once, presumably resulting in 'C' Battery having a mixture of both. Over the next two or three months it became clear that 135th Field Regiment had at last reached its turn for issues of new vehicles and equipment, including 8- and 15-cwt. trucks, 3-ton trucks and car-

Plate 136 *Gunners Hart* (Left) *and Smith* (Right) *of 344 Battery on recently-issued Norton motor-cycles at Catton, Norfolk, June 1940. Motor-cyclists were later issued with steel crash-helmets, 'pantaloons, D.R.' (breeches) and high-legged leather boots, and with Sten gun or pistol, rather than rifle.* (Regimental Collection)

Plate 137 *In F Troop's wagon lines at Lockerbie, early 1941. The Morris-Commercial 8-cwt. F.F.W.* (Left) *is the troop commander's O.P. vehicle 'RF', while the Guy 'Ant' 15-cwt.* (Right) *has no visible 'tac sign'.* (Regimental Collection)

riers, A.O.P. The full complement of motor-cycles was last to arrive, in March 1941. The issuing authorities were clearly out of step with those responsible for training and deployment, for the instructions to send parties to collect 25-pdrs. Mk. II on Mk. I Carriage and Trailers, Artillery No. 27 from the huge ordnance depot at Donnington, in Shropshire, arrived at the same time as the regiment was ordered to move to the Scottish borders. By a series of delayed moves and with personnel travelling in all directions, both objectives were achieved and by the end of January 1941, it seems that all 25-pdrs. and limbers had arrived.

A revised plan for the defence of East Anglia was due to come into effect around the turn of the year. The whole of 18th Division was to move into G.H.Q. Reserve in order to carry out mobile training. The division would be replaced in Norfolk in part by the newly-formed Norfolk County Division, which took command of 222 Infantry Brigade on the north Norfolk coast and two more coast defence brigades that carried the divisional frontage round as far as Lowestoft, and in part by 46th Division, which had completed mobile training and was to be based further inland as corps reserve. A 'warning order' for an impending move reached 135th Field Regiment on 19th December 1940. The destination was supposed to be secret but, according to Bombardier Austin, "the elderly lady who ran a small café opposite the village inn told some of our men over a cup of tea that we were moving to Scotland". Christmas was spent in Norfolk but in view of the impending move 'No parades today' was not sounded. Nevertheless, "Christmas dinner was again a grand affair". Then the regiment was relieved of its coast defence tasks by 147th Field Regiment and advance parties left on 1st January 1941. The main body began to move on 7th January, split into two parties, the tracked vehicles and a large number of men going by rail, while the wheeled vehicles and the sixteen 25-pdrs. already on strength moved by road, in very cold and difficult conditions, as part of the 18th Division convoy. By the middle of January, the regiment was established in billets, split between Lockerbie and Annan, in Dumfriesshire.

Mobile training was interrupted during January by the requirement to send parties to Donnington for the remaining 25-pdrs. and also by embarkation leave, which began on 22nd January. Bombardier Austin, who was a railway enthusiast with considerable knowledge, records with glee how, by ignoring the transport staff's instructions to change at Kettering and choosing his own route via Melton Mowbray, he and a party of friends from 336 Battery

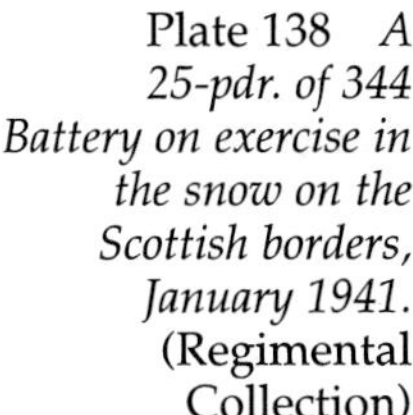

Plate 138 *A 25-pdr. of 344 Battery on exercise in the snow on the Scottish borders, January 1941.* (Regimental Collection)

Plate 139 *25-pdr. guns, certainly of 18th Divisional Artillery and believed to be of 135th Field Regiment, on exercise in Scotland, March 1941. Note how the firing platform* (secured to the top of the limber in Plates 20 and 22) *is now carried beneath the trail of the gun. Cartridge carriers are now being worn instead of basic pouches* (as in Plate 132).
(I.W.M. – H 8244–6)

Plate 140 *A troop of 25-pdrs., believed to be of 344 Battery, in action during an exercise in Scotland, March 1941. Whenever possible, the limber was dropped, or manhandled into position, on the left of the line of fire, so that the ammunition numbers, who always loaded from the left, had uninterrupted access.* (I.W.M. – H 8247)

reached Peterborough at 10.45, while those who had stuck to the instructions did not arrive until 16.00. Speculation as to the troops' destination once returned from leave was heightened by the issue of tropical clothing:

> "The cellular shirts were quite good. The shorts had a huge turn-up and were known as 'Bombay bloomers'. The jacket and slacks were identical to those issued to my Uncle Harry in the Boer War and the sun helmet was the Wolseley pattern . . . Cynics in the battery were adamant that the issue of tropical uniform meant for sure that the regiment was destined for Iceland". (Austin)

Very little detail of life and training on the Borders has survived. The War Diary records that March 1941 was filled with "higher exercises" – which was certainly the intention. Captain Halford-Thompson recalled the "very good – and very dangerous – wild fowling" and how he and Captain Peacock capsized a duck punt (with one-pound punt gun) "on a freezing January day . . . fortunately in only three feet of water". He also noted "a series of great exercises, one of which took us right along the border, almost into the suburbs of Edinburgh". Bombardier Austin's memoirs tell much the same story with details filled in from the other ranks' point-of-view – including an account of how "a voluptuous young lady who I will call Bubbles" complained that the previous unit in billets at Annan had "played bugle calls" but she had never heard 336 Battery do so. Not to be outdone, "We got Tich Underwood up early and he blew a rip-snorting Royal Artillery reveille on the trumpet, right under her bedroom window . . ." . The overall impression of Lockerbie and Annan is one of three months during which, in spite of the cold, everyone enjoyed themselves.

Once mobile training had finished at the end of March, 18th Division moved complete to Cheshire. Advance parties of 135th Field Regiment left for Macclesfield on 5th April and the main body had all moved into billets in the town by 11th April. Bombardier Austin described his billet:

> "Headquarters Troop [*336 Battery*] was billeted in what had been a hardware shop in Great King Street . . . double-tiered bunks on the ground and first floors – plate glass windows at the front. The ablutions were in a public house yard about three hundred yards diagonally across the road, in the open. It was too bad if it was raining when you went for a wash . . . It was some consolation that hot water supplies were in the hands of the publican's luscious daughter, who, alas, was aged only fourteen. It was not a very good billet at all.
>
> A few days after arriving, Bill Gilby and I were put in charge of the signals stores, which were established in two shops in Chestergate, opposite the Picturedrome. I looked after the line store and Bill the wireless store. Although it was a comfortable billet, we were at a disadvantage in not knowing the time of day and were often late for breakfast . . .".

The routine of training and life in billets, including bath parades and church parades continued until the regiment went to Trawsfynydd range in North Wales for three days at the end of April to fire the 25-pdrs. for the first time.

Early in May 1941 the Civil Defence authority in Liverpool requested military assistance in the event of further heavy raids on the city and 18th Division was ordered to provide the necessary manpower. On 4th May a recce party from 135th Field Regiment visited the sector in which they would carry out 'firewatching' duties and on 5th May the first firewatching party of nine officers and 295 other ranks, under command of Major Banham, left for the Launcelot Hey and Robert Street areas of the city. Bombardier Austin describes the first evening:

> "We were informed that we were to go on firewatching duties in Liverpool and in a very short time R.A.S.C. buses arrived. We travelled via Warrington and Prescott, along Edge Lane in Liverpool and by the tram depot to St. George's Square. Here our cooks set up their portable stoves and did us a nice stew . . . Our muster point was Gibraltar Row and from here air raid wardens took us in parties of four to show us the buildings where we would firewatch. Our party consisted of myself, Lance-Bombardier Day and Gunners Tokens and Walker. We were to firewatch in a hide and skin warehouse where the pong was so bad that we had to bivouac in the air-raid shelter in the basement of the Littlewood Building in Old Leeds Street. We were allowed to walk around until the air-raid siren sounded and we went to look at the pier-head, where the ferries left for Birkenhead and New Brighton. On return we decided to have a glass of beer at a public house that we had noted when being shown the hide warehouse, about half-way along Gibraltar Row . . . Time was now getting on and so we went to our bivouac . . . Soon civilians began to arrive and they insisted that we join in their refreshments. We refused and explained that we had orders not to accept food from civilians because of rationing. It was quite clear that they were seriously offended, so we accepted a sandwich or two and then the air-raid siren went off. It was 22.30 and our party rushed over to the hide warehouse. We went to the top floor, where incendiary bombs would be most likely to come through. This was to be Liverpool's most devastating night so far . . . 363 tons of high-explosive bombs were dropped and fifty thousand incendiaries. It was a lovely clear night and from the loading doors of the warehouse we could see incendiary bombs dropping on the railway yard adjoining Exchange Station, the flames dripping from signal posts like molten metal . . . Huge conflagrations gave the impression of the city being a vast inferno and the line of docks a massive curtain of flame and smoke, which was reflected in the river . . .
>
> At 04.30 the 'all clear' sounded. The previous evening the clocks had been put forward one hour to double summer time and when daylight came we made our way to Gibraltar Row . . . Firemen, who had really had an awful night, were asleep on the pavement . . . The city was in a state of chaos. No private cars were allowed in. The overhead railway had been put out of action by a previous air raid and the tram service was out of action on many routes, with overhead wires dangling down into the streets . . . We fell in for roll-call and at the end of the street we could see naval personnel extricating an unexploded mine from the balcony of the Northern Eye Hospital . . ."

That night the regiment sustained its first casualties from enemy action. Sergeant Hinds of 336 Battery was killed and two gunners of 344 Battery seriously wounded. Detachments of about three hundred officers and men from the regiment were again engaged on firewatching duties

Plate 141 *336 Battery march past the Mayor of Macclesfield during the War Weapons Week parade, July 1941. B.H.Q. Troop, led by Lieutenant P. K. Laing and 2nd Lieut. R Boult* (both saluting) *is followed by A Troop. A large number of men are wearing grenade collar badges* (see Plate 131). *The officers' version of 1937-pattern web equipment included pouches for compass and binoculars* (wearer's right) *and pistol holster and ammunition pouch* (wearer's left).
(Regimental Collection).

in Liverpool on the nights of 10th–11th, 11th–12th and 12th–13th May, but apparently without casualties or anything like the experiences of the night of 5th–6th.

Between firewatching duties, 336 Battery moved on 7th May from Macclesfield to new billets in mill buildings in Congleton. According to Bombardier Austin, the new billets for H.Q. Troop, 336 Battery were "The best we had had so far . . . washing facilities were actually in the barrack rooms – a line of wash-basins at the end and plenty of hot water. What luxury! . . . A and B Troops were in a mill on the opposite side of the street and C Troop were in a mill just over a little bridge over the River Dane . . . The gun park was in a meadow opposite B Troop's billet, but divided by the river . . . This area of Congleton was called Buglawton". The reference to C Troop of 336 Battery is interesting and is not the only one in surviving papers. It gives a strong indication, which is borne out by War Diary entries at the beginning of June 1941, that the reorganisation to three batteries which took place in November 1940 had (unlike the similar reorganisation in 86th Field Regiment) been regarded as purely experimental and had been reversed. The authority to form 499 Battery, as the third battery of the regiment was to be designated, was promulgated on 18th May 1941 and on 26th May Colonel Hudson held a conference on "reorganisation to three batteries" (344 Battery's Diary). The War Diary places the actual reorganisation at 1st June 1941, while 344 Battery's Diary records Captain Lord De Ramsey and three other officers as having been posted to the new battery, which occupied billets at Alderley Edge, on 3rd–4th June. Finally, Bombardier Austin wrote, "One glorious sunny afternoon in June, 499 Battery was reconstituted. No-one was allowed out until C Troop had packed everything up and left for Alderley Edge, where they were to become E Troop of the new battery . . .". Captain Daltry, who had commanded 'C' Battery, was promoted to command of 499 Battery.

During June, July, and August 1941 training continued, with some widespread 'schemes' taking batteries into Herefordshire, Shropshire and North Wales, but almost no detail of these exercises has survived. Bombardier Austin recorded the issue of the newly-approved 18th Division flash in July and the fact that "a lady living in the terraced houses opposite the battery office in Havanah Street (Congleton) would sew them on for a modest sum". At the beginning of August Major Sanders relinquished command of 344 Battery on joining the Ministry of Supply and Captain Peacock was promoted to command; and in the middle of the month 336 Battery moved from Congleton to Knowsley Park, outside Liverpool. It was at Knowsley, very early in September 1941, that Gunner Broadbent of 336 Battery received on-the-spot promotion to lance-bombardier, though all the indications are that his appointment was both acting and unpaid! Broadbent was on guard when the new commanding officer, Lieutenant-Colonel P.J.D. Toosey, first visited the battery. Never having seen him and being unwilling to take anybody's word for anything, he required the C.O. and the rest of his party to dismount from their vehicle and subjected their identity cards to close examination. Once he had reached battery headquarters, Colonel Toosey sent for Broadbent, who arrived with considerable apprehension only to find that he was presented with his 'tapes' rather than given the 'rocket' he expected.

After two years in command of 135th Field Regiment, Lieutenant-Colonel Hudson had handed over to Lieutenant-Colonel Toosey on 1st September 1941. Colonel Toosey was a Territorial officer who had been first commissioned in 59th (4th West Lancashire) Medium Brigade in 1927. By the outbreak of war he was commanding a battery of the same unit, with which he served in the British Expeditionary Force, gaining a Mention-in-Despatches. At 37 years of age, he was thirteen years younger than Colonel Hudson. Alexander (see Bibliography) describes Toosey as "energetic, personable and ambitious" and Hudson as "avuncular". It is no longer possible to obtain direct, objective evidence of the state of training in 135th Field Regiment in the autumn of 1941 but Davies (see Bibliography) records that on taking command Colonel Toosey "quickly discovered that he faced a fresh challenge of substantial proportions". In 1969, in response to a request for information about the situation at the time of handover of command, Colonel Toosey wrote as follows to the regimental historian:

> "When I took over the regiment I discovered that it contained the best possible human material – officers, N.C.Os. and men – but was sadly lacking in technical knowledge as a Gunner unit. We had a practise camp at Sennybridge about fourteen days before we left England. The results were disastrous. At the pow-wow afterwards there was no point in detailed criticism, so I merely said that 'if people like you cannot do better than this, we shall lose the war'. The reaction was instantaneous. Later that evening the three battery commanders came to me and said that if I would train them they would work night and day; and so they did, as a result of which after a very long sea voyage they were highly efficient by the time we reached Singapore . . ."

Davies repeats much the same story, while Alexander records that ". . . his bearing went down well with the troops, and the officers soon found they could take it or leave it. The older ones departed, and everyone else now felt Toosey's keen dark eye upon their successes and failures . . . With Toosey's arrival the feeling of fiddling while Rome burned left us".

'Orders to proceed overseas' (344 Battery Diary) reached the regiment on 22nd September 1941 in conformity with the War Office intention to move 18th Infantry Division to the Middle East. There was a great deal to be done in a very short time to complete all the mobilisation procedures and prepare for embarkation. As part of the measures necessary to ensure that all vehicles were Class I (fit for action), all the Morris and Guy gun towers were relegated to Class II (fit for training use only) and replaced by Canadian-built Chevrolet 'CGT' Quads. Guns and vehicles were loaded at Liverpool about two weeks ahead of the convoy's sailing date. They were accompanied by a small maintenance party. Signals and G. 1098 stores had to be crated ready for loading on to the ship in which the regiment would sail and, as far as possible, all ranks had to be allowed embarkation leave. For many this was their second embarkation leave and they were not pleased to hear that they would have to pay their own travel costs, since only one return was admissible for embarkation leave. Fortunately, this ruling was swiftly reversed and those who had set off having paid their own fares were reimbursed on return.

On 22nd October representative parties of three officers and fifteen other ranks from each battery, together with a detachment from R.H.Q., joined the 18th Division parade for inspection by King George VI. An order to remove all distinguishing badges had been received a week earlier but officers of the regiment had ignored it and continued to wear the Hertfordshire Yeomanry's bronze hart badge below the badges of rank on the shoulder straps of their battledress. The King noticed the hart on Captain Keane's uniform and asked him what it was, receiving the reply that it was "Our Yeomanry badge". "Good", The King is reported to have said, "I am glad to see that you are still wearing it and I hope you will continue to do so", following which, according to Captain Halford-Thompson, nothing more was heard about removing them.

Bombardier Austin, promoted from lance-bombardier to acting unpaid bombardier on 28th October, recorded:

Plate 142 *'Departure from Gourock, 29th October 1941'.* (Drawing by Gunner W.C. Wilder, dated Changi, 20th April 1942)

> "In the late hours of 29th October the battery fell in, in F.S.M.O.with kit bag, sea kit bag and sun helmet in a white bag . . . We marched through Knowsley Park and the only people who waved us goodbye were the Prescot Lodge gatekeeper and his wife and family . . . 344 Battery's departure from Macclesfield was quite different. The streets were lined with well-wishers . . ."

After arriving by rail at Gourock Pier the troops boarded Clyde steamers and were ferried, in 135th Field Regiment's case to the Polish ship *Sobiesky*. Once alongside, they climbed the companion way and half-way up handed their sea kit bags, stowed with gear 'not wanted on voyage', through a door to a baggage handling party, continuing to their mess decks, which had been rigged in the holds. Loading continued all night under floodlights while the soldier-passengers were divided into messes, taught how to sling their hammocks and given orders that for the first three nights at sea they were to sleep in full kit, including greatcoats, keeping their boots handy.

*Ten weeks at sea, November 1941–January 1942*

Convoy CT5, consisting of eight troopships – all civilian liners with well known names – with seven antique destroyers as escort, sailed on 31st November. While some officers may have known 18th Division's eventual destination, the troops apparently did not. They relied on rumour and imagination, fed by a few facts. They had, after all, been issued with tropical kit; the guns and vehicles had been repainted in sandy yellow; and some crates had been stencilled 'Basra'. Resourceful as ever, the signallers read the messages flashed between ships at this stage without gaining any clues and swiftly worked out, despite the zig-zag course, that the general heading was north-westerly. A new rumour that the division would reinforce the garrison of Iceland swept round the ship! Then, on 2nd November, they met an eastbound convoy escorted by the United States Navy and exchanged escorts. At the same time, troops were allowed to undress before going to sleep. By now, the heading was westerly and the rumour-mongers put about the idea that the division would land on the east coast of the United States and cross the continent by train, though their final destination, having reached the Pacific, was not explained. The facts were soon found to be different, when the troops embarked on *Sobieski* were told that at Halifax, Nova Scotia, they would transfer to U.S.S. *Mount Vernon*, another converted liner, which would carry the whole of 53 Infantry Brigade Group. The other two brigade groups would each sail on one ship and divisional troops, together with units attached for the voyage, would take up a further three ships. *Sobieski* docked stern to stern with *Mount Vernon* and advance parties left at once to recce the new accommodation. Other ranks were not allowed ashore, though sergeants managed a walk on the dockside, while officers, on venturing into town, discovered "a God-forsaken port, suffering from near prohibition. To get a drink one had to join a 'club'. I joined four" (Captain Halford-Thompson).

Bombardier Austin describes how the Bofors anti-aircraft guns were lifted from the *Sobieski* on to the *Mount Vernon*. (The gun detachments, from the Maritime Royal Artillery, were transferred too but soon replaced by men from A Troop, who "had great fun practising on balloons", according to Captain Halford-Thompson.) Austin continues:

> "That same evening the regiment were to transfer to the *Mount Vernon*. I was given a 7-lb. tin of bully beef and a large packet of sea biscuits and instructed that when I boarded the *Mount Vernon* I was to hand both to the cooks, following the standard practice in the British Army of joining with 'the unexpired portion of the day's rations', in this case for seven men.
>
> The time came to embark. Plimsolls had to be worn and boots carried . . . at the foot of the gangplank an officer . . . gave us a berthing ticket. Mine was 'bunk number .. , promenade deck forward'. I was carrying so much gear he had to put the ticket between my teeth. We entered the ship into what looked like the foyer of a luxury hotel. [*The 25,000-ton 'Mount Vernon' was the former liner 'Washington'.*] On the left was the entrance to the dining-hall, with lifts on either side of the doors. After depositing my kit I went to the dining-hall, where a meal was waiting for us. Phew! Turkey, cranberry sauce, Brussels sprouts, stuffing, nuts, oranges, coffee-flavoured ice cream . . . what a life! It was quite obvious that the Americans were not interested in the unexpired portion of the day's rations, even supposing that I could find the galley and the cooks . . .
>
> There were three sittings for meals . . . food trays were oblong with partitions. On occasions one partition contained rice. Now up to this time none of us had had rice as a vegetable. We honestly thought that the Americans did not know how to make rice pudding. We had been at sea quite a while [*The convoy sailed on 11th November.*] before we realised that the rice was meant to go with the gravy. The American jugs of tea were not all that good but their coffee was absolutely marvellous . . .
>
> There was no supper, and the sittings were changed over regularly, so if we changed from first tea to last breakfast one was jolly hungry when breakfast time came. Taking food from the dining hall was strictly forbidden, though we did sneak frankfurter sausages and bread and butter away sometimes to have as supper in our bunks, and on one occasion seven of us shared the tin of bully beef and the biscuits for supper. We were all astonished at the amount of food that the Americans threw away . . ."

The convoy stopped for three days off Port of Spain, Trinidad, where supplies were replenished by barge, then continued, skirting the eastern coast of South America and eventually

Plate 143 *Bombardier G.D. Austin* (Left), *Gunner R. Freeman and Lance-Bombardier J. Underwood in newly-issued khaki-drill uniform at Cape Town during the voyage to Singapore, December 1941. At this stage in the voyage 135th Field Regiment was still bound for the Middle East.*
(Regimental Collection)

altering course for Cape Town. On 23rd November *Mount Vernon* crossed the Equator. There were the usual ceremonies involving King Neptune, and everybody received U.S. Navy 'Crossing the Line' certificates. Then, on 27th November, Thanksgiving Day was celebrated "with a fantastic meal". The attack on Pearl Harbour and the United States' entry into the war was announced over the ship's public address system on 8th December. The convoy called at Cape Town for four days. Here, according to Bombardier Austin:

> "We were told that we could go on shore leave straight away. There was a mad rush to get ready and down the gangway we went in our Boer War jackets and the shorts with the astonishing turn-ups, known to the troops as 'Bombay bloomers' ... Before going ashore we had instructions that when evening came we were to unbutton the large turn-up on our shorts, turn it down and tuck it into the top of our hose tops. This would prevent us being bitten by mosquitoes at night and thus getting malaria. The good citizens of Cape Town enquired as to the reason for this strange garb and when we informed them of the anti-malaria reason they fell about laughing – malaria in Cape Town! ..."

After the relaxation of the first day a routine was established; the troops went on a route march in the morning, followed by leave in the afternoon. Such training as could be arranged on board was already well under way under the direction of Brigadier Duke, commanding 53 Infantry Brigade Group. Davies, following interviews with Colonel (by then Brigadier) Toosey, records that Brigadier Duke "ensured that training schedules were rigorously enforced", that Toosey "followed his lead with much enthusiasm", and that:

> "This meant that, in addition to the compulsory physical exercises undertaken by all on board, 135th Field Regiment also took part in special courses designed to improve their skills as Gunners. These took place on 'miniature ranges' which on Toosey's initiative were constructed out of canvas in two commandeered 'empty' spaces. They became so sophisticated that it was possible to teach men how to range and fire a gun with a puff of cigarette smoke blown up through the painted canvas to show where the shell had landed! For a change, the same model could be used to demonstrate infantry tactics and such items as the value of camouflage and how to take advantage of the ground when moving.
>
> The organisation of these activities and the establishment of a daily routine took much time and concentration, so the days passed quickly. Then, as the ships reached warmer climes, swimming-pools were erected on deck and the men were able to enjoy periodic, brief dips. Toosey thought that the voyage (apart from the congestion) resembled a peace-time cruise but in spite of all efforts a feeling of boredom gradually began to emerge ..."

Much the same story can be derived from the few words Toosey wrote, without the need to explain the detail, to the regimental historian in 1969:

> "... I had a miniature range built on the ship ... The voyage was used for technical training, and a lot was done, but the men, through no fault of their own, became somewhat soft physically ..."

On 13th December the voyage was resumed. Meanwhile, however, 18th Division's destination had been changed in response to events in the Far East. It had been decided on 11th December that the division would be diverted to India and placed at the disposal of the Commander-in-Chief, India, General Sir Archibald Wavell. The convoy was now expected to reach Bombay on 31st December. General Wavell's intention was that the troops should be disembarked at Bombay and their final destination settled later. The early reverses in Malaya, and particularly the heavy losses incurred by 11th Indian Division, prompted the Commander-in-Chief Far East to ask on 16th December for immediate reinforcements from India and to warn that 18th Division would be required in Malaya. In dealing with this question of reinforcements from India, General Wavell indicated that he had no objection to 53 Brigade Group of 18th Division, which he understood to be loaded in one ship, proceeding directly to Malaya. The *Official History* explains the decisions that then had to be made:

> "The proposed diversion of 53 Brigade Group gave rise to new difficulties. The brigade was in the American transport *Mount Vernon*, sailing in convoy with the remainder of 18th

Division. This convoy was due at Bombay about 31st December, and the divisional equipment and stores during the following week. If the *Mount Vernon* remained with the convoy, it was thought necessary that she should stay at least a week at Bombay so that the troops, who had been cooped up on board for nearly two months, would be able to stretch their legs ashore before going on to Malaya. This would mean that she would not leave Bombay before 10th January and could not therefore arrive at Singapore before the 24th at the earliest. The alternative was that the *Mount Vernon* should go to Mombasa to refuel, and then join, at sea, a convoy which was leaving Durban on 24th December direct for Singapore with reinforcements. This would give the troops only two or three days ashore at Mombasa and meant that they would arrive at Singapore without their transport or guns and with the minimum of equipment. The brigade would however arrive nearly a fortnight earlier.

The first course was obviously preferable, but at the urgent request of General Percival [*G.O.C. Malaya*] the Chiefs of Staff decided on 23rd December that, despite the inherent disadvantages, the *Mount Vernon* should go direct to Singapore, subject to American approval. Two days later this was given."

As a result, when just north of Madagascar *Mount Vernon* was diverted, alone and at best possible speed, to Mombasa, where she docked on Christmas Day. Shore leave was allowed while the ship took on stores and fuel. Four days later she left on an easterly course to join the convoy from Durban. After taking on fuel and water at the Maldive Islands, the convoy continued with reinforced escort. Establishing that one of the new escort ships was H.M.S. *Durban*, in which his father, whom he had not seen for two years, was serving, Gunner Gilby of 336 Battery, egged on by his friends among the battery signallers, including Bombardier Austin, persuaded the United States Navy to send a personal message. His father was actually on duty on the signal deck of *Durban* when *Mount Vernon's* signal lamp began "To Leading Signalman Gilby from . . .". Gunner Gilby got a dressing-down for failing to ask the favour through the 'chain of command' but reckoned it was worth it! (He was killed in action in Southern Johore.)

Batteries now held muster parades at which the troops were informed that they would disembark at Singapore. It is no longer clear whether officers already knew, but by modern standards the decision to confirm what must have been the strongest rumour does seem to have been made very late.

### *Southern Johore and Singapore Island, January–February 1942*

"A combination of good luck and good timing, allied with heavy rain and low cloud, enabled *Mount Vernon* to reach Singapore without damage" (Davies). She docked late in the morning of 13th January, in the middle of a substantial air raid – ninety Japanese bombers are reported to have been overhead but the bombs fell well wide of the docks. At 14.00 officers and men of 135th Field Regiment, in 'Christmas tree order' with kitbags and small-arms, made their way down the gang-plank, to be met by a tropical deluge which lasted until the small hours of the following morning. An advance party under the second-in-command left at once for the allotted accommodation at Nee Soon transit camp. Captain McMullen, battery captain of 344 Battery, was on the advance party; he recorded in an unpublished memoir:

"We left in two lorries and fetched up at Nee Soon camp – where we found that practically nothing had been made ready for us. The tents were pitched but there was no-one to show us round, no food or cooking utensils laid on, and nothing in the way of spades, mosquito nets, tables or benches, etc.

We got the tents allotted – officers were in separate lines – and eventually got food and utensils out of an anti-aircraft unit who had a permanent camp a couple of hundred yards away. The batteries began to arrive after an hour or so – everyone soaked to the skin – and we sent them off to the canteen for a cup of tea while we got a more substantial meal ready. After a bit our baggage started to arrive and continued to do so for most of the night. Half the batmen got lost and did not turn up until next morning. This was not their fault; the drivers, who were Australians, did not know their way about and several lots went astray. The officers' baggage began arriving about 23.00 and was dumped beside the road. I collected all mine by almost mid-night – still pelting with rain – and got to bed sometime between 02.00–03.00 . . .

The next morning we spent unloading baggage, drying the men's clothes and trying to

> get the water out of the tents. They were all pitched on a slope and consequently there were several rivers running through each tent. All our packing cases were stacked in large sheds near the football field and we had our own 'Q' office and stores further towards the lines and actually adjoining the wagon lines. Regimental and battery offices were in some garages opposite the officers' lines. We [344] had collected practically all our cases by the evening. Eventually we finished up two short. Unfortunately one contained cooking utensils but we managed to make them up from stuff in the camp. Our total number of packing cases for the battery came to 213, I think."

Meanwhile, the baggage parties had spent the night on *Mount Vernon* and continued working furiously into the morning of 14th January. Their meals were served on trestle tables on the dockside as the ship prepared urgently for sea. Civilian evacuees and Royal Air Force ground staff boarded and with least possible delay *Mount Vernon* – the regiment's home for nearly three months – cast off.

At noon on 14th January the commanding officer attended a conference called by the Brigadier, General Staff of Headquarters III Indian Corps. It became clear that there were sufficient guns in Singapore to equip the regiment, but only enough vehicles to provide two batteries with a very limited scale. Colonel Toosey resisted strongly the suggestion that one battery should be relegated to an infantry role at this early stage and went straight to Command Headquarters to fix the details of the hand-over of guns and vehicles. It was arranged by tossing a coin that 336 and 344 Batteries would be the first to be re-equipped – 336 Battery with 4.5-in. howitzers and 344 Battery with 25-pdrs. These two batteries were ordered to collect guns and vehicles the following morning and to be ready for action within 48 hours.

The whole of 15th January was spent in collecting guns and vehicles and passing them at once to battery fitters and L.A.D. so that they could be prepared for action. Captain McMullen recorded that the vehicles were "pretty assorted – several good 15-cwts. but more still pretty bad, good 30-cwt. gun towers, no 8-cwts. and only five motor-cycles per battery; banana wagons for 'B' Echelon". By the end of the day, R.H.Q. had 17 vehicles and the two batteries 27 each, with eight 4.5-in. howitzers and eight 25-pdrs. This had been achieved in spite of the fact that the "vehicle and gun dumps, etc. were useless – no-one seemed to realise there was a war on and everything stopped during air raids, which were pretty frequent . . . very short of M.T. tools and spares, ditto for guns" (McMullen). Lieutenant Alexander, writing as late as 1996 (see Bibliography), seems to enjoy recording that:

> "Toosey, with his guns still in Basra, or perhaps Bombay, now had to battle not with the Japs but with the local ordnance store to get hold of some 25-pdrs. They proved elusive, and a less zealous C.O. might have been content to wait in the fleshpots of Singapore until they materialised. Stuart Simmonds [*the regimental intelligence officer and principal aide to the C.O.*] who, for all his Wildean eye for paradox, could play the martinet as well as the next man, accompanied Toosey on his almost daily journeys to Ordnance, whose staff learned to dread their approach . . ."

As far as can be established, the 4.5-in. howitzers were Mk. I on Carriage Mk. I PA and came complete with limber. The 25-pdrs. appear to have been 'real' ones – Mk. II on Carriage, 25-pdr. Mk. I – rather than 18/25-pdrs. The gun-towing vehicles were American 1½-ton Chevrolet 4 × 4 trucks, fitted with winch. They had all been modified by the addition of a thick steel plate fixed across the front bumper and sloped back at an angle to protect the radiator. Their only draw-back, according to Bombardier Austin, was that the steering lock was too wide and when towing limber and gun they lacked the manoeuvrability of the purpose-built Quad. Austin also records that each battery received its proper establishment of three carriers, though he does not specify whether they were carriers, armoured observation post or a substitute.

The last word on re-equipment and drawing of necessary stores must lie with Captain Halford-Thompson who, in 1963, wrote in a letter to the regimental historian:

> "Somewhere in your history you should record, to the eternal damnation of the War Office, that when I took the regimental map-demand to Base Ordnance Depot I was issued with a bundle of one-inch maps of the Isle of Wight (which has some superficial resemblance to Singapore Island). I never did find a decent map of Singapore."

At 18.00 on 15th January, Colonel Toosey attended an O-group at Headquarters 53 Infantry Brigade and returned with orders that the regiment, less one battery, was to be ready to move by 18th January to the area of Ayer Hitam, on the mainland and some sixty miles north-west of the causeway across the Johore Strait. A recce party consisting of the commanding officer, with his intelligence officer, and the three battery commanders, was to accompany Brigadier Duke, commanding 53 Infantry Brigade, to Ayer Hitam the following morning, starting at 06.30. Finally, on 15th January, a contingent of officers of the Federated Malay States Volunteer Force arrived for attachment to the regiment in order to act as advisers on the local situation, interpreters and liaison officers. They were distributed amongst R.H.Q. and the batteries, where they generally fitted into 'B', rather than 'F', Echelon, and at once made themselves useful. The volunteers soon became part of the regiment, with which they served throughout the campaign. To Captain McMullen's evident delight, "Williams, Malay Volunteer who joined us as interpreter, managed to get several private cars to act as staff cars".

The recce party called for 16th January duly assembled under Brigadier Duke and, with the C.O. of 5th Norfolks, went first to Headquarters III Indian Corps at Johore Bahru. Here, they met Lieutenant-General Sir Lewis Heath, commanding III Indian Corps, and noted that, with the exception of Major Smith, the G.S.O. II assigned as their guide, "all concerned seemed despondent and tired" (Regimental Diary). They then moved on to Ayer Hitam to meet Major-General B.W. Key, commanding 11th Indian Division. "On the way up, the G.S.O. II gave the party a clear description of Japanese tactics and they got for the first time a glimpse of the low morale of some of the infantry. The impression gained already that the Japanese had complete air superiority was confirmed" (Regimental Diary). On meeting General Key, Brigadier Duke "quickly put [*him*] wise to the condition of his brigade", while Colonel Toosey "reported that his guns were being serviced and were unlikely to be ready for two days" (Harrison, see Bibliography). Colonel Toosey then met C.R.A. 11th Indian Division, Brigadier Rusher, and with him the 135th Field Regiment officers all visited the headquarters of 155th Field Regiment at Kluang. Here, the Gunners decided that it would be simplest to place 155th Field Regiment in support of 53 Infantry Brigade, who had been ordered into the line at once under command of 11th Indian Division. Taking account of the fact that 135th Field Regiment would not be ready for action until 18th January, the regiment would be best placed in corps reserve, with the probable role of supporting 28 Indian Brigade when the brigade re-entered the line. To the extent that 135th Field Regiment did not feature in General Key's deployment orders for the defence of the area north of Batu Pahat issued later the same day, Brigadier Rusher's decision was confirmed. The regiment's close relationship with 53 Infantry Brigade Group, which had been developed over many months, not least during the voyage out, when all units of the brigade group were embarked in *Mount Vernon*, was thus broken. As things turned out, 135th Field Regiment would not rejoin 18th Divisional Artillery at any stage of the campaign in Malaya and Singapore.

Re-equipment and preparation for action continued throughout the following day, 17th January. There were insufficient vehicles that were properly 'fitted for wireless' and efforts were made to convert 'general service' vehicles, but they were unsuccessful, partly because aerial wire was unobtainable but principally because nothing could be done to permit charging of the wireless batteries by means of the vehicle engine. The batteries themselves may not have been at their best after three months at sea. As all kinds of kit were acquired to put the regiment on a fully mobilised footing, so that which was not suitable for local use was withdrawn. Greatcoats and battledress went back to store and a limited issue of tropical kit was made to supplement the sand-coloured clothing which the men had already drawn in England. Their 'Wolseley' helmets were withdrawn too; apart from any other consideration, they disintegrated in the rain! An issue of bush hats was allegedly frustrated by Colonel Toosey, on the grounds that he would not have 135th Field Regiment mistaken for Australians, so the regiment went into action with the choice between the 'fore-and-aft' field service cap or the steel helmet.

While all this was going on at Nee Soon, which had became notorious as the area which took the 'overs' from Japanese air raids on Sembawang airfield, a mile or so to the north, Colonel Toosey and Major Daltry made a further visit to Headquarters III Indian Corps, under direct command of which 135th Field Regiment now came. General Heath pressed for the regiment to move at once to the mainland but Colonel Toosey managed to convince the corps commander that re-equipment and preparation for action would only be achieved on time (i.e., by the morning of the following day) if the regiment stayed in one place that was within easy reach of stores and workshops. Having established that there would be no move before the morning of 18th January, Colonel Toosey was given a probable role for the regiment, which, had it been put into effect, would have seen the two gun batteries about forty miles apart on opposite sides of Johore. One was to support 28 Indian Infantry Brigade at Pontian Kechil on the south-western coast and the other 2/17th Dogras at Kota Tinggi. (The splitting of already inadequate resources and the formation of ad-hoc groupings of units was as much a feature of the campaign in Malaya and Singapore as it had been in France and Flanders prior to Dunkirk.) The acceptance at corps headquarters that the third battery (499) would fight as infantry spurred Colonel Toosey to point out once more to the staff that trained personnel were being wasted and a useful increase in fire-power ignored for the sake of a comparatively small number of vehicles. The Regimental Diary records, though, that yet again "he did not receive much encouragement". After leaving corps headquarters, the commanding officer did a preliminary reconnaissance of the Pontian Kechil area, apparently without visiting Headquarters 28 Indian Infantry Brigade, for on return to Nee Soon he was summoned to meet Brigadier Selby, the brigade commander. Brigadier Selby confirmed that both the Pontian Kechil and Kota Tinggi areas should be recced and ordered the battery supporting his brigade to come into action during the night of 18th–19th January.

Next day (18th January), while Major Banham recced Kota Tinggi for possible occupation by 336 Battery, Colonel Toosey returned to Pontian Kechil taking with him Captain Cherry, commanding C Troop, 344 Battery. Brigadier Selby ordered C Troop to be in action by that evening in a 'coast defence' role – which was interpreted as a direct fire role on the beaches – and the commanding officer and Captain Cherry carried out the necessary detailed recces. On their way back to Nee Soon they called at corps headquarters and were given additional orders to occupy Pulau Pisang, an island some 15,000 yards off the coast, as an O.P. They also recced indirect-fire gun positions on the Pontian Kechil–Skudai road. C Troop moved out of Nee Soon with a thirty-strong local defence party from 499 Battery and were in action by 02.00 on 19th January.

Major Peacock (344 Battery) recced Pontian Kechil on 19th January and was asked by C.O. 2/2nd Gurkhas to deploy D Troop near the 34th milestone (i.e., 34 miles from Johore Bahru, on the road towards Pontian Kechil). At the same time, Major Banham and his troop commanders continued detailed recces of the Kota Tinggi area, still expecting that 336 Battery would deploy there. Those who were away from Nee Soon were fortunate, for the raids on Sembawang airfield had increased both in frequency and intensity. Bombardier Martin of 499 Battery recalled many years later that:

> "The Jap planes were 'Army 97' medium bombers in perfect formations of 27 at about 20,000 feet. There were usually two such formations, sometimes three, over the island at once. They were tackled by 1934-vintage Brewster 'Buffaloes' of the R.A.F. and R.A.A.F. but they could scarcely reach that height."

By the evening of 19th January it had been decided that Nee Soon "was not a healthy place for a concentrated artillery regiment" (Regimental Diary) and orders were given for all except 499 Battery to move to hides on the mainland at dawn the following day, there to await orders for deployment. With creature comforts in mind now that action was getting closer, but on the pretext of yet another road test and 'driver training', the signallers of 336 Battery made one last trip to Nee Soon village in a carrier and stocked up with tins of pineapple, condensed milk and tea!

As ordered, 344 Battery, less C Troop, moved early on 20th January to a hide at the twelfth milestone on the Skudai–Pontian Kechil road, some three miles west of Skudai village. From here, Major Peacock recced further positions in the area of Pontian Kechil. He also ordered an O.P. to be set up on Pulau Pisang in accordance with orders received earlier from corps headquarters (see above). This O.P. was occupied by a party under Lieutenant Gamble, G.P.O. of C Troop, who were accompanied by a platoon of 2/2nd Gurkhas. The island proved to be out of wireless range of the gun position but heliograph worked well by day. Attempts to communicate with the mainland by lamp at night were met by rifle-fire from the sea. For the week that the island served as a look-out the mystery of the rifle-fire was not solved. Headquarters 28 Brigade were convinced the Japs were making preparations to land by night but only later was it established that the Royal Navy operated patrols by motor-launch. There were R.N. liaison officers at brigade headquarters and higher but at no stage had anyone seen fit to consult them; neither did they pass on details of their patrols off an Army-held coast, as might reasonably have been expected.

Meanwhile, 336 Battery moved to a hide on the Mount Austin estate at Tebrau, north of Johore Bahru and conveniently situated on the road to Kota Tinggi. From here Colonel Toosey, Major Banham and A and B Troop Commanders recced anti-tank positions that would form part of a 'boulder' blocking the approach to Johore Bahru and the causeway south-westwards down the main road from Kota Tinggi. ('Boulder' was an Indian Army jungle-warfare term for a defensive position that was part strong-point, part fire- and patrol base.) But the best news that day concerned 499 Battery. During the course of yet another visit to corps headquarters, Colonel Toosey had wrung out of the corps commander the authority for vehicles to be released so that 499 Battery could join the coming battle as Gunners. The Base Ordnance Depot took its orders from Malaya Command, however, and not directly from General Heath, who was yet another 'customer', however high-powered. Major Daltry was responsible for finally convincing Malaya Command that his battery would be more use if armed with guns, rather than rifles, and collection of vehicles and guns began that evening. That was not all, for in the absence of suitable War Department vehicles, the depot issued requisitioned manure contractors' trucks as 'G' and 'M' vehicles. It took the whole of the next day to get them into a fit state for their new use, prompting some people to wonder whether the 'Q' staff at Malaya Command had not done it on purpose in order to have the last laugh on those who had pestered them unremittingly since arriving in the command.

The first full day on the mainland passed with little to record, except an order for Colonel Toosey to report to Brigadier Selby at Headquarters 28 Brigade early the following day, 22nd January. It was not until the evening of the 22nd, however, that it transpired that not only had 28 Brigade been taken under command of 11th Indian Division, but so had 135th Field Regiment, who were ordered to make contact with H.Q.R.A. of the division at once. To everyone's relief it looked as if the regiment would fight as a unit – and a three-battery unit, at that. All would become clear, or at least as clear as those concerned could make it, at an O-group to be held at Headquarters 28 Brigade the next day (23rd January). Representatives of Headquarters 11th Indian Division and H.Q.R.A. would both be present.

Lieutenant-General Percival had made clear to his senior commanders on 21st January that he intended to hold the enemy on the line Batu Pahat–Ayer Hitam–Kluang–Mersing. The 11th Indian Division would be responsible for holding Batu Pahat and for the defence of some sixty miles of coastline running from the Sungei Batu Pahat south-eastwards to the western entry to the Johore Strait. Vital lines of communication within the division's area of responsibility were the coast road from Batu Pahat to Pontian Kechil and the road that ran inland from Pontian Kechil to join the Ayer Hitam–Johore Bahru trunk road at Skudai. After changes in command due to come into effect at midnight on 23rd–24th January, Major-General Key would have at his disposal:

*15 Indian Brigade* (Brigadier Challen), consisting of the 'British Battalion' (an amalgamation of 1st Leicesters and 2nd East Surreys), 2nd Cambs and, joining on 24th January, 5th Norfolks. 2nd Cambs were deployed for the defence of Batu Pahat and the British Battalion were 'in depth' on the coast road.

*28 Indian Brigade* (Brigadier Selby), consisting of 5/14th Punjab, 2/2nd and 2/9th Gurkhas. The 2/2nd Gurkhas were deployed at Pontian Besar and Pontian Kechil and 5/14th Punjab and 2/9th Gurkhas were on the Skudai road about three miles east of Pontian Kechil.

*53 British Brigade* (Brigadier Duke), consisting of 6th Norfolks and 3/16th Punjab. These two battalions were due to move to the coast during the night of 25th–26th January and to deploy along the coast road between Senggarang and Benut, filling a serious gap between 15 and 28 Brigades.

*Divisional Troops*, including B Company 1/14th Punjab, who were occupying and continuing to develop a 'boulder' blocking position around the 22nd milestone on the Skudai–Pontian Kechil road, and 3rd Cavalry, whose armoured cars were patrolling the coast road, especially in the 'Senggarang–Benut gap'.

Artillery resources were minimal before 135th Field Regiment's arrival. Only one battery of

155th Field Regiment was under divisional command; it was deployed in support of 15 Brigade at Batu Pahat. The divisional anti-tank regiment – 80th Anti-Tank Regiment – was deployed throughout the divisional area.

Early on 23rd January, Colonel Toosey and Major Banham met the B.M.R.A. 11th Indian Division and were informed that the likely role for 336 Battery would be along the Batu Pahat–Pontian Kechil road. Recces were to be carried out at once and Colonel Toosey was to meet the C.R.A. at Ayer Hitam. Here, the commanding officer saw General Key and Brigadier Rusher and learned of the plan to move 53 Brigade, first from Ayer Hitam to Skudai and then along the west coast road to their deployment positions between Senggarang and Benut. Meanwhile, Major Banham, Captain Halford-Thompson (A Troop) and Captain Egar (B Troop) recced the coast road north-eastwards from Pontian Kechil but did not go beyond Benut. A despatch-rider was sent to 336 Battery in their hide at Tebrau, putting them at thirty minutes' notice to move to a hide which 344 Battery would prepare alongside their own near Skudai. By this time 344 Battery, less C Troop, had been in their 12th milestone hide for four days and were well settled, as described by Captain McMullen:

> "The hide provided quite good cover but was right up against the road and the ground became very churned up. However, after a prolonged hunt . . . we decided it was the best . . . We stayed here for five days and a very wet stay it was. It pelted for several hours each day and as one only had a mosquito net and a ground sheet it was not too easy to keep one's bed, let alone oneself, dry. However, Mason did very well and built me quite a good shelter of branches, etc. We managed to find some timber and a little corrugated iron and made a more or less waterproof kitchen and officers' mess.
>
> We had patrols out night and day and one gun on the road in the anti–tank role. Throughout our time there D Troop were busy preparing the 'boulder' position at the 20th [*22nd*] milestone.
>
> R.H.Q. delivered rations to us and we sent them on to C Troop. Ammunition, etc. I drew from the R.A.S.C. who were near the 19th milestone. The rations were good, the only shortage being bread, of which there was none – biscuits were issued instead. The meat ration was absurd – about twice as much as we had in England. Nobody wanted it in the hot and sticky climate. Our big difficulty was water; we had no water cart and it all had to be fetched in containers. There were very few places where we could be sure the water was good and so it all had to be boiled. Everyone had a quinine tablet once a day – generally given out at the evening meal."

During the night of 23rd–24th January 336 Battery moved from Tebrau to their new hide at Skudai and orders were sent to 499 Battery at Nee Soon bringing them forward to the Tebrau hide the next morning.

Before dawn on 24th January Colonel Toosey's tactical headquarters were set up alongside Headquarters 28 Brigade at Pontian Kechil. Early in the morning the C.R.A. gave orders for 336 Battery to support 53 Brigade in holding the road between Senggarang and Pontian Kechil and for 499 Battery to move up to Batu Pahat and take over the support of 15 Brigade from B Battery, 155th Field Regiment, who would rejoin their regiment. On receiving his orders, Major Banham reported to Headquarters 53 Brigade, who knew nothing about the plan that 336 Battery should support them in their defence of the coast road. Major Banham remained in the vicinity of brigade headquarters, however, and was eventually accepted, together with his battery, as a bona-fide addition to 53 Brigade's firepower. Colonel Toosey himself took the orders for the support of 15 Brigade to 499 Battery in their hide at Tebrau. The battery had been given 4.5-in. howitzers by Base Ordnance Depot and their limited range would have caused significant problems at Batu Pahat, so it was decided that E Troop of 499 Battery would exchange their 4.5s for the 25-pdrs. of D Troop, 344 Battery, whose hide at Skudai 499 would pass on the way to Batu Pahat. Later in the day 499 Battery were ordered to move at 04.00 on 25th January into a hide alongside 344 Battery at the 12th milestone near Skudai, there to effect the exchange of guns.

Brigadier Duke's deployment plan provided for 6th Norfolks (less A Company) to garrison Senggarang, supported by A Squadron, 3rd Cavalry, one section of A Troop, 336 Battery and a section of 287 Field Company, Royal Engineers, and for Rengit to be held by A Company, 6th Norfolks supported by the other section of A Troop. Brigade Headquarters would be located at Benut, which would be defended by 3/16th Punjab supported by C Squadron, 3rd Cavalry,

336 Battery (less A Troop) and 287 Field Company (less one section). Between 03.00 and 04.30 on 25th January 336 Battery left their hide on the Pontian Kechil–Skudai road and joined the 53 Brigade column as it passed. Captain Halford-Thompson was to command the section at Senggarang with 2nd Lieutenant Boult as G.P.O., while the section at Rengit would be commanded by Lieutenant Raynor with Lieutenant Stebbing as G.P.O. The head of the column reached Benut at about 04.00 and after a pause of some two hours 6th Norfolks and their supporting armoured cars, artillery and engineers moved on towards Rengit and Senggarang. By 08.00, Headquarters 53 Brigade had received a wireless report that the commanding officer of 6th Norfolks had reached Senggarang without incident. The same was not true, however, of the tail of his column – the rearmost platoon of 6th Norfolks, the section of A Troop and the engineer section – who had been ambushed some eight hundred yards short of the village. In the initial burst of fire, at least a dozen men of the Norfolks, including the platoon commander, were killed. As soon as he heard firing, Captain Halford-Thompson, who had gone into the village to recce a hide for the guns, turned his carrier round and sped back down the road. At the same time, Sergeant Leech of the Volunteer Armoured Car Company, who was escorting a follow-up convoy of ammunition vehicles, hurried forward. They arrived together at opposite ends of the "tragic shambles" (Harrison) and Sergeant Leech at once engaged the enemy, who were maintaining heavy fire from machine-guns and a mortar, with his own machine-gun. Under cover of this fire, Captain Halford-Thompson approached the leading gun and, finding that it was relatively unscathed, ordered the No. 1 to move down the road towards Senggarang and to come into action facing the scene of the ambush. He then went to the G truck, which was upside-down in the roadside ditch, and ascertained that 2nd Lieutenant Boult (whose 21st birthday it was) and his driver had both been killed. Next, still under heavy fire, he crossed the road to the second gun, which had also come to rest in the ditch. The No. 1 and another member of the detachment had been killed and several of the five surviving members wounded. Captain Halford-Thompson later recorded:

> "My excellent driver kept his head and managed to turn the carrier round and, under heavy fire . . . drew up alongside the upturned gun tower. The armour on a carrier is really wafer-thin and the Jap fire was making this one look like a colander by this time. We hastily bundled the survivors into and on to the carrier and, since one of the tracks had been hit [*practically destroyed by mortar-fire, according to Harrison*], limped away towards Senggarang. I then tried using the remaining 4.5-in. howitzer. It had rubber tyres and it was impossible to dig in the trail on the road. In consequence the gun bounced like a toy when fired. By this time some Norfolks had appeared and begun skirmishing in the area of the lost gun . . ."

Despite the difficulties in laying, the fire of the remaining gun was effective in silencing the enemy for a while and the follow-up convoy, carrying much-needed ammunition, was able to get through to Senggarang. Sergeant Leech then loaded more wounded into his armoured car, which reached Senggarang unscathed. On arrival he was ordered to escort a lorry loaded with wounded back to Pontian Kechil and while passing the scene of the earlier ambush was again attacked. He showed great gallantry in once more rescuing numbers of wounded and placing them in and on his armoured car, which he then used, moving at walking pace, to shield walking wounded who took cover on the 'lee side'. For his actions Sergeant Leech received the Distinguished Conduct Medal, while Captain Halford-Thompson's bravery at the first ambush forms the major part of the recommendation for his Military Cross.

Meanwhile, Lieutenant Raynor's section had arrived at Rengit, where they were dive-bombed and machine-gunned. During the morning Colonel Toosey visited Rengit and returned to Benut with the news that the garrison was well under strength because at least one platoon had failed to stop in Rengit and was now bottled up with the rest of 6th Norfolks in Senggarang. Furthermore, not only had the enemy cut the road immediately south-east of Senggarang but he was clearly in process of doing so just north-west of Rengit as well. On hearing this report, Brigadier Duke instructed Colonel Toosey to return to Rengit with a company of 3/16th Punjab to reinforce the garrison and with orders to Captain Campbell-Orde, commanding A Company, 6th Norfolks to attack north-westwards, supported by one of Lieutenant Raynor's guns, and clear the road. The attack was mounted early in the afternoon and the single gun fired 42 rounds, but the enemy were dispersed only temporarily. Indeed, not only did they seem to have a firm hold on the road out of Rengit towards Senggarang, but they were now reported on the road back to Benut as well.

While these efforts were being made to clear the road out of Rengit, Lieutenant-General Percival was holding a conference with Lieutenant-General Heath (III Corps), Major-General Gordon-Bennett (8th Australian Division) and Major-General Key (11th Indian Division). Here, taking account of representations from Generals Heath and Key that, in the face of such strong threats to their withdrawal routes, 15 Indian Brigade should be ordered to leave at once, General Percival decided upon a withdrawal across the whole Southern Johore front, by pre-arranged bounds, to Singapore Island. The date on which the last troops would cross the causeway was provisionally fixed as 31st January. Late that afternoon the codeword for withdrawal from Batu Pahat reached Headquarters 15 Indian Brigade and Brigadier Challen ordered the withdrawal to begin at 20.30. It had been arranged that he would take under temporary command the detachments of 53 Brigade at Senggarang and Rengit as he withdrew down the coast road to his destination, Benut.

At 06.00 on 26th January, 15 Indian Brigade reported that they had cleared Koris Corner, just over half-way between Batu Pahat and Senggarang. But the coast road was very far from being the open corridor, held by 53 Brigade, that had been intended. Still without news of his troops at Senggarang and Rengit, Brigadier Duke visited Rengit at 08.00 to establish the situation there, returning to his headquarters at Benut an hour later. The mixed Norfolks/Punjab garrison was holding the village but the road to Senggarang was held by the enemy. He had ordered a further attack, supported by the two guns of A Troop, to clear the road. By the time General Key reached Benut at 10.30 there was still no news from Senggarang, and no sign of progress out of Rengit.

The divisional commander accordingly decided to open the road to Senggarang using a special column. He did not wish to bring up any troops from divisional reserve (28 Indian Brigade), so Brigadier Duke assembled a scratch force based on a draft of 112 reinforcements for 6th Norfolks which had just reached Benut. Though nominally of company strength, the draft was not organised or trained to operate as a company and lacked automatic weapons and 2-in. mortars. In support of this 'company' were detailed a troop of the Volunteer Armoured Car Company, two carriers of 3/16th Punjab and two of 6th Norfolks, a section of B Troop, 336 Battery, a detachment of 287 Field Company, Royal Engineers and a number of motor ambulances for the eventual evacuation of 15 Brigade's casualties. The column was placed under command of Major Banham of 336 Battery and designated 'Bancol'. On arrival at Rengit, Bancol would be reinforced for the advance on Senggarang by A Company, 6th Norfolks and Lieutenant Raynor's section of A Troop. Major-General Key gave orders that Bancol was to open the road as far as Senggarang; there the column would come under Brigadier Challen's command for the return journey to Benut. Harrison records that General Key 'suggested' that beyond Rengit the infantry, who had lorries available, should advance on foot, with close support from the armoured cars and continuous artillery support from the two sections, which should advance by 'leap-frog' bounds (a well established method of ensuring that some guns were always 'on the ground' and within range of likely targets). Brigadier Duke was responsible for giving Major Banham his detailed briefing and orders.

The column left Benut at 12.30 and reached Rengit without incident. Here it was joined by A Company, 6th Norfolks, under Captain Campbell-Orde, who took command of the whole infantry component. After "ascertaining the situation" (Harrison), which should have included the news that a road-block was known to exist about half a mile from the village and that a platoon attack had failed to clear it earlier in the day, Major Banham ordered the column to advance. It was still led by three armoured cars, followed by the draft 'company', still in their lorries but with orders to debus and deploy if fired upon. The column had not gone more than two hundred yards when the leading armoured car was engaged by the enemy. All three armoured cars of the advanced guard returned fire and kept moving; the leading gun came into action and the infantry debussed into the ditch. After six casualties had been sustained, the enemy fire died away and Major Banham gave the order for the infantry to re-embus and for the column to move on. They had not covered more than a few hundred yards, however, before they encountered a road-block that could not be pushed aside by the armoured cars, two of which were holed by armour-piercing bullets. Fire was now opened from both sides of the road, as far back as the scene of the previous attack, and within two minutes the column was shattered. The infantry were mown down while still in their lorries – of the 112 reinforcements only eighteen survived. Attempts were made to bring the guns into action and return fire over open sights. Possibly only one was actually unhooked and it is not clear whether it was under the immediate orders of Lieutenant Raynor or Lieutenant Stebbing. As casualties fell fast among the detachment, it was ordered out of action and did succeed in reaching Rengit; both officers were killed. Another gun was saved by the initiative, bravery and skill of Bombardier Thompson of B Troop, who:

> "... when his driver had been killed and two sergeants mortally wounded, assumed command. He unlimbered the gun, climbed into the driving seat of the towing vehicle and manoeuvred it about on the extremely narrow road under continual fire. He then hooked in the gun, loaded the vehicle to its fullest capacity with wounded and unwounded Gunners and Infantry and drove back, huddling down below the armour with the side door slightly open to allow him to see the road through the gap between the door hinges ..." (Harrison).

The cool courage with which he saved the gun and many lives was eventually recognised by a Mention-in-Despatches.

Harrison records that Major Banham surveyed the dreadful scene on the road from his 'command post' – a carrier of 3/16th Punjab – and decided that it was his duty to reach Brigadier Challen and warn him of the likely opposition on the road between Senggarang and Rengit. The carrier commander, Naik (Corporal) Bakhtawar Singh, and driver, Lance-Naik Naranjan Singh, with whom Major Banham had no common language, responded with alacrity and considerable skill and drove through a hail of bullets to surmount the first obstacle – the road-block, built of logs and tar-barrels – in what would prove to be a nightmare steeplechase.

By now the greater part of 15 Brigade was concentrated in and around Senggarang, where Captain Halford-Thompson and his single gun were in action in support of the defenders of the southern outskirts of the village. Several attempts had been made to clear the first block on the road towards Rengit, none of them successful, and in the early afternoon Brigadier Challen was about to issue orders for a further attack by two battalions, when:

> "... suddenly, like a slow-motion picture of Reynoldstown jumping Becher's, a carrier topped the road-block, balanced precariously for a split second, tipped forward, landed safely and raced on ... It was Banham, or rather, it was Lance-Naik Naranjan Singh with his two passengers. This young Sikh driver had charged, hurdled or skidded round three major and three minor road-blocks in a hair-raising journey and, as a result of his gallantry, skill and perseverance, he had delivered Major Banham and Naik Bakhtawar Singh safely at Senggarang, his appointed destination." (Harrison)

Major Banham joined the brigade commander's O-group and reported that his carrier had 'blitzed' through or round six road-blocks. Only at the first – the nearest to Rengit – had he been fired on from the front. The others were all facing to meet troops moving from Senggarang towards Rengit. Brigadier Challen interrupted the O-group to confer alone with Major Banham, who described how strongly the road was held and expressed the opinion that wheeled vehicles would stand no chance of getting through the following day, especially in view of the number of derelict Bancol vehicles on the road. He further reported that Rengit was under attack as he left and told what he knew of the plans for withdrawal to the island, including the fact that the causeway would be blown in two or three days' time. Brigadier Challen then determined that, faced with the choice between fighting his way down the road in an effort to save some of his guns and vehicles, but undoubtedly at the cost of casualties, or abandoning guns and vehicles and avoiding battle by marching across country to rejoin 11th Indian Division, he would choose the latter. There followed a furious period of preparation for the trek, including the destruction of guns and vehicles. A Troop's remaining 4.5-in. howitzer could not be blown up because, according to Captain Halford-Thompson's memoir, "the village was by now full of wounded", so the detachment dropped the breech block in the river and carried the sights with them when they left. Leaving their wounded in the care of volunteers from 198 Field Ambulance, Brigadier Challen's 15 Indian Brigade started their journey towards the British lines at 18.15.

Captain Halford-Thompson described how he managed to get out of Senggarang and eventually rejoin 336 Battery at Benut:

"The sea was not far off and our party – Cecil Banham, our gunners and some Norfolks who attached themselves to us – did a recce towards the coast. It became very heavy going in the mangrove swamps. I was most disconcerted to have a 2-pound fish drop on my head from a mangrove. This was a climbing fish, of which we saw many more. Some who persevered towards the coast were lucky enough to be picked up by the Royal Navy in launches. We decided to cross the main road and stick to the land route. We came to a kampong [*village*] where the Malays were friendly and gave us water but the headman asked us to move on as quickly as possible as the Japanese were coming shortly to requisition all the bicycles in the kampong. We came to quite a substantial river and had to be ferried over it in canoes. Eventually, after about twelve hours we reached Benut . . ."

The Regimental Diary records the arrival of this party at Benut "during the late afternoon" of 27th January and estimates that they may have covered 25–30 miles on foot.

At Rengit, where the garrison consisted of a depleted company of 3/16th Punjab and two platoons of A Company, 6th Norfolks, backed by three guns of 336 Battery, all three survivors of Bancol and apparently without officers, Japanese pressure increased as the day (26th January) wore on. A concentrated attack on the headquarters area around the water-tower developed at about 15.30 after some two hours of mortaring and sniping. Towards evening, as the attack died down, a party of volunteers in a carrier and a truck left in an attempt to break through to Benut with a report on the situation in Rengit. Only two of the party reached Headquarters 53 Brigade and after hearing their report Brigadier Duke decided to make his way along the road towards Rengit to see for himself. He did so, accompanied by Colonel Toosey, in an armoured car of the Volunteer Armoured Car Company which was driven in reverse. They were prevented from further progress by a strong road-block about 1,200 yards south-east of Rengit, so they returned to Benut and Colonel Toosey went at once to Headquarters 11th Indian Division to report the situation. "There was", records Harrison, "little of value and nothing of cheer in the information which he was able to give". The Rengit detachment had seen no sign of 15 Indian Brigade and was itself closely engaged, cut off and out of communication with Benut, which was less than ten miles away.

The enemy continued to attack Rengit until midnight. The Norfolks' platoons north of the village were driven back to the water-tower with some losses but a determined attack on the tower at 20.30 was held, though the enemy got within thirty yards and a grenade battle followed in which casualties mounted steadily. A mortar bomb landed through the narrow doorway of the tower, which had been selected by Captain Pitt, Medical Officer of 135th Field Regiment, as his regimental aid post, and killed most of the wounded. By midnight it was evident that the 3/16th Punjab positions to the west of the village had been overrun and in the face of mounting casualties and dwindling ammunition, Lieutenant Calder, who had taken over command when Captain Campbell-Orde was wounded, decided that guns and vehicles should be disabled and the defenders should make their way to Benut. They crawled out along the roadside ditch at 01.00 on 27th January.

Headquarters 53 Brigade at Benut was now, for practical purposes, in the front line. The brigade was reduced to less than one battalion – 3/16th Punjab – supported by the last two guns of 336 Battery, the remaining section of B Troop, now under command of Captain Neal, Battery Captain of 336 Battery, who had been ordered forward from the battery's B Echelon in the hide near Skudai. Against the possibility that additional fire support would be required to cover withdrawal by elements of 53 Brigade, a section of C Troop, 344 Battery (25-pdrs.) was moved forward to the northern outskirts of Pontian Kechil.

Following orders from III Indian Corps that 11th Indian Division could withdraw from Benut after dark on 27th January (but retain its hold on Pontian Kechil), Brigadier Duke was given discretion to destroy the bridge at Benut and was ordered to hold the village until dawn on 28th January and then withdraw in stages to the Boulder Position, where his troops would form the divisional reserve. The withdrawal to Singapore Island was now clearly 'on' but firm orders or information were extremely hard to come by. Captain Lord De Ramsey, Battery Captain of 499 Battery, was ordered to return to the island to recce and prepare a harbour area for the regiment at the Island Golf Club. He was to move to the island at 15.00 unless ordered to the contrary in the meantime. As he was about to leave, a motor contact officer arrived with instructions that on no account was he to cross the causeway until he had obtained the precise location of the regimental harbour area from Headquarters III Corps. There followed three hours, not of the usual 'order, counter-order, disorder', but of complete absence of information or instructions after "futile encounters with staff officers who should have known" (Regimental Diary). Only after he had managed to corner the C.C.R.A. himself, was De Ramsey able to get definite orders to return to the island, where he would be able to obtain the precise location of the harbour area from rear corps headquarters.

It was as well that 53 Brigade had been ordered to remain in Benut throughout 27th January, for parties of men from Rengit arrived throughout the day – Lieutenant Calder's party, including men of 336 Battery, reached Benut soon after Captain Halford-Thompson's, described above. The first news of substantial elements of 15 Indian Brigade reached Benut soon after 18.00. Some 1,200 men had got to within about three miles and were resting, greatly exhausted, the other side of the Benut river. It was clearly important to keep the bridge open and Brigadier Duke was ordered to stand fast, retaining control of the bridge, until the party arrived. Then, at about 22.30, news reached divisional headquarters from Pontian Kechil that the brigade major of 15 Brigade had arrived there by sampan. He reported that another party were gathered on the coast some three miles north-west of Rengit. Arrangements were at once made for them to be taken off by the Royal Navy. In an effort to make himself useful, the ever-inventive Lieutenant Laing of 336 Battery took some men down to the mouth of the Benut river, where they built a huge bonfire as a beacon for naval craft and generally assisted as boatloads of evacuees arrived. The O.P. party from 344 Battery were still on Pulau Pisang and rendered valuable assistance to the Royal Navy by acting as a signal station. For his part in this operation, Sergeant Edwards, signals sergeant of 344 Battery was later mentioned in despatches. The evacuation of at least 1,500 men by sea took place over several nights. A large number of men managed to reach our lines as a result of their own endurance and initiative, rather than through the organised evacuation. Captain Egar, Troop Commander of B Troop, who had been forced to take to the roadside ditch with his carrier driver, Lance-Bombardier Castro, when Bancol was attacked, had reached Senggarang but had not joined up with Captain Halford-Thompson's party. Together, they commandeered a sampan on reaching the coast and gained 499 Battery's position on the Pontian Kechil–Skudai road during the afternoon of 28th January, each with stories of how he had prevented the other from drinking sea water in desperation.

During the night of 27th–28th January, Japanese patrols had approached the outposts of the defending battalion, 3/16th Punjab, at Benut but had made no attempt to press an attack. The bridge over the Benut river was blown at 07.30 and at 09.00 the two guns of B Troop with their command trucks – H and Y of battery headquarters – both "well loaded and sagging somewhat at the rear" (Austin), were ordered out of action. As they pulled out on to the Pontian Kechil road on the way to the regimental harbour area at Yio Chiu Kang – some distance from the golf course and known to all as 'Y.C.K.' – they heard a huge explosion as their dumped ammunition, which had been prepared for demolition by the Royal Engineers several days earlier, was blown up.

From 28th January until the whole regiment had crossed the causeway, there was significant activity as the withdrawal from Pontian Kechil to Skudai took place ('Forward') and as the deployment on the island gradually progressed ('Rear'). Major Pilling, Second-in-Command, had first been to Singapore with a party detailed by H.Q.R.A. 11th Indian Division during the afternoon of 26th January. Such orders as the party had received were "somewhat obscure" (Regimental Diary) but did eventually result in an indication of the sector allotted to the division for the defence of the island, but apparently no directions as to gun areas. About 48 hours later, Major Pilling was able to convey some very good news to Forward R.H.Q. and the batteries – the ship carrying the regiment's own guns and vehicles had now reached Singapore. Between them, Colonel Toosey and Major Pilling worked to ensure that both guns and vehicles reached the regiment and did not get dispersed in penny-packets as replacements for other units. By about 13.00 on 28th January the arrangements had been agreed and personnel of 336 Battery formed parties to reclaim the guns, under Captain Halford-Thompson, and the vehicles, under Lieutenant Laing. All the guns had to go through the base workshops for overhaul, starting first thing on 29th January.

Early on 28th January orders were received at forward headquarters that all troops in Johore would withdraw across the causeway during the night of 30th–31st January. On the western side of the peninsula 11th Indian Division was made responsible not only for conducting its own withdrawal along the Pontian Kechil–Skudai road but for holding 'Skudai corner' the junction with the trunk road to Ayer Hitam, until all troops on both roads had safely passed through. The division would then withdraw through two defensive lines, the inner line manned by the scratch 'Plymouth-Argyll' battalion, who were to become widely known as 'the last troops to cross the causeway'. In conformity with this plan, General Key ordered 28 Indian Brigade to hold Pontian Kechil until dusk on 29th January and then move back to a position astride the Skudai road at the 27th milestone, south of the Boulder Position. The northern, or right flank of both the 27th milestone position and the Boulder Position would be secured by the 3rd Cavalry, who would patrol the high ground of Gunong Pulai and the area of the Gunong Pulai reservoir. The almost totally depleted 53 Brigade, which had withdrawn from Benut to the Boulder Position the previous day, was to move to Singapore Island on the night of 29th–30th January.

The withdrawal of 28 Brigade from Pontian Kechil to Skudai Corner – a distance of just under thirty miles by road – would require considerable skill and co-ordination, especially if pressed by the enemy, and Colonel Toosey resolved that 135th Field Regiment would play a full part. Referring to "Toosey's tactics" along the Skudai road, Davies states:

> "The positions [*the guns*] successively occupied had been previously selected but there had been no time to undertake physical preparations. So far as possible they were sited at the southern end of forest clearings, so that when the Japanese emerged from the north, usually on bicycles, they presented an easy target . . . Then, once the initial thrust had been stopped, most of the guns were withdrawn to the next position with only one or two retained to deceive the enemy. These tactics proved to be quite successful in the circumstances; a large number of Japanese were killed and the pace of the advance was restricted to more manageable proportions. In addition, the reduction in the number of haphazard and unscheduled moves resulted in some limited relief for the already tired troops . . ."

But this passage is misleading, describing, as it does, an orthodox 'backward leapfrog' and while the "reduction in the number of haphazard and unscheduled moves" may have been welcome, 344 and 499 Batteries could hardly be described as "tired troops" – they had not yet fired a shot. What was important was that Colonel Toosey had ensured that B.Cs. and O.P. officers made proper contact with the battalions they were to support and engendered confidence while carrying out recces and making joint plans. This, 'silent registration' and the laying of miles of telephone cable in the four or five days between the batteries' arrival and the first Japanese probes against Pontian Kechil, was what made the difference between the piecemeal (and unsuccessful, however gallant) commitment of 336 Battery on the coast road and the near-text-book operations of 344 and 499 in the withdrawal to Skudai Corner.

At 09.00 on 29th January, according to the Regimental Diary, the enemy made contact with the outposts of 2/2nd Gurkhas at the 41st milestone, north of Pontian Besar. An ambush had

Plate 144 *'4.5-in. howitzer in action in Malaya, January 1942'. The scene, drawn from memory, shows one of the guns of D Troop, 344 Battery in action in the grounds of a girls' school at Pontian Kechil, 29th January 1942.* (Drawing by Gunner W.C. Wilder, dated Changi, April 1942).

in fact been laid on the coast road by a platoon of D Company, with fire support from D Troop, 344 Battery, and the procedures had been rehearsed. Unfortunately the ambush position was given away to the enemy by what appears to have been careless movement and the Japanese by-passed it. Two hours later D Company's main positions half a mile north of Pontian Besar were closely engaged with enemy parties attempting to advance between the road and the sea – possibly driven off the road by fire from D Troop, whose 4.5-in. howitzers were lined up across the balconied front of the girls' school at Pontian Besar. Sergeant Last described D Troop's first action:

> "Then at 09.15 came our first turn into action. We opened fire and continued at intervals until 17.45, firing one hundred rounds per gun. We were all fairly excited, for at one time we were on Charge 1. As the Jap planes came over to look for us we would stop firing and start again as soon as they were out of sight. It was a welcome relief to see Gunner Stan Keeble, our cook, come round with a dish of tea about noon. Some corned beef and biscuits went down well with this. Gosh, didn't we love to see old Keeble and his tea pail and hear his shout, 'Get your mess tins ready' . . . During some of the breaks we would tidy up round the guns and talk amongst ourselves. We would compare our firing here with the firing camps in England. Then our C.O. or the B.C. would come round and visit us, and we would ask them how the other troops were getting on. It may sound funny but we could never get to know what was going on apart from our own little circle . . ." (N.O.K. Newsletter).

Harrison suggests that D Troop's harassing of the road into Pontian Kechil from the north "imposed a salutary caution on the enemy", citing evidence given by isolated parties making their way back from Rengit and Senggarang and the fact that the troops holding Pontian Besar – 2/2nd Gurkhas – were "not in any way pressed up to 16.00, when they withdrew in accordance with the timed programme". D Troop came out of action at about 18.00 and C Troop an hour later, both troops joining the column that was to cross the causeway that night, 29th–30th January. The decision to halve the already reduced fire support available to 28 Indian Brigade, whose three battalions could now call only on 499 Battery, is curious and may not have been made by Colonel Toosey. There were certainly conflicting priorities. Traffic back to Singapore was slow and delays in hides north of the causeway considerable, since the crossing could only be made safely under cover of darkness. It was necessary, too, to get the batteries back to Singapore, rearmed with their own 25-pdrs. and deployed as part of the island defences. Fortunately 28 Brigade's role was to impose sufficient delay – now down to 36 hours – to allow the forces withdrawing through Skudai Corner to reach the causeway, and not to fight a prolonged defensive action on a 'stop line'.

By dark on 29th January, 5/14th Punjab had withdrawn from Pontian Kechil under cover of the guns of 499 Battery. Line had been laid from E Troop's position near the 26th milestone and Captain Keane, Troop Commander of E Troop, had accompanied the rearguard company as F.O.O. It did not prove necessary to call for fire and 5/14th Punjab moved through the next defensive position, held by 2/2nd and 2/9th Gurkhas, astride the road at the 27th milestone, and into brigade reserve a mile or so behind. At midnight General Key arrived at Colonel Toosey's forward headquarters close to E Troop's position with first-hand intelligence that the enemy were concentrating in the area of the water tower south-west of Pontian Kechil. This

Plate 145 *Members of D Troop, 344 Battery at Pontian Kechil, January 1942. This remarkable photograph was taken by Gunner G. Hawkwood, who managed to conceal the film throughout his two-and-a-half years as a prisoner of the Japanese and have it developed and printed on arrival in Britain.* (Regimental Collection)

Plate 146 *Sergeant Burns* (holding shovel) *of 344 Battery with his detachment, January 1942. It is not known how this photograph survived but it may have been on the same film as Plate 145.* (Regimental Collection)

target was out of range, so a section of E Troop (25-pdrs.) moved forward about a mile and a half and engaged it at extreme range – 13,200 yards. Meanwhile, the parties recovering the guns and vehicles had made good progress and Major Pilling had been given deployment areas for two batteries that would fit in with 11th Indian Division's sector, shortly to be occupied. The first two batteries to deploy would go into action immediately north of the Mandai–Nee Soon road and working parties, largely provided by 336 Battery, were detailed to start work the following morning, so that the positions could be occupied during the night of 30th–31st January.

It was perhaps around this time, possibly a day or so earlier, that Lieutenant Simmonds, the Intelligence Officer, had occasion to observe the attempts to sustain normality that were a feature of the short campaign. Alexander records that, following a visit from Colonel Toosey's forward headquarters, on the other side of the strait, to Headquarters Malaya Command at Fort Canning in Singapore, Simmonds decided to treat himself to dinner at Raffles Hotel before returning. Here:

> "His appearance in sweaty field kit caused consternation to the maitre d'hotel, but he was ushered to a corner behind some palms, well away from the band; and just to make quite sure he would not disconcert the diners in white tuxedos and mess kit, two more waiters appeared and delicately adjusted some screens round his table."

The final withdrawal of 28 Indian Brigade to Skudai Corner and thence across the causeway was, according to Harrison, "singularly uneventful", and "the timed leap-frog withdrawal in four bounds to Skudai Corner, which was to be denied to the enemy until midnight, proceeded undisturbed . . ." The Regimental Diary discloses a day of rather more activity. At 04.00 on 30th January Brigadier Selby briefed Colonel Toosey on the events of the previous evening and the early hours of the morning. There had been some contact with the enemy on the 'Waterworks Track', which ran through the jungle to the north of the Skudai road and the 3rd Cavalry patrols in the area of the Gunong Pulai reservoir had withdrawn, leaving this flank unprotected. In the face of the likelihood that the Japanese would use the track to outflank 28 Brigade and cut the road behind them, posing a serious threat to the guns, Brigadier Selby considered that as few guns as possible should be left in action in order to minimise the risk of them being cut off. The section of 4.5-in. howitzers of F Troop at the 20th milestone was accordingly sent back to Singapore at 06.00 and was replaced by one section of 25-pdrs. of E Troop, withdrawn from the position at the 26th milestone. At 09.00 the enemy began to probe the defences at the 27th milestone and were immediately engaged by the supporting section of E Troop, who fired intermittently until about 15.00, when contact was broken, with the infantry withdrawing to the Boulder Position and the two guns directly to Singapore. Only one section of E Troop now remained in action, at the 20th milestone. Telephone cable had been laid beside the road and Captain Keane, who left the Boulder Position with the infantry rearguard, was able to tap in at intervals as targets appeared – "constantly", according to the Regimental Diary. The section at the 20th milestone remained in action until 23.30, by which time only an armoured car screen remained between them and the enemy. They then withdrew with the commanding officer to the island, crossing the causeway at 01.00.

At the gun position on the Mandai Road work had proceeded all day. A large part of the effort had been devoted to clearing fields of fire, for the guns were to be deployed in a rubber plantation; some 70–80 trees had to be felled on each troop position. Eight of the regiment's own guns had been released from base workshops the previous evening and were collected at once but "owing to the chaotic state of the traffic, these guns were continually held up and diverted and did not reach the wagon lines until the early hours of the next morning" (Regimental Diary). On arrival they were handed over to 344 Battery, who carried out a daylight recce of the position which had been prepared for them, prior to occupation the same night. Digging in began as soon as the troop positions were occupied and the logs felled during the day were put to good use in the construction of overhead cover. The next morning (31st January), the remaining sections of 499 Battery arrived and the battery's guns were exchanged as more of the regiment's 25-pdrs. "trickled in" (McMullen) throughout the day, enabling 499 Battery to occupy their previously prepared position after dark. By the following morning (1st February), 344 and 499 Batteries were well established, with dug-in command posts, and three hundred rounds per gun had been dumped, but despite various promises it had not proved possible to recover all the regiment's vehicles. Owing to the need to replace casualties, 336 Battery were the last to rearm and had not yet deployed.

The island of Singapore had been divided into three 'areas'. The Northern Area, to be held by 11th Indian and 18th British Divisions under command of Headquarters III Indian Corps, stretched from a point just east of the causeway to the mouth of the Sungei Serangoon; from there round Changi Point and along the south coast to the Sungei Jurong constituted the Southern Area, held by 1 and 2 Malaya Brigades and the Straits Settlements Volunteer Force Brigade; the remainder of the coastline, right round to and inclusive of the causeway, formed the Western Area held by 8th Australian Division (two brigades) reinforced by 44 Indian Brigade. The 11th Indian Division, now reduced to 15 and 28 Indian Brigades was assigned the western part of Northern Area. From a point a few hundred yards east of the causeway the frontage on the Johore Strait extended round the Naval Base as far as the mouth of the Sungei Seletar. The divisional area was between five and six miles deep with the southern boundary just touching the Peirce Reservoir and running westwards towards Bukit Panjang. Initially, General Key deployed 28 Indian Brigade to hold the coast from near the causeway to the Naval Base and 15 Indian Brigade from the Naval Base to Sungei Seletar, a total distance of about 12,500 yards. The divisional reserve, located at Sembawang airfield, was 2/9th Gurkhas, detached from 28 Brigade. Harrison describes the reduced 28 Brigade's dispositions on 31st January as follows:

> "... 28 Indian Brigade held the six thousand yards of sea-front between the Dockyard [*the Naval Base*] and the causeway. B Company of 1/14th Punjab held the small bay west of the Dockyard and 2/2nd Gurkhas, with a machine-gun company of 9th R. Northumberland Fusiliers, covered the rest of the front, their left flank connecting with the right flank of 2/30th Battalion of 27 Australian Brigade four hundred yards east of the causeway. The 5/14th Punjab were in brigade reserve near the Naval Commander-in-Chief's house south of the Dockyard. The 135th Field Regiment (less 336 Battery which was refitting) with 4 Mountain Battery (now equipped with two 6-in. guns), under Lieutenant-Colonel Toosey's command, and one troop of 273 Anti-Tank Battery were in support of this sector. The 135th Field Regiment had the particular role of harassing the mouth of the Sungei Skudai and Johore Bahru; Colonel Toosey had also been ordered to answer calls from 27 Australian Brigade."

The next day the division was reinforced by 8 Indian Brigade, which was placed in divisional reserve astride the Naval Base–Nee Soon road just north of Sembawang airfield. The arrival of 8 Brigade enabled 2/9th Gurkhas to rejoin 28 Brigade, where they occupied the right of the brigade frontage and released the company of 1/14th Punjab to come under command of 5/14th Punjab, the brigade reserve battalion.

During the morning of 1st February, Colonel Toosey visited the regiment's O.Ps. On the right, 499 Battery were able to use a water-tower on the edge of the Naval Base, while 344 Battery, on the left, occupied a partially completed building overlooking the causeway. The Regimental Diary notes that while both positions offered excellent observation, "they were very obvious O.Ps." The two batteries also deployed F.O.Os. on the water's edge. Registration of likely targets and D.F. and S.O.S. tasks began and a counter-battery office was established at forward headquarters, the O.Ps. being urged to send in all possible scraps of information about likely enemy gun- and mortar positions. The next day (2nd February) registration of the

D.F. and S.O.S. tasks was completed and Colonel Toosey again visited the O.Ps. and called for fire on selected targets. Deployment orders for 336 Battery were received during the day and Major Banham made a detailed recce of an area south of Nee Soon in preparation for the arrival of his reconstituted battery. Their role was as yet "very indefinite – consisting largely of being prepared to support two separate brigades, 28 Brigade and 8 Brigade" (Regimental Diary).

In his history of 11th Indian Division, Harrison described the days of preparation prior to the Japanese invasion of the island:

> "Throughout its first eight days on the Island, from 31st January to 7th February, the division was hard at work 'getting set'. There was an enormous amount of work to be done, as the construction of shore defences, support lines, gun positions, defensive and tactical wire, underwater obstacles, and so on had been completely neglected since Singapore had been selected as the great Naval Base of the British Empire in the Far East fourteen years previously.
>
> The infantry slaved at the construction of defences, for which the divisional commander had laid down an order of priority. In the marshy area of the right sector and the concreted area of the Naval Base digging was impossible and stockades of sandbags revetted with galvanised iron sheets had to be built. All posts, including gun positions, were laid out for all-round defence; forward and support lines were built and wire was hurriedly erected; and ten days' reserves of ammunition and supplies were dumped in each company's area."

The final change in the divisional order of battle was made during the nights of 3rd–5th February, when 53 Brigade relieved 15 Brigade in the Naval Base–Seletar Creek sector and 15 Brigade left the division to move into Command Reserve.

The firepower in direct support of 28 Brigade was usefully increased on 3rd February. Two batteries were detached from 22nd Mountain Regiment, who were supporting 15 (later 53) Brigade, to come under command of 135th Field Regiment. One battery – 21 Mountain Battery (six 3.7-in. howitzers) – returned to 22nd Mountain Regiment after two days, but the other – 4 Mountain Battery (two 6-in. howitzers) – remained under command until almost the end of the fighting on the island. Their guns were first in action near Bukit Mandai and according to the Regimental Diary, the battery's O.P. was near the summit of the four-hundred-foot hill, much the highest ground in the north of the island but just outside the divisional area. The maximum range of the 6-in. howitzer was less than that of the 25-pdr. and varied according to the weight of the shell used – 85 pounds or 100 pounds – but given the general shortage of medium and heavy artillery, even a section would be worth-while on a brigade front.

It was during the first few days of the week of waiting and preparation that it was decided that units that had fought in Johore should send parties of men for short periods of relaxation in Singapore City. Bombardier Austin has recorded that in 336 Battery:

Plate 147 *6-in. howitzer of 4 Mountain Battery, Indian Army, in Malaya before the Japanese attack. 4 Mountain Battery was placed under command of 135th Field Regiment during the defence of Singapore Island.* (I.W.M. – KF 411B)

"... arrangements were made for us to visit Singapore – ten men at a time, for two hours only. On return the next ten would go, and so on ... So ten of us set off for Singapore, Raffles Square being the rendezvous. We had not been there many minutes when the air raid siren sounded and we spent a fair amount of our time in the shelter underneath the Fullerton Building ... At a book shop in the corner of Raffles Square I bought a copy of *Railway Wonders of the World*, a new monthly magazine which had not long ago appeared in England, and at a shop next door a strawberry-flavoured ice-cream, little realising that it was going to be a long time before I tasted another such delight.

One would not have thought from the atmosphere in Singapore that a war was going on only a few miles away. People were queuing at the cinema to see Greta Garbo and Ramon Navarro in 'Mata Hari' and 'The Ziegfield Girls' was on at the Alhambra. There were notices, 'Raffles Hotel tonight – Dinner 7.30–9.00 p.m.; Dance 8.00 p.m.' and 'Adelphi hotel – Grill Room; Dining Room. Table d'hote, Lunch, Dinner. Orchestral Selections by the Rellor Band' ..."

Early on 3rd February serious Japanese preparations for an assault on Singapore appeared to begin. A single aircraft made a low-level attack on the oil tanks in the Naval Base, setting one of them on fire. This fire, stoked at intervals by further bombing, and by shelling which began the following day and continued at intervals, lasted for three weeks, clouding out the sun at times and dropping oily soot throughout the divisional area. A heavy air attack on camps and installations around Nee Soon took place later in the day, killing four members of the regimental signals section and a despatch rider, who were laying telephone cable. A counter-battery programme, which grew as intelligence began to trickle in, began during the afternoon of 3rd February with a troop target against guns reported to be in action near Johore Bahru racecourse – the guns were evidently forced to move. The Regimental Diary records that contact was made with the counter-battery office at Headquarters III Indian Corps in an effort to obtain more intelligence of enemy gun- and mortar positions but the corps C.B. staff "never really functioned". Harassing fire tasks in the area of Tebrau Creek were engaged throughout the night of 3rd–4th February, setting a routine which, with counter-battery tasks during the hours of daylight, would be maintained for the next five days and nights.

The regiment was brought back up to full strength and fire-power when 336 Battery occupied their previously-prepared position south of Nee Soon early on 4th February. They joined in the counter-battery work which went on all day. The following day (5th February) the Regimental Diary noted:

"The counter-battery office, which was now established in a concrete dug-out, was beginning to function well and the regiment did a great deal of counter-battery work during the day. This work called for a large expenditure of Charge Super, which Malaya Command would only allow at the rate of ten rounds per gun per day, for this important role. Even this was exceedingly difficult to obtain.

From shelling reports, sound bearings and occasional flash bearings, it was concluded that the enemy's heavy-calibre guns were out of range of Charge 3 of our 25-pdrs."

What became an 'artillery duel' is described at some length by Harrison:

"On 5th February the mass of the Japanese artillery came into action ... The enemy's bombardment ... according to Japanese sources, 'is said to have been the heaviest concentration of fire ever put down by the Japanese army. The guns used were of all calibres, but the main punch came from modern 240-mm. howitzers which had been specially built for this very purpose ... For three days the artillery duel went on ...'

For two days and three nights this bombardment was concentrated almost entirely on the Naval Base, the gun positions and O.Ps. of 135th Field Regiment, and 27 Australian Brigade on the left flank of 28 Indian Brigade. In the divisional area the infantry who suffered most were B Company of 2/2nd Gurkhas, on the extreme left flank of the division, and the companies of 2/9th Gurkhas near the water tower, which was being used as an O.P. and, though never hit, proved a popular target for the enemy's guns.

Throughout this preliminary bombardment 135th Field Regiment performed yeoman service. They and the Sikhs of 4 Mountain Battery harassed the creeks on the Johore coast, which might be the assembly places for the enemy's landing fleet; they bombarded areas in which the Japanese infantry might be concentrating, including the town of Johore Bahru;

they strafed the railway station in the town; they hit back at the enemy's artillery with their counter-battery fire and by engaging his probable O.Ps., most conspicuous among which was the tower in Johore Bahru. The enemy did not like it; even the Chief of Staff of the Japanese Guards Division later described the effect of the divisional artillery's fire as 'very severe'.

Although 135th Field Regiment's cables were cut again and again, communication between guns and O.Ps. was never broken; Lieutenant-Colonel Toosey, whose regiment was expert in coast defence, on which it had been employed for many months in Britain awaiting the German onslaught, was fully prepared; he had duplicated all and even quadruplicated some of his lines; and the regimental signallers were busy day and night repairing under fire the frequent breaks.

The O.Ps. were almost continuously bombarded but they were never abandoned by their F.O.Os., notable among whom were Jemadar Jogindar Singh of 4 Mountain Battery and Captain Keane of 135th Field Regiment on Bukit Mandai. This hill was singled out for bombardment by the enemy's heavy guns and the massive overhanging rock below which the O.P. was located received 25 direct hits by heavy shells. However, though completely deafened and almost concussed by the shattering vibrations, these two officers remained staunch and unruffled at their posts, observing the flashes of the enemy's guns and directing their own counter-battery fire with such good effect that on more than one occasion the guns shelling the Naval Base were temporarily silenced.

The gun area and wagon lines of 135th Field Regiment (with its attached 4 Mountain Battery) were also heavily shelled, but the gun detachments and drivers remained staunch in their stoutly constructed and well camouflaged, timbered gun emplacements and their fire was never silenced . . .

Outstanding in courage was the commanding officer of 135th Field Regiment, Lieutenant-Colonel Toosey. Wherever things were hottest he would be found, be it an O.P., a sub-section emplacement, or an area in which his communications had been broken. He took practically no rest and his example was an inspiration to all ranks . . .

The divisional artillery might have been greatly handicapped by restrictions in the routine expenditure of ammunition. Originally the scale laid down was twenty rounds per gun per day; on 7th February this scale was halved. These restrictions proved a depressing opener of the eyes of those who had heard that ammunition reserves in Singapore were adequate for six months of siege. They were, of course, inapplicable in an emergency, and a saving clause permitting higher expenditure at the divisional commander's discretion was liberally interpreted by Major-General Key, who ensured that no good target remained unengaged."

On 8th February there was a marked crescendo in the enemy's bombardment but the focus of their attention was no longer the 11th Indian Division's sector, with the exception of the O.P. on Bukit Mandai. The Regimental Diary records:

"The Australian gun positions on our immediate left were heavily shelled at irregular intervals during the whole day, though most of the shells fell plus of their positions and nearer to this regiment. Since no reply appeared to be given to the shelling, our guns replied by bombarding heavily gun positions which by then had been fixed in the Johore Bahru area, with, it was thought, considerable success, as there was evidence of stopping at least two groups of guns firing . . . During the day the Australian artillery abandoned their positions and came into action in the regimental area."

The Regimental Diary attributes this concentrated attention on the Australian's gun positions to an incident which took place the previous night. A minor attempt at a crossing – probably a reconnaissance in force – was made by the enemy on the Australian front. The S.O.S. tasks were fired and defensive fire continued throughout the night, "thus exposing all their gun positions, which was to have an unpleasant sequel for them . . ."

Before darkness fell, Jemadar Jogindar Singh, 4 Mountain Battery's F.O.O. on Bukit Timah, reported landing craft in the mouth of the Sungei Skudai. They were engaged by his battery and 135th Field Regiment, whereupon they "hurriedly turned upstream and disappeared". Then the water-tower O.P. signalled that a party of Japanese were approaching the gap in the causeway. They were engaged and few escaped. After dark the artillery duel continued.

Major-General Key had visited the regiment during the afternoon and given "complete latitude" (Harrison) as regards ammunition expenditure. At the water's edge the forward posts were at constant alert, searching with Lyon lights and motor head-lamps for any sign of the enemy's approach. The divisional artillery harassed the creeks on the Johore coast and the far end of the causeway, with 135th Field Regiment concentrating mainly on the mouth of the Sungei Skudai. Patrols which crossed the strait reported no offensive activity opposite the division.

On the left of 11th Indian Division, however, the Japanese were making their first serious attempts at an assault landing, as the *Official History* records:

> ". . . After a lull at sunset, by which time all telephone lines [*in 22 Australian Brigade's sector*] had been cut, the enemy bombardment was renewed and greatly intensified. Neither Malaya Command nor Western Area Headquarters was, however, seriously perturbed by this, each apparently thinking either that it was the first of a number of days of softening up, or that the enemy would switch the bombardment back next day to the Causeway and north-eastern shores of the island. As a result no orders were given during the evening for artillery fire to be brought down on the probable enemy forming-up places. At about 10.30 p.m. landing craft were seen approaching the north-west coast, and soon the whole of the front between Tanjong Buloh and Tanjong Murai was being attacked . . ."

Very little information about the situation in Western Area reached 11th Indian Division. Harrison simply records that:

> "As 9th February progressed it became evident from reports received at divisional headquarters that 22 Australian Brigade had been completely overrun, and that the enemy's exploitation had assumed formidable proportions . . . At dusk it was reported that the Japanese were in occupation of Tengah airfield. This was infiltration with a vengeance."

In fact, by mid-morning the three battalions of 22 Australian Brigade had each been isolated and forced back from their original positions. Only remnants of the brigade gathered on the perimeter of Tengah airfield and it is described in the *Official History* as "for the time being no longer a cohesive fighting formation". By nightfall on 9th February, again according to the *Official History*, "it appeared that Western Area would be able temporarily to stabilize the position" and that with the four brigades disposed on the 'Jurong Line' (connecting the significant water obstacles, the Sungei Jurong in the south and the Sungei Peng Siang in the north and backing on to the trunk road from the causeway to Singapore City), the situation, "though far from satisfactory, was by no means hopeless". However, two Japanese divisions "had captured their first objectives, were firmly established on the island and were engaged in bringing over their reserves, transport and tanks as quickly as their resources in landing craft permitted".

Throughout 9th February the 11th Indian Division front was quiet and 27 Australian Brigade on the left of the division, with 2/26th Battalion deployed in and to the south of Kranji and 2/30th Battalion at the south end of the causeway and on the higher ground running along the coast to the south-west, were undisturbed except for bombardment. The left flank of 27 Australian Brigade was, of course, 'in the air' following the withdrawal of 22 Australian Brigade. The enemy's artillery fire continued into the night of 9th–10th February but routine patrols from 2/2nd Gurkhas, on the left of 28 Indian Brigade, maintained contact with 2/30th Australian Battalion, whose patrols reported 'All Quiet' and "gave no inkling of anything untoward up to 04.00" (Harrison). This is surprising for, according to the *Official History*:

> "During the day the Japanese intensified their artillery fire on the sector held by 27 Australian Brigade. By 18.00 most of the telephone cables in the forward areas had been cut and the defences near Kranji Pier had been almost completely destroyed. At about 20.30 the bombardment lifted and half an hour later a battalion of the Japanese 4th Guards Regiment, which had embarked in the Sungei Skudai, began its assault . . ."

Noting that only one battery was available to answer the Australians' calls for defensive fire, the *Official History* states that, "Nevertheless the Japanese at first made but little progress against stiff resistance". By midnight the three forward companies of 2/26th Battalion had been forced out of their positions but had concentrated some five hundred yards back, across the neck of the Kranji Peninsula, where they "repelled all attempts to dislodge them". During the afternoon of 9th February Brigadier Maxwell, commanding 27 Australian Brigade had discussed with the commanding officers of 2/26th and 2/30th Battalions a plan for their battalions to swing south-eastwards on to a line running from the 14th milestone on the Mandai Road to Bukit Panjang Village, and at midnight the brigade commander had authorised the commanding officer of 2/26th Battalion to initiate such a manoeuvre once certain demolitions had been carried out. This order was given at 04.00 on 10th February, with the result that "the causeway was . . . abandoned, the trunk road uncovered, the enemy allowed to consolidate his landings unopposed and a gap of some four thousand yards left undefended between 27 Australian Brigade and the flank of 11th Indian Division" (*Official History*).

There are discrepancies between the Regimental Diary and Harrison as to exactly how these events became known to 28 Indian Brigade and 135th Field Regiment. Harrison's account, which follows, is to be preferred:

> "At 04.30 on 10th February the Gurkha officer in command of the left platoon of 2/2nd Gurkhas on the extreme flank of the division's area was given a scrap of paper by two Australians. On it he read the scribbled words 'Position on Mandai Road near Bukit Mandai and 195 feature near 13 M.P.'. The platoon commander sent this mysterious message to company headquarters and was ordered to send a patrol to 2/30th Australian Battalion's area. The patrol returned and reported that it had found the battalion's forward right post empty . . .
>
> This was serious news. The enemy was now free to cross the Johore Strait west of the causeway undisturbed by small-arms fire, as the causeway would defilade his passage from the fire of 2/2nd Gurkhas, whose flank was now exposed and overlooked by the hills vacated by the 2/30th Battalion. This area was covered with rubber and scrub through which the enemy could move unobserved, and they were also free to penetrate . . . through the rubber and scrub south of the Naval Base in rear of 28 Indian Brigade."

Although the left flank company of 2/2nd Gurkhas made immediate and gallant efforts to regain Point 95 – a hill to their immediate left that had previously been occupied by the Australians – they were unsuccessful. By 10.00 Brigadier Selby had ordered the brigade reserve battalion, 5/14th Punjab to mount a company-strength attack to secure the hill. Meanwhile, General Key had ordered his reserve brigade, 8 Indian Brigade, to occupy the two-mile-wide gap between 28 Indian Brigade and 27 Australian Brigade running from Point 95 south to Point 120, then south-west to Point 168 and south to the Mandai Road. Fire support was to be provided by 135th Field Regiment, less 4 Mountain Battery, whose guns, at the 13th milestone on the Mandai Road, were now almost in the front line and were ordered to move to Nee Soon.

Major Banham, commanding 336 Battery, and Captain Egar, commanding B Troop, reported to Headquarters 8 Indian Brigade during the morning of 10th February with the news that 336 Battery had been placed in direct support of the brigade, with, of course, call on the other two batteries of 135th Field Regiment. Brigadier Trott's plan was in two stages. First, 2/18th R. Garhwal Rifles would move north-westwards from the reserve brigade position on the high ground about a mile and a half north of the 13th milestone on the Mandai Road and secure a forming-up point and start line from which they would advance, still north-westwards, towards the road from the southern end of the causeway to Mandai village (Woodlands Road). Then 1/13th Frontier Force Rifles would take over the advance and secure Point 168. The third battalion of the brigade – 2/10th Baluch – would remain on the high ground north of the Mandai Road as brigade reserve. The total advance would be about two miles. At about 10.00 the news reached Headquarters 11th Indian Division that the Garhwal Rifles had occupied the area of the forming-up point and start line without opposition. On hearing this, General Key moved forward to Headquarters 28 Brigade to discover that there was no news of C Company, 5/14th Punjab, who had been ordered earlier to move some three and a half miles from the reserve battalion's position south of the Naval Base and then secure Point 95. General Key ordered a second company to be committed to the recapture of Point 95 and D Company was despatched.

Shortly after General Key's return to divisional headquarters at mid-day, General Wavell and Lieutenant-General Percival arrived. This was General Wavell's last visit to Singapore as Supreme Commander South-West Pacific (the unified American–British–Dutch–Australian Command) and after leaving the island he sent a telegram to the Prime Minister which began, "Battle for Singapore is not going well" and concluded, "I have given the most categorical orders that there is to be no thought of surrender and that all troops are to continue fighting to the end ..." (*Official History*). At Headquarters 11th Indian Division the Supreme Commander was "not giving much away, except the confidence with which he invariably inspired those who were fortunate enough to meet him ..." (Harrison) but he requested General Key to send his congratulations to 135th Field Regiment and their attached 4 Mountain Battery "for the great part which they had played during the previous five days". The message reached Colonel Toosey by telephone from H.Q.R.A. the same evening and he visited each battery to pass it on.

As soon as the Supreme Commander had left, General Key heard from Brigadier Selby that 5/14th Punjab were out of touch with Headquarters 28 Brigade but that 2/2nd Gurkhas had reported that the commanding officer of 5/14th Punjab and D Company (the second company to be deployed) were established on Point 120, a few hundred yards south-east of Point 95, which was still in enemy hands. He left at once for Headquarters 8 Brigade to establish the situation there for himself. Contact with the Garhwal battalion had been lost but they were "evidently fighting hard in the Marsiling Estate, where considerable mortar- and small-arms fire could be heard". Behind, and also to the right of the Garhwalis, 1/13th F.F. Rifles were established, with their right forward company within sight, and sniper-shot, of Point 95. Soon afterwards an officer of 2/18th R. Garhwal Rifles arrived to report that their three forward companies were heavily engaged with greatly superior enemy forces and that the commanding officer had been killed. General Key ordered Brigadier Trott to be prepared to attack Point 95 with 1/13th F.F. Rifles if 5/14th Punjab's attempt to secure the hill failed, and to commit his reserve battalion, 2/10th Baluch, to move through 2/18th R. Garhwal Rifles at dawn the following day (11th February) and capture Point 130 as the left flank position for the brigade. Both attacks would be supported by 135th Field Regiment.

During the later afternoon it became clear that 5/14th Punjab were unable to attack Point 95 from Point 120; their way was barred by an impassable iron paling fence interlaced with barbed wire. The divisional commander accordingly confirmed that 1/13th F.F. Rifles were to attack the hill before nightfall. According to the Regimental Diary, it was arranged at about 16.00 that:

> "... the regiment should fire a concentration on Point 95 of ten minutes intense from zero hour (17.00) ...The concentration was duly fired and the attacking force then walked on to the hill entirely unopposed and established themselves there."

Bombardier Austin records with some pride that the guns of 135th Field Regiment averaged 63 rounds each during the ten minutes intense fire on Point 95 – against an official rate of fire of five rounds per minute. The resulting 1,500 rounds that fell on the hill can be compared with the regiment's total expenditure of 7,000 rounds fired in the 24 hours from 09.00 on 10th February.

At 19.00 on 10th February 27 Australian Brigade, whose right-hand battalion, 2/30th, were said now to be holding the vital Woodlands Road–Mandai Road junction at Mandai village, was placed under command of 11th Indian Division. The Australian brigade commander was told of 2/10th Baluch's dawn attack on Point 130, which would secure the Australians' right flank and leave 11th Indian Division with a hugely extended perimeter, stretching from Bukit Panjang village northwards to the causeway and then along the division's original frontage on to the Johore Strait. Divisional reserves were minimal.

Throughout the night of 10th–11th February the regiment fired H.F tasks while news of the forward battalions – none of it good – trickled in. Survivors of 2/18th R. Garhwal Rifles described their attempts to get through the Marsiling Estate to Point 168; the battalion was now at an effective strength of less than two companies. Plans were made for 2/10th Baluch to move west along the Mandai Road and attack Point 130 from the south, off a start line close to Mandai village. It then became clear that the Australians were not, as had previously been reported, holding the village. Finally, for no apparent reason 1/13th F.F. Rifles abandoned Point 95 before the planned relief by 5/14th Punjab which would establish a new left flank position for 28 Brigade. General Key ordered 1/13th to reoccupy Point 95 at 06.30 after another bombardment by 135th Field Regiment. The bombardment – five minutes intense – duly took place and 1/13th reoccupied the hill. There was no opposition from the Japanese but a confrontation with 5/14th Punjab, who had noticed that the hill was no longer in 8 Brigade's hands and were making plans to take it over themselves, was only narrowly avoided.

At 07.30 on 11th February 27 Australian Brigade was removed from command of 11th Indian Division. The Australians were still east of Mandai village and General Key decided to cancel the attack on Point 130 and instead ordered 2/10th Baluch to occupy a defensive position facing west astride the Mandai Road between the 13th and 14th milestones. B Troop was placed in direct support of the battalion and Captain Egar went forward as F.O.O. and soon found himself leading the advance. The second-in-command assessed that, with the enemy less than three miles away, and reportedly moving east in strength, the battery positions north of the Mandai Road were threatened. Two more F.O.Os. were accordingly sent to take up positions on the road to the west with a view to engaging the enemy with indirect fire before it became necessary to fire over open sights as they approached the guns. This initiative was formalised at about 09.30 when 135th Field Regiment was placed in direct support of 8 Indian Brigade and the guns were ordered to withdraw by troops to positions near Nee Soon. The first battery to move, 344 Battery, occupied previously recced positions in Nee Soon camp and were re-established by 16.00, having taken with them all the ammunition which had been dumped beside their previous gun pits. Captain McMullen recorded that the battery was shelled on arrival and that there was "general muddle and counter-orders". While 344 Battery were moving, the C.R.A. ordered the withdrawal to be accelerated and 499 Battery began moving at 13.00. The gun area originally allotted was becoming extremely crowded and Major Pilling went in search of other possibilities along Upper Thomson Road, south of the Nee Soon crossroads. He found positions in time for one troop of 499 Battery to be diverted to the new area before coming into action at Nee Soon.

The regiment did not fully occupy the Nee Soon–Upper Thompson Road position for reasons succinctly set out in the *Official History*:

> "As soon as he realised that 27 Australian Brigade could no longer be counted upon to protect his left flank, General Heath decided that the moment to abandon the Naval Base had arrived and ordered the final demolitions to be carried out. By 6.00 p.m. on 11th February the base had been evacuated; 53 Brigade had swung its left flank back and taken up a position from the Sungei Simpang facing north-west, covering the Sembawang airfield; 8 Brigade had withdrawn to a position just west of Nee Soon road junction and 28 Brigade had been placed in divisional reserve south of it . . ."

Harrison records that, "By dawn on 12th February the three brigades of the division were in their new positions", the last battalion arriving at 06.00. He amplifies the detail of the deployment and it becomes clear that much the greater part of the vulnerable north- and west-facing perimeter of Sembawang airfield was the responsibility of the battle-weary 8 Brigade, whose frontage then extended about another mile-and-a-half to cross the Mandai Road between Nee Soon village and the Seletar Reservoir. The much reduced 2/18th R. Garhwal Rifles had been placed in brigade reserve and 1/8th Punjab – a battalion that had been reconstituted with reinforcements that were only partly trained – had joined 8 Brigade. The brigade had also taken under command the units originally committed to the defence of Sembawang airfield – the 3rd Cavalry, 3 Field Company, R.E. and a detachment of the Karpurthala Battalion, I.S.F., together with some R.A.F. ground staff.

The Regimental Diary shows how these moves affected 135th Field Regiment:

> "Before this move [*to the regimental position at Nee Soon*] could be completed, orders were received for a complete change of front. The whole regiment was to go into action at Sembawang airfield – 336 Battery and the 6-in. howitzers were to cover the Mandai Road; 344 Battery were to cover Thomson Road; and 499 Battery were to cover the area of Seletar Creek. This move was completed by 17.30.
>
> At about 17.50 the C.O. visited H.Q.R.A. and there received orders for two batteries to pull out immediately and return to the wagon lines. It was decided that 336 Battery and 344 Battery should return that night as soon as possible – which they did – and 499 Battery were to remain in position to cover the Mandai Road.
>
> The second-in-command was sent to recce a regimental area in the neighbourhood of . . . Yio Chiu Kang, but as this area had already been allotted to 18th Divisional Artillery permission had first to be obtained and little or no recce could be done that night."

The probability of early withdrawal to Singapore had, according to Harrison, prompted General Key to 'thin out the artillery', leaving 155th Field Regiment, 22nd Mountain Regiment (less 4 Mountain Battery) and 499 Field Battery in support of the division.

Bombardier Austin remembered Sembawang airfield as "like the wreck of the *Marie Celeste* . . . with half-consumed cups of tea on the tables, half-eaten buns, chairs pushed back. The occupants had obviously departed in a hurry. When we left I noted some of our personnel triumphantly carrying R.A.F. camp beds". The chance to use a camp bed would have appealed to Bombardier Martin of 499 Battery, the only battery in action that night, who later wrote, "By this time we were practically asleep on our feet. Nevertheless, by using skeleton gun detachments, harassing fire was put down all night (four rounds per gun per hour at irregular intervals) while we all snatched some sleep in turn".

The events of the early morning of 12th February are described in the *Official History*:

> "In Northern Area, the Japanese began to press 8 Brigade shortly after dawn. This brigade held a position one mile west of Nee Soon with 2/10th Baluch astride the Mandai Road and 1/8th Punjab on their right. The Punjab battalion, which after it had been re-formed consisted almost entirely of untrained reinforcements, began to disintegrate. Since enemy penetration in this area would have isolated 53 Brigade, General Key brought up 2/9th Gurkhas and 499 Field Battery from 28 Brigade (then in reserve). The 1/8th Punjab's position was reoccupied and the situation restored."

Without giving details of the units supported, the Regimental Diary confirms that "during the morning 499 Battery were called upon to give considerable support to the infantry, who were holding Nee Soon village . . . By the accurate and quick response of this battery, and with the help of supporting fire from certain units of 18th Division, the enemy were held up".

While the operation to plug the gap left by 1/8th Punjab was continuing, orders arrived at Headquarters 11th Indian Division for the withdrawal of the division to a position in the north-eastern sector of a perimeter defence that was to be established round the outskirts of Singapore. The withdrawal was to begin at noon. There was, as yet, no detail of the division's deployment but 53 Brigade was to revert to command of 18th Division, taking 22nd Mountain Regiment (less 4 Mountain Battery) with them, and it seemed as if the divisional frontage would be held by a single brigade, leaving the second brigade as a substantial divisional reserve. General Key selected 8 Brigade, reinforced by 5/14th Punjab from 28 Brigade, to occupy the perimeter defence; 28 Brigade, now reduced to two battalions, of which one was detached to the defence of Sembawang airfield, would form the reserve. The 6-in. howitzers of 4 Mountain Battery were to move to corps control.

At about 10.30 General Key gave his orders for the withdrawal. The most northerly brigade – 53 Brigade – would move to a rearguard position south of Nee Soon village and 8 Brigade would withdraw through the rearguard during the later afternoon. At 12.45, C.R.A. 11th Indian Division ordered 336 Battery to be deployed in support of the rearguard. The battery received orders from elsewhere to leave their rearguard position at 18.00 but after further intervention by the C.R.A. it was arranged that one troop would stay in action until midnight. Harrison records that:

> "The withdrawal of the division proceeded smoothly, despite the short notice and a strong attack on 2/10th Baluch as the 2nd Cambridgeshires and 6th Norfolks passed through Nee Soon at 15.00. The Baluchis . . . staunchly withstood this attack, which was led by tanks, and the enemy was repulsed in a sharp action in which 499 Field Battery was at one time firing over open sights and a troop of 273 Anti-Tank Battery knocked out three tanks . . ."

In fact, the Japanese thrust was on a rather wider front than just the Mandai Road, astride which were the 2/10th Baluch's positions. F Troop were deployed east of Sembawang Road and within sight of Sembawang airfield when the enemy began breaking through on what was probably the section of the brigade frontage that had been taken over from 1/8th Punjab by 2/9th Gurkhas. Bombardier Martin later described the action:

> "This was nearly all Charge One firing. In the open-sights engagement my gun demolished the perimeter fence of Sembawang airfield, firing from our position just east of Sembawang Road. Thereafter, the infantry withdrew past us, our gun-towing vehicles were called up, and with the guns hooked in we continued to fire Charge One."

This spirited resistance enabled 53 Brigade to move without difficulty down Sembawang Road and through Nee Soon village to the rearguard position. They were followed by 8

Brigade, who disengaged in good order and were not closely pressed as they withdrew and moved towards their new positions. The guns, covered by F Troop, withdrew to the area of Yio Chiu Kang, then:

> "F Troop moved from Sembawang airfield through Nee Soon, narrowly escaping through this bottleneck. In broad daylight we moved along Yio Chiu Kang Road. At one halt, we – C Sub of F Troop – 'liberated' 14,000 cigarettes from an abandoned N.A.A.F.I. store, then stood tossing cartons to each 344 Battery truck as they overtook us. We drove through Chia Keng and Paya Lebar into the city outskirts as dusk fell". (Bombardier Martin)

At the rearguard position, Battery Headquarters and A Troop of 336 Battery remained in action until 18.00, when they moved out, followed by B Troop at midnight. Bombardier Austin recorded:

> ". . . when we left the gun position one of the Quads broke down, so under the supervision of Lieutenant Laing we all gathered round and tipped it head first into a monsoon drain . . . Our signal truck, a Bedford 15-cwt., towed two limbers and a 25-pdr. from this position. I was quite surprised – it managed the load quite easily. We left as darkness was falling . . ."

With consequences that were later to prove disastrous, the order to withdraw did not reach 499 Battery's B Echelon.

The *Official History* sets the scene for the final days in the defence of Singapore:

> "By the morning of 13th February, the occupation of the 28-mile perimeter covering Singapore was complete, except that part of 53 Brigade remained south of Nee Soon till noon . . . 2 Malaya Brigade held from Kallang airfield to Payar Lebar airstrip and 11th Division from there to a point on Braddell Road one mile west of Woodleigh. The 18th Division continued the line; 53 Brigade, now under its orders, held the Chinese Cemetery area north of Braddell Road . . .
>
> The withdrawal of 11th Division had been carried out none too soon, for after the failure of the Japanese 44th Guards Regiment to break through at Nee Soon, General Nishimura decided to contain the British forces at that point while he sent two battalions south . . . to cut Thomson Road behind the defenders. These enemy battalions reached their objective on 13th February, just after 53 Brigade had been withdrawn . . .
>
> By the morning of 13th February the battle for Singapore Island was irretrievably lost and it was only a question of time before capitulation would become inevitable . . ."

Harrison gives more detail of the deployment of 11th Indian Division:

> "The line inclusive Paya Lebar airstrip–inclusive Woodleigh crossroads was held by 8 Brigade with 5/14th Punjab on the right, 2/10th Baluch in the centre, 1/13th F.F. Rifles on the left and 1/8th Punjab, the Bahawalpur Infantry and Garhwal Battalion in brigade reserve. 28 Brigade, 3rd Cavalry and a detachment of the Karpurthala Battalion were in divisional reserve. The artillery remaining under divisional command now consisted of 135th and 155th Field Regiments and 80th Anti-Tank Regiment."

During the night of 12th–13th February, 28 Brigade had been heavily bombarded for some two hours in their harbour area near the wireless station and had suffered a number of casualties. At daybreak they moved into the divisional area and began digging a support line south of Braddell Road. After a hurried reconnaissance early in the morning, 8 Brigade completed occupation of their sector of the perimeter by noon. Enemy movement across that front was observed about an hour later.

As far as 135th Field Regiment were concerned, the morning of 13th February was spent "sorting out gun positions" (Regimental Diary). Both 11th Indian Division and 18th Division had been ordered to deploy their artillery in the same area – "on and around a large swampy waste area known as Toa Payoh, bounded by Serangoon, Balastier, Braddell and Thomson Roads" (Martin). The C.R.As. of the two divisions met to try to divide up the area but even so there was considerable difficulty in finding space for batteries. Captain McMullen spent the whole morning locating suitable positions for 344 Battery, which he managed to get into action early in the afternoon. Both troops of 499 Battery achieved a degree of cover from view, but no cover from fire, by placing their guns inside palm-thatch barrack huts. Bombardier Austin described 336 Battery's deployment:

"The battery position was beside Balastier Road . . . A Troop were in the open on what appeared to be the polo ground. [*It was; the polo ground is at the junction of Serangoon Road and Balastier Road.*] B Troop were better situated, two guns being in the front gardens of houses with camouflage nets over them and two guns in garages, where they shut the doors when they were not firing . . . The command post was in a building that was previously a Naval Store. The exchange was in an alcove, where Harry Simpson was handling calls as if on an exercise . . ."

The Regimental Diary records that by 12.00 part of the regiment was in action and that all guns were ready by 16.00. The regiment was still supporting 8 Brigade, with a battery in direct support of each of the forward battalions. Signal cable was in very short supply and emergency measures had to be taken to connect the O.Ps. with R.H.Q. and the guns. The O.Ps. ran lines to forward headquarters, from where the regimental signal section had laid a single line to 336 Battery's exchange – hence the reference to Harry Simpson (above) – and the battery was responsible for passing all messages on to the other two batteries, to rear headquarters and H.Q.R.A. At 15.15 Colonel Toosey met Brigadier Trott, commanding 8 Brigade, who asked for artillery support to be 'laid on' at once. As the cable network was not yet complete the gaps had to be bridged by despatch rider but "S.O.S. and D.F. tasks were prepared at once".

Harrison describes the situation in Singapore as darkness fell:

". . . All this time Singapore was being bombed and shelled. There was hardly a corner which was not a fair military target. Lorries stood herded in open parks and nose-to-tail in the streets. The perimeter, too large for the troops who were still standing, was all too small for the miscellany of administrative etceteras which aid the British army to victory but are merely a hampering burden in defeat; and there were guns here, there and everywhere. Many of the streets were blocked by craters or by a muddle of riven telegraph posts and tangled wire. Drainage and water systems were disrupted. Fifth columnists, Japanese infiltrators and panic-stricken members of our own forces vied with each other in causing alarm and despondency by their shooting matches within the city . . ."

At 21.00 on 13th February, according to Harrison, orders were received at Headquarters 11th Indian Division for the evacuation by sea of a representative party from divisional and brigade headquarters and one commissioned officer, one Viceroy's commissioned officer and thirty other ranks from each battalion not actively engaged with the enemy. These parties were to assemble at the Empire Dock at midnight, where a ship would be awaiting them. The Regimental Diary records that "at 23.00 the commanding officer was sent for by H.Q.R.A. and detailed to go on a special mission but, after a little difficulty, the divisional commander and the C.R.A. agreed to send a battery commander and Major O.H. Daltry (499 Battery) took his place". The "little difficulty" was described by Colonel Toosey in a letter to the regimental historian written in 1964:

"The idea of the escape party was that some young commanding officers should be got out in order to give some information on Japanese methods, and, I suppose, preserve them for future activities. [*Some sources suggest that the parties would have formed the basis for reconstituted units but this seems unlikely.*]

I found the whole thing quite extraordinary. Having been brought up on *Artillery Training, Volume II,* in which one is taught that in any withdrawal the commander is the last to leave, I felt the whole concept was wrong and so refused to go myself and sent Osmond Daltry instead."

Harrison's account continues:

". . . the whole scheme went awry. The docks were being shelled and the ship did not wait. The parties from the 11th Indian and 18th British Divisions were ordered to wait in the Y.M.C.A. until the morning. The building received several direct hits and a number of lives were lost. Those remaining were told that they must make for Sumatra in any craft which they could find, but the docks had already been combed by deserters and there were very few seaworthy boats left.

In Sumatra, Lieutenant-Colonel Warren of the Royal Marines awaited the arrival of the official evacuees. He had been sent there to organise an 'escape channel' across the island to Pegu, but none of the evacuees had been told and those that made their landfall on

PLATE V Sembawang Airfield, Singapore, 12th February 1942 – 25-pdrs. of 499 Field Battery prepare to withdraw after firing over open sights
*(From the water-colour specially painted for this work by Joan Wanklyn, 1999)*

Early in the morning of 12th February 1942, in the face of a steadily deteriorating situation, 11th Indian Division was ordered to withdraw to final defensive positions around the city of Singapore. In order to allow 53 Infantry Brigade, which was in some danger of being cut off, to pull back down the Sembawang Road and southwards through Nee Soon cross-roads, 8 Indian Brigade was ordered to hold the cross-roads against attack that was expected over a wide area, stretching from west round to north. The brigade was reinforced by 2/9th Gurkhas from divisional reserve, with 499 Field Battery in direct support. Throughout the morning and into early afternoon 8 Brigade held off all Japanese attempts to break through. Then, on hearing that the rest of the division had safely passed the cross-roads, they began their own withdrawal. The route for 2/9th Gurkhas lay across the abandoned Sembawang Airfield and from their position just outside the south-east corner F Troop of 499 Battery engaged tanks and infantry that were following up the Gurkhas with such effect that the battalion was able to break away. The open-sight action continued as the Gurkhas moved through the troop position and the enemy was further disorganised and delayed by several rounds fired after the guns had been hooked in and were awaiting the order to move.

This plate has generously been sponsored by McMullen and Sons Limited, supporters of Volunteers and Territorials in Hertfordshire for well over a century.

Sumatra at the right place did so fortuitously."

Major Daltry was seriously wounded while in the Y.M.C.A. building and command of 135th Field Regiment's escape party devolved upon W.O.II Waldock, B.S.M. of 499 Battery. A censored account of his successful evacuation of all his party was published in the *Hertfordshire Pictorial*:

"*Friday 13th February*

Ordered to stand by for special duty at 23.00. Left R.H.Q. at 23.30 under command of Major X, with fourteen other ranks from the regiment. Arrival at docks at 01.00 under shell-fire. No boats available to carry out job.

*Saturday 14th February*

Left the docks at 07.00 and went into a building to rest for the day as job could only be done under darkness . . . At about 22.30 a shell landed right inside the door, killing and wounding several, including Major X . . . We carried him out and, as luck would have it, an ambulance was just passing so we sent him on to hospital. We left the building then and spent the night looking for a boat but could not find one . . .

*Sunday 15th February*

Decided to look for boats in daylight, so took party into the docks. Enemy planes came over every fifteen minutes, systematically bombing the docks and anti-aircraft batteries. At 14.00 we were told . . . that we had the chance, if we cared to take it, of making a bid for freedom or remaining and being taken prisoner for certain . . . We had another look round and found one boat half full of water. It had been standing on the dockside for months and was badly warped. It had been thrown in the previous day. We were joined by Lieutenant Y who said we had until 15.15 to get out if we were going. We all got busy and bailed out the boat – the *Pyrrus Achilles*, 25–30 feet long. Rounded up a sail and oars, water and a few supplies and had a check of space for personnel. There was my party of fifteen, including myself, and Lieutenant Y and eleven Sikhs. Then we found room for five more – two Australians, two from the Royal Signals and one man of the Norfolks. We were 32 all told.

All set to leave at 15.10 hours, so off we paddled. As the Sikhs could not row, they had the job of bailing out – five with buckets and two with stirrup pumps. After the first 24 hours the woodwork swelled and bailing was reduced to two with buckets. Off we went, through the boom and two miles beyond, where we put up the sail. Fortunately we had one man [*Bombardier Adamson*] who could handle a sail and this saved us a lot of hard work. Our arms were all ready in case they were needed. Every man was armed with a rifle, tommy-gun or pistol and we had plenty of ammunition . . . The wind and tide were with us and by 20.00 Singapore was out of sight behind the islands, although the town was in flames and we could see the glare all through the night."

After a series of crises, but with no interruption from the enemy, the party landed on the east coast of Sumatra during the afternoon of 17th February. They were then forced to abandon their boat and make their way along the coast in hired sampans, finally making contact with the Dutch authorities on 22nd February. It was not until 1st March that they were able to board a destroyer which took them out to transfer – in the dark with a fairly high sea running – to a cruiser, on board which they reached Colombo on 5th March.

It was greatly to B.S.M. Waldock's credit that, having lost Major Daltry, the rest of the regiment's escape party all reached India. Here they were dispersed to other units with no apparent use being made of their experience. B.S.M. Waldock later confided to the regimental historian that the hardest part of all was that after the war it never really seemed to be accepted by those who had remained in action that the 'escapers' were carrying out orders and not acting on their own initiative. Their successful efforts to rejoin the British Forces in India against considerable odds were regarded by some as tantamount to desertion.

Meanwhile, in the Singapore defences, Captain Lord De Ramsey was promoted to command of 499 Battery and the gun positions were heavily shelled throughout the night of 13th–14th February. "The morning [*of 14th February*] passed quietly in the division's area, apart from continuous shelling . . . and occasional bombing", according to Harrison, but members of

135th Field Regiment may have felt that this understated the position. An observation balloon now overlooked the divisional area and the Regimental Diary records that, "All gun positions from that time onwards suffered most accurate and continuous shelling the enemy having the target of a lifetime". Efforts to shoot down the balloon came to nothing but the regiment achieved a small degree of success by taking bearings on the 'string' from various O.Ps. and engaging the point of intersection. This did result in the balloon being lowered for a time but "it was up again soon afterwards".

At 08.00 on 14th February B.Q.M.S. Cluff of 499 Battery made his way into Forward R.H.Q. carrying a piece of paper on which was scribbled "If you do not surrender at once all your prisoners will be killed". As previously noted, the order to withdraw into the Singapore perimeter had not reached 499 Battery's B Echelon. In a memoir sent to the regimental historian long after the event, Cluff recorded:

> "B Echelon, 499 Battery was in the wagon lines in a rubber plantation [*near Milestone 7 on the Yio Chiu Kang Road, according to Bombardier Martin*] until the morning of 13th February. At 09.00 Bombardier J.S. Allen was sent to contact R.H.Q. and must have run into a Jap advance as he did not return. Japs appeared at 13.00 and we pulled out before being seen. Captain C.H. Dakers [*attached from F.M.S.V.F.*] led the convoy, which was quickly surrounded by a Jap ambush. We were tied up, held in a basement and later taken back to a hut for the night. I was sent back to Singapore early next morning with a letter."

B.Q.M.S. Cluff, who had to walk through one of the regiment's own concentrations on the way towards 11th Division's lines, was taken to H.Q.R.A., who sent the ultimatum on to Headquarters Malaya Command. On the expiry of the 24 hours apparently allowed in the ultimatum, the thirteen men Cluff had left behind (including Captain Dakers and 2nd Lieutenant

Plate 148 *135th Field Regiment's 'Escape Party' photographed in India, 1942.* Back row (L.–R.) – *Gunners Briers, Pemberton, Thompson.* Centre row – *Gunners Muirhead, Daws, Hawkins, Wilkins, Burns.* Front row – *Sergeants Dexter, McCormack, B.S.M. Waldock, Sergeant McLay, Bombardier Adamson.* Absent – *Sergeant Pyne. On 13th February 1942 each major unit in Singapore was ordered to detail an escape party which would be evacuated from Singapore and would report on various aspects of the campaign. It might also have been used as a basis for reconstitution of a captured unit. Major O.H. Daltry was placed in command of 135th Field Regiment's party but he was seriously wounded on the dockside. It was left to B.S.M. Waldock, in the absence of any organised sea transport, to take command of the party, which then managed to reach Sumatra in a small boat and find onward transport to India.* (Regimental Collection)

Shelton, F.M.S.V.F.) were tied to trees and shot or bayonetted, according to rank. Remarkably, there were two survivors of this incident. One, whose name has not been recorded, managed, according to the Regimental Diary, to work lose his bindings and escape unharmed, reaching the regiment soon afterwards. The other, Gunner M.S. Carr, rejoined at Changi about a week after the capitulation with "a ghastly bayonet wound near the shoulder blades" (Austin). He had feigned death, thus avoiding further wounds, and had been looked after, at great risk to themselves, by a Chinese family.

Firing continued throughout 14th February, though the Japanese made no serious attempt to penetrate 11th Indian Division's front. On the division's left, 18th Division was strongly attacked and gave a little ground while offering resolute resistance. On the right the enemy tried to exploit the boundary between 8 Indian Brigade and the neighbouring 2 Malaya Brigade, perhaps with the objective of capturing the Payar Lebar airstrip. They made little progress on this flank and a counter-attack by 5/14th Punjab after they had lost their right forward position during the afternoon fully restored the original line. Part of the divisional reserve was deployed to maintain contact with the flanking brigade. There were signs that ammunition supplies were running low. Captain McMullen took three trucks through heavy shelling to the Base Ordnance Depot at Alexandra Barracks but found the ammunition dump on fire and was forced to return empty-handed.

Both Alexander and Austin record that during the evening of 14th February there were indications of a Japanese advance headed by tanks:

> "... the phone buzzed ... the message was 'Japanese tanks approaching along Thomson Road' ... Sergeant Hughes's gun of B Troop was detached and placed in an anti-tank role on Balestier Road, facing north. Balestier Road resembled photographs of France in the First World War – wrecked buildings and debris everywhere, with the trolleybus wires dangling down on the road, broken by enemy shell- and mortar-fire." (Austin)

The tank attack never materialised but shelling continued throughout the night and on the extreme right 5/14th Punjab repulsed a strong attack after a grenade battle lasting half an hour. To their right 2 Malaya Brigade pulled back, leaving the southward facing flank of 11th Indian Division along the Paya Lebar airstrip, now occupied by 3rd Cavalry and the Karpurthala Battalion, brought up earlier in the day from divisional reserve.

Before dawn on 15th February a report reached divisional headquarters that a company of 2/10th Baluch had 'gone over to the enemy'. They may have been tricked into surrendering rather than have deserted of their own accord. Nevertheless, when dawn broke and they could be seen assembled on a hill south of Paya Lebar village, the regiment was ordered to fire on them and, according to Harrison, did so. The gap left in the line was quickly filled by a company from the Garhwal Battalion. The morning began with the usual increase in shelling but activity on 11th Indian Division's front was relatively minor. A 'half-hearted' attack on the line held by 2/10th Baluch petered out under heavy defensive mortar-fire, while in 5/14th Punjab's sector the enemy captured 'Petrol Hill' but were quickly driven off by an immediate counter-attack by a detachment of 3/16th Punjab that was operating under command of 5/14th.

General Key, who had been summoned to a conference at corps headquarters at 11.00 returned to Headquarters 11th Indian Division at 13.00 with the news that it would "all be over at 16.00" and called an immediate O-group, at which, according to Harrison, Colonel Toosey was present. The divisional commander passed on the decision reached earlier by General Percival that his forces on the island should surrender. 'Cease-fire' had been arranged provisionally for 16.00. All equipment and guns were to be handed over intact. Harrison recorded that:

> "A gasp greeted this last remark. I asked to be excused and left the conference. Toosey followed me. 'I can take a lot but I can't take this', he said. I told him to cheer up; that the first seven years were always the worst; and that even 25-pdrs. sometimes blew up by accident. He brightened a bit at this and said, 'The trouble is that I cannot do it silently'. I told him that I did not understand what he was driving at and that, as far as I could see, the more noise the better.
>
> Later, thank God, General Wavell wirelessed orders from Java that all field guns were to be destroyed. Our two field regiments [*135th and 155th*] made a grand mess of theirs, and a hell of a lot of noise doing it."

About mid-day the guns began to run short of ammunition. The Base Ordnance Depot was now in enemy hands and there was no chance of replenishment. At 15.30, the Regimental Diary records, "the first official information that a surrender was in contemplation was received." This information did not reach batteries any too soon, as Bombardier Austin has noted:

> "During the early part of the day we had all been ordered to fix bayonets and prepare for hand-to-hand fighting. In the afternoon Captain Viney was preparing fire orders when a major of another unit came into the command post . . . He asked Captain Viney if he was preparing fire orders and, on receiving the answer 'Yes', replied, 'As senior officer present I forbid you to carry on. A cease-fire has been arranged and you may well kill some of our own men'."

Threatened with the visitor's revolver when he took no notice, Captain Viney agreed to send an officer to R.H.Q. to check. Lieutenant Tacchi, attached from F.M.S.V.F., left at once in his own sports car and returned with confirmation of the impending cease-fire. At 16.00 the regiment was ordered to destroy all guns and technical equipment. Bombardier Austin described events in 336 Battery:

> "We smashed up all our wireless sets and telephone equipment and smashed rifles by grasping the barrel and bringing the butt crashing down on to concrete. Then we buried the wreckage.
>
> With the 25-pdrs., we put a shell up the breech and one down the barrel and retired to a safe distance to pull the firing lever by means of trolley bus wire . . . We evacuated the residents of the houses behind B Troop's guns. One young man was unable to walk and our gunners carried him to safety. I thought that the guns would be blown to pieces but they were not. What happened was that the end of the barrel only was damaged, receiving a scalloped end – like the chimney of the 'Rocket' locomotive.
>
> We were all shaken by the day's events. Gunner Albert Smith sat on the pavement edge with his head in his hands, sobbing . . . I was not far from tears myself . . .
>
> We were instructed to destroy any American money that we had, and our 'crossing-the-line' certificates, which I regretted later, as the Japs took no interest in these items and when we were P.O.Ws. in Thailand the natives would give quite a good rate of exchange for U.S. dollars and British pound notes . . ."

At their position close to divisional headquarters, 499 Battery were less circumspect in destroying their guns and nearly killed the C.R.A. with a piece of metal which flew through the building occupied by H.Q.R.A. Half-an hour later, true to the spirit of 'Order, counter-order, disorder' which had dogged operations in Malaya and Singapore, orders were received to be prepared to carry on fighting – "a difficult problem, now that the guns had been destroyed" (Regimental Diary). Then, in an effort to ensure that the whole regiment was captured together, the commanding officer ordered his forward headquarters to join R.H.Q. in the gun area and the F.O.Os. were withdrawn from their battalions. Finally, the official 'cease-fire' was ordered for 18.30. One other rank was killed and two wounded during the last half-hour before it took effect. Then, except for the occasional shot, the battle for Singapore was over.

### *In Japanese hands, February 1942–August 1945*

Long after the event, members of 135th Field Regiment corresponding with the regimental historian had a single, common memory of the period immediately following the shock of the capitulation. It was "the wonderful experience of being allowed to sleep through the night for the first time in weeks" (Martin). In 336 Battery Bombardier Austin went out to his wireless truck to find his blankets, "which had not been undone for some time". There, something made him lift up the signaller's seat-cushion. Underneath he found a 1-inch map of the Peterborough area which had survived numerous inspections at home, the three-month voyage and the recent fighting. Captain McMullen recorded events in 344 Battery, which are confirmed by correspondents from the other batteries:

> "The next day [*16th February*] vehicles were lined up to be handed over. Ammunition, binoculars, etc. were collected and the Japs came round and inspected. [*On 336 Battery's*

Plate 149 *B.S.M. J. Burgess, 344 Battery.*
(Drawing by Gunner W.C. Wilder, dated Changi, 1942)

*position the inspecting officers enquired how the guns came to be damaged. Major Banham assured them that it was through Japanese shelling – a story they appeared to accept.*] We stayed where we were that night and moved out next day at about mid-day. All we were allowed as transport were two trucks and the water cart. One we loaded with food, the other with the men's kits, cooking utensils, etc. I left a lot of stuff behind – sheets, pyjamas, underclothes, etc., but managed to get camp bed and kitbag on the lorry. I gave away to the men all the cigarettes I could not carry – about a thousand – and we divided out about 1,200 dollars.

We started our march directly after lunch, B.Q.M.S. Locke having gone on ahead with the lorries. Joined up with a number of other units in the outskirts of Singapore and arrived at Changi as it was getting dark after about six hours' march. The men stuck it very well . . .

Locke had got a very good meal ready for us when we arrived, which we ate by the light of a fire and the sidelights of the water cart. The men slept in a building that night and officers out in the open. We rigged up mosquito nets and spent quite a good night. The next day the men moved into barrack rooms – rather squashed – and officers into N.C.Os.' billets in Quadrant Road.

All food was pooled after the first few days and we got no supplies from the Japs for about three weeks. Consequently our meals were pretty meagre. They consisted of: breakfast – tea and one biscuit; dinner – tea and three biscuits. With the biscuits we got butter and bully beef once a day."

Alexander describes conditions in Changi and carries the story beyond the first three weeks, to the point where Japanese-supplied rations became available:

"The commodious barracks, with their ample lawns, playing fields and parade grounds, had been designed on a generous scale for a population of about eight thousand. Fifty-one thousand British and Australian prisoners-of-war were marched there, while the Indian troops remained near the town. Bombing and demolitions had already destroyed the plumbing, and piped water was not restored for six weeks. We were left to sort ourselves out there, and eventually to wire ourselves in, and the whole military hierarchy soon managed to establish itself in a Heath-Robinson version of Fort Canning [*H.Q. Malaya Command*]. No amount of ingenious improvisation, however, could increase the miserable rations, and real hunger stalked the camp . . . "

Very shortly after arriving at Changi, Alexander succumbed to dysentery and was confined to the officers' quarters in Quadrant Road on a diet of liquids only. By the time he had recovered three weeks later he had "missed the first bout of starvation that hit us between combat rations and 'prison fare'. He described the daily menu thus:

"Breakfast – rice pap, sometimes 'limed', often mouldy and pepped up with garden fertiliser which Ailwen [*Captain Lord De Ramsey*] assured us was harmless and full of vitamins, a teaspoon of tinned milk and sugar, an army biscuit, a flat teaspoonful of marmalade, and plain tea; lunch – rice, a tin of bully between sixteen, a sweet of rice and grated coconut; supper – rice-flour pasty (the 'flour'milled by the transmission of a truck), beef tea from our minute cold-storage Jap beef ration, citronella water and a rice-and-fertiliser biscuit."

Bombardier Austin's account of his experiences as a prisoner-of-war, now in the Regimental Collection, goes into some detail of the vitamin-deficiency diseases that were common in Changi and goes on:

> "Some fertiliser made of ground peanut shells was found. The medical officers said that this was rich in Vitamin 'B' and so some foul-tasting biscuits were made from it, and also a drink using yeast to ferment it. We used to line up at mealtimes for a spoonful of this drink . . . there was a slight improvement in vitamin-related complaints as a result."

By all accounts life, however uncomfortable, began to settle down at Changi into what might be described as 'prison-camp routine'. Units remained responsible for discipline and stayed together, divided, in 135th Field Regiment's case into batteries, and retaining the officers–N.C.Os.–men hierarchy, which still extended to messes. During March it was decided that Roberts Barracks, part of a military hospital which had been occupied by the regiment, would be turned into an extension to the hospital, so the regiment moved to an area known as 'India Lines', within the barrack complex, where they were accommodated in tents. Some working parties were sent out but there was a good deal of free time and the usual round of classes, lectures and sport was instituted. At the end of April:

> ". . . a regimental art exhibition was held in a marquee in India Lines. All sorts of remarkable items turned up – knitted pullovers, plenty of drawings and paintings, including a series of coloured paintings depicting a London Underground journey as seen from the driver's cab. Lance-Bombardier Rush exhibited a display of knots and splices neatly fastened on a board."

Concluding one of his descriptions of the diseases that beset the troops in Changi, Bombardier Austin states that, "There were daily funeral processions to the cemetery, which was on the road to Singapore". It must have been in one of these processions that members of 135th Field Regiment escorted a coffin to a grave that was to be recorded as 'Private W.D. Airey'. In the coffin the regiment had placed a copy of the diary which Colonel Toosey had compiled, with help from other officers, immediately following the capitulation, nominal rolls of those who had survived the fighting and those known to have been killed, to be missing or to have been evacuated wounded, and recommendations for decorations. The coffin was dug up after the Japanese defeat, giving Captain Halford-Thompson's Military Cross "a somewhat posthumous air", as he put it, and leading eventually to Mentions-in-Despatches for Captain Keane, Lieutenant Simmonds, Sergeant Edwards and Bombardier Thompson. Colonel Toosey's D.S.O. was the only award that was known to have been made before the 'buried' recommendations were announced in 1946. He had received notification of the 'immediate' award of the D.S.O. a few days after the capitulation in "a little note in pencil from General Beckwith-Smith". Colonel Toosey's diary, referred to throughout this chapter as the 'Regimental Diary' might have survived without the burial; several people made copies and may have succeeded in secreting them throughout their captivity. The compilation of the diary, which does have occasional inaccuracies as to date, was, however, of the greatest importance, since none of the official war diaries of the campaign have survived.

During the first week of May 1942 Colonel Toosey was ordered to take a party of five hundred all ranks from 135th Field Regiment to join a 3,000-strong force under Brigadier Duke (whom the regiment had known as Commander 53 Infantry Brigade Group) that was to build the Japanese memorial to their troops lost in the battle for Singapore. The principal feature of the memorial, a Shinto shrine, was to be on an island in the MacRitchie Reservoir. The shrine was to be approached on roads newly laid across a golf course on the lower slopes of Bukit Timah. The regimental party was to be accommodated in Sime Road Camp (earlier the site of Headquarters Far East Air Force), which was conveniently close to the work. Alexander described the move to Sime Road:

> "In our weakened condition we found the 23-mile march hard going, although our heaviest packs went by truck. The Chinese tossed bread rolls to us and a few senior officers man-

Plate 150 *'The prisoners' church at Bukit Timah'.* (Drawing by Gunner W.C. Wilder, dated Singapore, 1942)

aged to buy food. The guards were considerate, even lending their bicycles to the weakest of us. But, in spite of regular halts, by the time we reached Sime Road several had fallen by the wayside and our marching had become a shamble.

The effort proved to have been worth it. [*The camp's*] badly shelled wooden huts were sprinkled with decaying bodies, but by the time we had cleaned up and repaired the huts its advantages became plain . . .

. . . The food situation improved again and we turned our attention to other creature comforts . . . We were eventually made to wire ourselves inside an official perimeter, but we had plenty of space and saw little of the Japanese . . . after three weeks someone discovered an electric substation within the perimeter, together with drums of cable and other supplies. A technical squad was formed, repairs were made and electricity laid on to the huts – and, at their request, to the Japs' guardroom. Fired by success, the squad went on to develop water services from some old mains, and an improvised pumping station . . ."

By the middle of June 1942, the Japanese had decided that all officer prisoners of the rank of colonel or above should be sent to Japan. Brigadier Duke therefore handed over command of Bukit Timah Camp (Sime Road) to Colonel Toosey. In his 'Report on Malay and Thailand Prisoner-of-War Camps', written in September 1945, a copy of which is in the Regimental Collection, Colonel Toosey described the conditions and the routine in the camp. Thanks to Brigadier Duke's efforts in the first six weeks, the camp was clean, makeshift water and electrical supplies had been arranged and living conditions were generally reasonable. The troops were divided into three units, each with its own commanding officer – some eight hundred Australians, the 500-strong party from 135th Field Regiment, now under the command of Major Peacock, and the remainder, described as "18th Division infantry and other troops". The work was not hard, though the hours were very long – from 08.00 to 19.00 – usually with one day's holiday a week. All officers and men working were paid ten cents a day. Rations were a great improvement on Changi, with meat, vegetables and rice arriving every day in sufficient quantities. Supplies from the Red Cross in South Africa reached the camp during September–October. Entertainments included a good library, a concert party, a 'race course' under the direction of Major Peacock and Captain Northcote of 135th Field Regiment, lectures and classes and a flourishing canteen, also under Captain Northcote's direction. A clandestine wireless provided reliable news. "In retrospect", Colonel Toosey wrote, with three years' experience, "Bukit Timah was our best camp. Here, conditions approached a more or less normal standard for prisoners-of-war. Also we were learning how to adapt ourselves to an entirely new mode of life."

When the main body of the regiment moved from Changi to Sime Road early in May, a number of officers and men remained in Changi, many of them in hospital and some in key appointments – Captain Lord De Ramsey was appointed 'Director of Agriculture' for

Plate 151 *'Japanese shrine on the golf course, Bukit Timah'.* (Drawing by Gunner W.C. Wilder, dated September 1942)

Singapore and ran the prisoners' gardens and pig farms on the island for the rest of the war. It was those who remained in Changi who experienced the 'Selarang Incident'. Bombardier Austin retained a copy of the statement covering the incident which he made to a debriefing officer on board the troopship *Orduna*, on which he returned to Britain:

"On 30th August 1942 the Japanese produced forms of promise not to escape, accompanied by their Order No. 17, which stated that all ranks were to be allowed to sign this form if they so wished. In our army it is our duty to try to escape and to hinder the enemy. The offi-
[202] cers and men in the Changi camp treated the forms with contempt and refused to sign.

Plate 152 Left – *The prisoners' gardens, Singapore, 1942. Some military prisoners-of-war remained in Singapore until liberated in 1945. Their gardens were a very important source of vegetables, which were used to supplement the totally inadequate issue of rations, almost entirely rice.*
Right – *Captain O.J.G. McMullen, Battery Captain of 344 Battery, who played a large part in the organisation of the prisoners' vegetable gardens in Singapore.* (Water-colour annotated 'P.O.W. Camp, Singapore, 1942')
(Regimental Collection)

Plate 153 *The 'Selarang Incident', when, following a general refusal to sign an undertaking not to attempt to escape, more than 17,000 British and Australian prisoners-of-war were crowded into Selarang Barracks, near Changi, Singapore, September 1942.*
Top – *General view of the barracks.*
Bottom left – *Scene on the barrack square during heavy rain.*
Bottom right – *An officer signs the undertaking not to escape following the decision by British commanders that the undertaking was being given 'under duress'.* (Regimental Collection)

The next evening the Japanese held a complete roll-call of prisoners in Changi. This was the first time they had completely checked our numbers and it was suspected that some sort of reprisal was about to be taken.

On 1st September the Japanese said we were to be punished and that we were to move to Selarang Barracks by 18.00 that evening. No handcarts were to be used and everything had to be transported by hand. The scene on the road was similar to that of refugees in Belgium. In our case, two men [*Bombardier Austin and his friend 'Ginger' Patterson*] carried their kit and the wood ration for our small party's cookhouse on a stretcher. Despite the Japanese order about trucks, some men actually arrived with motor vehicles running under their own power. There was an ambulance, water truck and several ex-Chinese contractors' wagons. It was amazing how these men had managed to keep these vehicles hidden from the Japanese since the fall of Singapore. Goats were also included in the procession. Selarang Barracks were some 250 yards square and in this area were to be congregated about 17,000 men. With only one water tap, washing was obviously out of the question. No food was issued by the Japanese for four days. Diptheria had broken out and also dysentery. No one was allowed to step on the road encircling the barracks and there were machine-guns mounted at each corner. In order to lie down and sleep it was necessary for two men to sleep opposite one another with their feet under each other's armpits.

Squads of men were working in shifts all night and day digging latrines through the tarmac of the barrack square. At all times there were great queues at the latrines and urinals, mixed up amongst which were the cookhouses and livestock – ducks, chickens, pigs, etc. – and also men sleeping.

Colonel Harris [*of 148th Field Regiment*], various padres and other officers were forced to witness the execution of four men, two British and two Australian, who had attempted to escape. The execution was most brutal. It took 27 shots from the firing squad [*made up of renegade Sikhs formerly of the Karpurthala Battalion*] to kill the men . . . They refused to be blindfolded or to accept cigarettes and died bravely.

During all this time Colonel Holmes had continually negotiated with the Japanese, who had by now threatened to bring in the hospital patients as well if we did not sign. Eventually they altered their order 'men were to be given the opportunity to sign' to 'men must sign' . . ."

Lieutenant-Colonel E.B. Holmes, of the Manchester Regiment, was the Commander British and Australian Troops, Changi following the removal of officers of the rank of colonel and above to Japan. He undertook a formidable responsibility in dealing with the crisis and, following advice from the senior medical staff that the situation could not be allowed to continue, he ordered all ranks to sign the undertaking not to escape. While himself accepting full responsibility for the order to sign, Colonel Holmes relied on the fact that the form had been signed under duress to negate any contractual value.

Events at Selarang were closely followed in Colonel Toosey's work camps at Bukit Timah. Here, the duress so apparent at Selarang was deemed to have force as well, and all ranks signed a non-escape certificate which was equally considered to have no value. By early September it was evident that work on the shrine and its approach roads would soon be finished and there were rumours that the prisoners were shortly to be moved. The destinations varied from 'a special camp in the Cameron Highlands where we shall be out of the way and left to ourselves' to a fairly accurate indication of 'railway-building in Thailand'. At the beginning of October the shrine was inaugurated with proper ceremony. To Lieutenant Alexander it looked "pleasingly unmilitary, with its airy Buddist archways and lacquered red sacred bridge leading through the landscaped grounds of the golf club to the wigwam-shaped sanctuary and oratory".

The regiment was further dispersed in October 1942 and it becomes impossible to account for more than a general picture of the prisoners' life for the three further years until liberation. A crucial document in keeping track of the larger element is Colonel Toosey's 'Report on . . . Prisoner-of-War Camps', quoted below:

"We left Bukit Timah during the last days of October 1942 on our journey to Thailand. Before leaving, prisoners were organised into battalions of 650 men. My battalion was made up of about four hundred men of my own regiment and was completed by detachments of Norfolks, Suffolks and 18th Divisional R.A.S.C. We were handed a good supply of Red Cross clothing by the Japanese, which served to equip ninety per-cent of the party with one of each essential article, including boots. We were also fortunate enough to be able to take with us a good supply of Red Cross medicines and some food.

Our final destination proved to be Ban Pong in Thailand. The journey by rail took four days and nights and was most uncomfortable. It was our first journey under Japanese organisation and, though later we were to suffer much harder conditions, it came as a severe shock. We were packed 31 to a metal wagon, including all our baggage. The food arrangements on the journey were sufficient to keep us alive but were very badly organised. We were, luckily, able to buy from the Malays and Thais throughout the journey. Our guard consisted of one Japanese sergeant and four other ranks.

We arrived at Ban Pong at 04.00 and were unloaded, formed up for inspection by Colonel Ishi, and then marched a short distance – some two and a half kilometres – to the Ban Pong staging camp. This camp was one of the worst I ever met. [*A description follows, including the fact that the whole camp was under some two feet of floodwater.*] Fortunately we only stayed one night . . .

The next day we left Ban Pong Camp and were taken to Tamarkan Camp, fifty kilometres away, in transport – being the first party to move in this manner.

Tamarkan [*now Tha Makham*] Camp was situated on the Meklow river [*now Mae Khlaung or Kwae Yai*] about three miles from Kanburi [*Kanchanaburi*] . . . It was started in early October 1942 by a party of two hundred all ranks under the command of Major Roberts, 80th Anti-Tank Regiment, R.A. This party was joined on 20th October by 110 all ranks of 2nd Argyll and Sutherland Highlanders under command of Captain J.D.L. Boyle of that unit. Five huts were completed, plus cookhouse and Japanese quarters.

My party arrived on 26th October, followed on 27th October by a party of Gordon Highlanders, British Battalion and Royal Artillery commanded by Major R.G. Lees, Gordon Highlanders. The camp strength was now 1,500 and it increased by November, with the addition of small parties, to 1,600 – all British. About 15th February 1943 a party of one thousand Dutch arrived from Java. The camp was extended at that time by four huts to make room for them. [*A table showing the camp staff includes Captain Northcote and R.S.M.Coles of 135th Field Regiment as Officer i./c. Canteen and Camp R.S.M.*]

We were told the day after our arrival that our job was to make a wooden and concrete bridge across the river and to construct about two kilometers of railway embankment on either side of the bridge. This work would take between nine months and one year. It had by now become clear to me that, whether we liked it or not, this work had to be done. I therefore addressed the troops, giving them my views, and told them that good discipline was essential and that they should work cheerfully to keep their spirits up, while we [*i.e., the officers*] would do our best to ensure they got good food and fair treatment. They responded as usual – cheerfully. [*Under the normal conventions covering prisoners-of-war, commissioned officers could not be required to work. On the railway officers began by supervising the men's work, sometimes taking up tools to join in voluntarily. Towards the end of December 1942 the Japanese issued an order that all officers should work. It was judged by senior officers, including Colonel Toosey, that resistance to this order would result in more harm than good, and from then on officers worked alongside their men.*]

The work outside was supervised by Japanese engineers who lived in the camp adjoining ours. The work was on the task system but on many occasions if the task was completed earlier than expected a further task would be given to eke out the day. I complained on all occasions when this happened and finally succeeded in having the work kept within bounds, the average working day being from 09.00 until 18.30 with one-and-a-half to two hours break in the middle of the day. At this time the ration scale was:

| *Grams per man per day* | |
|---|---|
| Rice | 700 |
| Vegetables | 600 |
| Meat | 100 |
| Salt | 20 |
| Sugar | 20 |
| Oil | 15 |

The combination of long working hours and insufficient diet soon brought our sick as high as four hundred serious cases.

In conjunction with Major Lees I had many interviews with the Japanese, telling them that if they wished the work to be completed according to the schedule they must:

(a) increase the rations;
(b) give the troops regular working hours; and
(c) allow one holiday a week.

With the assistance of Sergeant-Major Saito, who had obviously handled troops before, (b) and (c) above soon came into force and the rations improved slightly. These measures caused an immediate drop in the sick figures. Work continued in this manner until May 1943, when all work was stepped up to complete the railway throughout by a certain date. This period was the time when most of the deaths in Thailand occurred and was known as the 'Speedo' period. Work in Tamarkan became very hard but owing to the proximity of the camp to the work and the supply of food we did not suffer any serious casualties, though at times men were working eighteen hours a day.

Fortunately for all concerned, my party had brought a good supply of drugs from Singapore. The Japanese issue was entirely negligible. In the early days the general ailments were malaria, vitamin deficiency, tropical ulcers and some dysentery. The hospital consisted of part of one of the huts screened off, and it reflects great credit upon the medical officers that a successful appendix operation was performed in the open air.

We were beginning to realise the urgent need of anti-fly precautions, hygiene and general cleanliness. Hygiene and sanitation were improving all the time and with this improvement dysentery was gradually brought under control. During the whole period October 1942 to May 1943 . . . only nine deaths occurred. Most of these patients would have died under peace-time conditions. A small hospital was built and opened by 1st January 1943.

Few men had either mosquito nets or blankets and we were lucky that the type of malaria found locally was not a severe one. The accommodation generally consisted of the usual bamboo and attap huts, each man being allotted 75 cms. bed space."

A great deal has been written and published on the subject of the 'Burma Railway', and particularly on the 'Bridge over the River Kwai'. The few details that follow are included in order to place the work of the prisoners-of-war of 135th Field Regiment in a factual context. They have been extracted from an unattributed article in Edition No. 26 of *After The Battle*, published in 1979. The same edition included an article by Kevin Patience entitled 'Guide to the Death Railway', which considers the remains of the railway, as they stood in 1978–79, and the cemeteries established along the line by the Commonwealth War Graves Commission.

Plans had been drawn up before the war by the governments of Thailand and Burma to link the railway systems of the two countries by means of a single-track line running from Nompuradokku (known to the prisoners as Nong Pladuk) in Thailand to Tambyuzaya in Burma. The route, about 260 miles through jungle-covered mountains, had already been surveyed by Swiss engineers, whose plans were available to the Japanese. From Nompuradokku the line ran for some 35 miles through relatively flat country to cross the Mae Khlaung river at Tha Makham, about three miles north of Kanchanaburi. Two bridges were built at Tha

Plate 154 *'Building the Wan Po Viaduct'.* (Drawing by Gunner W.C. Wilder, dated 1943)

Makham, where the wide, fast-flowing river proved a difficult obstacle. The first bridge, which was of timber trestle construction and was not intended to be permanent, was completed in February 1943. The permanent, eleven-span steel bridge on concrete piers was finished two months later. At Kaopon (known to the prisoners as Chungkai), on the far side of the bridges, the Chungkai cutting had to be excavated. The line then continued some 35 miles up the valley of the Khwae Noi river (or Little Kwai) to Wampo, where a huge wooden viaduct had to be built to skirt the cliffs that formed the river's eastern bank. It is the southern portion of the line, about sixty miles long, from Nompuradokku (Nong Pladuk) to Wampo (sometimes called Wang Po) that was best known to members of 135th Field Regiment. While the prisoners based at the southern end of the line were working their way northwards, a force of Australians pushed south from Tambyuzaya (Thanbyuzayat), across the border between Burma and Thailand at the Three Pagodas Pass, and down the valley of the Khwae Noi. The two groups met at a point about 165 miles from the southern end on 17th October 1943 and the line was quickly opened to through traffic. Both during and after the construction phase the line was a target for Allied bombers and numerous attacks were mounted, especially against the bridges and the depots and marshalling yards that were established at the southern end of the railway:

> "The raids became more frequent after the line was opened in October 1943, necessitating the retention of prisoners to repair and maintain the track. In one raid on Nong Pladuk alone, where the prisoners were located amongst sidings holding petrol, ammunition and store trains protected by anti-aircraft defences, 95 prisoners were killed and three hundred wounded.
>
> The twin bridges at Tha Makham were a prime target but not until the eighth attack on 13th February 1945 were both the wooden and steel bridges hit, although repairs were immediately begun using prisoner-of-war labour. By April the wooden by-pass bridge was back in use and an attack to destroy it was mounted [*on 3rd April*] by aircraft of the United States 7th Bomb Group . . .
>
> On 24th June 1945, both the bridges, which had been repaired, were hit again by British pilots, putting the railway out of commission for the rest of the war . . .
>
> The three blown sections of the steel bridge were repaired by a Japanese firm as war reparations. However, as the 22-metre spans had proved an obstacle to the huge timber rafts plying the river, the two damaged piers were removed and replaced by a single support carrying two box-girder bridge sections. This enabled the navigable gap to be increased to 33 metres. The wooden bridge, being an even worse barrier to river traffic, was dismantled."

As work progressed, it was necessary to move parties out of the base camps and into work camps established at intervals alongside the line. Thus, while the major part of 135th Field Regiment arrived at Tamarkan Camp with Colonel Toosey's 'battalion', they were split up in the following months and the regiment can no longer be accounted for as a unit. After the completion of the two bridges the majority of fit men were moved to work further up the line. Tamarkan camp was then turned into a hospital camp, with Colonel Toosey still in command. Chungkai, across the river, also became a hospital camp. It was at about this time – mid-1943 – that the camps made contact with the 'V' Organisation, a very gallant joint enterprise between interned Britons and Thais, described at some length by Davies (see Bibliography), that arranged for drugs and money to be smuggled into the camps. Without the help of 'V' the number of deaths would have been immeasurably greater, for absolutely no reliance could be placed on the Japanese for the provision of any form of medical aid.

While a force of prisoners was retained in Thailand after the completion of the railway in October 1943 for maintenance and repair work and to work in the sidings and goods yards, many of the prisoners were dispersed to other labouring jobs – in Thailand and in French Indo-China, in Formosa and in Japan. Officers, who, as described above, had hitherto lived in the same camps as the men and shared the work, were concentrated at Kanburi Camp in January 1945, moving to Nakon Nyok in June 1945.

Five important accounts of the experiences of individual members of 135th Field Regiment have survived, four of which have already been referred to above. They are Colonel Toosey's 'Report on Malay and Thailand Prisoner-of-War Camps'; Lieutenant Alexander's *Sweet Kwai Run Softly*; Gunner Wilder's *P.O.W. Sketch Book*; Signalman Caplan's *From Gorbals to Jungle* (see

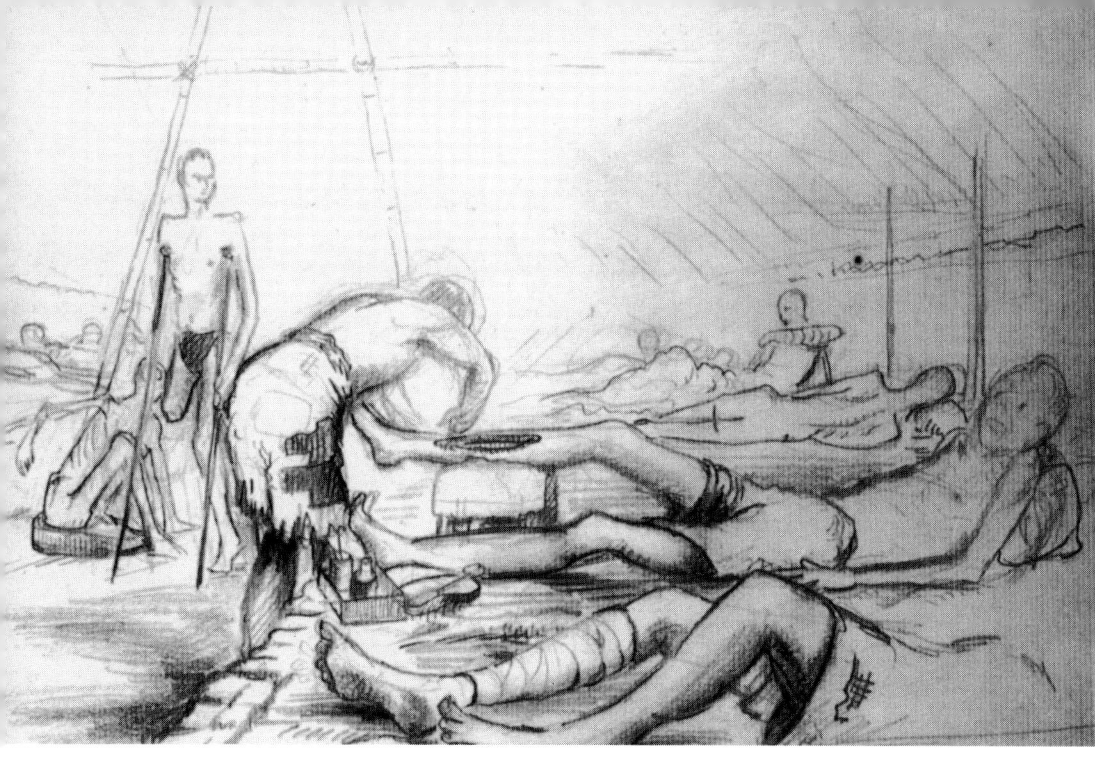

Plate 155 *'Hospital Scene, Chungkai, Thailand'.* (Drawing by Gunner W.C.Wilder, dated 1943)

Bibliography); and the series of letters and commentaries which constitute one side of a long-running correspondence between Bombardier Austin and the regimental historian which, together with his '336 Battery History', are in the Regimental Collection. Shorter, but no less valuable memoirs by Captain Halford-Thompson and R.Q.M.S. Beech are also in the Regimental Collection.

The placing, at a stroke, of almost the whole of 135th Field Regiment 'in the bag' (as the expression was, and generally has been since) led very quickly to the formation of the 135th Field Regiment, R.A. Regimental Association of Next-of-Kin. Within a few days of the news of the fall of Singapore, Major Sanders, who had commanded 344 Battery from the outbreak of war until Y-Listed with a broken leg in August 1941 and was now convalescing based at Corpus Christi College, Cambridge, had written to the Officer-in-Charge of Field Branch Records asking if arrangements could be made for him to extract an up-to-date list of the non-commissioned members of the regiment and their next-of-kin. Despite a rather evasive reply, Major Sanders went to the record office at Foots Cray in Kent:

> ". . . taking with me Miss Majorie Dalley from the Bursary, Corpus Christi College, for short-hand purposes. We were received by the Officer-in-Charge of Records (a colonel), who explained that he had no power to grant my request but perhaps as I had come so far I would be interested to see round the Record Office.
>
> We walked through a few rooms and on the way he observed casually, 'as a matter of fact, your regimental records are up on that shelf over there!' Shortly afterwards he remarked, 'I say, you must find it rather tiring on those crutches, wouldn't you like to sit down?' We took the hint and he left us. We then went to work hard for two or three hours and the attached roll [*now in the Regimental Collection*] was the result . . . " (Major Sanders)

Major Sanders and Miss Dalley returned with great satisfaction to Cambridge, which was, of course, very conveniently situated between the regimental centres at Hitchin and Peterborough, having promised not to divulge how they had come by the names. Officers' Records were not prepared to turn a similar 'blind eye'.

By early April 1942 a circular letter, complete with reply-postcard that would form part of a card index of nearly seven hundred names was ready for despatch. The replies showed overwhelming support for the idea and the embryo committee – Colonel Hudson, Mrs Toosey, Mrs Pilling, the wives of the three battery commanders and Captain Cherry's mother, supported by the Reverend Hector Morgan, the Regimental Padre prior to embarkation – was brought into being. The first printed newsletter was sent out during May 1942, forerunner of a series of fourteen which ended in January 1946.

There is no doubt that the association and its newsletter played an important role in helping the prisoners' families face their "mutual anxiety with mutual fortitude" (from the circular inviting next-of-kin to join) but the newsletter does make curious reading nearly sixty

Plate 156 *'Camp Scene, Nong Pladuk, Thailand'.* (Drawing by Gunner W.C. Wilder, dated May 1944)

years later, in an age when news from a battlefield reaches people's homes within hours. At no stage is it admitted that B.S.M. Waldock's party had been ordered to leave. They are mentioned in Newsletter No. 1 as "known to be away from Singapore" and listed in No. 3 (September 1942), where they are described as having "escaped". By March 1943 (No. 5) "All officers of the regiment are known to be prisoners except Lieutenant Raynor (missing) and Lieutenant Boult (killed in action)". In No. 7 (July 1943) it is announced that many members of the association "have now received postcards from their relatives in the regiment". The postcards, most of which had taken between four and six months to arrive, reported "good health, good treatment and reasonable food". The Christmas 1943 edition (No. 9), however, notes with regret that "we have nothing further to report since our last leaflet regarding the whereabouts of our prisoners. Even the Red Cross have been unable to obtain further news . . . ".

The secretary's report for the year ended December 1943, which was not printed in the newsletter, states that up to 31st December 1943 390 non-commissioned officers and men had been properly notified as prisoners-of-war and that four were known to have died while prisoners. Nearly four hundred were still to be officially accounted for. Real news of the prisoners' whereabout does not seem to have reached their next-of-kin until the summer of 1944. The 'July Mail' is described in No. 11 (August 1944) as having contained "very many letters from camps No. 2 and No. 4, from whom we have heard so little before". Among the cards was found "news of many men of the regiment from whom nothing at all has been heard since the fall of Singapore".

After No. 11 (August 1944) the newsletter was not published again until March 1945. Edition No. 12 contained a letter to the association from Lance-Bombardier Castro "lately returned from No. 4 Camp, Thailand". Castro had been on the way to Japan with a party of prisoners in the Japanese passenger-cargo ship *Rakuyo Maru* when the ship, sailing in convoy, was torpedoed by the United States submarine *Sealion* in the early morning of 12th September 1944. The *Rakuyo Maru* remained afloat for several hours but the prisoners were prevented at gun point from getting on to rafts or floating wreckage while the Japanese crew and guards were picked up by the escort vessels. It was not until the afternoon of 15th September that another submarine of the attack group discovered survivors on a makeshift raft and called *Sealion* to help in rescuing any more that could be found. Between them the two submarines and two more specially called to the area recovered 159 British and Australian survivors, including Lance-Bombardier Castro. It is not clear when he arrived in Britain but Castro lost no time in contacting the Next-of-Kin Association, news of which had reached the prisoners in Thailand. However, he had signed a special security undertaking at the War Office and was "not allowed to give any information on certain subjects, and none at all to the Press". He was also forbidden to speak in public. His letter, and a typed but undated record of a meeting with Mrs Peacock and Mrs Neal of the association committee, fail completely to give a realistic account of conditions in Thailand. It must be presumed that Lance-Bombardier Castro was under instructions not to reveal the true situation. Possibly he was able to give greater detail in what were treated as private conversations. Certainly newsletters published after March 1945 appear to take a more gloomy, or realistic, view of the conditions in which the prisoners were living and working, of the fact that they would be far from fit when they eventually returned, and of the likelihood that large numbers would not return.

Two more prisoners from 135th Field Regiment reached home before the end of the war with Japan, but neither of them seem to have communicated with the Next-of-Kin Association. If they did, there is no record in the newsletter and no papers have survived. Captain Halford-Thompson's memoirs include the following passage, which unfortunately does not date the incident:

> "Having survived quite a lot, we then had to cope with Allied bombing, R.A.F. and U.S.A.A.F. The R.A.F. were at least fairly accurate; the Americans favoured more widespread delivery. The railway bridges were the targets and our camps were always near them. The Japs would not let us dig adequate trenches in which to take cover and there were a considerable number of casualties from these raids . . . Another raid dropped a bomb which blew Lance-Sergeant Pateman over the bamboo fence. He came to fifty yards or so outside the camp to find himself being addressed by an English-speaking Siamese who urged him to accompany him. The Siamese was a member of Force 136, the Far East arm of the Special Operations Executive. We all knew at the time that if anybody tried to escape the local population would hand him back to the Japs for execution. Pateman tried to get back into the camp but eventually followed the Siamese. Within three weeks he was flying out of the country and soon reached home, where he saw my mother and told her I was still alive."

The return to Britain of Gunner Dellar is a happy aside in the following extraordinary account by Gunner A. J. Wilkins of his experiences after leaving Chungkai, following the completion of the railway, and being sent to Singapore for passage to Japan:

> "The journey took six months. We left Singapore (1,200 P.O.W. on board, including about thirty from 135th Field Regiment) and off Borneo the ship broke down. The convoy went on without her and we eventually got to Manilla, travelling only part of each day, usually in sight of land. We stayed in the ship in Manilla Bay for about three months. The Japs made several attempts to sail but each time the engine packed up and in the end they lightened the ship by unloading the cargo of bauxite. During this period there were very many deaths and conditions became quite frightful. Gunners Lawrence, Hill, Robson, Warner and Newland of 135th Field Regiment died and were buried at sea during this time.
>
> Eventually we sailed but we were attacked [*by United States bombers*] at about 10.00 the next day (I think), I know I was down below in the lower hold when the whole side of the ship caved in and I was swept back by a towering wall of water. Gunner White (135) was standing by my side – I never saw him again. I made my way under water to the open part of the hold and came up with my head level with the feet of the men standing in the upper hold. I remember seeing B.S.M. Cannon (135). I then recall the ship sliding backwards and downwards, taking me down with her. Eventually I came up again and in time got on a raft. After about six hours paddling we got ashore at a place I believe was called San Fernando, just north of Manilla . . .
>
> Those of us who got ashore were rounded up and kept in the upper room of a house. I remember only Gunner Dellar (135) being with me. Others were picked up by Phillipino fishing vessels . . . We were taken to a P.O.W. camp at Cabanatan, full of American P.O.Ws., where we were made to work extremely hard in the manioc fields. [*Here Dellar was left behind sick, eventually to be rescued by the Americans. He got home about six months or so early.*] We were then moved to the old Spanish prison at Bilibid, back in Manilla.
>
> Aboard the next ship – a terrifying experience. The whole convoy was sunk except us. We were beached and left overnight. The Americans came and finished us off next morning. Into the sea again and once more ashore. It was now [*after*] Christmas 1944.

Plate 157 *'Hut Interior, Nong Pladuk, Thailand'.* (Drawing by Gunner W.C. Wilder, dated May 1944)

Following some really incredible hardships [*I was*] eventually shipped on to Formosa . . . Finally, I met some chaps on Formosa – survivors of the first ship, I think, and on we went in ship No. 4 to Fukuoka, Japan, arriving on 11th February 1945 . . . I believe the camp we were taken to was at Omuta, across the bay from Nagasaki. It was a coal-mining camp – very severe discipline.

Of the 1,200 who embarked at Singapore, only fifteen men reached Japan."

News of the progress of the war and of the increasing likelihood of liberation reached the prisoners through contact with the local Thai population and from the clandestine wireless sets which most camps had. Some time early in 1945 Bombardier Austin was with a group of prisoners trekking from Tha Makham southwards towards a new camp at which an airfield was to be constructed. During the journey:

". . . We reached the town of Petchaburi. It was a nice town with a very beautiful temple with a number of pagodas. A Thai rushed out of a shop and gave one of our men a bottle of ringworm ointment. Another, trotting by in pony-and-trap, said in a stage whisper and looking straight ahead, 'Germany nearly finished' . . ."

Eventually, the warrant officers in charge of the various detachments at the airfield camp, known as Pagoda Camp, Petchaburi, who continued the now long-standing practice of being very sparing with 'hard' news in order to safeguard the clandestine contacts, felt able to forecast that the war might be over "in about a week". Bombardier Austin made notes of events as liberation neared:

*"15th August 1945*

Today parties went to work on the airfield as usual but all work on camp jobs stopped. Men jokingly said, 'Oh, the war must be over', but never really believed it was. Tonight the Japs held a celebration. We did not know what to make of this. They also mentioned 'going to paradise and taking the prisoners with them'. Actually, in the morning they were all in a drunken heap.

*16th August 1945*

No work at all today. Something has gone wrong with the Japs. A buzz of excited conversation fills the camp. Normally the Japs would have come into the huts shouting 'No speak'.

*17th August 1945*

Still no work. Mr. Mashuska, the interpreter, told us that Mr. Churchill had been thrown out and that we now had a Labour government.

*18th August 1945*

. . . That evening Lieutenant Davidson had us all on parade and announced the end of the war . . .

*19th August 1945*

The concert party put on the best show ever – 'Atlantic Interlude', written in the camp by Jack Kirby . . .

*20th August 1945*

. . . Our warrant officers seized the Japanese Red Cross store. There were many parcels dated 1941 and 1942, mostly, I noticed, from Stepney and Bermondsey, and large stocks of sorely-needed medical equipment.

*21st August 1945*

Today we decided to make a Royal Artillery flag. The blue background was Lance-Bombardier Greenwood's P.T. shorts, which had to be forcibly taken from him. He was so proud that he had kept them throughout his time as a prisoner-of-war but the chaps said, 'Don't be so b....y daft. There are bales of new uniform about to arrive by parachute!'. I cannot remember where the red came from. The yellow was from a duster equally proudly looked after by Gunner Bert Dabnor but given up willingly in his case. I embroidered a gun with wool picked from a blanket, and a field dressing I had kept was undone to make a fringe. The flag was hoisted by the youngest Gunner, a lance-bombardier from another regiment, the ceremony being supervised by B.S.M. Burgess of 344 Battery. [*The flag is now in the Regimental Collection.*]

*26th August 1945*

We had a memorial service today, in the pretty little cemetery, and a parade. Photographs were taken by a Thai photographer.

*27th August 1945*

. . . A British paratroop captain arrived in camp. He had been parachuted in May, north of Kanburi, with a mule. While we were listening to his news an American parachutist also arrived. He too was dropped in May and had a camp full of Thai guerillas not far from our camp. The six men who had escaped from our camp earlier had been taken to him by his Thai confederates . . .

Events now began to move fast . . . Harry Neave, Bill Smith and Jenkins arrived in camp from Singora, dead beat, with stories of terrible hardship and work on bridges – building them up as the Liberators knocked them down . . .

*28th August 1945*

Gunner Jenkins told us that he had been on a party making a road from Wam Po to Mergui. Out of 35 of our regiment on this party, seventeen died . . . It was an awful story of privation and death . . .

*29th August 1945*

Brigadier Miles, a medical officer, arrived with a Jeep and trailer, at which we stared in amazement, never having seen one before . . . The first Dakota arrived with supplies and took twenty stretcher cases back to Rangoon . . . The airfield we had built was the best they had used, they said . . .

*30th August 1945*

More planes arrived and began to move the hospital – sixteen stretcher cases or 24 walking patients. More supplies landed.

*31st August 1945*

On our toes with excitement. Nearly our time to go.

*1st September 1945*

We went for a wash and changed into new uniform, plenty of which had arrived, with plimsolls. How strange to get used to footwear again . . . I was surprised at how calm I was at my first flight, though somewhat apprehensive to note that the plane's door is missing . . . . . . when the plane stopped an ambulance backed up to the door, into which we fell in a heap.

We were taken to a canteen, where dainty chicken sandwiches were laid on – our first bread for three-and-a-half years. We sat looking at them for quite a while. Then Sammy Greenwood, who had a stammer, said, 'I s..suppose s..somebody had b..better make a f..f......g s..start!'and grabbed a sandwich, and we all then tucked in . . . peaches and cream, too. From the canteen we were taken to the 38th British General Hospital – into white sheets – six years to the day after I was called up on 1st September 1939."

Other accounts tell much the same story. A final irony was the death of two members of the regiment as the planes in which they were being evacuated from Thailand crashed. Gradually, as ship-loads were put together at Rangoon, the liberated prisoners trickled back to Britain. The decision had been made to send them back by sea to allow them to recuperate to the greatest possible extent during the voyage. But the journey was not a bracing, curative experience for everybody. Gunner Wilder, returning on the troopship *Orbita*, found that conditions reminded him of the voyage to the Far East on *Mount Vernon* four years previously. "We are crowded right below", he recorded, "Nothing to do but lie and sweat. Shall be glad to get home".

They came home as individuals, and 135th Field Regiment, Royal Artillery did not ever reassemble as a unit. For most, though, the regimental service of remembrance and thanksgiving held at St. Mary's Parish Church, Hitchin just before Christmas of 1945 was the regiment's final parade.

Plate 158 *Returning from the Far East, November 1945. Bombardier P. Searle of 135th Field Regiment* (Right) *relaxing with another former prisoner in the Silver Bowl, San Francisco, en route for Britain. Both are wearing the ribbons of the 1939–45 Star and the Pacific Star, earned through their service in Malaya and Singapore in 1942.*
(Regimental Collection)

Chapter 6

# *The War-formed Unit – 191st Field Regiment, R.A., December 1942–December 1944*

*Formation and training, December 1942–May 1943*

In December 1942 a further eleven field regiments were added to the list of 'war-formed' artillery units. They were numbered from 185th to 195th and all were formed around cadres drawn from other units, rather than by conversion of existing units or by change of arm. In 42nd Armoured Division both regiments of the divisional artillery – 86th (Hertfordshire Yeomanry) and 147th (Essex Yeomanry) Field Regiments – were ordered by W.O.U.M. 20/Artillery/6092 (A.G.6a) of 16th December 1942 to provide cadres of approximately battery strength for a new regiment, to be numbered 191st. The new unit would start to form on 21st December in accommodation vacated by 86th Field Regiment (see Chapter 4) in Hovingham and Slingsby, in Yorkshire. The designation 'Herts and Essex Yeomanry' seems to have been adopted within the first few days after formation.

Major J.R. Cochrane, Second-in-Command of 147th Field Regiment, was promoted to command 191st. Major R.C. Hulbert was posted from a staff appointment to become second-in-command; Captain W.B. Godfrey, who had been assistant adjutant of 86th Field Regiment was appointed adjutant and Lieutenant (Q.M.) F.C. Peters arrived fresh from his commissioning course as quartermaster. In *View from the Bridge*, his history of 191st Field Regiment, Lamb (see Bibliography), who will frequently be quoted in this chapter, records the formation of the three batteries:

"By 21st December the skeleton of the regiment was organised and officers, W.Os. and senior N.C.Os. were assigned to their batteries . . . The three batteries were numbered 532, 533 and 534. The nucleus of 532 Battery was provided from 413 Battery of 147th Field Regiment, and in similar fashion the personnel for 533 Battery were drawn from 462 Battery of 86th Field Regiment. 534 Battery was staffed by a roughly equal number from each . . .

The battery commanders of 413 and 462 more or less took up where they had left off in their old regiments . . . Major Perkins, surrounded by a host of Essex Yeomen, conducted the affairs of 532 Battery as though nothing had happened, while Major Higgens, who had reared the St. Albans battery of the Hertfordshire Yeomanry with a kind of paternal irascibility through the Munich convulsions of 1938, continued to follow the same irrepressible vein . . .

The organisation of 534 Battery soon took shape. The battery commander was Captain N. Norman-Butler of the Essex Yeomanry and his promotion from captain to major was confirmed a few days later . . .

Christmas intervened briefly and thereafter things began to move . . . The departure of 86th Field Regiment was immediately followed by the arrival, in five 3-tonners, of the first of the infantry. One hundred and twelve men of 30th Battalion The Wiltshire Regiment . . ."

The early weeks of 191st Field Regiment are recorded in great detail in a series of progress reports annexed to the War Diary. By 30th December there were 23 officers and 380 other ranks on strength but no equipment had yet been issued, necessitating borrowing from the 'parent' regiments. The vehicle strength stood at 44 motor-cycles and a few trucks. A week later the other rank strength had risen to 473; regimental classes for signallers and command post and O.P. assistants had started and eight 25-pdr. guns had arrived, together with towing vehicles and limbers. Very little G.1098 equipment had been issued but bootmaker's, tailor's and hairdresser's shops had been staffed and opened. By the end of the third week, the other rank strength had reached 630. Equipment was reported to be "coming through well" but the most urgent requirements for training purposes were still wireless sets and rifles. A dance band had been formed within the regiment; the first dance had been held and it was planned that dances would become a weekly event.

The next report, dated 4th February 1943, shows that 533 and 534 Batteries had their full establishment of 25-pdrs. Mk. II, while 532 Battery had eight 18/25-pdrs. However, the 25-pdrs. had some ten modifications outstanding and each gun needed about two days in workshops. The fact that guns may not have been up-to-date with modifications did not prevent them being fired, however, and on 1st and 2nd February each troop had carried out live-firing practice on the nearby Spaunton Moor range. According to Lamb, "There were safety officers behind every tree and the troop leaders were fully occupied in a continual race from gun to gun, checking line before each shot". The first shoots were at relatively close range, and the gunners themselves could see the fall of shot. Trainee signallers and 'specialists' – command post and O.P. assistants – were employed in their intended roles, occasioning the odd "stifled curse from a harassed G.P.O." but proving to all that the combination of guns, communications and technical wizardry could, and did, result in 'rounds on the ground'.

The fifth, and last, report was submitted after the regiment had been in course of formation for exactly three months. There were 33 officers against an establishment of 36, while other ranks were thirty over establishment at 667. The overbearing was expected to reduce to a deficiency of twelve after nineteen O.Rs. assessed as unsuitable for the Royal Artillery had been posted out, together with others transferring to the Royal Engineers and the Intelligence Corps and a number who were expected to be accepted for O.C.T.U. The regiment's Light Aid Detachment, R.E.M.E. had been formed but had not yet received any vehicles or equipment. Among the various trades and classifications the only serious deficiency was in signallers, of which the regiment was 29 short. It was reported that it was "quite impossible to find any more signallers from the resources within the regiment as they have already been combed out. Further, there are amongst the 107 on strength quite a fair number who will never make good signallers". Specialist, gun-layer and driver training was clearly going well and six hundred other ranks had fired the 'Full R.A. War Course' with the rifle, resulting in 180 first-class shots and over two hundred second-class. Further live-firing practice had culminated in the firing of some lines of a quick barrage after the regimental survey section had passed both fix and line to batteries. Anti-tank practice had taken place too. Field training had included driving at night without lights and occupation of harbour areas, and each battery had practised bivouacking and cooking in the field. All outstanding modifications had been carried out on the guns, which were now going back to workshops in relays to have muzzle brakes fitted. There were still vehicle deficiencies; the shortage of 15-cwt. trucks, especially, was preventing proper collective training. In summary, though, Colonel Cochrane reported that he was "satisfied with the progress made by the regiment and with its present state – with the important exception of the signallers".

At the end of March 1943 42nd Armoured Division, under command of which 191st Field Regiment remained throughout the period of build-up and training, moved into Southern Command. The regiment was accommodated at Trowbridge Barracks, as described by Lamb:

> ". . . while the original barracks was not large enough to accommodate a complete regiment, temporary buildings had been added. Each of the three batteries occupied a 'spider', which was simply a large office bungalow surrounded by living huts, all of which were connected by corridors. Each troop was allotted a single living hut and this also contained the troop office and stores. In the central bungalow, in addition to the battery office and stores, there were to be found the latrines, baths and ablutions. Regimental Headquarters took over most of the original building, which included centralised mess rooms, dining-hall and medical centre. An excellent N.A.A.F.I. canteen was installed on the first floor above the dining-hall, and a Nissen hut, placed conveniently near the back gate, contained a wet bar and the bombardiers' mess.

After the primitive bleakness of Hovingham, all of this was sheer luxury and, predictably, following a suitable interval which allowed everyone to become accustomed to the new conditions, a number of innovations were introduced. Guard mounting was now to be carried out with considerably greater ceremony ... with guard orderlies and the orderly officer in attendance. Casting aside all his good resolutions of December, the R.S.M. took to presiding over a daily assembly on the parade ground ..."

By now, 'collective', rather than 'individual' training was in full swing. Lamb reckons that the regiment was about one month ahead of the training schedule and records that:

"During the last week of April each battery headquarters was busily occupied with the C.O.'s latest task. Each would devise a twelve-hour scheme which was to be performed by one of the other two batteries at Westdown on 29th April ... the enterprise degenerated into a competition between the batteries ... [*but*] ... all of these miniature exercises were tackled very creditably on the ground.

... The following week each battery carried out a 36-hour exercise arranged by R.H.Q. ... The regiment was now preparing to tackle the first of a series of regimental exercises and on 10th May 24 men of the Royal Signals under 2nd Lieutenant E.H. Richards arrived to man the rear link. At the same time, the problems of supply eased slightly and new wireless sets were installed in the battery and troop command vehicles. Thus reinforced, the regiment departed for Okehampton on 11th May, where there would be a steady introduction to the techniques of regimental shooting."

Although training at regimental and higher levels was not yet complete, 191st Field Regiment had joined 42nd Armoured Divisional Artillery in replacement of 86th Field Regiment (see Chapter 4) on 3rd May 1943.

### *Waiting for action, May 1943–May 1944*

After their few days at Okehampton the regiment returned to Trowbridge and at the end of May moved with the whole of 42nd Armoured Division to the Portsmouth–Southampton area. Here, according to Lamb, "the object of the exercise was to create the impression that large numbers of troops were massing close to the south coast ...". The deception planners were making a last attempt to persuade the enemy that the invasion of Europe would take place during the summer of 1943, while in reality sights were now being set on the spring of 1944.

As if to welcome 191st Field Regiment as full members of 42nd Armoured Divisional Artillery, but perhaps more with a view to seeing what sort of unit had been taken on, the division laid on Exercise 'Macra' starting on 10th June. Captain M.G. Bond, who contributed the chapter on 191st Field Regiment to Gee's history of the Essex Yeomanry (see Bibliography) recorded events during June, July and August 1943:

"It was on West Down [*Salisbury Plain*] that the regiment first showed its paces to the military world at large. In June a 'gallop exercise' took place, starting on West Down with 30 Armoured Brigade and finishing at Sennybridge in Wales with 71 Infantry Brigade. In this exercise the infantry and tanks were on the ground and live ammunition was used. The regiment was in competition with a very worthy rival – 147th – but so conspicuously did 191st distinguish themselves during the opening days of this first and exacting test that on the last day, when a troop salvo was fired on to a village some three miles off the range, this was attributed to 147th. Such is the value of a good reputation!

Throughout July and August, brigade, divisional and artillery exercises continued. In divisional exercises 147th normally worked with 30 Armoured Brigade and 191st with 71 Infantry Brigade – 532 Battery was affiliated to 1st Highland Light Infantry, 533 Battery to 1st Oxfordshire and Buckinghamshire Light Infantry and 534 to 1st East Lancashire Regiment.

Meanwhile, at Trowbridge, training continued during the intervals and the commanding officer arranged regimental sports by way of variation ... One event in the competition was a three-and-a-half mile run over the downs above Westbury for thirty men per troop; the first twenty men per troop to count. The C.O. accompanied the runners ... in one of the tanks which had just been issued to the regiment. These were Crusaders, armed with a 6-

pdr. gun, speedy, and with first-class suspension. But the armour was light, the diamond-shaped turret cramped, and the chain-driven fan mechanically unsound. About a month after they were issued they were replaced by Cavaliers, a version of the Cromwell, with the Cromwell turret [*used on some marks of Churchill*], but with a Nuffield Liberty engine instead of the Cromwell's Rolls-Royce engine. These, also, were not entirely free from mechanical trouble, but some at least were able to give good service and provided valuable experience until finally withdrawn in the following March.

In August, it became known that 42nd Armoured Division was to be broken up to provide specialist units. This was not a surprise, but it precipitated the problem of the regiment's future and the probability of a move from Trowbridge. At this time most of the formations due for the Second Front were already at full establishment, and the prospect of being attached to an Army Group Royal Artillery (or A.G.R.A.) as an army field regiment seemed, at the time, uninteresting and unbecoming after a role in an armoured division. Still worse was the awful possibility of conversion to a reinforcement unit.

Meanwhile, with the future unsettled, activities continued with unabated intensity. For eighteen days in the month of August the regiment was out on some scheme or exercise . . .".

With this uncertain future hanging over them, the regiment returned to Okehampton on 9th September for ten days. Hardly had they arrived, however, when an urgent call came for a battery to move at once to the Milford Haven area, where 79th Armoured Division were conducting a long series of trials and exercises to establish the role of specialised armour – mine-clearing and bridgelaying tanks and various armoured vehicles to be used by the Royal Engineers – in an assault landing. It was arranged that 532 Battery should move immediately to Linneyhead. Here, according to Captain Bond:

". . . there was no rest, but the work, though hard, was interesting, and the experience of great value to troop commanders, G.P.Os. and gun numbers. Probably more ammunition was fired by the battery during their five weeks at Linneyhead than during all previous practices.

. . . The role was to give support to 27 Armoured Brigade in squadron battle practice and to provide the reality of fire for two big exercises – 'Siegfried' and 'Europa'. These two exercises were performed almost daily, with countless small variations. 'Europa' was a rehearsal for the invasion of the beaches, and specimen beach obstacles were erected and experiments carried out, not only in dealing with the expected opposition but in getting the tanks through minefields and over sand-dunes. While 'Europa' generally took place in the early morning, 'Siegfried' [*which rehearsed breakout through a prepared and well organised line*], took place after dark . . .

In working with . . . 27 Armoured Brigade, troop commanders had the inestimable benefit of firing in support of tanks and infantry without safety officers and without supervision . . . On 12th October the battery's work was done. After firing, on the penultimate morning, the balance of ammunition unexpended – 130 rounds per gun – in twenty minutes, the battery set out . . ."

The rest of the regiment had completed their practice at Okehampton – "as varied a programme of shoots as one could possibly hope for . . . [*followed by*] a succession of Mike targets and complex fire plans" (Lamb) – by 19th September. They could not, however, return to Trowbridge, which was already in process of handover to the United States Army. By an admirable piece of sleight-of-hand, Colonel Cochrane obtained temporary use of the requisitioned Warner's holiday camp at Seaton in Devon. Work continued, especially to improve trade classifications, but "every spare moment was filled in with some recreational pursuit or other . . . [*and*] all in all this was a happy fortnight for everyone" (Lamb). At the end of this 'holiday' the regiment returned briefly to Trowbridge, where they received orders to move on 10th October to a hutted camp at Newlands Corner, near Epsom. "The prospect of spending another winter in such spartan surroundings was not a very pleasant one", Lamb recorded, but at the very last minute the instructions were changed. A despatch rider overtook the advance party's column on the Guildford by-pass with orders to move instead to Ramillies Barracks, Aldershot. Here, as part of the 'British Increment, First Canadian Army', they would come under command of 2nd Canadian A.G.R.A.

Plate 159 *The embroidered sleeve badge adopted by 191st Field Regiment in April 1943. Based on a purely Essex badge worn by 147th Field Regiment, the 191st Field Regiment's badge incorporated the Hertfordshire Yeomanry's hart as well as the three seaxes of Essex. Very unusually, a version of this sleeve badge was later used by the Commonwealth War Graves Commission as a headstone badge for the graves of members of 191st Field Regiment* (see Plate 171).
(Regimental Collection)

Orders to mobilise put an end to speculation on the regiment's future. They were, it seemed, guaranteed a place in Twenty-First Army Group for the expected invasion of Europe. On 21st October, Brigadier Huckvale, commanding 2nd Canadian A.G.R.A., visited 191st Field Regiment to inspect progress with the mobilisation programme. Lamb comments that, as the first Canadian commander to have a British unit serving under him, the brigadier's visit must have been "an intriguing experience". This would particularly have been so in the matter of badges, for in addition to the normal rank and trade badges and red-and-blue arm of service strip, all ranks wore the regiment's own badge on both sleeves of their battledress. This badge had been 'introduced' by Colonel Cochrane in defiance, or possibly in ignorance, of A.C.Is. which stipulated that regimental flashes should bear no "badge, emblem, lettering or figures", soon after the regiment arrived at Trowbridge. Captain Bond describes it:

> "... This flash ... was modelled on 147th Field Regiment's flash. But whereas 147th wore a red diamond flash with the three Essex seaxes, the 191st flash was a green diamond bearing a shield with the Essex seaxes and surmounted by the hart of the Herts Yeomanry. The 'goat and cutlasses' was a colourful and attractive sign. All ranks were proud of it and it helped to make the regiment known."

The same design was used on the regimental flag, six of which were made and flown by Regimental Headquarters and the batteries in camp in England and later, when opportunity arose, in North-West Europe. (The flag flown by 533 Battery is now in the Regimental Collection.)

The flash and the flag, which would undoubtedly have been flown for the brigadier's visit, were at least consistent with the new regiment's title. What the visitor made of officers who met him wearing service dress, and thus the original cap, collar or shoulder-strap badges of the parent regiments, is not on record but, wisely perhaps, he took no action. It was necessary, however, for 191st Field Regiment to change the serial number on their red-and-blue vehicle signs to conform to the series used by 2nd Canadian A.G.R.A. and to adopt the First Canadian Army vehicle marking instead of that used by 42nd Armoured Division. The Canadian sign was an oblong equally divided into black, red and black horizontal stripes, which normally had a yellow maple leaf superimposed on the centre. In 191st Field Regiment's case, however, the maple leaf was not used.

In the middle of November 1943 the regiment moved out of Ramillies Barracks and into billets in Sutton, in Surrey. Less than a week after their arrival, they set off with the rest of 2nd Canadian A.G.R.A. for exercises on the ranges at Otterburn and Redesdale in Northumberland. The journey north took three days and was immediately followed by two days of battery and regimental exercises before all units came under A.G.R.A. command. Lamb records that 191st Field Regiment played a leading and highly successful part. Two weeks with the other units of the A.G.R.A. provided ample opportunity for all ranks to meet their Canadian opposite numbers, often over a pot of coffee, which featured in the Canadian Army's rations and life in much the same way that tea did in the British Army. The regiment thus became "absorbed into the life and affairs of First Canadian Army".

The first anniversary of formation, 21st December 1943, found 191st Field Regiment taking part in a major demonstration on Salisbury Plain, where four field regiments and one medium regiment supported a battalion in the attack. They returned to Sutton in time for Christmas, which was spent quietly, with news of the impending change of their commanding officer. On 27th December it became known that Lieutenant-Colonel Cochrane, who had built the regiment up into a highly competent unit over the past twelve months, was to join the headquarters of British Increment, First Canadian Army as G.S.O.1 (Staff Duties and Training). In the course of a rather longer tribute to Colonel Cochrane, Lamb remarks that he had inspired in the regiment "a deep consciousness of belonging to an exclusive brotherhood in which giving of one's best was an acquired habit, rather than an occasional strenuous effort". "This spirit", he says, "was the legacy inherited by Lieutenant-Colonel M.W. Hope when he arrived in Sutton . . .". Colonel Hope was a Regular officer who had attended the Royal Naval Staff College and had spent most of the war to date working in staff and training appointments in Combined Operations. He joined on 1st January 1944 and assumed command the next day. First impressions, according to Lamb, were that he "offered a strange contrast with his predecessor in many ways, the most striking of which was the entirely false impression he gave of the kindly headmaster with the ready smile". Events would prove he was an ideal choice to carry the regiment through the training for the invasion of Europe and to lead it in action.

January 1944 was a busy month from all points of view. Anti-tank practice at Lydd was followed by calibration at Larkhill, and cooks, clerks, storemen and signallers were routed out of various hiding places for training in local defence of the gun position. Lamb records that "the P.I.A.T. [*projector, infantry, anti-tank – a spring-powered forerunner of the anti-tank rocket launcher*] and the Bren [*light machine-gun*] were both dealt with to exhaustion, and a whole morning was spent messing about with mines and booby-traps". But the clearest indicator, if any were needed, of the regiment's forthcoming part in an amphibious landing came in the last week of January when roads and other suitable spaces in Sutton were marked out with the internal dimensions of landing craft, together, of course, with the bow doorway and ramp, and the whole regiment began loading and unloading drills. Captain Bond noted that, "Practising first by day and later by night, a compact, speedy and systematic loading was achieved".

Another indication of the esteem in which 191st Field Regiment was held, despite its lack of seniority and extreme youth, was received at the end of January 1944, when the regiment was offered the opportunity to redesignate as 6th Field Regiment in order to replace the original 6th Field Regiment, which had been lost in the Far East. After discussion with the senior members of the regiment, in the knowledge that affiliations with the Yeomanry and the counties of Hertfordshire and Essex would be severed and that with them would go much of the *esprit-de-corps* which had originally prompted the offer, Colonel Hope replied that the regiment did not wish to become 6th Field Regiment. Lamb notes, not entirely with tongue in cheek, that the only dissident voice was the quartermaster's. He was fed up with 191's position in the orderly queue inevitably imposed by the staff and would have welcomed a change that in practice would have brought the regiment to the front, cutting waiting time considerably and no doubt vastly improving the choice! Eventually, 189th Field Regiment, which had been formed without Territorial affiliations, became 6th Field Regiment.

Changes to the order of battle for the assault formations landing under command of I Corps, which included the Canadian landing on 'Juno' Beach, were made during February 1944. It was decided that 2nd Canadian A.G.R.A. would not land until late in the build-up programme for Twenty-First Army Group. However, it was necessary to reinforce the divisional artillery of the assaulting Canadian division, 3rd Canadian Infantry Division, as soon after the initial landing as possible. For this purpose 6th (formerly 189th) and 191st Field Regiments left 2nd Canadian A.G.R.A. and joined I Corps' 4th A.G.R.A. Both units were assigned to 3rd Canadian Infantry Division and future exercises were either with that division or with 51st (Highland) Division, which was the immediate follow-up formation. It was accordingly with the artillery of 3rd Canadian Division that the regiment was inspected by Commander-in-Chief Twenty-First Army Group, General Sir Bernard Montgomery, at Holmsley airfield on 28th February. The general had a special word with one or two of the regiment's veterans who were sporting the ribbon of the Africa Star and gave his usual 'knock them for six' speech, after which, Lamb records, "No one doubted for a moment that this was what would happen".

Plate 160 *Senior N.C.Os. of Regimental Headquarters, 191st Field Regiment, before leaving for France, May 1944.* Standing (L.–R.) – *Lance-Sergeant Whybrow (Clerk), Sergeant Riley (Royal Signals), Sergeant Lingard (Chief Clerk), Sergeant White (L.A.D., R.E.M.E.), Sergeant Wherry, Sergeant Fenner (Royal Signals), Sergeant Mobbs (Technical Storeman), Sergeant Goddard.* Seated – *W.O. II (R.Q.M.S.) Kitchener, W.O. I (R.S.M.) Brown, Lieutenant-Colonel M.W. Hope, Major A.G. Proudlock (Second-in-Command), W.O. I (A.S.M.) Fry (L.A.D., R.E.M.E.).* (Regimental Collection)

Shortage of landing craft would eventually dictate that 191st Field Regiment would not land on D-Day, but at this stage a 'wet' landing was expected and much of February was spent in learning to waterproof guns and vehicles. On 1st March the first trial of the regiment's waterproofing skills took place on Walton Common. This was followed by an exercise on 'assault scales'. Lamb records that, for the purpose of the exercise "only the bare essentials were loaded, but the combined value and bulk of personal property left behind in the quarters at Sutton was positively frightening". He also states that, "Among the earliest casualties in the drive to reduce the regiment's laden weight were the Cavalier tanks which had served as armoured O.Ps. for each troop". When they needed tanks, O.P. officers would (and, indeed, did) obtain them from the armoured formations they were supporting. The exercise involved embarkation and landing by night, a move from the beach to an assembly area and occupation of a gun position, still under cover of darkness. Final live-firing exercises took place at Sennybridge at the end of March and on Salisbury Plain in April. Here were practised the first 'Victor' targets, on which all the available artillery of I Corps fired. By the last week of April it was apparent to all that the invasion was imminent. Privilege leave had been stopped and another loading exercise carried out at Southampton Docks. An active service postal address was introduced too, together with the first stage of censorship of outgoing mail.

Follow-up formations for the I Corps beaches were due to embark at various ports in the Thames estuary and at Harwich, so on 30th April 191st Field Regiment moved into the corps concentration area in Essex, Regimental Headquarters and 533 Battery to Ramsden Hall, near Billericay, 532 Battery to Great Baddow and 534 Battery to Little Baddow. During the first week of May the final exercise 'Fabius V' was held. The regiment's part consisted of moving from their billets to a marshalling area at West Ham Stadium, where "amid the cindered dust . . . all the administrative paraphernalia of embarkation was rehearsed" (Captain Bond). The guns and vehicles were then loaded on to a liberty ship at the Royal Albert Docks, unloaded and driven back to the regimental area. Lamb records that, "Although preparations were being pushed along, the mood was one of holiday" and after 'Fabius V' "the regiment settled down to the quiet life – cricket, swimming or country walks, all adding up to produce an appetite for the pilgrimage to the village inn during the evenings". A visit by C.C.R.A. I Corps, who addressed all ranks in the cinema at Billericay on 12th May, was followed the next day by a joint visit by the Lords Lieutenant of Hertfordshire and Essex, Viscount Hampden and Colonel Sir Francis Whitmore.

After a final 'dry' exercise in the form of an inter-troop deployment and gun-drill competition, waterproofing began on 18th May. On 23rd May leave was restricted to a radius of 25 miles and by 26th May all vehicle deficiencies had been made up. Receipt of the codeword 'Cornelius' on 28th May placed the regiment at six hours' notice to move. Lamb continues the story:

> "The order to move out was finally received on the afternoon of Friday, 2nd June at two o'clock . . . when the appointed time arrived, all ranks appeared to be present, although a few were definitely out of breath, and the regiment moved off in the direction of London. It was not a great distance but the roads were congested with military traffic and it was 03.30 before the column of guns arrived at its destination after crawling for several hours through the suburbs of north-east London.
>
> Marshalling Area T1 was situated in a public park at Snaresbrook, on the southern fringe of Epping Forest – a vast enclosure containing large numbers of ridge tents, completely surrounded by a barbed wire fence . . .
>
> The officers of each unit in the camp were given a preliminary briefing during the course of the morning [*of 3rd June*] and were allowed to leave the camp in order to travel to Snaresbrook School, where details of 'Overlord' were unfolded for the first time. The actual date of the operation was not disclosed but it was realised by all who attended that the long awaited invasion was now only a few hours away, and they returned to their units with 'Top Secret' written all over their faces . . .
>
> On Sunday [*4th June*] the regiments' vehicles and guns were driven away, leaving everyone feeling a trifle naked. Ration packs were handed out, together with some large thick paper bags and the first free issue of cigarettes . . . The following morning French money was handed out to each man . . ."

Then, following the announcement of the landings in Normandy on the morning of 6th June, "Marshalling Area T1 emptied in a matter of hours as a continuous stream of 3-tonners conveyed the 'guests' to the Port of London, where the loaded ships were waiting". The regiment embarked at the Royal Albert Docks at 18.00.

### *From Normandy to the Netherlands, June–December 1944*

After dark on 6th June the ships on which 191st Field Regiment were embarked left the dock and steamed down-river to spend the night off Southend, where the convoy carrying Follow-Up Force 'L' was assembling. Throughout 7th June more ships continued to join the convoy, while B.Cs. briefed their batteries on the regiment's intended role in support of 9 Canadian Infantry Brigade of 3rd Canadian Infantry Division. The brigade expected to be to the west of Caen, which would already be in our hands. The next morning the convoy sailed at 08.00, passing through the Straits of Dover under cover of a smoke-screen towards mid-day, bound for Rendezvous Area 'Z' or 'Piccadilly Circus', south-east of the Isle of Wight. The density of sea traffic, which had to be passed from Area 'Z' through swept channels in the huge German minefield, stretching from Boulogne almost to the Cotentin Peninsula, was such that the regiment's ships did not drop anchor, until just before dawn on 9th June (D + 3). There was yet another day of waiting, only 1,500 yards off the beaches. Hatches were uncovered during the afternoon but, according to Lamb:

> "It was not until 18.30 that the L.C.Ts. finally pulled alongside . . . and 532 Battery commenced the tricky business of transferring the guns and vehicles, ready for the run ashore. This was one activity which the regiment had not been able to practise under conditions approximating to the real thing; therefore it was no mean achievement that nobody finished up in the water."

Captain Bond records that most of the regiment were lucky to land in relatively shallow water and only in one vehicle – belonging to the L.A.D. – did the waterproofing fail. He continues:

"The regiment landed about half a mile west of Courseulles-sur-Mer and collected beyond the village of Graye-sur-Mer at the assembly area above the River Seulles. At this stage only a light scale of vehicles was allowed. Two guns per troop were drawn by ammunition 3-tonners instead of Quads and one [*O.P.*] party from each battery had to walk ... In the assembly area immediate de-waterproofing was carried out but it was not until dusk [*about 22.00*] that Colonel Hope sent back from divisional headquarters the orders for deployment.

Disembarkation was somewhat unmethodical and, while all G.P.Os. and C.P.Os. were still afloat, the first guns ashore (532 Battery) were put into action before midnight by Major Pearson and the Regimental Survey Party. The gun area [*close to Cainet*] was about six miles south of the assembly area, in the sector where 7 Canadian Infantry Brigade had pushed across the Caen–Bayeux road at Bretteville-l'Orgueilleuse."

By the end of the next day (10th June) all the regiment were ashore, though the last troop did not reach the gun area until darkness was falling.

F.O.Os. deployed on 11th June in support of No. 46 Commando and the North Shore Regiment of 8 Canadian Infantry Brigade, who were clearing the enemy from the villages along the River Mue – Cairon, Lasson, Rosel and Rots. After some stiff fighting, supported by concentrations from the regiment, all objectives were captured before nightfall and new F.D.Ls. established along the Mue. The expected counter-attack did not materialise until the evening of 12th June, continuing at intervals throughout the night, but well placed D.Fs. discouraged each attempt. On the morning of 13th June 9 Canadian Brigade moved into the line on the left of 8 Canadian Brigade and the regiment was switched to support of 9 Brigade. The guns moved to Barbières, immediately east of Thaon. Lamb records:

"All the indications pointed to a fairly long stay and the guns were dug in at once. Each battery established one O.P. on the brigade front – 533 Battery supporting the Stormont, Dundas and Glengarry Highlanders at Vieux Cairon, 532 Battery supporting the Highland Light Infantry of Canada at the western end of the Les Buissons estate and 534 Battery supporting the North Nova Scotia Highlanders at the eastern end of Les Buissons, overlooking the road from Colomby to Épron.

The troop commanders of each battery shared the O.P. duties on a fifty-fifty basis, one crew resting while the other put in a 24-hour stint, but after the D.F. tasks were registered there was not much firing in the first few days. Ammunition was arriving piecemeal and had to be conserved as much as possible."

This routine, described by Captain Bond as "the regiment's gentle introduction to battle", continued for several days. On 15th June the 'Second Residue' arrived with the remaining vehicles and on 17th June a little local excitement was provided by the attack on the radar station at Douvres, about a mile-and-a-half behind the gun position, which was still held by the Germans. A violent bombardment persuaded the garrison to surrender but several 'overs' – rounds of solid shot – fell in the gun area. On F Troop's position the target records were carried away, necessitating complete recalculation – but perhaps with the over-riding thought that the damage might have been much worse. At the 'sharp end' things were a little less tranquil, especially at night, when harassing fire was the norm and at the slightest excuse either side would loose off small-arms and mortars.

On 18th June the regiment moved from Barbières to an area close to Bretteville-l'Orgueilleuse, from where they were due to exercise a dual role, continuing to support 9 Canadian Brigade while preparing to take part in the barrage which would precede Operation 'Epsom'. This southward thrust around the western edge of Caen, across the Rivers Odon and Orne was ultimately directed at the high ground north-east of Bretteville-sur-Laize, ten miles south-south-east of Caen. It was to be undertaken by VIII Corps, whose divisions were newly arrived and had not yet been committed to battle. Over seven hundred guns were assembled to support the initial attack, which had been delayed by several days as a result of the storm which had raged in the Channel between 19th–22nd June, causing huge dislocation to the build-up of troops and stores. 'Epsom' would now start on 26th June. Lamb describes 191st Field Regiment's part in the operation:

"The weather was much improved by 24th June and preparations for 'Epsom' were accelerated. The complete 15th (Scottish) Division was now concentrated one thousand yards behind the start line ... There were now ten field regiments and five medium regiments massed in the immediate area, ready to deliver a shattering barrage . . . when the operation commenced. . . . Final briefing took place on the afternoon of 25th June and the remainder of the day was spent in contemplation of the task ahead.

The morning of 26th June dawned fine and warm but with a certain amount of ground mist and for this reason home-based bombers of the R.A.F. were forced to abandon attempts to soften up the strong German positions on Carpiquet airfield and in the area of Verson . . .

At 07.30 the barrage opened up from over three hundred guns – a 'gentle' fall of one round per minute from each gun for the first ten minutes followed by one minute of intense fire, which produced a concentration equal to one round to each yard of the assault front. The infantry of 15th (Scottish) Division advanced through 8 Canadian Brigade's front at 07.42 and started picking their way through the shambles of the enemy positions on their way to the Odon.

The barrage continued for another two hours and forty minutes with a fifteen minute rest at 08.45, during which the guns were allowed to cool off and the gun-pits were cleared in preparation for the resumption at 09.00. In the quietness of this interval, muffled sounds of gunfire drifted back from the direction of the Odon, indicating that the Germans were resisting the advance. The unbelievable din of the barrage started again at 09.00, and at 10.20 the gunners straightened their backs and pulled out their earplugs. In a few minutes under three hours the regiment had expended the amazing amount of almost 11,000 rounds of high-explosive.

The 15th Division made good progress up to the line of the River Odon on this first day of the operation, and the armoured force followed through to commence the second phase – the drive to the Orne. But after the success of the initial assault by the infantry, 11th Armoured Division and 4 Armoured Brigade encountered strong opposition from the enemy on the east bank of the Odon, where German armour, playing an almost static role, soon blunted the spearhead of the advance. 'Epsom' was eventually held to a draw about a mile to the north-west of Esquay on the hill feature 112 . . ."

The next day, their part in 'Epsom' finished, 191st Field Regiment returned to support of 9 Canadian Brigade from their old positions at Barbières.

The remaining days of June and the first three days of July passed quietly, with the occasional call for a concentration in the area of Carpiquet. On 4th July, 8 Canadian Brigade made a further attempt to capture Carpiquet village and the airfield to the south. The regiment joined in the barrage and were 'on call' for subsequent support. The Canadians were to a great extent successful, capturing all but the hangar area of the airfield, which, garrisoned by 150 men of 12th Panzer Division, held out for another five days.

An operation codenamed 'Charnwood' was now planned for 8th July. On that day, I Corps, strongly reinforced, was to clear Caen as far as the River Orne and establish bridgeheads across the river south of the city (*Official History*). The three infantry divisions of the corps would attack simultaneously, 3rd British Division from the north-east, 59th Division from the north, and 3rd Canadian Division from the north-west. The infantry would be supported by 27 Armoured Brigade and 2 Canadian Armoured Brigade, reinforced by flail, flamethrowing and engineer tanks of 79th Armoured Division. The artillery of two divisions in addition to those of I Corps was made available, together with 3rd and 4th A.G.R.As., and naval gunfire would be provided by a battleship, a monitor and two cruisers. Heavy bombers were to be used for the first time for tactical support of the operation.

Lamb's account of the battle for Caen, for which 191st Field Regiment were placed in direct support of a single battalion of 9 Canadian Brigade – the Stormont, Dundas and Glengarry Highlanders – opens with a description of the bombing of the German defences in the north of the city the previous night and follows events during 8th and 9th July:

"At 21.45 the long drone of a vast armada of heavy bombers [*there were more than 450*] brought everyone from their command posts and bivouacs to cheer them on their way to the target area, and even in the forward positions the infantry clambered hastily from their dug-outs in order to get a better view as they dropped their bombs and wheeled away to the left on the homeward flight. After they had passed, the dense columns of smoke rising from the town indicated a busy night for the Germans and ensured that they would be anything but fresh-faced when the assault was launched in the morning . . .

. . . The 3rd Canadian Division, on the extreme right, faced south-east and east from the valley of the River Mue, where progress in the initial stages of the assault would certainly be an uphill business from every point of view. Between Vieux Cairon and the Château les Buissons the topography undoubtedly favoured the defence . . .

The I Corps barrage commenced at 04.20 and continued for one hour and a half. Even before the initial barrage lifted, the first success of the day had been reported. At 05.40 the 59th Division had cleared the Germans out of La Bijude and were consolidating in preparation for the second phase.

The F.O.Os. of 191st Field Regiment were at this time lining up with the Canadian infantry at Vieux Cairon, where the Stormont, Dundas and Glengarry Highlanders waited in the half-light of dawn for the order to cross the start-line . . . For the purpose of 'Charnwood' all the wireless sets of the regiment were linked on a single frequency, thus enabling the commanding officer to follow the progress of operations without interruption for the whole of the day . . .

Before first light Colonel Hope, accompanied by the battery commanders, arrived at the battalion headquarters of the Stormont, Dundas and Glengarry Highlanders and the troop commanders quietly rehearsed in their minds their parts in the operation. Some were attached to companies of the Canadian battalion, while others were installed in the Sherman tanks of the 10th Armoured Regiment [*The Fort Garry Horse*] . . .

Captain Hollis [*E Troop Commander*] appeared to have drawn the short straw. His assignment for the day was with the leading company of the battalion, where he could enjoy an uninterrupted view of the battle. It was almost 07.00 before the snipers stole away into the fields to take up their positions on the flank of the company. At last the infantry moved forward in a series of bounds, taking a line of approach from the south of Vieux Cairon with the object of penetrating the enemy position at Gruchy [*the battalion's first objective*] with a right-flanking movement. The difficult nature of the ground, and the discovery of a large minefield in the direct path of the assault, brought the Canadians to an abrupt halt just short of the crest and they were forced to dig in while a solution was evolved . . . Captain Hollis was called forward to arrange some measure of close support and the advance was resumed.

After the early success at La Bijude, 'Charnwood' was now running behind schedule and it was 08.00 before . . . 3rd British Division reported Lébisey to be clear of enemy troops. 09.00 came, and with it the news that the North Nova Scotia Highlanders were in possession of Buron and pressing against the German defences east of Gruchy . . . From this moment the conflict at Gruchy became a bitter and close struggle in which both sides lost many casualties. However, a charge by a troop of Canadian Shermans led by a Bren-gun carrier eventually forced the Germans to retire through the village towards Cussy and Authie and the infantry moved on to the forward edge of Gruchy to regroup in readiness for the third phase. [*The Official History records that, 'What probably settled the issue here was the somewhat unorthodox action of about sixteen Bren carriers of the divisional reconnaissance regiment which suddenly charged, in cavalry fashion and with all guns firing, right into the middle of the German position'.*]

The regiment's observers continued to support the forward troops for the remainder of the day and efforts were made to lay and maintain telephone lines from Rosel and Cairon to the freshly-dug trenches where the troop commanders lurked with their signallers in the midst of a tangle of maps and wireless equipment. Even the noisy retaliation of the German mortars failed to upset the normal routine of most parties and the carrier drivers usually contrived to maintain a supply of hot tea. The maintenance of line communications was much less successful . . .

Battalion Headquarters was on the move after a long wait for news of the success of the initial assault on Gruchy . . . A late lunch was taken and the Stormont, Dundas and Glengarry Highlanders rested while the remainder of the brigade moved forward to Authie. By this time Mâlon and St.-Contest had been taken by the 59th Division . . .

In the middle of the afternoon the Highlanders' right-hand company stalked through the cornfields under cover of a barrage from 191st Field Regiment with the object of taking the Château de St.-Louet from the north. The capture of Authie had left the château totally isolated but the Germans still showed no inclination to call it a day. However, the new barrage proved to be the last straw . . . When the Canadians over-ran the positions they met very little resistance . . . [*Captain Bond records that, 'The fire of the regiment was conspicuously accurate, and at the Château de St.-Louet the infantry advanced to within one hundred yards of the cascade of shells falling on the front of the enemy's position. When the fire lifted the Canadians overwhelmed the enemy before they could recover from the neutralising effect'.*]

The last objective of the day [*for 9 Canadian Brigade*] was Franqueville, just to the north of Carpiquet . . . The North Nova Scotia Highlanders in Authie sized up the prospects and decided that the occasion called for additional support from the artillery. Colonel Hope immediately called Major Pearson [*532 Battery*] . . . [*who*] sped away in his Jeep . . . On his arrival in Authie he found that the battalion had already moved off and he spent more than half an hour searching before he finally contacted the company commander who was to direct the attack on Franqueville. A plan was worked out and the infantry advanced . . . Almost at once the attack came under heavy fire from German mortars and Major Pearson's party sought refuge beneath a burnt-out Panther tank. This was not a very satisfactory situation and there was a danger that the Jeep with the wireless equipment aboard might be put out of action. Therefore the party edged back . . . until the mortaring eased up . . .

The infantry were by now in Franqueville but the mortar-fire resumed with increased intensity, threatening to drive the attackers all the way back to Authie. Major Pearson dismounted and sent his Jeep back and waited with a 38 set while the infantry mustered for a new attack. He did not have long to wait, for ten minutes later the battle was over. A plan for defensive fire was arranged on the spot, ensuring that the Canadian front would hold, and the third phase of 'Charnwood' came to a close.

. . . During the afternoon of 8th July aerial reconnaissance showed that the roads leading away to the south-east of Caen were jammed with enemy vehicles departing from the battle area. One of the last tasks of the day was a Victor target [*all available guns of I Corps*], which added considerably to the confusion that reigned in the south-eastern suburbs."

It is clear from the *Official History* that the actions described above represent those of 9 Canadian Brigade, whose part in the day's fighting ended with the capture of Franqueville. A second brigade (the *Official History* does not say which) passed through 9 Brigade in the early evening, advancing on Cussy and Ardenne. By 20.30 Cussy was captured and an armoured counter-attack beaten off. Ardenne was occupied the next morning without opposition. By nightfall on 8th July the forward troops of 3rd Canadian Division and 3rd British Division on the wings of the attack were only two miles apart. The corps commander accordingly ordered these two divisions to carry on with the clearance of the centre of Caen while 59th Division dealt with resistance that continued in the north of the city.

The events of the next day, 9th July, are described at length by Colonel Hope in a report annexed to the War Diary. His exasperation at the slow pace of 3rd Canadian Division's advance into Caen from the west is very clear. Although he is at pains to point out that the Canadians were playing their first real street-fighting 'according to the book', there is throughout an implied criticism that more aggressive reconnaissance would have demonstrated that the Germans had no intention of making a further stand north of the Orne and that the cumbersome tactics of ensuring that every house was searched for snipers could have been set aside. As a result of his enthusiasm (or impatience) Colonel Hope and Major Pearson reached the centre of the city alone and well ahead of the Canadians, as described by Lamb:

"The Stormont, Dundas and Glengarry Highlanders, which 191st Field Regiment were still supporting [*though now at the extreme limits of wireless communication and with no opportunity to bring the guns forward*], were ordered to spearhead the advance of 3rd Canadian Division . . . the C.O. and Major Pearson accompanied the leading troops of the battalion through the western suburbs but soon became bored with the slowness of the advance and ventured on ahead of the infantry. This almost led to their undoing as they drew the fire of a group of Germans defending a road-block. [*Major Pearson was pinned in a doorway and Colonel Hope, shouting to him to remain where he was, went back to seek help.*] . . . The C.O. returned, riding on the hull of an armoured car and followed by a troop of Shermans . . . The Germans vanished from the scene without delay, leaving a clear field for the advance to continue. The crew of the armoured car declined to proceed any further without orders from their own commander but the men of the 10th Armoured Regiment were less argumentative and agreed to join the two part-time infantrymen in their independent operation. Progress into the centre of Caen now proceeded with increased momentum [*though Colonel Hope became increasingly impatient of the tanks' slow progress and eventually left them behind*] until these irregulars reached the Abbaye aux Hommes, where between two and three thousand refugees had taken up residence since D-Day. Here, in the nine-hundred-year-old abbey, Colonel Hope mounted the pulpit and informed the throng of French civilians that they were now relieved and in doing so received credit for liberating the town . . .

Extricating themselves from the jubilant scenes at the abbey, the C.O. and Major Pearson pressed on towards the north-east, where they met troops of the Royal Ulster Rifles who were leading the 3rd British Division into the town . . .

During the course of the morning the regiment had fired in support of 8 Canadian Brigade, who made another assault on Carpiquet, the last German position west of the Odon. By 12.45 the whole area of Carpiquet, including the hangars, had been cleared of the enemy and the battle for Normandy was moving out of range of the guns of 191st Field Regiment for the first time in a month . . . They were moved in the afternoon to new positions east of Rosel . . . The troop commanders immediately drove through Caen to search for likely O.Ps. overlooking the Faubourg-de-Vaucelles, across the river . . ."

Caen west of the Orne was, in accordance with the objectives of Operation 'Charnwood', in Allied hands, and the Canadians had brought their line forward to the Odon west of its junction with the Orne. The final phase, of establishing bridgeheads east of the Orne, was set aside for the time being. Those bridges that had not been blown by the Germans as they withdrew were blocked by rubble or denied by enemy positions on the far bank, and to prevent further Allied progress 1st S.S. Panzer Division had been moved nearer to Caen. The regiment remained in the Orne–Odon sector for one further day (10th July) firing several concentrations on enemy pockets south of the Orne. Then, on 11th July, came a complete change of front.

The battle for Caen marked the end of any 'gentle introduction' to war, as far as 191st Field Regiment were concerned. Their supported battalion, the 'Glens', suffered heavy casualties, especially in the companies that had led the assault on Gruchy. The O.P. teams were extremely lucky, having shared much of the enemy's fire, especially the mortaring, in having none. Long after the event the regiment's first honours for services in action, gazetted on 21st December 1944, included the Military Cross for Captain Laycock, commanding C Troop, 533 Battery, who had been F.O.O. with A Company of the 'Glens' during the attack on Gruchy. Even later, in the Cease-Fire List announced in January 1946, it became clear that Captain (by then Major) Hollis's Military Cross was in part attributable to his gallantry in the 'bitter and close struggle' for Gruchy. French honours were offered to Twenty-First Army Group in celebration of the liberation of France and 191st Field Regiment received two awards of the Croix de Guerre – to Major Pearson, commanding 532 Battery, for his services with the North Nova Scotia Highlanders at Franqueville and subsequently in the advance into Caen, and to Lance-Sergeant Holland, also of 532 Battery, who, when the North Nova Scotia Highlanders had suffered heavy casualties at Franqueville, displayed outstanding courage and leadership in organising the evacuation of wounded, assisting in the clearing of the village and in helping to prepare the newly-won position against counter-attack.

Regrouping following the battle for Caen took place on 11th July, when 191st Field Regiment came under command of 4th A.G.R.A. and was ordered to move to Biéville-sur-Orne, four miles north-north-east of Caen. Here, on 12th July, they relieved 150th Field Regiment in support of 6th Airborne Division. The division's integral field artillery consisted only of one air-landing light regiment armed with 3.7-in. howitzers and they were severely dependent upon external artillery resources, such as those that could be provided by the A.G.R.As., if they were to fight for any length of time after an initial airborne assault. In addition to 3 and 5 Parachute Brigades and 6 Airlanding Brigade, the division had under command 1 and 4 Special Service Brigades, each consisting of four commandos. The 6th Airborne Division had landed east of the River Orne as part of the D-Day assault and, now reinforced by the two Special Service brigades, held the bridgehead won earlier. This had, according to the *Official History*, "been consolidated and was now firmly held [*but*] had not yet been substantially expanded". The forward line stretched south from the mouth of the Orne, with Sallenelles, Bréville and Le Mesnil all in Allied hands, then along the western edge of the Bois de Bavent to join the neighbouring formation south of Escoville.

B.C.'s and O.P. parties from 532 Battery joined 4 Special Service Brigade – Nos. 41, 46, 47 and 48 (Royal Marine) Commandos – on the extreme left of the line between Sallenelles and

Le Plein. To their right 533 Battery supported 1 Special Service Brigade – Nos. 3,4 and 6 Commandos and No. 45 (Royal Marine) Commando – in the orchards near Amfréville and Bréville and the wooded area as far as Le Mesnil. There was very little activity on the 6th Airborne Division front. A major operation, codenamed 'Goodwood' would take place shortly and all resources were devoted to assembling the armoured force which was due to break out southwards from the Orne bridgehead and strike down to the east of Caen. The opportunity was accordingly taken to rest as much as possible, to send relays of men to the mobile bath unit and to enjoy fresh rations, rather than tinned. On 16th July the regiment handed their support tasks back to 150th Field Regiment for 36 hours 'out of the line', during which parties made for the beaches at Luc-sur-Mer and Colleville, as well as finding any number of 'local brews' to sample.

The rest ended at midnight on 17th July, when 191st Field Regiment came under command of 51st (Highland) Division for the opening stages of Operation 'Goodwood'. The role of I Corps (3rd and 51st Infantry Divisions and 6th Airborne Division) in 'Goodwood' was limited to extending, and then guarding, the eastern (or left) flank of the operation. The three armoured divisions of VIII Corps (7th, 11th and Guards Armoured) would cross the existing front-line between Escoville and Ste.-Honorine with the objective of occupying the line Vimont–Secqueville–Garcelles–Verrières, some eight miles south of their start-line, while II Canadian Corps would capture Caen south and east of the Orne and bring into use the bridges connecting the two sides of the city. An important, but unpublicised, objective of 'Goodwood' was to engage as much German armour as possible on the allies' eastern flank while the United States armies began their break-out in the west. The operation would open on 18th July with a huge programme of bombing by British and United States heavy and medium bombers which would be assisted by a 'flak-suppression' programme fired by the British and Canadian artillery on known enemy anti-aircraft positions.

The flak-suppression programme began before 05.30 on 18th July and within minutes the first of more than two thousand bombers, that would drop more than eight thousand tons of bombs, were over their targets. As the heavy bombers left the area at 06.15, the guns of the three corps, supplemented by naval gunfire, began a 'milk round' lasting an hour and ten minutes in which they engaged every known enemy battery within range. During this bombardment the attacking formations moved up to their start-lines. H-hour was at 07.45 and the leading troops set off behind barrages and timed concentrations. The regiment did not deploy forward observers during 'Goodwood' but played a full part in the artillery programmes, starting with flak suppression on the factory area around Colombelles on the north-eastern outskirts of Caen. The 'Goodwood' battles continued for three days. By the end of 20th July both sides had fought to a standstill, with the Allies still short of their original objectives by between one and three miles. Although the operation had not attained all that was intended, the *Official History* concludes that it "had achieved its main purpose in that it had greatly improved our position on the eastern flank and had kept the enemy's armoured divisions fighting there". The regiment must have 'run out of range' over much of the front during the afternoon of the first day. There were no plans to move them forward on a battlefield which was very congested and they remained in action at Biéville firing at the targets that were within range, and no doubt with a considerable defensive fire task, until mid-day on 20th July.

During the afternoon of 20th July 191st Field Regiment crossed the Orne with orders to support 3rd British Infantry Division from a gun area just south of Herouvillette. The 3rd Division had held the left flank of the 'Goodwood' break-out and during the battle had pushed their front south-eastwards from Escoville along the edge of the Bois de Bavent as far as the crossroads west of Troarn, but without capturing Troarn itself. On their right they held the village of Banneville-la-Campagne. Lamb described the new gun area as "two-and-a-half miles behind the axis of the 3rd Division . . . One mile east of the gun positions loomed the Bois de Bavent, a densely wooded area of several square miles in which the enemy was securely established on the high ground overlooking the left flank of 3rd Division". His account continues:

> "Just after 16.00 [*on 20th July*] the weather broke and the ground, which had until now been hard and dusty, suddenly became a sea of mud as a torrential thunderstorm saturated the battlefield . . . On the gun positions, efforts to dig in were decisively abandoned and energies directed towards keeping guns, ammunition and gunners as dry as possible. In spite of the discomfort of this situation all calls for fire were met promptly . . . Late in the evening

rum was issued and the rain halted temporarily . . . It started again before midnight.

. . . A chapter of misfortunes was just beginning for 191st Field Regiment. With the coming of darkness, the German mortar batteries in the Bois de Bavent opened up on the gun area, causing many casualties. Mortar bombs fell among the trees close to the guns, scattering shrapnel over a wide area and perforating the tarpaulin sheets which sheltered the gunners. One of these set fire to ammunition stacked on 532 Battery's position and only the prompt action of the gunners prevented a greater disaster. Cases of cartridges, burning away with a noise like frying sausages, were dragged away from the high-explosive shells before the fire reached them and blew the gun position apart. To make matters worse, if this was possible, shots from one of the detachments fouled the trees close to one of the other guns, underlining the problems of crest clearance. In the detachments which were not affected by these unhappy affairs the task of harassing the enemy continued throughout the night . . .

When light returned in the morning the extent of the regiment's misfortunes became apparent. A complete detachment of [*A Troop*] 532 Battery had been wiped out during the night . . . and the regiment had suffered nineteen casualties. Two gunners were killed outright and four others died of their wounds later."

By the morning of 21st July 3rd Division was in the outskirts of Troarn and 534 Battery was moved to a position just south-east of Escoville. Here, during the afternoon, the battery wagon lines came under fire from a bold 88-mm. self-propelled gun which emerged from the Bois de Bures. Two gunners were wounded, one of them dying shortly afterwards. Further back, on 22nd July, continued mortaring of 532 Battery's position, which killed one more gunner and wounded two others, forced B Troop to move to an alternative position. Harassing fire tasks continued by day and night but attempts to press forward on 3rd Division's front, even as far as Troarn, were abandoned.

The regiment was transferred to support of 6th Airborne Division on 26th July. The general line of fire changed from south to east and there was some shifting of troop positions as a result, but Herouvillette and Escoville continued as 'home'. Once more it was the regiment's task to support two brigades, such was the shortage of artillery. The B.C. and O.Ps. of 532 Battery deployed with 1 Special Service Brigade and those of 533 Battery with 3 Parachute Brigade (8th and 9th Parachute Battalions and 1st Canadian Parachute Battalion). Captain Bond, then commanding A Troop, 532 Battery recorded that:

". . . At very few places was it possible to see one hundred yards and the F.D.Ls. were always in close proximity to the enemy . . . It was impossible to carry out any orthodox O.P. work but the extensive enemy mortaring gave opportunities for the operation of an elaborate and effective counter-mortar organisation.

Numerous harassing fire tasks were carried out but the few observed shoots required special accuracy. Crest clearance was always a delicate calculation, and one farm frequently engaged was only eighty yards from the point of observation.

It was the unhappy fate of the troop commanders in 533 and 534 Batteries to crawl up a dirty chimney above the pottery works at Le Mesnil, which provided the only general view over the Bois de Bavent to the River Dives."

Captain Bond also captured briefly, but with some interesting domestic detail, the atmosphere and routine that prevailed during the three further weeks that the regiment spent at Herouvillette and Escoville:

"The 'Gun End' continued to receive frequent attention from the enemy, and the village of Herouvillette became so unhealthy that R.H.Q. – rather to the secret pleasure of batteries – was forced to evacuate and dig in in the open country. Only the officers' mess remained beside the cross-roads, and from the flagpole the shell-pocked regimental flag continued to fly.

The shelling was, however, a less constant inconvenience than the mosquitoes. Millions of these giants zoomed and swarmed in swaying pillars throughout the long evenings and from their persecution there was little escape. At night they penetrated in thousands into the slit trenches in which men tried to sleep. By day they were supported by flies, who no doubt throve on the inevitable garbage of war and caused the bout of 'Normandy Stomach' to which some of the regiment fell victim.

The daily rations were still based on the Compo Pack – the pack of rations designed for fourteen men for one day. This was all tinned food, and included cigarettes, boiled sweets and soap. Among the tins were bacon or sausage, 'M. and V.', steak-and-kidney pudding, or stewed pork; rice pudding, treacle pudding or tinned fruit; butter, jam and biscuits. The biscuits were the only unpopular item, being regarded as dry, hard and lacking in bulk. The more adventurous had always supplemented their rations with new potatoes or an occasional egg – some detachments kept hens – and the O.P. parties had the pick of the livestock that, for a time, ran wild in forward areas. But there was general approval when bread and fresh meat were issued in lieu of biscuits and the tinned meats. This brought to an end 'individual' cooking by detachments over petrol fires, and troop, command-post and wagon-line cookhouses were reconstituted.

Meanwhile, in preparation for things to come, a new tarmac road was built across 532 Battery's position, and the minefield, which had cost the battery a Quad and a 15-cwt., was finally cleared.

. . . The regiment had time to consider these wider issues [*i.e., the progress of the war*] as the days passed at Herouvillette and the thunder of battle rolled away to the south. The enemy to the east fell silent. Gunners ceased to keep their steel helmets handy, and the dusty staffs of the command posts emerged into the glare to write their interminable letters – for so they seemed to censoring officers. Overhead the Air O.P. kept watch over the enemy batteries. Ears no longer strained for the warning whistle of the shells . . .

Meanwhile ammunition expenditure remained at about one hundred rounds per gun per day, and harassing tasks were carried out at night to interfere with the enemy supplies. These nightly tasks were often executed by roving guns. Occasionally a propaganda shoot was fired, or red smoke put down for the Typhoons, and the flare shell used in the big II Canadian Corps attack on 7th–8th August was tried out by the regiment on 6th August.

To give a complete break, the C.O. put a troop off duty each day and opened the rest centre at Riva Bella between Ouistreham and Lion-sur-Mer. In seaside villas, which were cleared of mines, three officers and forty other ranks could go for three days to absolute freedom from the routine and dreariness of the gun lines."

Much happened while 191st Field Regiment supported 6th Airborne Division on the extreme left of the Allied front between 20th July and the middle of August. On 23rd July Headquarters First Canadian Army, which had by then arrived in France, began to take over responsibility for operations on the British–Canadian left, leaving Second Army (the other half of General Montgomery's Twenty-First Army Group) to control the right, as far as the boundary with the United States Twelfth Army Group. Until February 1945 there were only three Canadian divisions in North-West Europe, forming, with other formations as required, II Canadian Corps, which came under command of First Canadian Army almost at once. First Canadian Army always included at least one British corps – I Corps was the first British formation to come under Canadian command, as soon as the army headquarters became operational – and this gave rise to a good deal of confusion. Forces under command of First Canadian Army were often referred to in the press as 'Canadian Forces', when they were in fact British. (General Barker, commanding the British 49th Division used to get particularly angry when his division's achievements were attributed to 'Canadian Troops' – as they were, for instance, at the capture of Le Havre – and several times wrote to higher headquarters to try to persuade the public relations branch to set the matter straight.) On 25th July the United States First Army began to attack southwards on the extreme western flank. The American front had progressed sufficiently to allow expansion to two armies (First and Third) on 1st August and by 16th August United States divisions had reached the line Dreux–Chartres–Orleans in a massive sweep eastwards, while at the same time pushing north towards the line Argentan–Flers, which formed the southern edge of what was to be known as the 'Falaise Pocket'. Falaise fell to II Canadian Corps on 16th August and, as pressure on the Falaise Pocket increased, the German formations holding the coastal strip, roughly from Troarn to the River Seine at Rouen, seeing the possibility of being cut off, began to make preparations for withdrawal across the Seine.

As early as 7th August, General Gale, commanding 6th Airborne Division, had been ordered by Headquarters I Corps (now under command of First Canadian Army) to plan for the advance of his division in the event of a German withdrawal from the coastal strip towards the Seine. While First Canadian Army was concentrating on the battle to close the Falaise Gap, and an eventual thrust eastwards, it would be the task of its left-flanking formation – the considerably reinforced 6th Airborne Division, which now had a Belgian and a Dutch brigade under command, as well as the two Special Service brigades – to maintain unceasing pressure on the enemy's right flank. In *The Red Beret*, Saunders (see Bibliography) summarises admirably what faced the division and outlines the tactics General Gale decided to adopt:

> "The main difficulty of the advance to the Seine apart from shortage of transport and the opposition that the enemy might put up, lay in the nature of the ground to be covered. It was traversed by at least three rivers, each of them flooded, and since they were near their journey's end, wide, deep and sometimes tidal. There were two main roads running to the Seine, one inland through Troarn, Dozulé, Pont-l'Évêque, Beuzeville and Pont-Audemer; the other following the sea coast through Cabourg, Trouville and Honfleur. Both traversed a rolling land, its many hills covered with woods, between which lay fields of pasture divided each from each by thick hedges. The rivers were the Dives, bordered by marshes, the derelict Dives Canal running beside it, with, in the background, a range of hills overlooking the whole waterlogged plain; the River Touques and the River Risle, both of which flowed through deep-cut valleys. The distance from Troarn to the Seine was thirty-five miles as the crow flies, and forty-five by road. Every yard of the country could easily be defended, and was ideal for fighting a series of delaying actions. These were certainly to be expected, at least at the outset, from an enemy who, though heavily defeated, was still fighting vigorously, and might well continue to do so to the end.
>
> Of the two possible ways to the Seine, General Gale chose to take the bulk of his forces along the inland road through Troarn to Pont-Audemer, though this would entail crossing a valley about 8,000 yards wide full of streams and swamps, with a main water obstacle, a double river, the Dives and its Canal, running at right angles across the path of the advance. His chief concern was artillery support, or rather its lack. 'I had,' he records, 'a most fantastic assortment of stuff.' This was made up of the light regiment belonging to the 6th Airborne Division, carried originally to action in gliders, two field regiments, a battery of medium guns, and a heavy anti-aircraft regiment transformed for the moment into field artillery. The Belgian Brigade possessed one battery of 25-pdrs. . . ."

Signs of the enemy's withdrawal were detected on 16th August and orders for 6th Airborne Division's follow-up operation, codenamed 'Paddle', were issued. The advance began the following morning. In the Bavent sector, 191st Field Regiment began by supporting 1 Special Service Brigade. In the dull, sunless, misty morning, No. 4 Commando began the advance through the woods towards the village of Bavent with forward observer parties accompanying the leading troops. Booby traps had to be avoided but there was no active opposition and by mid-morning Bavent was occupied and orders given to the regiment to move forward to the area of the village. The advance continued, with the brigade moving up to the River Dives between Varaville and Bricqueville, and in the afternoon the regiment moved again, into positions south-west of Robehomme. Calls for fire were minimal; during the whole day there was only one regimental concentration – to disperse a German rearguard west of Varaville – and one rather prolonged smoke-screen to cover the withdrawal of a patrol that had been cut off on the left of the brigade front. By nightfall, Nos. 3 and 6 Commandos had taken over the line along the west bank of the Dives. Support for 1 Special Service Brigade continued during the morning of 18th August as the brigade exploited across the river but later switched to 3 Parachute Brigade, who had crossed the Dives at Bures late the previous day, as they planned to attack down the main road from Soustrainville to Dozulé.

The ground over which 3 Parachute Brigade was due to advance was overlooked by the enemy on hills a short distance to the east, so the attack took place after dark. By midnight 1st Canadian Parachute Battalion had captured crossings over the canal which runs along the eastern edge of the Dives valley and 9 Parachute Battalion had moved through, with the railway station at Dozulé as their objective. By morning the battalion was in partial possession of Dozulé but under observed shell-fire which caused more than fifty casualties. Rather than remain to assist, however, forward observer parties from 191st Field Regiment were withdrawn around mid-day and moved to support of 4 Special Service Brigade, who were due to take over the attack on Dozulé. The guns, meanwhile, moved to Bassenville. It would again be a night attack and the brigade would attempt a right-flanking movement from the south, rather than a renewed assault eastwards down the road. The two leading commandos, Nos. 46 and 48, would be supported by 534 Battery and 532 Battery respectively. The O-group called by the commanding officer of No. 46 Commando was caught by heavy mortar-fire. Six of the group were killed and several others, including Major Norman-Butler, commanding 534 Battery, were wounded. Captain Hollis stepped up to command 534 Battery (an appointment later confirmed with his promotion) and the attack proceeded much as planned. While No. 46 Commando dealt with the village of Dozulé itself, No. 48 Commando made a wide sweep through the thickly wooded hills to the south and, after sharp skirmishes in the early morning of 20th July, pushed an enemy horse-drawn battery off Point 120 to the south-east of the village. According to Captain Bond, "the guns got away, but the enemy left behind some of their horses and limbers and also their supper". Once Dozulé was in the hands of 4 Special Service Brigade, 191st Field Regiment was transferred once more to support of 3 Parachute Brigade. For his part as a forward observation officer during No. 46 Commando's attack on the high ground immediately overlooking Dozulé, Captain Richardson of F Troop, 534 Battery was awarded the Military Cross. His work was particularly significant because the assaulting troops had no wireless communications of their own and were entirely dependent on use of the Gunner net.

The next German defensive position was along the ridge which crossed 6th Airborne Division's main eastward axis at Annebault. At 07.00 on 21st August the advance was resumed with 3 Parachute Brigade, now considerably reliant on 191st Field Regiment for assistance with transport, of which they had none, in the lead. The change in the nature of the ground to be crossed, and the likely effect on pursuit operations, is evident from a study of a contoured map and well described by Lamb:

> "The pursuit was now in fairly difficult artillery country, where the problems of reconnaissance and survey were almost as strenuous as the subsequent task of manhandling the guns into positions from which they could be safely fired. Among the forward troops of the parachute battalions conditions for the observers were little better, and in the attack on Annebault it was continually necessary for F.O.Os. to transmit their orders by 38 set to the more powerful 22 set [*in their vehicle*], by which they were relayed to the gun position. To maintain this line of communication throughout the operation, it was often necessary also to manhandle Jeeps through hedges and across ditches when the transmissions from the 38 sets became subdued by the proximity of trees and tall hedges."

With support from 534 Battery which was later described in the citation for Major Hollis's Military Cross, 8th Parachute Battalion succeeded in clearing Annebault during the afternoon of 21st August. The guns moved twice during the day, as, with 9th Parachute Battalion now in the lead, the brigade pressed on through La-Haie-Tondue in order to secure a line from which 5 Parachute Brigade could mount a river-crossing assault against Pont-l'Évêque.

During the night of 21st–22nd August, 5 Parachute Brigade moved through 3 Parachute Brigade and continued their advance until they reached that part of Pont-l'Évêque that lies west of the River Touques. The town is divided by the river, which flows through two channels about two hundred yards apart. The railway embankment running along the eastern bank of the river provided a further obstacle, while the town is dominated by high ground on both sides of the river. Harcelrode (see Bibliography) gives a detailed account of 5 Parachute Brigade's gallant attempt to seize Pont-l'Évêque, from which the following outline has been extracted:

> "... the 13th Parachute Battalion was tasked with infiltrating into the town and securing a bridgehead across both channels of the river. Meanwhile, 12th Parachute Battalion was to effect a crossing south of the town and to secure both the railway embankment and the feature of St.-Julien, which controlled the approach from the south ...
>
> At 15.00 that afternoon A Company of 12th Parachute Battalion advanced under the cover of smoke, laid down by the guns of 150th and 191st Field Regiments, R.A., which were in support, across open ground towards two fords over which it would cross the river. All went well to begin with and the company had advanced some four hundred yards before it came under fire. Once it appeared that A Company ... had reached the fords ... B Company started its advance. Unfortunately ... A Company had missed the fords but was

unable to inform the commanding officer because the company commander's wireless set had been hit . . . While the rest of the company took cover in ditches on the west bank, A Company commander and nine men swam the river and succeeded in dislodging the enemy from the railway embankment but soon found they were running low on ammunition.

By this time, the cover provided by the smoke was lessening and B Company was pinned down in a hedgerow by machine-gun- and shell-fire from the St.-Julien feature to the south and from the high ground to the east of the river . . . More smoke was called for and was laid down on the St.-Julien feature, the railway embankment and the railway station. This enabled B Company to move further forward to some dykes but here it was pinned down again. At this point, A Company commander . . . and his small group [*who had run out of ammunition*] . . . withdrew to the west bank.

. . . [*Now*] with 12th Parachute Battalion's two leading companies pinned down between the start-line and the river, and with the enemy once more in possession of the railway embankment from which all approaches were dominated, Commander 5 Parachute Brigade realised there was no chance of success being achieved in daylight and ordered the attack to be broken off. From 17.00 until dark, A and B Companies were forced to remain in their very exposed positions with no smoke from the supporting artillery [*who had used all available smoke ammunition*] . . . After dusk . . . they were able gradually to withdraw, having lost sixteen killed and approximately fifty wounded.

Meanwhile, 13th Parachute Battalion [*supported by B.C. and F.O.Os. of 533 Battery*] had managed to penetrate the town and cross the bridge spanning the western channel of the river. However it was unable to clear the main street which led to the bridge crossing the eastern channel, having encountered determined resistance from enemy troops in well prepared positions. [*Even with the help of four Cromwell tanks of 6th Airborne Armoured Reconnaissance Regiment, the battalion were unable to fight their way through the blazing ruins of the town centre.*] . . . and at 19.00 the battalion was ordered to consolidate its positions in the town. [*After discussion between brigade and divisional headquarters*] it was agreed that 12th Parachute Battalion should withdraw . . . into brigade reserve and 7th Parachute Battalion would assume responsibility for the western and southern approaches to the town.

On the morning of 23rd August . . . a patrol of 13th Battalion managed to cross the eastern channel of the river without meeting any opposition [*by means of the single remaining girder of one of the two bridges*] . . . [*There now seemed to be*] a better chance of establishing a bridgehead on the far bank and 13th Battalion was ordered to carry out a crossing as quickly as possible. [*Three companies crossed the single girder. One provided a firm base covering the commanding officer's tactical headquarters, while the other two attempted to make progress through the eastern part of the town.*] There then ensued some vicious street fighting in which the battalion had to fight hard for every yard of ground because the enemy were in well-prepared positions and were giving a very good account of themselves . . .

[*During the afternoon of 23rd August*] Commander 5 Parachute Brigade realised that the bridgehead on the far bank was too weak for the attack to have any chance of success. He therefore ordered the battalion to withdraw across the river through a firm base set up by 7th Battalion . . ."

Operations by 4 Special Service Brigade to outflank Pont-l'Évêque during the night of 22nd–23rd August and again during the night of 23rd–24th were planned, with 191st Field Regiment assigned to support the brigade, but both operations were cancelled. At dawn on 24th August patrols from 7th Parachute Battalion discovered that the enemy had abandoned the town during the night. The battalion was ordered to push forward at once along the road to Pont-Audemer. With 191st Field Regiment still in support, 5 Parachute Brigade advanced without meeting any opposition until the road–railway crossing below Le Vieux-Bourg about three miles east of Pont-l'Évêque. The opposition here was swiftly overcome and the high ground overlooking the road secured. The brigade was then ordered to halt and 1 Special Service Brigade moved through to take the lead.

It is unfortunate that so little is known of 191st Field Regiment's part in these three days of hard fighting. Captain Bond records that F.O.Os. from 150th Field Regiment supported 12th Parachute Battalion in their efforts to cross the river south of the town. The 13th Battalion's attempts to fight through the centre were shared by Major Higgens and F.O.Os. from 533

Battery. The citation for the Military Cross awarded to Major Higgens records how he went from place to place in the burning town under heavy fire in order to gain observation and bring fire from the battery to bear, and states that "his actions undoubtedly assisted in preventing a serious situation from deteriorating".

Describing events on 24th–25th August, Lamb records:

> "The enemy now fell back towards the marshy area of Pont-Audemer, fighting a long succession of rearguard actions against 5 Parachute Brigade, who continued to surprise them before a solid defensive line could be established. The real value of the regiment's contribution to the rapid advance at this stage of Operation 'Paddle' was in its transport as much as its firepower, and the paratroopers were able to maintain constant contact with the enemy by fully utilising the regiment's vehicles, thus depriving him of time to consolidate.
>
> In the evening of 24th August 1 Special Service Brigade took up the running [*supported by 191st Field Regiment*] and continued the advance against light opposition in the darkness of the night. Then, when daylight returned, No. 48 Commando [*of 4 Special Service Brigade, who, with support from 191st Field Regiment, had taken over the lead in conjunction with 3 Parachute Brigade*] pressed home the advantage with a series of attacks on hurriedly raised defences south of Beuzeville. Once again the regiment faced enormous problems in the close, wooded country and Private Denny, A.C.C. was killed on 532 Battery's gun position when a premature burst from one of the guns sprayed the field kitchen with splinters. In spite of the difficulties, and it may be interesting to note that at one period only one troop of guns could be deployed, the regiment continued to answer calls for fire relayed by as many as four wireless sets. By now, the troop commanders' drivers were seriously considering whether it might be a good idea to commandeer wheel-barrows for the transport of the heavy radio equipment!"

One of those drivers, Gunner Murphy of F Troop, 534 Battery gained the regiment's only Military Medal for his work supporting the commandos south of Beuzeville on 24th August. The commandos were working without transport in very thick and difficult country and Gunner Murphy drove his Jeep and operated his wireless set all day in exposed positions amongst the forward troops under considerable mortar-, shell- and small-arms fire. The citation records that by his bravery and devotion to duty Gunner Murphy "enabled artillery support to be brought at once to the commandos, who were closely engaged and suffered many casualties throughout the day."

During the evening of 25th August General Gale received orders which placed Pont-Audemer, a major crossing point on the River Risle and the next obvious objective, inside the left-hand boundary of 49th Division's advance. While 4 Special Service Brigade, still supported by 191st Field Regiment, advanced on St.-Maclou, other elements of 6th Airborne Division staged a race with the leading troops of 49th Division to reach the bridge at Pont-Audemer before it was destroyed by the Germans. On the morning of 26th August troops of the Dutch Brigade mounted on tanks of 6th Airborne Armoured Reconnaissance Regiment reached the bridge first, but too late to prevent the enemy from blowing the demolition charges. The 6th Airborne Division was then taken out of the line and began to make preparations for their long overdue return to England. Captain Bond recalls the intense tiredness which was by now overcoming everybody in the division, but especially commanders at all levels, who "had had an endless series of marches, reconnaissances, orders groups and then battles". The regiment was hardly less weary. In the ten days since the start of Operation 'Paddle', 191st Field Regiment was switched between supported brigades nine times. Each change required adjustment to new plans and new methods, fresh allocation of F.O.Os. to supported units, and changes in codes for use on the wireless net of those units – all this in difficult country with almost every vehicle in demand for tasks other than those to which it was normally assigned.

Colonel Hope saw no need for the regiment to rest, however, and, according to Lamb, "departed on one of his mystery tours after lunch on 26th August and succeeded in having the regiment taken under command by 49th Division". Although C.R.A. 49th Division was later to discover that this arbitrary switch from 6th Airborne to 49th Division did not meet with the approval of C.C.R.A. I Corps, the regiment was ordered to join 49th Divisional Artillery in a gun area some miles south of Pont-Audemer – a seventeen mile road move. The War Diary records, with pride that can still be felt, that the order to move was received at

18.45, the first troop was in action at 21.15 and the regiment ready at 22.30. An Uncle target was called at 22.40 and the 49th Divisional Artillery was left dumbfounded when the newcomers got the ranging! The next day F.O.Os. from 191st Field Regiment supported 49th Divisional Reconnaissance Regiment's advance to the bank of the Seine at Quillebeuf and Vieux-Port, north and north-east, respectively, of Pont-Audemer. Here, in the early afternoon, the enemy "gave up all pretence of resistance" west of the Seine (Lamb). The regiment then reverted to command of 4th A.G.R.A. and moved into a harbour area near Routot for three days' rest (29th–31st August).

The time spent at Routot was the first spell that the regiment had spent fully 'out of the line' since mid-July. Colonel Hope could not stand the inactivity, however, and on the evening of 30th August drove north the few miles to the Seine with Lieutenant Wallich (a fluent German speaker) and crossed the river in a boat, having ascertained that the Germans had already left Caudebec-en-Caux, the small town on the opposite bank. They spent half-an-hour talking with members of the local resistance forces and stressed the need for information to be collected on the German defences at Le Havre, returning with the news that, while they continued to hold Le Havre, the enemy had evacuated a huge belt of country, reaching as far up the Channel coast as Dieppe.

Within First Canadian Army priority in crossing the Seine was given to II Canadian Corps, who would cross in the immediate area of Rouen and move on Dieppe and the coastal strip to the north-east. Their crossing began on 27th August and on 30th August Canadian troops entered Rouen and began using two road bridges in the city centre. On the Canadians' left, I Corps "hurried to get over the river by any means it could find" (*Official History*). Once across the Seine, I Corps would move north on St.-Valéry-en-Caux, which the 51st (Highland) Division was due to liberate, and west on Le Havre, which 49th Division would contain while forces were assembled to capture the city and port.

On 31st August, 191st Field Regiment was ordered to support 4 Special Service Brigade which would attempt reconnaissance of the huge area between the axes of 51st Division, making for St.-Valéry and 49th Division, hooking westwards towards Le Havre. No bridge had yet been built downstream of Rouen and I Corps were establishing a raft-crossing at Duclair, where there was already a civilian ferry-crossing. Lamb described 191st Field Regiment's experiences whilst crossing the Seine:

> "By an unhappy coincidence, that annual phenomenon, the tidal bore occurred on the morning of 31st August, and for several hours the turbulence caused the greatest difficulty to the engineers who were manning the ferries . . . the first raft to reach the centre of the river swung out of control . . . and capsized, throwing its cargo into the water. Captain Stinson, embarking on his first outing as E Troop Commander, was a strong swimmer and soon returned to the surface. Gunner Dudley was dragged down amid a tangle of signal equipment and drowned, despite desperate efforts to rescue him from the river bed . . .
>
> . . . There was no sense in tempting providence too far and no more vehicles were committed to the ferries, [*Captain Bond records that the other O.P. parties' Jeeps did cross.*] but it was important that the regiment should cross over without undue delay in order to give effective support to 4 Special Service Brigade. Major Proudlock was therefore instructed to search for a bridge higher up the river.
>
> The commanding officer was sleeping at Headquarters 4 Special Service Brigade when the second-in-command called him by wireless to report that only two bridges remained intact in the area of Rouen and that there was a long waiting list of units . . . 191st Field Regiment stood fairly low on the list of priorities and would not be able to cross until late in the afternoon [*of 1st September*]. 'Find another bridge', replied the C.O., and went back to sleep.
>
> Major Proudlock, somewhat remarkably, succeeded . . . He eventually discovered a railway bridge leaning at a crazy angle over the swollen river the near centre of Rouen. During the morning the regiment drove bumpily over the sleepers, followed by the bulk of the transport of two infantry divisions."

Having crossed the Seine, the regiment followed up the advance of 4 Special Service Brigade, who were 'swanning' unopposed through the French countryside. According to Saunders in *The Green Beret* (see Bibliography), "The enemy were dead, captured, or miles away in headlong retreat, and the chief danger was receiving a bunch of roses in the face while

Plate 161 *Quads of C Troop, 533 Battery leave the town square of Fécamp, on the Channel coast, north-west of Rouen, in search of petrol, while the guns submit to the admiration of the locals, 2nd September 1944.*
(Regimental Collection)

travelling at forty miles an hour in a Jeep". The route out of Rouen was through Barentin and Pavilly. At Yvetot the regiment harboured for the night, except for 533 Battery, who accompanied No. 47 (Royal Marine) Commando in a rush to Fécamp, to ensure, as 51st Division were doing at St.-Valéry, that the little harbour had not been designated a 'channel port' by the Germans and garrisoned accordingly. It had not, and the commandos took the town over from the hastily retreating Germans on the morning of 2nd September. During the afternoon 533 Battery rejoined the regiment at Epretot, a few miles east of Le Havre, where, under command of 49th Division – this time with the C.C.R.A.'s blessing – they were preparing for the operations to liberate the city.

The defences of Le Havre were formidable, as described in the *Official History*:

> "... Starting from the Lézarde valley where it passes Montivilliers and continuing to the coast near Octeville was a wide and almost unbroken anti-tank ditch, strengthened by extensive mine-belts and wire and covering numerous field-works and strong-points with concreted dugouts. From the crest of the southern plateau two forts covered the town and harbour entrance, and on the coast near the Cap de la Hève the Grand Clos battery threatened approaching ships. The German garrison (under-estimated at some 8,700) was well equipped with artillery and mortars; the conformation of the ground and the German defences made it a difficult position to capture."

For the attack I Corps disposed 49th and 51st Infantry Divisions, 33 Armoured Brigade, 34 Tank Brigade, elements of 79th Armoured Division under command of Headquarters 30 Armoured Brigade and 4th and 6th A.G.R.As. The preliminary bombardment began on 5th



Plate 162 *Panoramic view of vehicles and guns of 533 Battery harboured in the town square of Fécamp before joining 49th Division for the siege of Le Havre, 2nd September 1944.* (Regimental Collection)

September by sea (H.M.S. *Erebus*) and by air and continued the next day and on 8th September. Bad weather interrupted all operations on 9th September and delayed the start of Operation 'Astonia' until 10th September when bombardment was resumed by sea (H.M.S. *Warspite* and *Erebus*) and air. During their final attack just before H-hour, Bomber Command brought the total of bombs dropped to 'soften up' the defences to more than nine thousand tons. The German garrison commander was twice offered the opportunity to surrender but declined to do so.

H-hour was fixed for 17.45 on 10th September. The 49th Division, with 34 Tank Brigade under command, would attack the north-eastern and eastern defences, beginning just east of Fontaine-la-Mallet and stretching to Harfleur, and 51st Division, with 33 Armoured Brigade under command, would attack the northern defences, from Octeville-sur-Mer to Fontaine-la-Mallet. Having taken part in the massive harassing-fire and counter-battery operation which preceded the attack, 191st Field Regiment was ordered to support 34 Tank Brigade (7th and 9th R.T.R. and 107th Regiment, R.A.C.), one regiment of which was placed under command of each brigade of 49th Division. Captain Bond gave a concise account of the two days' fighting which resulted in the fall of Le Havre:

"Heavy bombing attacks were the prelude to the assault, which began in the evening against enemy positions south-west of Montivilliers, by 56 Brigade Group. This group, which included 7th R.T.R. with F.O.Os. from 533 Battery, made good progress despite the extensive obstacles and bad going, and during the night part of 147 Brigade (with 107th Regiment, R.A.C. and F.O.Os. from 534 Battery) passed through on to the plateau east of the town of Le Havre and above the River Lézarde.

It was not until nearly dawn [*on 11th September*] that 146 Brigade (with 9th R.T.R and 532 Battery) began their attack on the 'reverse slope' positions east of Harfleur. Darkness prevented the effective use of tanks and the infantry were held up by anti-personnel mines and machine-gun fire. Later, mine-clearing flail tanks and flame-throwing tanks, and some very heavy artillery concentrations, were employed. By mid-day the positions were over-run and a column could be launched through Harfleur to the docks.

With Colonel Hope somewhere in the van, 147 Brigade was steadily, if slowly, winkling out strong-points, while 56 Brigade had penetrated the Forêt de Montgéon. The 51st Division was also progressing but it was 56 Brigade which made the news on 12th September. Breaking through into the centre of the town, a detachment of tanks took the main German headquarters, complete with commander [*reputedly in his pyjamas, but wearing his medals!*] and staff at 11.30. The citadel fell, and by 15.00 fighting in Le Havre was over.

The garrison had been 11,000 men. The defences were elaborate, a position of natural strength having been laid out with extensive minefields, obstacles and concrete defence posts. In two days the town had fallen at little cost to the attackers; this constituted the quickest and cheapest reduction of any of the channel ports.

This was in part due to the excellence of the British equipment and technique in siege warfare. Flails dealt with the minefields and flame-throwing tanks had a devastating effect on morale. A comparable factor was the weight of artillery fire, and the regiment's F.O.Os. were instrumental in giving support within the 49th Division's boundaries. The regiment were in close touch with the entire divisional front, for the F.O.Os. on the regimental net were with the forward troops of each brigade and, through the tank nets, in contact with each battalion. Concentrations of half a dozen artillery regiments were promptly switched against any sign of resistance. The 533 Battery log records the engagement in just under 35 hours, of 86 targets, many of which lasted five, ten, or even thirty minutes."

The regiment's part in the capture of Le Havre and his own gallantry while accompanying Commander 34 Tank Brigade as artillery adviser during the street-fighting on 11th September resulted in the award of the Distinguished Service Order to Colonel Hope. The citation concludes with the words, "Throughout these two days this officer was in the van whenever artillery support in street-fighting looked like being required. He displayed most marked gallantry and inspiring leadership under fire". Lamb describes the lighter side of celebrating the capture of Le Havre:

"After supporting 'Astonia' from the gun positions at Epretot for two days, 191st Field Regiment pulled up sticks in the early evening and moved to the outskirts of Le Havre to join in the celebrations which followed. In a secluded railway cutting just outside Harfleur, the vehicles were placed in harbour for the night and jubilant French civilians brought their various offerings of wine and brandy. A good time was had by all . . ."

After a few days 'out of the line', first at Yvetot, then at St.-Nicholas-d'Aliermont, a few miles south-east of Dieppe, the regiment was ordered on 19th September to move to support 4 Special Service Brigade, part of the force investing the now isolated port of Dunkirk, which was still held by a German garrison some 12,000 strong. The besieging force was under command of Headquarters 107 Anti-Aircraft Brigade, and during the time that 191st Field Regiment was involved in the siege the main infantry force was provided first by 4 Special Service Brigade, then by 154 Infantry Brigade of 51st (Highland) Division, who took over from the commandos on 27th September. The role of the investing force was to prevent a break-out, rather than capture the port. Lamb describes the regiment's part in the siege:

> "On the morning of 21st September the three batteries of 191st Field Regiment went their separate ways and moved into the damp fields to the rear of the commando troops – 532 at the distillery at Mille Brugge [*immediately west of Bergues*], 533 Battery at Loon-Plage, to the west of Dunkirk, and 534 Battery facing the bastion at Bergues. The regiment's role promised a dull period and the weather lived up to this promise from the very start. The autumn mist greeted the gunners every morning at 'Stand-to', and the moment that 'Stand easy' was given saw such an unaccustomed flurry of activity, with everyone slapping their arms vigorously and double-marking time to bring back the circulation. The static role allowed the drivers to continue the good work of catching up on their tasks in the vehicle lines and, with the Belgian border only a few miles to the east, transport was arranged to convey small parties to that other battlefield at Ypres . . .
>
> For several weeks the supply lines which were serving the Twenty-First Army Group had been under strain due to the inadequacy of port facilities . . . the efforts of the Royal Navy in bottling up the channel ports with mines before D-Day still kept the ports of Calais and Ostende almost completely out of action and the port of Antwerp was also ineffective, since the Germans still held strong positions on the Scheldt estuary . . . For this reason supplies for the force investing Dunkirk were being landed at Fécamp, many miles to the west, and the R.A.S.C. detachment which was serving 191st Field Regiment ran a daily column to convey ammunition and rations from a supply dump two miles inland from the port. The system worked very well on the whole, although the distance involved was considerable and it was necessary to maintain a shuttle service in order to keep the guns firing." [*The War Diary records daily harassing-fire and counter-battery tasks during the period 21st–30th September.*]

The Highlanders were considerably under strength and following their arrival the regiment provided some of the standing patrols on the siege perimeter but the routine remained tedious and it was a relief to all, especially Colonel Hope, when orders arrived on 8th October for 191st Field Regiment to rejoin I Corps Troops at Turnhout, in Belgium. Colonel Hope moved ahead of the regiment to Headquarters I Corps but on arrival found that he had been temporarily attached to Headquarters 4 Special Service Brigade, then preparing for the operations to seize the island of Walcheren. Lamb records that Colonel Hope "dropped everything and joined Force 'T' headquarters in Bruges after despatching a message instructing Major Proudlock to take over command of the regiment. Major Higgens then became acting second-in-command and Captain Woodbridge took over command of 533 Battery".

The regiment handed over their tasks on the Dunkirk perimeter to 150th Field Regiment on 8th October and set off on 9th October on the 130-mile drive to Turnhout, which they reached the following day. Here they were ordered to support an armoured force which combined the Royal Dragoons (armoured cars) with elements of 147th Regiment, R.A.C. and which was holding a sixteen-mile front on the western 'shoulder' of the Nijmegen Salient, from Poppel (south of Tilburg, which was still in German hands) to Hilvarenbeek and then along the Wilhelmina Canal to Best, north of Eindhoven. The batteries deployed at Hilvarenbeek (532), Diessen (533) and Middelbeers (534), where they remained for nearly ten days. On the 11th October 532 Battery was called upon to provide some men to act as infantry in conjunction with a patrol of Royals armoured cars which was to raid an enemy post. They returned with twelve prisoners and the enemy abandoned the post but in the shelling and mortaring which

Plate 163 *Captain D.J. Stinson of 534 Battery* (at the 'donkey's ears'), *with his O.P. ack, Gunner Martindale, observing during the siege of Dunkirk, October 1944.* (I.W.M. – B 10593)

followed the raid there were three casualties, one of whom later died – the regiment's last death attributable to enemy action. The War Diary records the next few days as "holding and harassing the enemy on the line of the canal between Hilvarenbeek and Oirschot". With a little more feeling, Lamb wrote that:

> "In the late evening [*of 11th October*] the first snow of the winter started falling gently. For a week the regiment stood on guard behind this thinly held front, occasionally despatching 'Scale 3' into the enemy positions to the north-east. But the role was one of waiting, as it had been at Dunkirk, and the real war seemed to have slipped away from the regiment once again . . ."

On 16th October 1944 Field-Marshal Montgomery issued a new directive which gave priority to opening the port of Antwerp. First Canadian Army was ordered to "concentrate all available resources" on these operations and to redirect its right wing so that it could "exert a more direct influence on the battle for possession of the area Bergen-op-Zoom–Roosendaal–Antwerp". While securely holding the ground in its possession, Second Army was to concentrate "its whole available offensive power . . . in a strong thrust westwards on the general axis Hertogenbosch–Breda, with [*its*] right flank on the Meuse" (*Official History*). With both armies concentrating their offensives on the same area, I Corps, still under command of First Canadian Army, could now be released from the task of protecting Second Army's western flank and ordered to attack northwards.

An operation which would take I Corps through Breda, Roosendaal and Bergen-op-Zoom and thence to the south bank of the Maas (Meuse) was planned to start on 20th October. Initially two divisions, 4th Canadian Armoured Division on the left, and 49th Division on the right would break out from a start-line that ran approximately from Putte just north of Antwerp to Brecht, north-east of the city. The follow-up formations were 104th United States Infantry Division, which was temporarily under Canadian command, and 1st Polish Armoured Division. Once more, 34 Tank Brigade was placed under command of 49th Division, and, as at Le Havre, 191st Field Regiment was ordered to support 34 Tank Brigade. Accordingly, on 19th October the regiment moved from their dispersed positions south of the Wilhelmina Canal to a regimental area at St.-Leonard, east of Brecht. On arrival they learned that 34 Tank Brigade would be used as the basis for 49th Division's own 'armoured spearhead', rather than in the more conventional support of the infantry brigades, as had been the case at Le Havre. Headquarters 34 Tank Brigade would command the force, to be known as 'Clarkeforce' after the commander of 34 Tank Brigade, Brigadier W.S. Clarke. It would comprise 107th Regiment, R.A.C., 49th Divisional Reconnaissance Regiment, a troop of flame-throwing tanks, two armoured engineer sections and an infantry component – initially one company, later a battalion. Artillery support for Clarkeforce would be provided by 191st Field Regiment and 248 (S.P.) Anti-Tank Battery, both of which were under command. *The Story of 34 Tank Brigade* (see Bibliography) summarises the role of Clarkeforce in 49th Division's Operation 'Rebound', which began at 07.30 on 20th October:

"... to launch through a gap, north of St.-Leonard, to be made by 49th Division [*supported by 9th R.T.R.*], advance northward in order to protect the right flank of 4th Canadian Armoured Division, and to gain ground as a spearhead to 49th Division, whose main bulk would follow up and take over as opportunity occurred. The divisional commander's briefing was wide in its terms and gave O.C. Clarkeforce the fullest freedom to operate over a generous area of country to the east of where the Canadian flank was expected to move ..."

Operation 'Rebound' started with a barrage – small by most previous standards – fired by the four field regiments of 49th Division reinforced by two medium regiments. The division's attack was headed by 56 Infantry Brigade, supported by 9th R.T.R., who advanced on Stapelheide and seized the village as a start-line for Clarkeforce's attack on Loenhout, some two miles further north. Finding Loenhout strongly held, Clarkeforce left it to be dealt with by 147 Infantry Brigade and moved on. The forward elements reached 'Stone Bridge', on the road from Loenhout to the main Antwerp–Breda road, in time to prevent its total demolition. Then, reaching the main road, they turned south-westwards and took the surprised garrison of Wuestwezel from the rear. The fight for 'Stone Bridge' took most of the afternoon with, according to Lamb, "frequent demands for more and more shell-fire on the eastern approaches [*which*] kept the regiment's guns busy all through the afternoon", but resulted in the enemy withdrawing before demolition could be completed. Captain Bond describes the next move:

"As soon as the handful of Germans in Wuestwezel had been rounded up, the tanks continued their advance. After leaving by the Esschen road in the blackness of the night they were held up in the morning south of Nieuwmoer. The woods were thick and much of the low-lying ground was impassable, but after a bombardment the village was occupied – not, however, without some loss."

Meanwhile, 147 Brigade, with 11th Royal Scots Fusiliers in the lead, had moved up to Wuestwezel from the south, despite some delay imposed by a blown bridge, in order to relieve Clarkeforce.

The day had been a busy one for the regiment. In the early stages of the advance F.O.Os. were deployed with 56 Brigade as well as with Clarkeforce. A 'step-up' move to keep pace with the forward troops began when 532 Battery deployed to Brecht during the day. The remaining two batteries moved during the evening, one to Brecht and the other some two thousand yards further forward to Stapelheide. It was by now clear that 49th Division's axis of advance would be restricted by huge areas of flooded low-lying land on either side. The road from Wuestwezel through Nieuwmoer, Esschen and Nispen stood clear of the floods and was the vital causeway between the division's start-line south of Brecht and their objectives, Roosendaal and eventually Willemstad.

The second day of 'Rebound' (21st October) saw Clarkeforce battling to capture Nieuwmoer, while to their rear 2nd Essex of 56 Brigade, supported by 9th R.T.R. dealt with Loenhout, which had been contained and by-passed the previous day. Loenhout was occupied before mid-day after a short action, and the guns of 191st Field Regiment were ordered forward to positions near Wuestwezel, using the Loenhout–'Stone Bridge' road. Lamb described the move and subsequent events:

"... as the Germans retired from Loenhout, the first enemy counter-attack was launched on the area of 'Stone Bridge' from the north just as the advance parties of 533 and 534 Batteries ... were ... crossing to the west of the river to provide closer support to Brigadier Clarke's battlegroup. 533 Battery's Y truck and two other vehicles were brewed up by a troop of self-propelled 88s and a motor-cycle was destroyed, but everyone managed to abandon their sinking craft, and no casualties were caused. 532 Battery had succeeded in making the crossing earlier and now found themselves temporarily isolated from the remainder of the regiment with the German armour approaching from the direction of Breda. The Leicesters [*1st Leicesters of 147 Brigade*] took the early weight of this counter-attack and for a while there was a danger that Clarkeforce, exploiting from Wuestwezel, might be chopped off at the neck. But this attack was beaten off and both sides gathered their forces for a resumption later. During the next two hours more German armour arrived from the north-east and elements of several adjacent units raced up to reinforce the Leicesters. The second counter-attack came at three in the afternoon, causing great anxiety to the British force deployed to the north of the bridge. Although casualties were suffered by the Leicesters, their headquarters platoon succeeded in knocking out two self-propelled guns which blocked the only approaches to 'Stone Bridge', thereby defeating the object of the attack. During this second assault 532 Battery was called upon to deploy in an anti-tank role and had the rare experience of delivering solid shot over a range which gradually diminished until only twelve hundred yards intervened."

Prevented by the action around 'Stone Bridge' from entering Wuestwezel from the north-east, 533 and 534 Batteries' gun groups back-tracked and reached their new deployment positions by a long detour through Brecht. Clarkeforce were pressing their attack on Nieuwmoer and, according to Captain Bond, "the F.O.Os. continued to call for support and, despite the distractions and difficulties in the gun area, response remained quick and accurate". His account continues:

"At last light on 21st October six tanks had been lost in an attempt to break out to the north of Nieuwmoer, where a deep ditch and a vast wood restricted manoeuvre. The maximum concentration was called for. Major Proudlock succeeded in engaging every gun within range – the full artillery of 49th Division, 68th Medium Regiment, certain units of 4th Canadian Armoured Division and an A.G.R.A. from over the adjoining formation boundary. A twenty-minute concentration from these guns – about two hundred, ranging from field to heavy – devastated the roadside woodland and next morning the advance continued unopposed."

By the morning of 22nd October, the danger of a successful counter-attack by the Germans was judged to have passed. The next objective was Esschen and Clarkeforce, approaching from the south-east, joined 4th Canadian Armoured Division, who were moving in from the west, in an effort to 'pinch out' the town, which was captured by the Canadians later in the day. The regiment, who had assisted the advance of Clarkeforce "with the help of small fire plans and impromptu shoots by the F.O.Os. with both H.E. and smoke" (Captain Bond) then moved up to Nieuwmoer (less 532 Battery, who moved the following day). They arrived in the new gun area without incident, even though there were still pockets of enemy along the route. The entire recce party of another field regiment were 'put in the bag' during the day, as were most of B Echelon of 107th Regiment, R.A.C. These pockets gave particular trouble in the farms and hamlets to the east of the Nieuwmoer–Esschen road and complete dominance of the area was not achieved until well into 23rd October. The division then began to concentrate south of Esschen, having handed over a large part of the area already captured to 104th United States Infantry Division, who would join the advance between 49th Division and 1st Polish Armoured Division on the far right.

Although it was not known whether they would maintain a robust resistance or merely impose delay, it was now clear that the enemy were holding the area north of Esschen in some strength. The 49th Division therefore paused for a short time in order to regroup and plan Operation 'Thruster', which would cover the next phase of the advance to the Maas, with Roosendaal as the principal objective. In preparation for the attack, 191st Field Regiment moved a little further forward, to Visschenheuvel. In the early stages of Operation 'Thruster', which was due to start during the night of 25th–26th October, 56 Brigade would advance northwards from Esschen and capture Nispen. Once 56 Brigade were clear of Esschen and had secured their start-line for an attack through Nispen from the west, Clarkeforce would begin moving north-westwards towards Wouw, intending to execute a left hook into, or to the north of, Roosendaal. At the briefing on Operation 'Thruster' air photographs were circulated which disclosed the presence of a huge anti-tank dyke. This, according to Lamb "extended for about three miles from Wouwsche on the left to Tolberg on the right and protected the important feature at Wouwsche Hil, which commanded the otherwise flat, undulating panorama for many miles in all directions". Lamb continues by describing the opening of the operation:

> "The evening of 25th October brought 191st Field Regiment to the support of 56 Brigade and 9th R.T.R., who were to probe the defences of Nispen. This village was found to be poorly garrisoned and the British force was morally obliged to capture it in spite of the fact that this objective was earmarked for disposal on the following day. However, the early capture of Nispen brought an initial advantage to Clarkeforce, which returned to the battle on the morning of 26th October. 9th R.T.R. was quick to follow through in the wake of the retreating enemy and the road to Brembosch was cleared before daylight returned.
>
> F.O.Os. of 191st Field Regiment rejoined 107th Regiment, R.A.C. and 1st East Riding Yeomanry before dawn and awaited the signal to move into the attack on Brembosch, to the north-west. The advance duly commenced against a series of strong rearguard actions by a force consisting almost wholly of infantry. The bulk of the German armour was now massed behind the great barrier of the anti-tank ditch and only a small number of self-propelled guns remained to support the infantry. It was soon apparent that the contribution of the German gunners was sadly handicapped by a shortage of ammunition and as the attack was pressed home more and more 88s withdrew from the battle. The enemy infantry, however, acquitted themselves very well in the circumstances, and disputed every yard of ground . . . Even on the outskirts of Nispen, where the reserve squadron of 107th Regiment, R.A.C. waited for orders to take over the running, the volume of small-arms fire from the German infantry brought some uncomfortable moments . . ."

With Nispen in our hands, 191st Field Regiment were able to move forward to gun positions on the northern outskirts of Esschen.

By the early afternoon of 26th October the battle had reached the anti-tank ditch, which had been crossed in places, and Clarkeforce was meeting stubborn resistance from enemy armour in the area of Wouwsche Hil and Haaink, a mile-and-a-half to the north-east. It took a further day to push the Germans off these two strong-points and concentrated artillery fire was instrumental in so doing. Major Proudlock was awarded the Distinguished Service Order for his work in support of Clarkeforce. The citation concentrates on the battle for Wouwsche Hil, where, it says:

> "He displayed great personal courage under fire in his successful efforts to apply the fire of four field, two medium and two heavy anti-aircraft regiments in support of the leading armoured units of Clarkeforce, which were constantly engaged and suffered considerable casualties from skilfully handled enemy self-propelled guns. Repeatedly, when the situation appeared critical and our armour was under heavy direct fire, Major Proudlock positioned himself where he was best placed to control the fire of the supporting artillery grouped under him without thought of his own safety and when enemy fire in his vicinity was heavy and accurate . . ."

Lamb summed up the position after Wouwsche Hil had fallen:

> "By the night of 27th October Clarkeforce had driven the enemy from Wouwsche Hil and Haaink and was in the built-up area of Oostlar by the morning of 28th October. The regiment had by now moved forward once more to the area of Nispen in order to support the operations of Clarkeforce and for the whole of this difficult task on the north of the great ditch had been engaged in a series of massive 'stonks' on the area of Wouwsche Hil and far beyond to the outskirts of Oostlar . . ."

The next day (28th October) Clarkeforce, with 56 Brigade following up closely, was directed through Oostlar towards Wouw, while 146 Brigade, supported by 9th R.T.R. developed a left hook that would take them through some outlying villages and into the western outskirts of Roosendaal. Throughout the day 191st Field Regiment "divided its efforts between these two separate forces" (Lamb). By 20.00, however, Clarkeforce had taken Wouw and turned eastward towards Roosendaal and the F.O.Os. had returned to the gun area, now only three miles south-west of Roosendaal, and were expecting orders for an assault on the town the next day. During the night of 28th–29th October it was discovered that much of the armour opposing 49th Division was withdrawing. Over the next two days Roosendaal, which proved to be only lightly held, fell to a combined attack from west, south and east, with the outlying villages to the west, where enemy self-propelled guns were able to deploy, giving more trouble than the

Plate 164 *An O.P. officer of 191st Field Regiment observes fall of shot from an upper-storey window on the Belgian-Dutch border and shouts corrections to his signaller inside the house, October 1944.* (I.W.M. – B 11472)

town itself. As operations to clear Roosendaal continued, the regiment moved, first to Wouw and then, as the enemy withdrew northwards, into the northern fringes of Roosendaal itself, where:

> "In the evening of the first day there [*31st October*], the Dutch civilians who had remained in their houses during the battle . . . appeared at the gun positions with offers of accommodation for the chilly night which lay ahead . . . the weather had been cold and damp . . . which made the comfort of a warm parlour extremely attractive for the gunners after many hours of chilly exposure on the gun positions. There was little that the people of this town could offer apart from a seat beside the fire, and, although they asked for nothing in return, most detachments had a 'whip-round' for spare tins of food or cigarettes and chocolate, which they placed shyly on the parlour table as they entered." (Lamb)

The final objective in 49th Division's sector was the ancient, fortified town of Willemstad. It lies on the south bank of the Hollandsch Diep, some ten miles north of Roosendaal, across an expanse of flat, low-lying land criss-crossed by drainage ditches, with the River Mark about half-way between the two towns. The ground was unsuitable for an 'armoured spearhead' and Clarkeforce was disbanded, 107th Regiment, R.A.C. reverting to their more usual role of close support of an infantry brigade and 49th Divisional Reconnaissance Regiment returning to command of Headquarters 49th Division. The division, according to Lamb, deployed on a wide front for the last step to the banks of the Maas – a continuation of 'Rebound' and

Plate 165 *A 25-pdr. gun of 191st Field Regiment in action during the attack on Roosendaal, October 1944. By this time, 25-pdr. guns had been modified by the addition of a muzzle brake, which reduced the recoil and enabled increased muzzle velocity to be achieved when firing 'Charge Super'.* (I.W.M. – B 11471)

Plate 166 *A member of the Belgian resistance, the 'Armée Blanche', shows off her Luger pistol to members of 191st Field Regiment, and doubtless regales them with 'war stories' as well, October 1944.*
(I.W.M. – B 11470)

'Thruster' code-named 'Humid'. Lamb continues:

> "From here the nature of the ground offered no natural defences for the enemy, whose retreat was delayed only by the compression of their numbers into a relatively narrow strip of damp and marshy land between Roosendaal and the river [*Maas*]. The trend of German movement was now in an easterly direction, towards the few remaining bridges which carried the enemy armour out of South Holland. At the same time, the flat undulating farmland . . . gave no bonuses to the British force. The unspectacular expression "working forward from Oud Gastel [*three miles north of Roosendaal*] on 1st November" really is a gem of understatement. For two days the infantry stumbled along muddy ditches which led them on a zig-zag course from one isolated farmstead to the next, while the armour crept slowly forwards across waterlogged fields drawing off the enemy's fire.
>
> The guns of 191st Field Regiment remained on the outskirts of Roosendaal giving general support to 49th Division as they inched forwards towards the river in that uncomfortable advance."

During the night of 2nd–3rd November 56 Brigade forced crossings of the River Mark at Barlaque and Stampersgat against strong opposition and held them against counter-attack, allowing 146 Brigade to follow through. A further three days' fighting brought the division within a short distance of Willemstad, where the divisional artillery, including 191st Field Regiment, supplemented by 4th Canadian Armoured Divisional Artillery and two medium regiments, concentrated to the south and south-west of the town. The regiment deployed in open fields near Fijnaart. In an effort to avoid the destruction of the town and inevitable casualties to the inhabitants, General Barker invited the garrison commander to surrender. His offer was refused but the Germans did agree to allow civilians to leave. They came crowding out and were taken away in transport provided by the division. There turned out to be no need for an assault the following morning (6th November), for while 49th Division had been busy with the refugees from the town, the garrison had withdrawn across the river.

By now the enemy retained only a small bridgehead south of the Maas, around the southern end of the two bridges which crossed the river at Moerdijk. On 7th November, therefore, 104th United States Division left to return to American command elsewhere and 49th Division were ordered to extend their frontage eastwards along the Maas until in contact with the enemy's right. The positions vacated by the 'Timberwolf' Division were accordingly taken over by 146 Brigade, supported by forward observers from 533 Battery and plans were made for the brigade to co-operate with 1st Polish Armoured Division in an attack on the Moerdijk bridgehead. Lamb described events:

[244]

Plate 167 *Lieutenant-Colonel M.W. Hope at the 'sharp end' during his attachment to 4 Special Service Brigade for the attack on Walcheren, October 1944.* (Regimental Collection)

> "During the evening of 7th November, 4th Polish Armoured Division moved noisily up towards Moerdijk Bridge and introduced itself to the German defenders in unmistakeable terms . . .
>
> Representatives from 191st Field Regiment duly reported for duty at Headquarters 4th Polish Armoured Division before dawn on 8th November, only minutes before the impatient Poles advanced across their start-line. It had been expected that no time would be wasted over courteous exchanges here but the sheer pace of the initial assault exceeded all expectations. At the regiment's gun positions near Zevenbergen [*four miles south of Moerdijk*] the speedy exploitation from the bridgehead could almost be visualised as ranges steadily increased from 7,000 yards to 12,000 yards in less than three hours.
>
> This operation brought an end to fighting south and west of the River Maas, and the regiment was withdrawn from action on 10th November . . ."

Unfortunately, the Poles had not been quick enough to prevent the Germans from destroying the Moerdijk bridges.

For a short time the regiment rested at Etten, between Rosendaal and Breda. C.C.R.A. I Corps then ordered a composite battery of three troops to deploy to S'Gravenmoer in support of 22nd Canadian Armoured Regiment (The Canadian Grenadier Guards), who were mopping up odd pockets of enemy marooned south of the Maas. The composite battery, under command of 532 Battery Headquarters, left Etten on 13th November. The following day F Troop of 534 Battery moved to "a lonely farm to the south of Willemstad" (Lamb) in support of 18th Armoured Car Regiment (12th Manitoba Dragoons), the armoured car regiment of II Canadian Corps, who were patrolling the south bank of the Maas centred on Willemstad. Lamb records that Captain Richardson "established an O.P. in the clock tower of a church and commenced a long, lonely vigil . . .". Lamb also notes that "Major Pearson's composite battery was engaged in a sudden flurry of counter-battery shoots on 22nd November, before it was withdrawn from action and settled into a new billetting area at Roosendaal". On 28th November, B Troop of 532 Battery and D Troop of 533 Battery moved to St.-Philipsland and Dinterloord, respectively, supporting a thinly-spread screen from 51st Division watching the islands of Duiveland and Overflakkee across the grey waters of the Lower Scheldt. Captain Bond described the scene and the atmosphere:

> "The advent of winter had changed conditions. Villages and buildings, which attracted shell-fire, had been avoided in Normandy: but later troop positions, like company areas, were sited with convenient access to houses and barns. The long hours of darkness imposed a restraint which kept men together for considerable periods, huddled over stoves which had been 'liberated' and which travelled on the tops of the Quads. Perhaps it was this enforced monotony, or perhaps just exhaustion from the active summer months, which brought out in the army as a whole a sense of weariness. The high hopes of autumn were disappointed; the rigours of winter had to be faced."

To add to the gloom, on 30th November Colonel Hope was summoned to meet C.C.R.A. I Corps at Tilburg. Here, the bald facts were put to him – the shortage of infantry reinforcements was such that 50th Division was to be disbanded, together with a proportion of units under command of A.G.R.As. As a very junior field regiment raised during the war, 191st Field

Regiment would have to yield to the seniority of Regular and Territorial regiments and would be disbanded. The younger men would be drafted to infantry units as reinforcements; the older men and some urgently needed specialists in artillery trades would be dispersed to other regiments. Lamb described the events which followed:

> "That evening B, D and F Troops received orders to rendezvous with the remainder of the regiment at Roosendaal the following morning ... By mid-day the news was out. The Colonel explained in as few words as possible that the regiment had just suffered the worst possible misfortune. Then he brightened up slightly and added, 'We won't be returning any ammunition. It was meant for the Hun and we'll damned well see that he gets it'.
>
> Early on the morning of 2nd December the guns were driven to the south bank of the River Maas. The Germans on the opposite bank then went through their most confused hour as 191st Field Regiment bade them farewell, first with a succession of fairly ordinary bombardments with H.E. 117, then the complete repertoire of smoke – red, white and blue – and finally the regiment's holding of armour-piercing shot thudded flatly into the north bank of the river. Before the smoke cleared the guns were on their way back to Roosendaal . . .".

That same day (2nd December) operational commitments were handed over to 90th Field Regiment and, "during the afternoon . . . the men of the regiment occupied themselves busily with white spirit, soap and water, determined to leave an impression of cleanliness, if not godliness, behind them in their final appearance as a unit . . ." (Lamb), for the regiment's disbandment parade was to be held in Roosendaal the next day.

After an inspection by Lieutenant-General Sir John Crocker, Commander I Corps, who was accompanied by the Commander Corps Royal Artillery, Brigadier Manners-Smith, the regiment marched past General Crocker and continued to church for a farewell service. Here, they surprised the townspeople by singing 'Glorious things of thee are spoken . . .' to the tune of the German national anthem. The Army Film and Photographic Unit recorded the event at some length; film and stills are now in the Imperial War Museum. Then the officers of the regiment entertained the visitors (some say 'drowned their sorrows') with oysters and champagne and in the evening the Royal Artillery Band, who had travelled from Woolwich for the occasion, played for a regimental dance. Captain Bond recorded the last few days:

> "On Monday [*4th December*] the vehicles, cleaned for the last time, took the road into Belgium, to three villages near Dixmude, twenty miles east of Dunkirk.
>
> Equipment was handed in. Drafts left. By the middle of December only the rear party remained. Then they too went to other units and to fresh appointments, and 191st (Herts and Essex Yeomanry) Field Regiment, R.A. lived on only in spirit."

There is little to add to these eye-witness accounts. The disbandment parade had been overshadowed by the death the previous evening in a traffic accident of Captain Richardson, who had commanded F Troop, 534 Battery throughout the campaign and was the regiment's only fatal officer casualty. On a happier note, Colonel Hope recommended the adjutant, Captain Butler and the R.S.M., W.O. I Brown for appointment as Members of the Order of the British Empire in what amounted to a 'Disbandment Honours List'. He was successful on both counts, though the announcement of these awards did not take place until June 1945.

Lamb provides an appropriate tailpiece. After recording that most of the technical assistants and driver-operators were transferred, still wearing their regimental sleeve badges, as observer teams to the newly-formed counter-mortar organisation in 43rd, 49th and 52nd Divisions, he continues:

> ". . . let it not be thought that the spirit of the 191st was allowed to slip away without a struggle. On 28th March 1945 the counter-mortar officer's staff of 52nd (Lowland) Division drove into harbour four miles east of Xanten bridge for a 36-hour rest. The C.R.A. stood at the roadside receiving a long-drawn-out salute. During the following morning the counter-mortar officer received a summons from the brigadier. Two hours later he returned in a state of considerable agitation . . . after lunch . . . he visited each section and instructed his men to 'Take those damned badges off your sleeves b. . . . . quickly if you don't want to see me cashiered'. Colonel Cochrane's emblem had just been carried across the Rhine!"

Plate 168
*Disbandment parade of 191st Field Regiment at Roosendaal, Holland, 5th December 1944.*
Top – *Lieutenant-General Sir John Crocker, K.C.B., C.B.E., D.S.O., M.C., commanding I Corps, inspects 532 Battery, accompanied by Major Pearson.*
Bottom – *The Corps Commander in conversation with Lieutenant-Colonel M.W. Hope, D.S.O. after the parade. Brigadier L.C. Manners-Smith, C.B.E., C.C.R.A. I Corps* (Left) *and an unidentified officer listen in.*
(I.W.M. – B 12471–6)

Plate 169 *The commanding officers of the Hertfordshire Yeomanry field regiments in action, 1942–1945.* Top left – *Lieutenant-Colonel (later Major-General) G.D. Fanshawe, D.S.O., O.B.E., 86th Field Regiment* (Photograph taken c. 1955); Top right – *Lieutenant-Colonel (later Brigadier) R.C. Symonds, D.S.O., 86th Field Regiment;* Bottom left – *Lieutenant-Colonel (later Brigadier) P.J.D. Toosey, D.S.O., O.B.E., 135th Field Regiment* (Photograph taken c.1955); Bottom right – *Lieutenant-Colonel (later Brigadier) M.W. Hope, D.S.O., 191st Field Regiment.*

(Regimental Collection)

# *Epilogue – Last Post and Reveille*

It will have been seen from the three preceding chapters that the achievements of the Hertfordshire Yeomanry field regiments and those of the war-formed Herts and Essex Yeomanry, though very different, were considerable. In North-West Europe, 86th Field Regiment, who themselves showed every sign of simply getting on with the job in hand without paying undue attention to what would now be described as 'their place in the league tables', had in fact earned themselves the description "among the very best of the field regiments in theatre". The chance, unhappy in so many ways, that sent 135th Field Regiment to Malaya, and to capture in Singapore, itself presented extraordinary opportunities for service and for achievement, which were seized to the full, though frequently went unrecognised. And 191st Field Regiment, who could so easily have settled for 'a short life and a happy one', as was the lot of many war-formed units, were able to ensure that wherever they went during their six months in action their presence was felt and they made a real contribution to the outcome of the battle.

Chance, assisted by whatever selection system operated at the time, dealt a remarkable hand of officers to command the three regiments in action. None of them were 'home-grown' Territorials; indeed all but one were Regulars. Each turned out to be the man that the moment required and each has paid handsome tribute to the officers and men under his command. These tributes have invariably been reciprocated many times over by members of the three regiments, who have demonstrated to the regimental historian huge pride in their service with the unit but at the same time have spoken of 'their' commanding officer with both respect and affection. In final tribute to them all, these officers' portrait photographs appear together opposite in recognition of the part that they played in enabling their regiments to add so significantly to the Hertfordshire Yeomanry's long list of achievements and honours.

These achievements were attained at considerable cost in lives; no figures for those whose lives were affected, sometimes permanently, by wounds or the results of mistreatment while prisoners-of-war have been kept. In North-West Europe 86th and 191st Field Regiments lost,

Plate 170 *The Commonwealth War Graves Commission's designs for headstone badges for the graves of members of 86th Field Regiment* (Left) *and 135th Field Regiment* (Right). (Commonwealth War Graves Commission)

Plate 171 *Design for the headstone badge for 191st Field Regiment. The regiment is unique in having a headstone badge based on an embroidered sleeve badge, rather than an authorised cap or collar badge.* (Commonwealth War Graves Commission)

respectively, 43 and fifteen all ranks, including attached, who were killed in action or died of wounds or through accidents. The figures for 135th Field Regiment are higher – 67 killed in action or died of wounds and 159 who died while prisoners or from causes directly related. These include those lost at sea in transit to Japan, those killed in the Allied bombing of installations close to their camps and those whose aircraft crashed during the early stages of their return. The regiments' dead lie in Commonwealth War Graves Commission cemeteries in France, Belgium, The Netherlands, Germany, Malaysia, Singapore, Thailand, Burma and Japan, with a very few in cemeteries in the United Kingdom. Those who have no known grave are commemorated on memorials at Bayeux in Normandy and in Singapore. The names of many additional members of 135th Field Regiment would have been included on the Singapore Memorial, as having no known grave, but for the efforts of their comrades of all ranks to keep records of where they were buried and of the date and cause of their death. Happily, the Commission chose to use the hart in the headstone badges for 86th and 135th Field Regiments, though their artist was allowed too much licence in interpreting the beast

Plate 172 *The graves of Captain H.M. Pamphilon of 86th Field Regiment in St. Charles-de-Percy War Cemetery in Normandy* (Left) *and Gunner G. Barry of 191st Field Regiment in Ranville War Cemetery, also in Normandy* (Right). (Regimental Collection)

Plate 173 *The two types of headstone used for graves of members of 135th Field Regiment in Commonwealth War Graves Commission cemeteries in the Far East – Sergeant W.C. Bryant's grave* (Left) *is in Kranji War Cemetery, Singapore and Gunner H.L. Marshall's* (Right) *is in Kanchanaburi War Cemetery, Thailand.* (Regimental Collection)

and produced a design which is not recognisable as the regimental badge. Very unusually, the Commission agreed to the use of a headstone badge incorporating the features of 191st Field Regiment's sleeve badge, though again a strict interpretation was not carried out and the regiment's title has been added, so that it appears twice on the headstone.

At home, the Hertfordshire Yeomanry, whether as 'Old Comrades' or as members of the post-war successor units (see below), ensured that those who gave their lives would not be forgotten within their county. On 19th September 1954 the Lord Lieutenant of Hertfordshire unveiled a memorial tablet, only a few feet away from those for the South African War and the First World War, in the north aisle of St. Albans Abbey. The tablet recorded the four units – 86th, 135th and 191st Field Regiments and 79th Heavy Anti-Aircraft Regiment – that had carried the Hertfordshire Yeomanry's name during the Second World War. On a table below the tablet was placed a memorial book in which are inscribed the name of all officers and men of these units who died. In 1995, in commemoration of the fiftieth anniversary of the end of the Second World War, the three regimental memorials, together with the guidon of the Hertfordshire Yeomanry and the 1939–45 Memorial Book, were refurbished and moved a few feet eastwards into the new War Memorial Chapel. Regrettably, it may now be said, the 1939–45 Memorial Book only contains the names of those who were commissioned or enlisted in the Royal Regiment of Artillery. Not until 1972, when the Hertfordshire Yeomanry and Artillery Historical Trust published their *Hertfordshire Yeomanry and Artillery Roll of Honour* (since followed by two supplements – see Bibliography), were the names of the men who died while serving with the 86th and 135th Field Regiment Signal Sections, Royal Corps of Signals or 86th and 135th Field Regiment Light Aid Detachments, Royal Electrical and Mechanical Engineers, or those of attached personnel of the Army Catering Corps or the Federated Malay States Volunteer Force, listed with the units of which they formed part. Much more recently, the regimental historian has found evidence of further names that it may be necessary to add to 135th Field Regiment's roll. It is hoped that it will be possible to do this through a third supplement to the *Roll of Honour*.

It is apparent that commanding officers and those higher up the chain of recommendation set very high standards for honours and awards. Some details of those gained in action have been included in preceding chapters. A full list, with citations, appears in *Hertfordshire Yeomanry and Artillery Honours and Awards* (to which one supplement has been added and another is in preparation – see Bibliography). As in the First World War, a very interesting variety of honours, British and Allied, were bestowed on extra-regimentally employed officers. It is not possible to trace other ranks who were mobilised with 86th or 135th Field Regiments, but were decorated (or, indeed, lost their lives) after commissioning or transfer to other units. The conditions of award of both the Efficiency Decoration (Territorial) and the Efficiency Medal (Territorial) were changed in 1942 to provide for embodied service during the Second World War to count double. The war lasted almost exactly six years, so all personnel who joined the

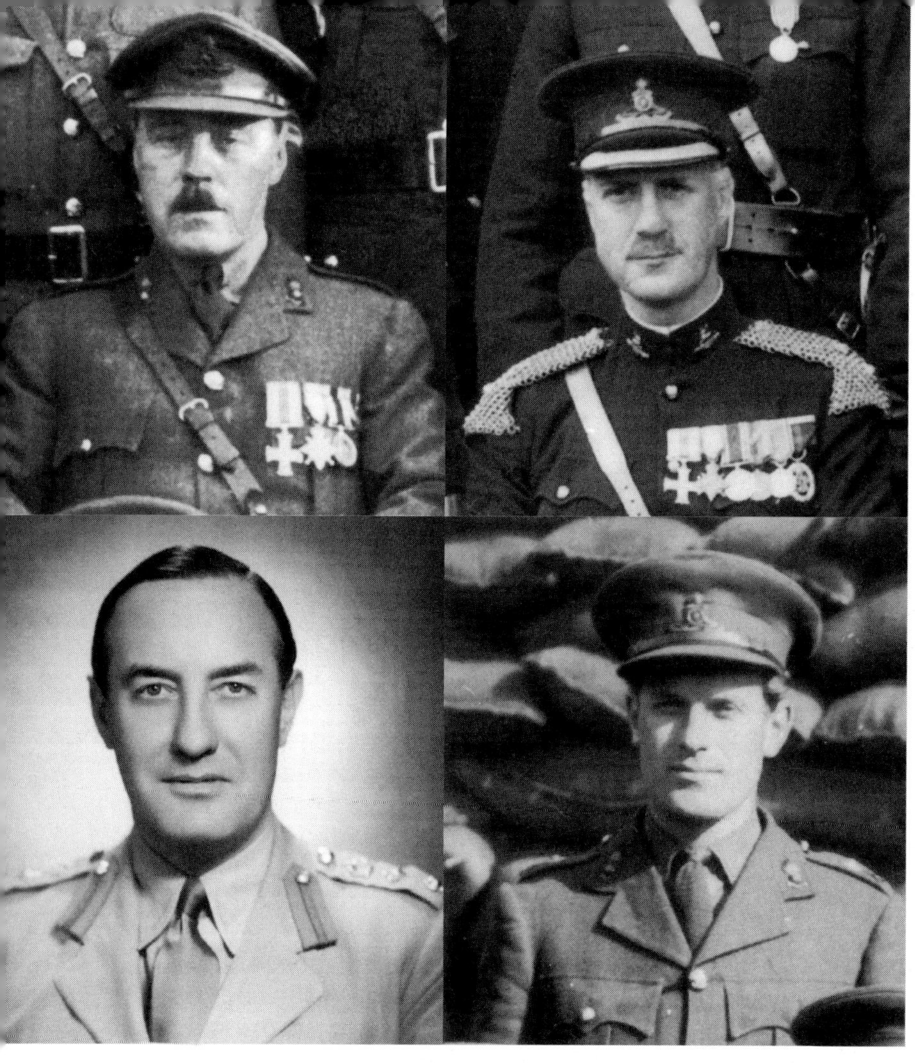

Plate 174 *Some of the officers who were decorated for services after leaving 86th Field Regiment.*
Top left – *Brigadier Sir Geoffrey Church, Bt., M.C., T.D., appointed C.B.E. as C.R.A. 54th Division;*
Top right – *Colonel W.R.D. Robertson, M.C., T.D., who served on the Munitions Assignment Board in Washington and was made an Officer of the United States Legion of Merit;* Bottom Left – *Colonel H.M. O'Connor, appointed O.B.E. and an Officer of the United States Legion of Merit in recognition of his two years' work as representative in Washington of the London Controlling Section, responsible for the deception plan covering Operation 'Overlord';* Bottom right – *Lieutenant-Colonel M.R. Norman, appointed O.B.E. and awarded the United States Medal of Freedom for his services in the War Cabinet Secretariat and with the London Munitions Assignment Board.*
(Regimental Collection)

Territorial Army before 3rd September 1939 and continued to serve, even for a few days, after 3rd September 1945, completed the necessary twelve years service and became eligible for the Decoration or Medal, as appropriate. Officers who received the Decoration are listed in *Hertfordshire Yeomanry and Artillery Honours and Awards* but it has proved impossible to compile a complete list of other ranks who were awarded the Efficiency Medal.

As explained in Chapter 1, units of the Territorial Army were placed in suspended animation on ceasing to be effective through demobilisation or, in 135th Field Regiment's case, capture. War-formed units, 191st Field Regiment among them, were disbanded. Accordingly, both 86th and 135th Field Regiments existed on paper after the war's end, though, in conformity with War Office Letter 20/Gen./5689 (T.A.1) of 10th October 1938 (see Chapter 1), their numbered batteries did not. Even as 86th Field Regiment were going through the winter of 1945–46 with the Army of Occupation, a shadow of their former selves and without their guns, in the War Office thoughts were being directed to raising a reorganised Territorial Army with as little delay as possible. Within the Royal Regiment of Artillery, too, efforts were at last being made to devise a system of numbering all units in a common series, thus finally ending the confusion which existed between units with similar designations.

The composition of the post-war Territorial Army was discussed at length, especially between the War Office and the Territorial Associations, during the second half of 1946. On 1st January 1947 the units comprising the proposed order of battle were reactivated from suspended animation, to exist without personnel until commanding officers and permanent staff had been selected and posted, generally during April. Recruiting opened on 1st May 1947. Some three hundred units of the Royal Artillery were to be raised but only 75 were in the Field Branch. The overwhelming majority of units were for air defence, either in a reconstituted Anti-Aircraft Command or for deployment with a future expeditionary force.

A comprehensive renumbering scheme for the whole of the Royal Regiment of Artillery was introduced in the Territorial Army to coincide with the reactivation of units on 1st January 1947, and in the Regular Army on 1st April 1947. Details were first published in A.C.I. 229/1947 and repeated in full in *Royal Artillery Notes*, No. 41 of February 1947. Territorial units were numbered in a series starting with 235 and ending with 670, according to a table of precedence based on their seniority in the *Army List* on 1st January 1938, or on the date of their conversion to Royal Artillery, or of formation, if later.

Representatives of Hertfordshire Territorial Association who attended a meeting called by Headquarters East Anglian District early in September 1946 learned, no doubt with shock, that the first circulated draft of the War Office plan for the re-formation of the Territorial Army would place only two companies of infantry in the county (as part of a battalion of the Bedfordshire and Hertfordshire Regiment with headquarters in Bedfordshire). It was planned, however, that Hertfordshire would be responsible for raising one field regiment, one heavy and one light anti-aircraft regiment, a searchlight battery, an A.G.R.A. headquarters and a corps counter-battery staff, all in the Royal Artillery, together with an ordnance field park. The reaction of the Hertfordshire Association was, predictably, to make the strongest efforts at the highest possible level to ensure that the Hertfordshire Regiment was not written out of the order of battle, and to pass the comment that there would be too many artillery units in the county. Some rethinking within the War Office, which took account of these representations, resulted in the announcement at an Eastern Command conference on 29th October 1946 that the county would be responsible for a field regiment and a heavy anti-aircraft regiment of the Royal Artillery – successors to 86th Field Regiment and 79th Heavy Anti-Aircraft Regiment; a whole infantry battalion – successor to 1st Battalion The Hertfordshire Regiment; and a new transport company of the Royal Army Service Corps. The 54th (East Anglian) Division was not included in the immediate post-war order of battle and the one field regiment to be raised in Hertfordshire would be under command of 89th A.G.R.A. No place could be found for the successor to 135th Field Regiment, which was not reactivated from suspended animation, and Hertfordshire's historic, but sometimes difficult, link with Peterborough was thus broken.

Early in December 1946 Hertfordshire Territorial Association had heard that the reactivated 86th Field Regiment would take the title '286th Field Regiment, Royal Artillery (East Anglian) (Hertfordshire Yeomanry)'. Brigadier Sir Geoffrey Church, previously Honorary Colonel of 86th Field Regiment, and soon to be confirmed as Honorary Colonel of 286th, gave the opinion (it is not clear whether with or without consultation with other officers of the regiment) that the 'East Anglian' designation should be dropped, and a meeting of the Association's Finance and General Purposes Committee resolved on 13th December to ask for the new title to be simply '286th Field Regiment, Royal Artillery (Hertfordshire Yeomanry)'. All concerned must have reacted very swiftly, for when the new titles were published in A.C.I. 229/1947 and in *Royal Artillery Notes*, No. 41, the bracketed designation 'East Anglian' did not appear. While it is possible to sympathise with the desire to make a potentially cumbersome title roll as easily as possible off the tongue, with hindsight the decision to remove 'East Anglian' should be regretted. At a stroke all evidence of the 'pure Gunner' ancestry of the unit disappeared; and throughout the post-war period the tendency has increasingly been to emphasise the Yeomanry's history and achievements at the expense of those of 4th East Anglian Brigade, R.F.A., and the 1st and 2nd Hertfordshire Batteries.

Major R.D. Cribb, who, it may be remembered, had led the party which left 86th Field Regiment to join 19th Field Regiment in July 1940, and had since served in North-West Europe with 121st Medium Regiment, gaining a Mention-in-Despatches, was appointed to command 286th Field Regiment with effect from 1st May 1947. Recruiting for the regiment began in June, when, as will be seen in the final volume of this series, a good sprinkling of those who had worn the black beret and the hart badge, and followed the fortunes of 86th Field Regiment from Normandy to Northern Germany, were persuaded to return.

Appendix 1

# *Principal Acts of Parliament, Regulations and Orders relating to the origin, raising and maintenance of Territorial units of the Royal Artillery, 1920–1946 and the Home Guard, 1940–1945*

| | |
|---|---|
| *1907*<br>7 Edw. VII c.9 | *Territorial and Reserve Forces Act*<br>Authorises the Crown to raise and maintain the Territorial Force consisting of such numbers of men as may be fixed by Parliament. Sets out the underlying provisions for administration by County Associations, organisation and training (maximum 18 days annually for mounted units) and provides for regulations to be issued by the Secretary of State. The Territorial Force to be embodied only after the call-out of the Army Reserve, and only for service in the United Kingdom, except in the case of those units or individuals who have volunteered to serve abroad. Units of the Imperial Yeomanry and the Volunteer Force to be transferred to the Territorial Force by Order in Council once the administrative machinery has been established in their counties.[1] The Volunteer Act, 1863 remains available for the raising of volunteer forces in addition to the Territorial Force. Enables the enlistment of men who have not served in the Regular Forces into the Army Reserve as 'Special Reservists'. Provides for the transfer by Order in Council of units of the Militia to the Special Reserve. |
| *1921*<br>11 & 12 Geo.V c.37 | *Territorial Army and Militia Act*<br>Redesignates the Territorial Force as the 'Territorial Army' with effect from 1st October 1921. Repeals powers to raise or maintain any additional Auxiliary Forces (notably those conferred by the Volunteer Act, 1863 and the Militia and Yeomanry Act, 1901). Redesignates the Special Reserve as the 'Militia', also with effect from 1st October 1921. |
| *1939*<br>2 & 3 Geo. VI c.24 | *Reserve and Auxiliary Forces Act*<br>Makes further, and temporary, provision to enable the Reserve and Auxiliary Forces of the Crown to be called out for service as may be found necessary. Enables call-out of "all or any" members of the Reserves by Order in Council if the Secretary of State is satisfied that their service is urgently required for ensuring preparedness for the defence of the Realm against any external danger. Members of the Territorial Army called out under the Act to be deemed to have been embodied for purposes of the Territorial and Reserve Forces Act, 1907. |

| | |
|---|---|
| *1939*<br>2 & 3 Geo.VI c.25 | *Military Training Act*<br>Makes temporary provision for rendering men between the ages of 20 and 21 years liable to undergo training in the Armed Forces of the Crown. Excuses from registration or call-up men who before 27th April 1939 have enlisted in or been appointed to commissions in any of His Majesty's Reserve or Auxiliary Forces. Men called up for full-time training to be deemed to have been enlisted as 'militiamen' under Section 30 of the Reserve Forces Act, 1907 for a period of four years. |
| *1939*<br>2 & 3 Geo.VI c.62 | *Emergency Powers (Defence) Act*<br>Enabling legislation for the series of 'Defence Regulations' promulgated as Statutory Rules and Orders (S.R.& O.), including those for the raising and maintenance of the Home Guard (see below). |
| *1939*<br>2 & 3 Geo.VI c.68 | *Armed Forces (Conditions of Service) Act*<br>Provides, "notwithstanding anything in the Territorial and Reserve Forces Act, 1907", for embodied personnel of the Territorial Army to be "ordered to go out of and liable to be carried out of" the United Kingdom or to be transferred without consent to another corps or posted to another unit. |
| *1939*<br>2 & 3 Geo.VI c.90 | *Military and Air Forces (Prolongation of Service) Act*<br>Extends existing Reserve and Auxiliary Forces engagements "until the end of the emergency". |
| *1940*<br>S.R. & O., 1940, No. 748 | *Defence (Local Defence Volunteers) Regulations*<br>Provides for the establishment of a force to be called the Local Defence Volunteers, to consist of such men as may voluntarily undertake to serve without pay. Instructions relating to organisation, training, duties, etc. to be issued by the Army Council. Members of the L.D.V. shall not, unless mustered to resist invasion, be required to give whole-time service or live away from home and shall not be required to enroll for a period exceeding that of the present emergency. Members of the L.D.V. to be members of the Armed Forces of the Crown and be subject to military law. |
| *1940*<br>S.R. & O., 1940, No. 1383 | Amends S.R. & O., 1940, No. 748 to provide for the Local Defence Volunteers to be known by the alternative title 'Home Guard'. |
| *1940*<br>S.R. & O., 1940, No. 2017 | *Home Guard Officers' Commissions Order, 1940*<br>Revoked by S.R. & O., 1941, No. 186. |
| *1941*<br>S.R. & O., 1941, No. 186 | *Home Guard Officers' Commissions Order, 1941*<br>Refers to the Order of 1927 regulating the issue, form and effect of commissions in the Land Forces and provides for officers of the Home Guard to be granted commissions in the form set out in the schedule. Commissions to be notified in the *London Gazette* or "in such other manner as the Army Council may decide".[2] |
| *1942*<br>S.R. & O., 1942, No. 91 | Amends S.R. & O., 1940, No. 748 to provide that the force established thereunder shall be known by the title 'Home Guard' and the title 'Local Defence Volunteers' shall not be used. Empowers the Minister of Labour and National Service to direct male persons to enroll in the Home Guard and introduces penalties for non-compliance or absence from parade. |

NOTES

1. Order in Council dated 19th March 1908 published as A.O. 70/1908 and in the *London Gazette* of 20th March 1908.
2. Home Guard commissions and subsequent promotions, etc. were announced in Home Guard Orders within each command.

Appendix 2

# *Battery Establishments and Organisation*

*The 4-gun horse-drawn battery (Peace Establishment), 1920–30*

Provisional establishments, which have not been traced and may not have survived in detail, governed the re-raising of Territorial units in 1920. It is known that a four-battery field artillery brigade had a total establishment of 26 officers and five hundred other ranks. It can accordingly be deduced that a single battery must have had an establishment very similar to the 4-gun 15-pdr. battery shown in Appendix 2 of *The Hertfordshire Batteries, R.F.A.* A new permanent Peace Establishment of five officers and 101 other ranks, shown in detail in Table 1, was introduced in March 1922 and remained in force until units were officially transferred to mechanised establishment in the early 1930s.

*The 4-gun mechanised battery (Peace Establishment), 1930–38*

Although some Territorial brigades trained with mechanised draught between 1927 and 1929, the decision to introduce a mechanised establishment was not promulgated until January 1930 (W.O.L. 20/Artillery/4798/A.G.1 dated 9th January 1930). Units were directed to adopt either the 'completely mechanised' or the 'partly mechanised – mounted battery staff but mechanised draught' establishment at once. The completely mechanised establishment, to which batteries of 86th Field Brigade conformed, is shown in detail in Table 2. The considerable reduction in other ranks' posts was obtained by the removal of all mounted drivers and horse-holders and their replacement by less than half that number of drivers for cars and lorries. All ready-use ammunition was to be carried in the gun-towing vehicles, so ammunition wagons were struck off the establishment. No War Establishment specific to the Territorial field brigade was issued but it had been planned since 1920 that Territorial units would mobilise with 6-gun batteries, involving an increase from 84 all ranks to 145 and the reintroduction of first-line ammunition carriers, other than the towing vehicles, in the form of an additional towing vehicle with limber and ammunition wagon in each section. The 4-gun completely mechanised Peace Establishment introduced in 1930 was reissued at intervals between 1931 and 1937, the only change being a reduction of two other ranks between 1933 and 1937. The scale of vehicles available for training in camp was minimal and various devices were used to supplement it. These included borrowing from neighbouring Regular units, the use of members' civilian motor-cycles and the pooling of the brigade's vehicles so that two batteries could exercise in the field while the other two carried out instruction in camp, the allocation being reversed on alternate days.

*The 12-gun battery (War Establishment) 1938–1940*

The adoption of the new regimental establishment (two batteries, each of three 4-gun troops) was promulgated by W.O.L. 20/General/5689 (T.A.1) of 10th October 1938, which was followed shortly afterwards by details of training scales of new vehicles and guns (see Chapter 3). The expansion of the Field Force in the spring of 1939 called for units to move on to War Establishment for personnel, so the Peace Establishment, if it was ever issued, was overtaken almost at once. Mobilisation in September 1939 was on the basis of the two-battery, 24-gun regiment, probably to W.E. III/1931/9/4, but shortages of guns and vehicles were such that this was never attained. In any case, it was known by October 1940 that the organisation of a field regiment was to be changed from two 12-gun batteries to three 8-gun batteries and many units adopted a provisional three-battery organisation at once.

*The 8-gun battery (War Establishment), 1941–1945*

Although provisionally taken into use by many units during the autumn of 1940, the new regimental organisation and establishment of three 8-gun batteries (each two troops of four guns) was not officially adopted until March 1941, when the establishment was issued as W.E. II/1931/7A/3. The new organisation afforded greater tactical flexibility without any loss of fire-power in the regiment as a whole and all troops were brought on to the same scale of vehicles and wireless sets. By the time batteries were officially reorganised to two troops, the issue of 25-pdr. guns was more or less complete, though the 18/25pdr. had not yet been fully replaced by the 25pdr. Mk. II on Carriage Mk. I, and many units had two, sometimes three, makes of 'Quad' field artillery tractor on charge. Field service, as opposed to training, units were gradually brought to 'mobilised' scales of homogenous equipment during 1941. The establishment on which batteries of 135th Field Regiment mobilised for service abroad in the autumn of 1941 is shown in Table 3.

The number of personnel employed in a towed field battery hardly changed between March 1941 and the end of the war. Within the totals, the only significant changes were the transfer of the cooks from the Royal Artillery to the Army Catering Corps and the introduction of the trade of driver-operator, as a result of which eighteen signallers were reclassified from non-tradesmen to tradesmen. As far as vehicles and equipment were concerned, the main visible changes were the introduction of the Jeep (car, 5-cwt., 4x4) as X2 and for the battery- and troop sergeant-majors and, of course, the substitution of the No. 19 wireless set for the No. 11 and the issue of man-pack sets – No. 18 and No. 38 – for use at the O.Ps.

*The 8-gun self-propelled battery (War Establishment), 1943–1945*

War Establishments for self-propelled field regiments were not issued until September 1943 (W.E. VIII/490/1 – 25-pdr. Bishop and W.E. VIII/515/1 – 105-mm. M7 Priest) and October 1943 (W.E. II/19OA/1 – 25-pdr. Sexton). There was no underlying difference in the role and organisation of a self-propelled battery, as compared with a towed battery, and hence very little difference in the establishment of personnel. A self-propelled 25-pdr. detachment was only four, compared with six in a towed detachment and there was a requirement for larger numbers of driver-mechanics, driver-mechanics (A.F.V.) and driver-operators, and fewer drivers, I.C. The inventory of guns and vehicles was, of course, substantially different, with a much larger proportion of F.F.W. vehicles and No. 19 wireless sets, including, by 1944, one set on each of the guns. The establishment on which batteries of 86th Field Regiment served in North-West Europe was W.E II/190A/2 which came into effect on 25th May 1944 and is shown in detail in Table 4. There was no significant difference in personnel but the vehicle establishment reflected the intention to issue F.F.W. 15-cwt. half-tracks – M14s were eventually issued – in substitution for carriers, armoured O.P. and some 15-cwt. trucks. Further Jeeps were also to be issued. It can safely be said that 86th Field Regiment never fully conformed to W.E. II/190A/2. However, the extent to which this was the regiment's choice rather than the result of anomalies in the supply system cannot be determined. As described in Chapter 4, half-tracks issued as ammunition vehicles were converted to command posts well before F.F.W. vehicles arrived. Battery commanders always used tanks rather than half-tracks, with Jeeps as X2, while troop commanders seem to have retained carriers, armoured O.P. in addition to their O.P. tanks throughout the campaign. At the gun end there is no evidence that Jeeps, which were always in short supply, were issued to batteries, rather than for use in Regimental Headquarters, so battery- and troop sergeant-majors retained their motor-cycles.

*Table 1*

A Territorial Field Battery, R.A. (Two sections, each of two 18-pdr. guns or two 4.5-in. howitzers), Peace Establishment, 1922–1928.

| | Battery Headquarters | Two Sections (each) | Total, Battery |
|---|---|---|---|
| *Personnel* | | | |
| Majors | 1 | .. | 1 |
| Captains | 1 | .. | 1 |
| Subalterns | 1 | 1 | 3 |
| W.O.IIs (B.S.M.) | 1 | .. | 1 |
| B.Q.M.Ss. | 1 | .. | 1 |
| Sergeants (Nos.1) | .. | 2 | 4 |
| Farrier-sergeants | 1 | .. | 1 |
| Trumpeters | 2 | .. | 2 |
| Signals N.C.Os. | 1 | .. | 1 |
| B.Cs.' assistants | 1 | .. | 1 |
| G.P.Os.' assistants | 1 | .. | 1 |
| Bombardiers | .. | 4 | 8 |
| Surveyors, R.A. | 4 | .. | 4 |
| Saddlers | .. | 1 | 2 |
| Artificers, R.A. | 1 | .. | 1 |
| Farriers | 1 | 1 | 3 |
| Signallers | 6 | 2 | 10 |
| Rangetakers | 1 | .. | 1 |
| Cooks | .. | 1 | 2 |
| Storemen | 1 | .. | 1 |
| Clerks | 1 | .. | 1 |
| Stable orderlies | 1 | .. | 1 |
| Pay sergeants' assistants | 1 | .. | 1 |
| Batmen | 3 | 1 | 5 |
| Limber gunners | .. | 2 | 4 |
| Gunners | 6 | 7 | 20 |
| Gunners (for vehicles) | 1 | 12 | 25 |
| Total all ranks | 38 | 34 | 106 |
| *Guns and Vehicles* | | | |
| Carriages, gun or howitzer, with limbers | .. | 2 | 4 |
| Wagons, ammunition, with limbers | .. | 2 | 4 |
| Wagons, G.S. | 1 | .. | 1 |
| *Horses allowed for Annual Training* | | | |
| *Riding* | | | |
| Officers | 3 | 1 | 5 |
| W.O.s., sergeants and coverers | 3 | 4 | 11 |
| Trumpeters | 2 | .. | 2 |
| Signals N.C.O. and signallers | 4 | .. | 4 |
| B.C.s.' and G.P.Os.' assistants | 2 | .. | 2 |
| Horseholders | 4 | .. | 4 |
| *Light draught* | | | |
| Guns | .. | 12 | 24 |
| Ammunition wagons | .. | 8 | 16 |
| Wagons, G.S. | 2 | .. | 2 |
| Spare, draught | .. | 2 | 4 |
| Total horses | 20 | 27 | 74 |

[Source: *Peace Establishments, Part II, Section II (Territorial Army) 1927–28* (notified in Army Order 335/1927)]

*Table 1 (continued)*

Possible organisation for training at annual camp

| Battery Headquarters | | Gun Group | | First Line Group | |
|---|---|---|---|---|---|
| | Horses | | Horses | | Horses |
| B.C. | 1 | Battery | 1 | *A Sub wagon* | |
| B.C.'s assistant | 1 | leader | | 2 drivers | 4 |
| Rangetaker | 1 | | | | |
| Orderly | 1 | *A Sub-* | | *B Sub wagon* | |
| 2 horseholders | 2 | *Section* | | 2 drivers | 4 |
| | | No. 1 (Sgt.) | 1 | | |
| Signals sergeant | 1 | Bombardier | | *C Sub wagon* | |
| O.P. terminal (T.1) | | 4 gunners | | 2 drivers | 4 |
| (2 signallers) | 2 | 3 drivers | 6 | | |
| Horseholder | 1 | | | *D Sub wagon* | |
| | | *B Sub-* | | 2 drivers | 4 |
| G.P.O. | 1 | *Section* | | | |
| G.P.O.'s assistant | 1 | No. 1 (Sgt.) | 1 | *Wagon Lines* | |
| 2 surveyors | 2 | Bombardier | | Battery captain | 1 |
| Battery terminal (T.2) | 2 | 4 gunners | | Farrier-sergeant | 1 |
| (2 signallers) | 2 | 3 drivers | 6 | Artificer | 1 |
| 2 horseholders | 2 | | | Maint. terminal | |
| | | Section | | (T.4) | 2 |
| B.S.M. | 1 | commander | 1 | (2 signallers) | |
| Maint. terminal (T.3) | | | | Horseholder | 1 |
| (2 signallers) | 2 | *C Sub-* | | | |
| Horseholder | 1 | *Section* | | | |
| | | No. 1 (Sgt.) | 1 | | |
| Duties in camp | | Bombardier | | | |
| | | 4 gunners | | | |
| | | 3 drivers | 6 | | |
| B.Q.M.S. | | | | | |
| Cooks | | *D Sub-* | | | |
| Storeman | | *Section* | | | |
| Clerk | | No.1 (Sgt.) | 1 | | |
| Pay assistant | | Bombardier | | | |
| Batmen | | 4 gunners | | | |
| | | 3 drivers | 6 | | |

[Source: *Artillery Training, Volume I – Drill*, 1932]

*Table 2*

A Territorial Field Battery, R.A. (Two sections, each of two 18-pdr. guns or two 4.5-in howitzers), Peace Establishment, 1937.

| | Battery Headquarters | Two Sections (each) | Total, Battery |
|---|---|---|---|
| *Personnel* | | | |
| Majors | 1 | .. | 1 |
| Captains | 1 | .. | 1 |
| Subalterns | 1 | 1 | 3 |
| W.O.IIs (B.S.M.) | 1 | .. | 1 |
| B.Q.M.Ss. | 1 | .. | 1 |
| Sergeants (Nos. 1) | .. | 2 | 4 |
| Trumpeters | 2 | .. | 2 |
| Tradesmen: | | | |
| Fitters | 1 | .. | 1 |
| Non-tradesmen: | | | |
| Signals N.C.Os. | 1 | .. | 1 |
| Signallers | 12 | .. | 12 |
| B.Cs.' assistants | 1 | .. | 1 |
| G.P.Os.' assistants | 1 | .. | 1 |
| Rangetakers | 1 | .. | 1 |
| Gun detachments | .. | 10 | 20 |
| Limber gunners | .. | 2 | 4 |
| Officers' Mess | 1 | .. | 1 |
| Sergeants' Mess | 1 | .. | 1 |
| Cooks | .. | 1 | 2 |
| Storemen | 1 | .. | 1 |
| Clerks | 1 | .. | 1 |
| Pay sergeants' assistants | 1 | .. | 1 |
| Officers' servants | 3 | 1 | 5 |
| Sanitary dutymen | 1 | .. | 1 |
| Water dutymen | 1 | .. | 1 |
| Drivers, I.C. | 4 | 5 | 14 |
| Gunners, Spare | 2 | .. | 2 |
| Total, all ranks | 40 | 22 | 84 |
| *Guns* | | | |
| Carriages, gun or howitzer, with limbers | .. | 2 | 4 |
| *Vehicles allowed for annual training* | | | |
| Lorries, 30-cwt., 6 × 4 | .. | 2 | 4 |
| Cars, 5-seater, 4 × 2 | 3 | .. | 3 |
| Cars, 2-seater, 4 × 2 | 2 | .. | 2 |
| Motor-cycles | 1 | .. | 1 |

[Source: *Peace Establishments, Part II, Section II (Territorial Army) 1936–37* (notified in Army Order 59/1937)]

*Table 2 (continued)*

Possible organisation for training at annual camp

| Battery Headquarters | | Gun Group | |
|---|---|---|---|
| Car, 2-seater | B.C.<br>Driver | | Battery leader[1] |
| Car, 5-seater | B.C's assistant<br>Rangetaker<br>O.P. terminal (T.1)<br>(2 signallers)<br>Driver | Lorry, 30-cwt., $6\times4$ | *A Sub-Section*<br>No. 1 (Sgt.)<br>Bombardier<br>4 gunners<br>Driver |
| Motor-cycle | Signals sergeant | Lorry, 30-cwt., $6\times4$ | *B Sub-Section*<br>No. 1 (Sgt.)<br>Bombardier<br>4 gunners<br>Driver |
| Car, 2-seater | G.P.O.<br>Driver | | Section commander[1] |
| Car, 5-seater | B.S.M.<br>G.P.O.'s assistant<br>Battery terminal (T.2)<br>(2 signallers)<br>Driver | Lorry, 30-cwt., $6\times4$ | *C Sub-Section*<br>No. 1 (Sgt.)<br>Bombardier<br>4 gunners<br>Driver |
| Car, 5-seater | Maint. terminals<br>(T.3, T.4)<br>(each 2 signallers)<br>Driver | Lorry, 30-cwt., $6\times4$ | *D Sub-Section*<br>No. 1 (Sgt.)<br>Bombardier<br>4 gunners<br>Driver |
| Duties in camp | | | |
| | B.Q.M.S.<br>Cooks<br>Storeman<br>Clerk<br>Pay assistant<br>Batmen | | *Travelling with the guns*<br>Battery captain[1]<br>Artificer<br>2 surveyors |

1. Travels with the guns or may use civilian car or motor-cycle.

[Source: *Artillery Training, Volume 1 – Drill*, 1932; *Artillery Training, Volume I, Pamphlet No.2 – Battle Drill and Manoeuvre for the Reconnaissance and Occupation of Positions* . . . 1938]

*Table 3*

A Field Battery, R.A. (Two troops, each of four 25-pdr. guns), War Establishment, March 1941.

| | Battery H.Q. | Two Troops (each) | | | Total, Battery |
|---|---|---|---|---|---|
| | | Troop H.Q. | Two Sections (each) | Total, Troop | |
| *Personnel* | | | | | |
| Majors | 1 | .. | .. | .. | 1 |
| Captains | 1 | 1 | .. | 1 | 3 |
| Subalterns | 2 | 2 | .. | 2 | 6 |
| W.O.IIs (B.S.M./T.S.Ms.) | 1 | 1 | .. | 1 | 3 |
| B.Q.M.Ss. | 1 | .. | .. | .. | 1 |
| Signals sergeants | 1 | .. | .. | .. | 1 |
| Sergeants (Nos.1) | .. | .. | 2 | 4 | 8 |
| Tradesmen: | | | | | |
| Fitters, motor vehicle | 1 | .. | .. | .. | 1 |
| Fitters, gun | .. | 1 | .. | 1 | 2 |
| Driver-mechanics | .. | .. | 2 | 4 | 8 |
| Equipment repairers | 1 | .. | .. | .. | 1 |
| Motor mechanics | 1 | 1 | .. | 1 | 3 |
| Technical storemen | 1 | .. | .. | .. | 1 |
| Non-tradesmen: | | | | | |
| Ammunition numbers | 5 | .. | .. | .. | 5 |
| Batmen | 10 | .. | .. | .. | 10 |
| Clerks | 2 | .. | .. | .. | 2 |
| C.P.Os.' assistants | 4 | .. | .. | .. | 4 |
| Cooks | 5 | .. | .. | .. | 5 |
| Drivers, I.C. | 16 | 5 | 3 | 11 | 38 |
| Gun numbers | .. | .. | 10 | 20 | 40 |
| G.P.Os.' assistants | .. | 2 | .. | 2 | 4 |
| A.A. L.M.G. numbers | 4 | 2 | .. | 2 | 8 |
| Motor-cycle orderlies | 3 | .. | .. | .. | 3 |
| O.P. assistants | 1 | 1 | .. | 1 | 3 |
| Sanitary dutymen | 1 | .. | .. | .. | 1 |
| Signallers | 14 | 13 | .. | 13 | 40 |
| Storemen | 1 | .. | .. | .. | 1 |
| Water dutymen | 1 | .. | .. | .. | 1 |
| Total, all ranks | 78 | 29 | 17 | 63 | 204 |
| *Guns and Vehicles* | | | | | |
| Motor-cycles | 6 | 3 | .. | 3 | 12 |
| Cars, 2-seater, 4 × 2 | 1 | .. | .. | .. | 1 |
| Carriers, armoured O.P. | 1 | 1 | .. | 1 | 3 |
| Trucks, 15-cwt., 4 × 2, G.S. | 3 | 2 | .. | 2 | 7 |
| Trucks, 15-cwt., 4 × 2, personnel | 2 | 2 | .. | 2 | 6 |
| Trucks, 15-cwt., 4 × 2, water | 1 | .. | .. | .. | 1 |
| Lorries, 3-ton, 4 × 4 | 8 | .. | .. | .. | 8 |
| Tractors, field artillery | .. | .. | 3 | 6 | 12 |
| Trailers, artillery, No. 27 | .. | .. | 4 | 8 | 16 |
| 25-pdr. guns | .. | .. | 2 | 4 | .. |

*Table 3 (continued)*

## Organisation in the field

**Battery Headquarters (Command)**

| | | |
|---|---|---|
| X | Carrier,<br>Amd. O.P. | Major<br>2 signallers<br>O.P.A.<br>*Wireless set No. 11* |
| X2 | Car,<br>2-seater | Driver, I.C. |
| MC1 | Motor-cycle | Orderly |
| H | 15-cwt.,<br>4 × 2, F.F.W. | Subaltern (C.P.O.)<br>2 C.P.O. As.<br>2 signallers<br>Driver, I.C.<br>*Wireless set No. 11* |
| MC2 | Motor-cycle | Orderly |
| MC7 | Motor-cycle | Signals sergeant |
| M1 | 15-cwt.,<br>4 × 2, pers. | 5 signallers<br>Driver, I.C.<br>*Mechanical cable layer* |
| Y | 15-cwt.,<br>4 × 2, G.S. | Subaltern (A.C.P.O.)<br>2 C.P.O. As.<br>Driver, I.C. |
| K1 | 15-cwt.,<br>4 × 2, F.F.W. | Captain<br>3 signallers<br>Driver, I.C.<br>*Wireless set No. 11* |
| MC8 | Motor-cycle | Orderly |
| K2 | 15-cwt.,<br>4 × 2, pers. | Bombardier clerk<br>2 signallers<br>2 A.A. L.M.G. numbers<br>Driver, I.C.<br>*A.A. L.M.G. and 1,000 rounds*<br>*A. Tk. rifle and 200 rounds* |
| MC11 | Motor-cycle | B.S.M. |

**Battery Headquarters (Administration)**

| | | |
|---|---|---|
| Amn1 | 3-ton, 4 × 4,<br>G.S. | 5 ammunition numbers<br>Driver, I.C.<br>*184 rounds ammunition* |
| Amn2 | 3-ton, 4 × 4,<br>G.S. | 4 batmen<br>Driver, I.C.<br>*184 rounds ammunition* |
| Amn3 | 3-ton, 4 × 4,<br>G.S. | 4 batmen<br>Driver, I.C.<br>*112 rounds ammunition*<br>*Camouflage stores* |
| P | 3-ton, 4 × 4,<br>G.S. | Driver, I.C.<br>Spare driver, I.C.<br>*Petrol* |
| Q1 | 3-ton, 4 × 4,<br>G.S. | B.Q.M.S.<br>Clerk<br>Storeman<br>Driver, I.C.<br>*'Q' stores* |
| Q2 | 3-ton, 4 × 4,<br>G.S. | Motor mechanic<br>Technical storeman<br>Equipment repairer<br>Driver, I.C.<br>*M.T. stores* |
| Q3 | 3-ton, 4 × 4,<br>G.S. | Bombardier cook<br>2 cooks<br>Sanitary dutyman<br>Driver, I.C.<br>*Cooking sets and rations* |
| Q4 | 3-ton, 4 × 4,<br>G.S. | 2 A.A. L.M.G. numbers<br>2 cooks<br>2 batmen<br>Driver, I.C.<br>*A.A. L.M.G. and 1,000 rounds*<br>*A. Tk. rifle and 200 rounds*<br>*Cooking sets and rations* |
| Q5 | 15-cwt.,<br>4 × 2, Water | Water dutyman<br>Driver. I.C. |
| MC12 | Motor-cycle | Fitter, M.V. |

**Two Troops (each)**

| | | | |
|---|---|---|---|
| RA | RB | Carrier,<br>Amd. O.P. | Captain<br>2 signallers<br>O.P.A.<br>*Wireless set No. 11* |
| GA | GB | 15-cwt.,<br>4 × 2,<br>F.F.W. | Subaltern (G.P.O.)<br>G.P.O. A.<br>2 signallers<br>Driver, I.C.<br>*Wireless set No.11* |
| MC5 | MC6 | Motor-cycle | T.S.M. |
| MC3 | MC4 | Motor-cycle | Signals bombardier |
| M2 | M3 | 15-cwt.,<br>4 × 2,<br>pers. | 4 signallers<br>Driver, I.C.<br>*Hand cable layer* |
| TLA | TLB | 15-cwt.,<br>4 × 2,<br>pers. | Subaltern (T.L.)<br>G.P.O. A.<br>Motor mechanic<br>2 A.A. L.M.G. numbers<br>Signaller<br>Driver, I.C.<br>*A.A. L.M.G. and 1,000 rounds*<br>*A. Tk. rifle and 200 rounds* |
| M4 | M5 | 15-cwt.,<br>4 × 2,<br>G.S. | 3 signallers<br>Driver, I.C.<br>*Hand cable layer* |
| MC9 | MC10 | Motor-cycle | Fitter, gun |
| A<br>B<br>C<br>D | E<br>F<br>G<br>H | Tractor, F.A.,<br>4 × 4<br>Trailer, artillery, No. 27<br>25-pdr. gun | Nos. 1,2, 3 and 4<br>Driver-mechanic<br>Driver, I.C.<br>*56 rounds ammunition*<br>*12 A.P. shot* |
| AB<br>CD | EF<br>GH | Tractor, F.A.,<br>4 × 4<br>2 × Trlr., artillery, No. 27 | Nos. 5 and 6 of both guns<br>2 drivers, I.C.<br>*88 rounds ammunition* |

[Source: *War Establishment II/1931/7A/3* (notified in A.C.Is. 12th March 1941)]

*Table 4*

A Self-Propelled Field Battery, R.A. (Two troops, each of four 25-pdr. Sexton S.P. guns), War Establishment, May 1944.

| | Battery H.Q. | Two Troops (each) | | | Total, Battery |
|---|---|---|---|---|---|
| | | Troop H.Q. | Two Sections (each) | Total, Troop | |
| *Personnel* | | | | | |
| Majors | 1 | .. | .. | .. | 1 |
| Captains | 1 | 1 | .. | 1 | 3 |
| Subalterns | 2 | 2 | .. | 2 | 6 |
| W.O.IIs (B.S.M./T.S.Ms.) | 1 | 1 | .. | 1 | 3 |
| B.Q.M.Ss. | 1 | .. | .. | .. | 1 |
| Signals sergeants | 1 | .. | .. | .. | 1 |
| Sergeants (Nos.1) | .. | .. | 2 | 4 | 8 |
| Tradesmen: | | | | | |
| Artificers, R.A. (or fitters, gun) | .. | 1 | .. | 1 | 2 |
| Clerks | 2 | .. | .. | .. | 2 |
| Driver-mechanics | 1 | .. | 1 | 2 | 5 |
| Driver-mechanics (A.F.V.) | .. | 2 | 2 | 6 | 12 |
| Driver-operators | 6 | 4 | 2 | 8 | 22 |
| Equipment repairers | 1 | .. | .. | .. | 1 |
| Technical storemen | 1 | .. | .. | .. | 1 |
| Vehicle mechanics | 3 | 1 | .. | 1 | 5 |
| Non-tradesmen: | | | | | |
| Ammunition numbers | 6 | .. | 1 | 2 | 10 |
| Batmen | 6 | 2 | .. | 2 | 10 |
| Clerks | 2 | .. | .. | .. | 4 |
| C.P.Os.' assistants | 4 | .. | .. | .. | 4 |
| Drivers, I.C. | 14 | 3 | .. | 3 | 20 |
| Gun numbers | .. | .. | 6 | 12 | 24 |
| G.P.Os.' assistants | .. | 2 | .. | 2 | 4 |
| L.M.G. numbers | 8 | 2 | .. | 2 | 8 |
| Motor-cycle orderlies | 3 | .. | .. | .. | 3 |
| O.P. assistants | 1 | 1 | .. | 1 | 3 |
| Sanitary dutymen | 1 | .. | .. | .. | 1 |
| Signallers | 4 | 10 | .. | 10 | 24 |
| Storemen | 1 | .. | .. | .. | 1 |
| Water dutymen | 1 | .. | .. | .. | 1 |
| Total, all ranks, R.A. | 70 | 30 | 14 | 58 | 186 |
| Attached: | | | | | |
| Electricians, R.E.M.E. | 1 | .. | .. | .. | 1 |
| Cooks, A.C.C. | 6 | .. | .. | .. | 6 |
| Total, all ranks including attached | 77 | 30 | 14 | 58 | 193 |
| *Guns and Vehicles* | | | | | |
| Motor-cycles | 7 | 1 | .. | 1 | 9 |
| Cars, 5-cwt., 4 × 4 | 1 | .. | .. | .. | 1 |
| Trucks, 15-cwt., 4 × 2, G.S. | 1 | .. | .. | .. | 1 |
| Trucks, 15-cwt., 4 × 2 Water | 1 | .. | .. | .. | 1 |
| Trucks, 15-cwt., half-track, F.F.W. | 5 | 3 | .. | 3 | 11 |
| Trucks, 15-cwt., half-track, with winch | .. | .. | 1 | 2 | 4 |
| Lorries, 3 ton, 4 × 4, G.S. | 8 | .. | .. | .. | 8 |
| Tanks, O.P./C.P. | .. | 2 | .. | 2 | 4 |
| Carriers, tracked, starting and charging | 1 | .. | .. | .. | 1 |
| 25-pdr. S.P. guns | .. | .. | 2 | 4 | 8 |
| Trailers, 1-ton, 2-wheeled, G.S. | 4 | .. | .. | .. | 4 |

*Table 4 (continued)*

## Organisation in the field

**Battery Headquarters (Command)**

| | | |
|---|---|---|
| X | Tank,<br>O.P./C.P. | Major<br>O.P.A.<br>2 driver-operators<br>*2 × W.S. No.19* |
| X2 | Car, 5-cwt.,<br>4 × 4 | Batman<br>Driver, I.C. |
| MC1 | Motor-cycle | Orderly |
| H | Tank,<br>O.P./C.P. | Subaltern<br>(C.P.O.)<br>C.P.O. A.<br>2 driver-operators<br>*2 × W.S. No.19* |
| MC2 | Motor-cycle | Orderly |
| MC7 | Motor-cycle | Signals sergeant |
| M1 | Half-track,<br>F.F.W. | 5 signallers<br>Driver, I.C.<br>*Mechanical cable layer* |
| Y | Half-track,<br>F.F.W. | Subaltern<br>(A.C.P.O.)<br>2 C.P.O. As.<br>Driver, I.C. |
| K1 | Half-track,<br>F.F.W. | Captain<br>2 driver-operators |
| MC8 | Motor-cycle | Orderly |
| K2 | 15-cwt.,<br>4 × 2, G.S. | 2 L.M.G. numbers<br>Clerk<br>C.P.O.A.<br>*L.M.G.*<br>*P.I.A.T.* |
| | Carrier, tracked, starting and charging | Corporal-electrician, R.E.M.E.<br>Vehicle mechanic<br>Driver-mechanic<br>Driver, I.C. |
| MC9 | Motor-cycle | B.S.M. |

**Battery Headquarters (Administration)**

| | | |
|---|---|---|
| Amn1 | 3-ton, 4 × 4,<br>G.S. | 3 ammunition numbers<br>Driver, I.C.<br>*152 rounds ammunition* |
| Amn2 | 3-ton, 4 × 4,<br>G.S. | 3 ammunition numbers<br>Driver, I.C.<br>*152 rounds ammunition* |
| P1 | 3-ton, 4 × 4,<br>G.S., with trailer | Vehicle mechanic<br>Batman<br>Driver, I.C.<br>*Petrol* |
| P2 | 3-ton, 4 × 4,<br>G.S., with trailer | 2 L.M.G. numbers<br>Batman<br>Driver, I.C.<br>*Petrol*<br>*2 L.M.Gs.* |
| P3 | 3-ton, 4 × 4,<br>G.S., with trailer | 2 L.M.G. numbers<br>Driver, I.C.<br>*Petrol*<br>*2 L.M.Gs.* |
| Q1 | 3-ton, 4 × 4,<br>G.S., with trailer | B.Q.M.S.<br>Clerk<br>Storeman<br>Sanitary dutyman<br>Driver, I.C.<br>*'Q' stores* |
| Q2 | 3-ton, 4 × 4,<br>G.S. | Storeman (technical)<br>Equipment repairer<br>3 batmen<br>Driver, I.C.<br>*M.T. stores* |
| Q3 | 3-ton, 4 × 4,<br>G.S. | 2 L.M.G. numbers<br>Corporal cook, A.C.C.<br>5 cooks, A.C.C.<br>Driver, I.C.<br>*Cooking sets and rations*<br>*2 L.M.Gs.*<br>*P.I.A.T.* |
| Q4 | 15-cwt,<br>4 × 2, Water | Water dutyman<br>Driver I.C. |

**Two Troops (each)**

| | | | |
|---|---|---|---|
| RA | RB | Tank,<br>O.P./C.P. | Captain<br>O.P.A.<br>Driver-operator<br>Driver-mech. (A.F.V.)<br>*2 × W.S. No. 19* |
| GA | GB | Tank,<br>O.P./C.P. | Subaltern<br>(G.P.O.)<br>G.P.O. A.<br>Driver-operator<br>Driver-mech. (A.F.V.) |
| MC5 | MC6 | Motor-cycle | T.S.M. |
| MC3 | MC4 | Motor-cycle | Signals bombardier |
| M2 | M3 | Half-track,<br>F.F.W. | 5 signallers<br>Artificer, R.A., or fitter, gun<br>Driver, I.C. |
| TLA | TLB | Tank,<br>O.P./C.P. | Subaltern<br>(Troop leader)<br>Batman<br>G.P.O. A.<br>2 driver-operators |
| M4 | M5 | Half-track,<br>F.F.W. | 4 signallers<br>Vehicle mechanic<br>Batman<br>Driver, I.C. |
| A<br>B<br>C<br>D | E<br>F<br>G<br>H | S.P.<br>25-pdr.<br>Sexton | Sergeant<br>(No. 1 of gun)<br>Nos. 2–4 of gun<br>Driver-operator<br>Driver-mechanic (A.F.V.)<br>*102 rounds ammunition* |
| AB<br>CD | EF<br>GH | Half-track,<br>with winch | Ammunition numbers<br>Driver-mechanic<br>*64 rounds ammunition* |

Note: All F.F.W. vehicles, including S.P. guns, carried W.S. No. 19.

[Source: *War Establishment II/190A/2* (notified in A.C.Is. 14th June 1944)]

# Appendix 3

# *Extracts from the Monthly Army List, 1922–1939 and Lists of Officers, 1939–1945*

*1. May 1922*

Territorial officers of the Royal Field Artillery were not listed by brigades until November 1921, by which time the designation '86th (East Anglian) (Hertfordshire Yeomanry) Brigade' was in use. The empty square brackets beneath the title were intended to contain the individual precedence of brigades but it proved too difficult to calculate and, in any case, a new *de facto* precedence had been established by numbering brigades in sequence following the precedence of the Territorial divisions (see Chapter 1). The brigade is still seven officers below establishment and Major-General The Marquess of Salisbury has yet to be transferred from 4th East Anglian Brigade to be joint honorary colonel with Colonel Abel H. Smith. The crossed swords symbol indicates that an officer has served "in any of the several theatres of war overseas" but it has not yet been applied to the names of seven officers who are known to have qualified.

86th (East Anglian) (Herts. Yeomanry).

[ ]

28, St. Andrews Street.
Hertford.

*Hon. Colonel.*
p.s. Smith, A. H., TD (*Lt.-Col.ret.T.F.*) 26Sept.16

*Lt -Colonel.*
⚔Lawrence, G., *D.S.O.*, *t.a.* 16Feb.20

*Majors.*
342 Halsey, R., TD (H). *t.a.*, (*Bt. Lt.-Col.*) 11Aug.21 6July20
344 Goldie, B. A. H. 6July20 16Feb.18
343 ⚔Currie, J. M. 26Nov.20
341 ⚔Church, G. S., *M.C.* 2Mar.21

*Captains.*
342 Lutyens, E. J. T. 30Nov.20
344 ⚔Robertson, W. R. D., *M.C.* 14Dec.20
343 ⚔Bushman, G. N., *M.C.* 21Jan.21

*Lieutenants.*
342 Albany, S. O., *M.B.E.* 1July17
342 Harradence, R. G. 28July17
341 Dixon, G.W. 17Aug.18
342 Richardson, F. N. 29Apr.21
344 Green, T. L. L. 28Aug.21

*2nd Lieutenants.*
344 Heathcote, M. A. U. 2Dec 20
Banham, C. F. W. 16Mar.22

*Adjutant.*
⚔Noakes, S. M., *D.S.O.*, Maj. R.F.A. 12Aug.20

---

Cadet Unit Affiliated.
Beccles Cadet Corps, R.F.A.

*2. January 1925*
Following the amalgamation of the Royal Horse and Royal Field Artillery with the Royal Garrison Artillery, 86th Brigade is now listed under 'Royal Artillery – Territorial Army – Field Brigades'. Precedence is now determined by the numerical order of brigades and the possibility of showing individual precedence derived from the Royal Garrison Artillery of the Volunteer Force has been abandoned and the square brackets removed. Addresses of batteries are now included and their bracketed 'Herts' designation shown. The symbol *'t.a.'* beside officers' names indicates that they are members of Hertfordshire Territorial Army Association, the full membership of which was shown in a half-yearly supplement to the *Monthly Army List*. The supplement also listed officers of the Territorial Army Reserve of Officers, where appropriate by units. Attached officers of the Royal Army Medical Corps were not listed with their units, as had been the case before the First World War, but were included in the section covering the Royal Army Medical Corps with the unit to which they were attached shown in brackets after their names. Captain A. Gregson Williams is shown as attached to 86th Field Brigade, R.A. The establishment for a Territorial field brigade did not include a veterinary officer or a chaplain.

**86th (East Anglian (Herts. Yeomanry).**

H.Q., and 342nd (Herts.) Batt., 28, St. Andrews Street, Hertford; 341st (Herts.) Batt., Riding School, Harpenden Road, St. Albans; 343rd (Herts.) Batt., Clarendon Hall, Watford; 344th (Herts.) Batt. (How.), Bearton Camp, Hitchin.

*Hon. Colonels.*
⚔*Salisbury,* Rt. Hon. the Marq. of, K.G., G.C.V.O., C.B., TD (*Hon. Maj.-Gen.*) *A.D.C.* 17/2/00
*Smith, A. H.,* TD 26/9/18

*Lt.-Colonel.*
⚔Lawrence, *Hon.* G., *D.S.O., t.a.* 16/2/20
*bt. col.* 16/2/24

*Majors.*
343 Halsey, R., TD, *t.a.* 6/7/20
*bt. lt.-col.* 11/8/21
344 Goldie, B. A. H., *t.a.* 6/7/20
16/2/18
341 ⚔Church, G. S., *M.C.* 2/3/21
342 ⚔Lutyens E. J. T. 3/10/23

*Captains.*
344 ⚔Robertson, W. R. D., *M.C.* 14/12/20
343 ⚔Bushman, G. N., *M.C.* 21/1/21
342 Albany, S. C., *M.B.E.* †3/10/23
341 Richardson, F. N. 14/11/23

*Lieutenants.*
344 Green, T. L. L. 28/8/21
342 ⚔New, L. P. 1/6/22
344 Heathcote, M. A. U. 2/12/22
341 Ellery, H. W. O. 11/7/23
342 Gooderidge, T. W. W. 4/8/23
344 Banham, C. F. W. 15/3/24

*2nd Lieutenants.*
343 Salinger, F. S. 28/3/23
341 Norbury, R. J. 5/5/24
342 Henderson, N. B. 12/7/24

*Adjutant.*
⚔Griffith, A. L. P., *D.S.O.*, Capt. (*bt. maj.*) R.A. 13/11/23

*3. November 1938*

The November 1938 edition of the *Monthly Army List* was corrected to 29th October 1938 and is the last edition to show under 86th Field Brigade the officers who transferred with effect from 1st November 1938 to 79th Anti-Aircraft Brigade (Majors Green and Barry, Captains Fremantle and Morgan Smith, Lieutenants Weall and Hanbury and 2nd Lieutenant Crisfield). The bracketed designations of batteries have been changed in accordance with Army Order 168 of 1937 (see Chapter 3). The commanding officer, Lieutenant-Colonel W.R.D. Robertson, M.C., T.D., is shown as a student at the Imperial Defence College.

**86th (East Anglian) (Herts Yeomanry).**

H.Q. and 342nd (Hertford) Bty., 28, St. Andrews Street, Hertford; 341st (St. Albans) Bty. Riding School, Harpenden Road, St. Albans; 343rd (Watford) Bty., Clarendon Hall, Watford; 344th (Hitchin) Bty. (H.), Bearton Camp, Hitchin.

*Hon. Colonel.*

*Goldie, B. A. H.*, C.B.E., T.D. (*Bt. Col. ret. Terr. Army*), *t.a.* 21/2/31

*Lt.-Colonel.*

⚔Robertson, W. R. D., *M.C., T.D.* (*Imp. Defence Coll.*) *t.a.* 1/4/36
1/1/34

*Majors.*

341 ⚔Green, T. L. L., *T.D., t.a.* 1/1/30
342 ⚔Coghill, *Sir* M. N. Patrick S., *Bt.* (*Capt. Res. of Off.*) [L] *t.a.* 18/1/35
344 Banham, C. F. W. 1/4/36
343 Barry, I. W. G. 18/4/37

*Captains.*

344 Keane, G. 18/1/35
342 Fremantle, F. D. E. 1/4/36
343 Smith, J. B. M. 4/12/36
341 Tabor, J. B. S. 7/11/37

*Lieutenants.*

342 Cribb, R. D. 10/2/31
343 Weall, J. L. G. 11/7/35
344 Wells, E. D. 9/6/37
342 Hanbury, R. N. 10/7/37
341 Boyes, W. E. 19/1/38

*2nd Lieutenants.*

341 Briggs, J. A. 20/1/35
2/7/33
344 Halford-Thompson, P. T. 18/1/36
344 Cherry, D. W. 7/4/36
H.Q., King, K. S. 8/4/36
24/11/33
344 Crisfield, J. S. 9/4/36
5/7/35
343 Higgens, R. S. W. 21/4/37
342 Jones, J. C. 21/4/37
343 Cory-Wright, A. J. J. 18/8/37
Swann, K. G. 4/6/38

*Adjutant.*

Fanshawe, G. D., Capt. R.A. 15/11/35

*4. March 1939*

Although instructions had been issued in October 1938 that 336 Battery of 84th Field Brigade was to join 86th Field Brigade, which was about to reorganise as 86th Field Regiment, the officers of 336 Battery continued to be shown separately until March 1939. The six officers listed all joined 86th Field Regiment.

**§ 84th (1st East Anglian).**

H.Q., Drill Hall. All Saints Green. Norwich; 336th (Northamptonshire) Bty. (H.). Lincoln Road, Peterborough.

*Hon. Colonel.*

⚔*Stradbroke*, The Earl of, K.C.M.G., C.B., C.V.O., C.B.E., V.D., T.D. (*Col. ret. Terr. Army*) *t.a.* 1/4/08

*Major.*

336 ⚔Ramsay, W. A., *t.a.* 17/3/35

*Captain.*

336 Stephenson, J. L., *t.a.* 25/4/37

*Lieutenants.*

336 Deacon, J. P. 6/8/35

336 Neal, J. M. 1/7/36

336 Crick, P. C. 18/4/37

2nd *Lieutenant.*

336 Crick, M. A. 24/3/37

**Cadet Norfolk Artillery.**

*5. April 1939*

Since 1st November 1938, 86th Field Regiment has had only two 3-troop batteries – 342 and 344 – but the four original batteries are still shown at the top of the regiment's entry, including 343 Battery, which is noted as "in course of conversion", even though 79th Anti-Aircraft Regiment now has a full entry. The battery numbers in front of officers' names require complete revision. Lieutenant-Colonel Robertson, who has the '*i.d.c.*' symbol after his name following completion of his course at the Imperial Defence College, is now held supernumerary to the regimental establishment while posted to a staff appointment.

FIELD REGIMENTS—*contd.*

**86th (East Anglian) (Herts Yeomanry).**

H.Q. and 342nd (Hertford) Bty., 28, St. Andrews Street, Hertford; 341st (St. Albans) Bty. Riding School, Harpenden Road, St. Albans; §§343rd (Watford) Bty., Clarendon Hall, Watford; 344th (Hitchin) Bty. (H.), Bearton Camp, Hitchin.

*Hon. Colonel.*

*Goldie, B. A. H.*, C.B.E., T.D. (*Bt. Col. ret. Terr. Army*), *t.a.* 21/2/31

*Lt.-Colonel.*

⚔*Robertson, W. R. D.*, O.B.E., M.C., T.D., *i.d.c.* (*Supern.*) *t.a.* 1/4/36 1/1/34

⚔Coghill, *Sir* M. N. Patrick S., *Bt.* (*Capt. Res. of Off.*) [L] *t.a.* 17/1/39

*Majors.*

⚔Ramsay, W. A., *t.a.* 17/3/35

344 Banham, C. F. W. 1/4/36

*Captains.*

344 Keane, G 18/1/35

Stephenson, J. L., *t.a.* 25/4/37

342 Cribb, R. D. 6/11/37

341 Tabor, J. B. S. 7/11/37

*Lieutenants.*

Deacon, J. P. 6/8/35

Neal, J. M. 1/7/36

Crick, P. C. 18/4/37

344 Wells, E. D. 9/6/37

Gardner, A. R. 11/1/38 1/10/36

341 Boyes, W. E 19/1/38

344 Halford-Thompson, P. T. 18/1/39

*2nd Lieutenants*

341 Briggs, J. A 20/1/35 2/7/33

344 Cherry, D. W. 7/4/36

H.Q., King, K. S. 8/4/36 24/11/33

Crick, M. A. 24/3/37

344 Higgens, R. S. W. 21/4/37

342 Jones, J. C. 21/4/37

343 Cory-Wright, A. J. J. 18/8/37

342 Swann, K. G. 4/6/38

344 Russell, M. J. W. 25/1/39

Anderson, W. A. 18/3/39

Powell, H. A. R. 22/3/39

*Adjutant.*

Fanshawe, G. D., Capt. R.A 15/11/35

*6. June 1939 (Half-Yearly Supplement)*

The regimental entry under 'Territorial Army Reserve of Officers – Regimental List' shows nine officers. A tenth officer, Captain M.A. Unwin Heathcote was held in Class I of the 'General List'. 2nd Lieutenant Berry had, in fact, rejoined the Active List in April. All the remaining officers except Captain Rees were recalled at the outbreak of war, and all except Captain Darling rejoined, at least for a short time, 86th or 135th Field Regiment.

**86th (EAST ANGLIAN) (HERTS. YEO.)**

**Class I.**

*Captain.*

Norbury, R. J. 22/11/30

*Lieutenants.*

**McMullen, O. J. G. 24/11/29**

**Darling, R. C. N. 16/12/29**

**Class II.**

*Major.*

⚔Lutyens, E. J. T., *T.D.* 3/10/23

*Captain.*

⚔Rees, N. O. 1/3/39 25/8/26

*Lieutenants.*

**Anderson, J. H. 29/5/26**

**Cribb, C. F. 15/4/34**

2nd *Lieutenants.*

Berry, M. F. 20/8/38

Crick, G. A. 8/2/39

*7. September 1939 (Security Edition)*
The 'Security Edition' was not on sale to the public, since it would have been of some help to enemy intelligence services attempting to construct the British Army's order of battle. It was corrected to 25th August 1939 and thus included almost all Territorial officers who were embodied and mobilised on 1st September 1939. This was the last edition of any *Army List* to show officers of the Royal Artillery by regiments. Had they appeared in further editions, the entries for 86th and 135th Field Regiments would have required considerable revision. The batteries are not all correctly shown at the head of the columns (see page 65) and the officers not correctly distributed. Dates of appointment or promotion would also have been added. The symbol beside '135th' indicates that the title is provisional.

Five officers who, in addition to all those listed, were embodied with 86th/135th Field Regiment, are missing. They are 2nd Lieutenant E.G. Scammell (incorrectly listed under 79th Anti-Aircraft Regiment), Lieutenant-Colonel J. Hudson, M.C., T.D. (appointed 18th August 1939), 2nd Lieutenant H.M. O'Connor (appointed 1st September 1939) and Lieutenant J.C. Chaytor and 2nd Lieutenant A.P. Hay (appointed 2nd September 1939).

**86th (East Anglian) (Herts Yeomanry).**

H.Q. and 342nd (Hertford) Bty., 28, St. Andrews Street, Hertford; 344th (Hitchin) Bty. (H.), Bearton Camp, Hitchin.

*Hon. Colonel.*

*Goldie, B. A. H.*, C.B.E., T.D. (*Bt. Col. ret. T.A.*), *t.a.*

*Lt.-Colonel.*

⚔Coghill, *Sir* M. N. Patrick S., *Bt.* (*Capt.Res. of Off.*) [L]*t.a.*

*Majors.*

⚔Ramsay, W. A., *t.a.*
344 Banham, C. F. W.
Smith, J. B. M.
342 Cribb, R. D.

*Captains.*

Buxton, J. F.
344 Keane, G.
Stephenson, J. L., *t.a.*
Tabor, J. B. S.
344 Deacon, J. P.
344 Neal, J. M.
344 Wells, E. D.
Boyes, W. E.
344 Crick, P. C.
344 Higgens, R. S. W.
342 Jones, J. C.
Sanders, T. R. B.
Wootten, F. W. W.

*Lieutenants.*

H.Q. Gardner, A. R.
Briggs, J. A
344 Cherry, D. W.
H.Q., King, K. S.

*2nd Lieutenants.*

Crick, M. A.
Cory-Wright, A. J. J.
342 Swann, K. G.
344 Russell, M. J. W.
342 Anderson, W. A.
Powell, H. A. R.
Laing, P. K.
Berry, M. F.
Humbert, A. C.
Norman, M. R.
Cleminson, J. A. S.
Perry, S. D.
Turner, D. G. A.
McClintock, D. C.
Egar, S.
Turner, P. A.
Cory-Wright, M.
Daltry, O. H.
Dearden, H. S.
De Ramsey, *The Lord*
Marsh, E. B.

*Adjutant.*

Prior, H. R. R., Capt. R.A. 8/5/39

*Quarter-Master.*

⚔Felstead, P. E., *lt.*

**§135th.**

H.Q., Hitchin, 336th (Northampton) Bty., Lincoln Road, Peterborough; 341st (St. Albans) Bty., Riding School, Harpenden Road, St. Albans.

*Lieutenants.*

Wentworth - Fitzwilliam, W. T. G.
Peacock, H. M.

*2nd Lieutenants.*

Bees, H. W.
West, R. T.
Smyth, R.
Morgan, H. G.
Viney, D. G.
Woodbridge, R. A. P.
Horberry, W. R.
Hay, G. A. R.
Pryor, R. M. M.
Butler-Henderson, L.
Norman, H. W.
Walkerley, C. V.

*Adjutant.*

Halford-Thompson, T. P., *capt.* 8/5/39

## 86th AND 135th FIELD REGIMENTS, R.A. – OFFICERS, OCTOBER 1939

### 86th Field Regiment, R.A.

Regimental Headquarters

*Commanding Officer:*
Lieutenant-Colonel Sir Patrick Coghill, Bt.

*Second-in-Command:*
Major J.C. Chaytor

*Adjutant:*
Captain H.R.R. Prior, R.A.

*Assistant Adjutant:*
2nd Lieut. H.M. O'Connor

*Quartermaster:*
Lieutenant (Q.M.) P.E. Felstead

*Medical Officer:*
Captain R.H. Mortis, R.A.M.C.

341 Field Battery

Major J.B. Morgan Smith
Captain F.W.W. Wooton
Captain J.B.S. Tabor
Captain R.S.W. Higgens
Captain J.A. Briggs
Lieutenant K.S. King
2nd Lieut. A.J.J. Cory-Wright
2nd Lieut. M.J.W. Russell
2nd Lieut. E.G. Scammell
2nd Lieut. A.C. Humbert
2nd Lieut. H.W. Bees
2nd Lieut. R.A.P. Woodbridge
2nd Lieut. P. Thorp
2nd Lieut. H.W. Norman

342 Field Battery

Major R.D. Cribb
Captain M.A. Unwin Heathcote
Captain R.J. Norbury
Captain W.E. Boyes
Captain J. Carew-Jones
2nd Lieut. K.G. Swann
2nd Lieut. W.A. Anderson
2nd Lieut. H.A.R. Powell
2nd Lieut. J.A.S. Cleminson
2nd Lieut. M.R. Norman
2nd Lieut. S.D. Perry
2nd Lieut. D.C. McClintock
2nd Lieut. P.A. Turner
2nd Lieut. L. Butler-Henderson

### 135th Field Regiment, R.A.

Regimental Headquarters

*Commanding Officer:*
Lieutenant-Colonel J. Hudson, M.C., T.D.

*Second-in-Command:*
Major E.J.T. Lutyens, T.D.

*Adjutant:*
Captain T.P. Halford-Thompson

*Assistant Adjutant:*
2nd Lieut. P.K. Laing

*Quartermaster:*
Lieutenant (Q.M.) A.E.W. Noakes, R.A.

*Medical Officer:*
Lieutenant-Colonel A. Gregson Williams, O.B.E., T.D., R.A.M.C.

336 Field Battery

Major C.F.W. Banham
Captain J.L. Stephenson
Captain E.D. Wells
Captain J. M. Neal
2nd Lieut. G.A. Crick
2nd Lieut. M.A. Crick
2nd Lieut. S. Egar
2nd Lieut. W.R. Horberry
2nd Lieut. D. G. Viney
2nd Lieut. H. M. Peacock
2nd Lieut. W.T.G. Wentworth-Fitzwilliam
2nd Lieut. The Lord De Ramsey
2nd Lieut. E.B. Marsh
2nd Lieut. A.P. Hay

344 Field Battery

Major T.R.B. Sanders
Captain G. Keane
Captain J.P. Deacon
Captain P.C. Crick
Captain D.W. Cherry
Lieutenant O.J.G. McMullen
Lieutenant M.F. Berry
2nd Lieut. M. Cory-Wright
2nd Lieut. R. Smyth
2nd Lieut. R.M.M. Pryor
2nd Lieut. C.V. de B. Walkerley
2nd Lieut. O.H. Daltry
2nd Lieut. H.S. Dearden

### Commands and Staff, Late 86th Field Regiment, R.A.

Brigadier Sir Geoffrey Church, Bt., M.C., T.D.
Lieutenant-Colonel W.R.D. Robertson, O.B.E., M.C., T.D.

### Extra-Regimentally Employed

Major W.A. Ramsay, Major J.F. Buxton
Lieutenant C.F. Cribb, Lieutenant A.R. Gardner
2nd Lieut. D.G.A. Turner, 2nd Lieut. H. Morgan, 2nd Lieut. Hon. G.A.R. Hay

Plate 175 *The officers of 86th Field Regiment at Chiseldon, July 1939.* Back row (L.–R.) – *2nd Lieuts. P.A. Turner, R.T. West, H.M. Peacock, D.C. McClintock, M.R. Norman, K.G. Swann, E.G. Scammell, R.A.P. Woodbridge, L. Butler-Henderson, R. Smyth, A.C. Humbert, Lord De Ramsey, W.R. Horberry, C.V. de B. Walkerley.* Fourth row – *2nd Lieuts. O.H. Daltry, H.W. Bees, M.A. Crick, H.G. Morgan, M.J.W. Russell, H.W. Norman, S.D. Perry, H.A.R. Powell, Hon. G.A.R. Hay, D.G.A. Turner, Lieut. M.F. Berry, 2nd Lieuts. A.J.J. Cory-Wright, H.S. Dearden, E.B. Marsh, M. Cory-Wright.* Third row – *Lieut. D.W. Cherry, Lieut. (Q.M.) P.E. Felstead, Lieuts. A.R. Gardner, K.S. King, Captains P.C.*

*Crick, W.E. Boyes, F.W.W. Wooton, E.D. Wells, J.M. Neal, 2nd Lieut. P.K. Laing, Captain J.P. Deacon, Lieutenant J.A. Briggs, 2nd Lieuts. W.A. Anderson, D.G. Viney, S. Egar.* Second row – *Captains T.P. Halford-Thompson, G. Keane, Rev. (C.F.IV) C.T.R.C. Perowne, Lt.-Col. E.E. Charles (Herts T. & A.F.A), Majors J.F. Buxton, J.B. Morgan Smith, Lt.-Col. Sir Patrick Coghill, Bt., Major R.D.Cribb, Captains T.R.B. Sanders, J.L. Stephenson, R.H. Mortis, R.A.M.C., J. Knox (H.A.C.), H.R.R. Prior, R.A. (Adjutant).* Front row – *2nd Lieuts. R.M.M. Pryor, R.S.W. Higgens, J. Carew Jones, P. Thorp.*
(Regimental Collection)

## 135th FIELD REGIMENT, R.A. – OFFICERS, 15th JANUARY 1942

### REGIMENTAL HEADQUARTERS

*Commanding Officer:*
Lieutenant-Colonel P.J.D. Toosey
*Second-in-Command:*
Major J.R. Pilling, M.C.
*Adjutant:*
Captain M.P. Northcote
*Quartermaster:*
Lieutenant (Q.M.) H. Pratt

*Intelligence Officer:*
2nd Lieut. E.H.S. Simmonds
*Survey Officer:*
2nd Lieut. D.S. Pitcher
*Medical Officer:*
Captain C.S. Pitt, R.A.M.C.
*Chaplain:*
Rev. (C.F. IV) V.S. Robertson, R.A.Ch.D.

*Officer Commanding 135th Field Regiment Signal Section, Royal Signals:*
2nd Lieut. G.H. Hoerder, R. Signals
*Officer Commanding 135th Field Regiment Light Aid Detachment, R.A.O.C.:*

### 336 FIELD BATTERY, R.A.

Battery Headquarters

*Battery Commander:*
Major C.F.W. Banham*
*Battery Captain:*
Captain J.M. Neal†
*Command Post Officer:*
Lieutenant D.G. Viney*
*Asst. Command Post Officer:*
2nd Lieut. R. H. Boult

A Troop

*Troop Commander:*
Captain T.P. Halford-Thompson*
*Gun Position Officer:*
Lieutenant R. Raynor
*Troop Leader:*
Lieutenant W.S. Horberry*

B Troop

*Troop Commander:*
Captain S. Egar*
*Gun Position Officer:*
Lieutenant R.E.A. Stebbing
*Troop Leader:*
Lieutenant P.K. Laing*

### 344 FIELD BATTERY, R.A.

Battery Headquarters

*Battery Commander:*
Major H.M. Peacock*
*Battery Captain:*
Captain O.J.G. McMullen*
*Command Post Officer:*
Lieutenant M.A. Crick†
*Asst. Command Post Officer:*
2nd Lieut. E.A. Furbear

C Troop

*Troop Commander:*
Captain D.W. Cherry*
*Gun Position Officer:*
2nd Lieut. J.C. Gamble
*Troop Leader:*
2nd Lieut. C.D. Moser

C Troop

*Troop Commander:*
Captain G.M. Campbell
*Gun Position Officer:*
Lieutenant M. Cory-Wright*
*Troop Leader:*
2nd Lieut. G.J. Haskell

### 499 FIELD BATTERY, R.A.

Battery Headquarters

*Battery Commander:*
Major O.H. Daltry*
*Battery Captain:*
Captain The Lord De Ramsey*
*Command Post Officer:*
Lieutenant G.A. Crick†
*Asst. Command Post Officer:*
Lieutenant S.A. Hall

E Troop

*Troop Commander:*
Captain G. Keane*
*Gun Position Officer:*
Lieutenant T.R. Macgregor
*Troop Leader:*
2nd Lieut. A. Haldenby

F Troop

*Troop Commander:*
Captain H.S. Dearden*
*Gun Position Officer:*
Lieutenant A.P. Hay*
*Troop Leader:*
2nd Lieut C.S.J. Searles

### FIRST LINE REINFORCEMENTS

Lieutenant E.S. Munro, Lieutenant F.H. Wilkinson, 2nd Lieut. S.C. Alexander, 2nd Lieut R.E.B. Smith

* Commissioned into 86th Field Regiment prior to 3rd September 1939
† Commissioned into 84th Field Regiment and transferred to 86th Field Regiment prior to 3rd September 1939

## 86th FIELD REGIMENT, R.A. – OFFICERS, 6th JUNE 1944

### REGIMENTAL HEADQUARTERS

*Commanding Officer:*
Lieutenant-Colonel G.D. Fanshawe, O.B.E.
*Second-in-Command:*
Major J.B. Morgan Smith*
*Adjutant:*
Captain R.R. Thornton
*Assistant Adjutant:*
Lieutenant J.M.M. Wood
*Technical Adjutant:*
Captain N.M. Pickford

*Quartermaster:*
Captain (Q.M.) P.E. Felstead, M.B.E.*
*Intelligence Officer:*
Lieutenant J. Prentis
*Survey Officer:*
Lieutenant D.M. Coultas
*Medical Officer:*
Captain A.B. Hegarty, R.A.M.C.

*Officer Commanding 86th Field Regiment Signal Section, Royal Signals:*
Lieutenant J. Hindshaw, R. Signals
*Officer Commanding 86th Field Regiment Light Aid Detachment, R.E.M.E:*
Captain S.A. Revie, R.E.M.E.

### 341 FIELD BATTERY, R.A.

Battery Headquarters

*Battery Commander:*
Major G.A. Loveday
*Battery Captain:*
Captain R.J. Kiln
*Command Post Officer:*
Lieutenant R. Dorey
*Asst. Command Post Officer:*
Lieutenant C.B. McCaie

A Troop

*Troop Commander:*
Captain E.W.C. Hall
*Gun Position Officer:*
Lieutenant J.A. Craston
*Troop Leader:*
Lieutenant S.R. Kalbraier

B Troop

*Troop Commander:*
Captain S.D. Perry*
*Gun Position Officer:*
Lieutenant S.J. Beck
*Troop Leader:*
Lieutenant A.K. Birrell

### 342 FIELD BATTERY, R.A.

Battery Headquarters

*Battery Commander:*
Major K.G. Swann*
*Battery Captain:*
Captain C. Hankins
*Command Post Officer:*
Lieutenant H.L. Dovey
*Asst. Command Post Officer:*
Lieutenant J. Bartlett

C Troop

*Troop Commander:*
Captain G.G. Street
*Gun Position Officer:*
Lieutenant D.M. Mathers
*Troop Leader:*
Lieutenant E.C. Smallman

D Troop

*Troop Commander:*
Captain J.G. Ash
*Gun Position Officer:*
Lieutenant W. Gear
*Troop Leader:*
Lieutenant A.L. Dorling

### 462 FIELD BATTERY, RA

Battery Headquarters

*Battery Commander:*
Major E.G. Scammell*
*Battery Captain:*
Captain H.W. Norman*
*Command Post Officer:*
Lieutenant P.D. Deshon
*Asst. Command Post Officer:*
Lieutenant B.P. Heaton

E Troop

*Troop Commander:*
Captain R.D. Turnbull
*Gun Position Officer:*
Lieutenant G.P. Eisen
*Troop Leader:*
Lieutenant J.A. Carpenter

F Troop

*Troop Commander:*
Captain H.M. Pamphilon
*Gun Position Officer:*
Lieutenant G.H. Jamieson
*Troop Leader:*
Lieutenant V.R.H. Yarnell

### FIRST LINE REINFORCEMENTS

Lieutenant R. G. Godsmark, Lieutenant H. Treble

* Commissioned into 86th Field Regiment prior to 3rd September 1939

## 191st FIELD REGIMENT, R.A.– OFFICERS, 3rd DECEMBER 1944

### Regimental Headquarters

*Commanding Officer:*
Lieutenant-Colonel M.W. Hope
*Second-in-Command:*
Major A.G. Proudlock
*Adjutant:*
Captain F. Butler
*Assistant Adjutant:*
Lieutenant H. Foster

*Quartermaster:*
Captain (Q.M.) F.D. Peters
*Intelligence Officer:*

*Survey Officer:*
Lieutenant W. Wallich
*Medical Officer:*
Captain S. Conlan, R.A.M.C.

*Officer Commanding 191st Field Regiment Signal Section, Royal Signals:*
Lieutenant K.W. Gardner, R. Signals
*Officer Commanding 191st Field Regiment Light Aid Detachment R.E.M.E.:*

### 532 Field Battery, R.A.

Battery Headquarters

*Battery Commander:*
Major G.M.R. Pearson
*Battery Captain:*
Captain G.A.W. Gold
*Command Post Officer:*
Lieutenant A.E. Lawrence
*Asst. Command Post Officer:*
Lieutenant H.D. Laws

A Troop

*Troop Commander:*
Captain M.G. Bond
*Gun Position Officer:*
Lieutenant P.C. Wilbur
*Troop Leader:*
Lieutenant R. Berey

B Troop

*Troop Commander:*
Captain N.F. Biglands
*Gun Position Officer:*
Lieutenant D.C.C. Watson
*Troop Leader:*
Lieutenant R.S. Couper

### 533 Field Battery, R.A.

Battery Headquarters

*Battery Commander:*
Major R.S.W. Higgens*
*Battery Captain:*
Captain R.A.P. Woodbridge*
*Command Post Officer:*
Lieutenant A.E. Warren
*Asst. Command Post Officer:*
Lieutenant R. Holden

C Troop

*Troop Commander:*
Captain J.M. Yeoman
*Gun Position Officer:*
Lieutenant J.W. Dowlen
*Troop Leader:*
Lieutenant G.S. Whyte

D Troop

*Troop Commander:*
Captain P.A. Turner*
*Gun Position Officer:*
Lieutenant G. Whitten
*Troop Leader:*
Lieutenant G.T. Pennell

### 534 Field Battery, R.A.

Battery Headquarters

*Battery Commander:*
Major E.V. Hollis
*Battery Captain:*
Captain J.F. Duncan
*Command Post Officer:*
Lieutenant C.H.W. Hodges
*Asst. Command Post Officer:*
Lieutenant G.E. Thurston

E Troop

*Troop Commander:*
Captain D.J. Stinson
*Gun Position Officer:*
Lieutenant J.R. Stanley
*Troop Leader:*
Lieutenant P.R. Heaton-Ellis

F Troop

*Troop Commander:*
Captain G.S. Richardson
*Gun Position Officer:*
Lieutenant E.G.G. Shimell
*Troop Leader:*
Lieutenant G. Iveson

* Commissioned into 86th Field Regiment prior to 3rd September 1939

# Appendix 4

# *The Defence Force, 1921*

The threat to public order during the 1921 coal miners' strike was judged to be so great that the government called out the Regular Army Reserve and made extensive preparations to back civil power by military. Embodiment of the Territorial Force was considered but undertakings had been given when recruiting reopened in 1920 that Territorials would not be used for the maintenance of public order. The cabinet accepted advice not to follow call-out of the Regular Army Reserve by embodiment of the Territorial Force, as would legally have been possible to deal with "grave national emergency", and the Prime Minister appealed on 8th April 1921 for loyal citizens to enlist for a temporary period of full-time service, not to exceed ninety days, with the Regular Army, in new units to be called 'Defence Units'. Enlistment, which was for service in the United Kingdom only, was open to those discharged from military service; to serving officers and men of the Territorial Force; and to certain categories of civilians with specialist qualifications.

Dennis (see Bibliography) describes the decision to raise the Defence Force as "the most transparent of devices". So it may well have seemed. Defence Force units were based on Territorial drill-halls, despite some opposition from Associations, and carried the titles of the Territorial units occupying those drill-halls, differenced only by 'Defence Force' in brackets. Regular P.S.Is. were transferred to the new organisation without consultation and serving Territorials were 'specially invited' to enlist. The commissions or engagements of serving Territorial officers and other ranks were deemed to lapse on joining the Defence Force but they would be subject to automatic renewal, on application, when the period of full-time service ended. It was later announced that service in the Defence Force would count as the whole of Territorials' 'efficiency' obligation for annual bounty, as far as camp and drills were concerned, leaving only the small arms classification if it had not previously been fired.

Disbandment of the Defence Force, which had reached a total strength of over 40,000, but had hardly been used, was announced on 2nd July 1921 and took place over the next two weeks. Two days after the announcement the War Office finally made clear that those who had joined from the Territorials would have to re-engage within one month of discharge if their service was to qualify them as 'efficient' (see above). In addition, it was announced that members of the Defence Force who had not previously been Territorials would be granted a considerable concession if they joined a Territorial unit within one month of discharge. They, too, could qualify as 'efficient' and thus receive the annual bounty, subject only to firing the small arms classification. The recruiting potential was substantial and Associations took advantage of it, though Dennis records that large numbers of those enlisted directly from the Defence Force were later discharged from the Territorial Army as 'undesirable'.

Undesirable recruits apart, the Defence Force does not seem to have had a long-term adverse effect on the Territorial Army, as might have been feared. To some extent, also, lessons were learned from the "most transparent of devices" (i.e.,the use of Territorials under another name as a means of ensuring internal security) and applied when reinforcements for the police were next needed. At the time of the General Strike in 1926, embodiment of the Territorial Army was discarded as an option at an early stage but Territorials were invited to enroll in the 'Civil Constabulary Reserve', operating in plain clothes and under the control of the Home Office. While this stratagem failed to separate the Territorial Army entirely from involvement in 'Aid to the Civil Power', it, and, at least as importantly, the swift collapse of the strike, avoided such damage as had earlier been attributed to the Defence Force. Between 1927 and 1939 the question of how, if at all, the Territorial Army should be used in circumstances of internal unrest, was not seriously considered, and by 1931 the Chiefs of Staff had

*War Office,*
*9th May,* 1921

DEFENCE FORCE.

REGULAR FORCES.

ROYAL REGIMENT OF ARTILLERY.

*R.H. & R.F.A.*
86*th Brig., R.F.A.* (*D.F.*).
To be temp. Lt.-Col.:—
G. Lawrence, D.S.O. 9 Apr. 1921.

To be temp. Majs.:—
9 Apr. 1921.
R. Halsey, T.D.
J. M. Currie.
B. A. H. Goldie.

To be temp. Capts.:—
9 Apr. 1921
S. C. Albany, M.B.E.
C. N. Bushman, M.C.
G. S. Church, M.C.

To be temp. Lts.:—
9 Apr. 1921.
E. N. C. Symonds, M.C.
L. F. M. Richardson.

11 Apr. 1921.
R. G. Harradence.
T. W. W. Gooderidge.
A. G. Agnew.
J. N. Cowley.
F. N. Casey.

G. W. Dixon. 12 Apr. 1921.

15 Apr. 1921.
M. Routledge.
T. L. Green.

To be temp. 2nd Lt.:—
N. Heathcote. 11 Apr. 1921.

Plate 176 *The first announcement of officers' commissions in 86th Brigade, R.F.A. (Defence Force) as it appeared in the* London Gazette *of 9th May 1921.*

concluded that it was most unlikely that either the Regular or the Territorial Army would be called upon to assist the Civil Power.

### *86th Brigade, R.F.A. (Defence Force)*

In common with other major 'teeth arms' units of the Territorial Force, 86th Brigade, R.F.A was called upon to raise a Defence Force counterpart – 86th Brigade, R.F.A. (Defence Force) – and officers and men were subject to the invitation described above, which was reinforced by a letter from the Lord Lieutenant of Hertfordshire published in local newspapers. No doubt, there were also pressures of *esprit de corps*, if the Defence Force unit was to uphold the standards and traditions of the Territorial unit. Lieutenant-Colonel Geoffrey Lawrence, all four battery commanders, five other officers out of the seven then on strength, and the medical officer were granted temporary commissions in the Defence Force, the majority dated 9th April 1921, which must be considered as the date on which the new unit was raised. A further eight officers were commissioned, of whom one had previously served with the Hertfordshire Yeomanry and two with 4th East Anglian Brigade, R.F.A. On 16th April the *Hertfordshire Mercury* reported that "the Brigade of Artillery is up to full strength". Returns made to Hertfordshire Territorial Association show a fall in other rank strength of the Territorial brigade of about 150, which must be largely attributable to transfers to the Defence Force brigade, so it seems that there were as many as 350 direct enlistments of former servicemen, if the brigades had the same establishment (five hundred other ranks).

Neither the local papers nor the minutes of Hertfordshire Territorial Association record where 86th Brigade, R.F.A. (Defence Force) was stationed during its three months' existence, or what, if any, training officers and men received in 'Aid to the Civil Power'. Webster (see Bibliography) devotes several pages to a description of the neighbouring 5th Battalion The

Bedfordshire and Hertfordshire Regiment's routine in the former Royal Air Force camp at Cardington, but there were no such convenient, unoccupied sites in Hertfordshire. The *Hertfordshire Mercury* of 30th April 1921 records, however, that:

> "The Defence Force units raised in the county at the time of the threatened general strike are still in being and recruits are undergoing training. In the case of members of the Force who are still following their civil employment, this training is being given in their leisure hours".

Disregarding the complexities of the War Office and civilian employers both obtaining value for their money, this report could indicate that the Defence Force batteries never left their drill-halls and that, because of the lack of sleeping accommodation, soldiers may have returned to their homes at night when not on duty.

The officers of 86th Brigade, R.F.A. (Defence Force) relinquished their commissions between 5th and 14th July 1921, with the latter date counting as the date of disbandment of the unit. All the officers who had transferred from the Territorial unit returned, bringing with them three more whom they had persuaded to sign on as Territorials. As far as can be derived from the strength returns submitted to Hertfordshire Territorial Association, as many as 150 other ranks, possibly considerably more, who had enlisted directly into the Defence Force brigade, all of them having previously served in the Armed Forces, were similarly persuaded to become Territorials. How many of these turned out to be 'undesirables', it is impossible to say, but no adverse comments on these recruits are recorded in the minutes of Hertfordshire Territorial Association.

## Appendix 5

# *The Home Guard, 1940–1944*

The requirement for additional troops for the defence of the British Isles in the face of the threat of imminent German invasion led to the appeal by the Secretary of State for War on 14th May 1940 for volunteers to join a new force to be known as the 'Local Defence Volunteers'. In the absence of any suitable legislation (see Chapter 1 and Appendix 1) powers were taken under the blanket 'Defence Regulations' by the passing of the Defence (Local Defence Volunteers) Regulations on 17th May 1940. An additional regulation, passed on 31st July 1940, permitted the use of the alternative title 'The Home Guard'. For the first nine months of its existence, although the Home Guard was recognised as part of the Armed Forces of the Crown, no arrangements were made for the commissioning of officers or for conferring and delegating powers of command and discipline. This evident deficiency was corrected with effect from 1st February 1941 by the passing of the Home Guard Officers' Commissions Order on 12th February and from that time officers held the King's Commission and there was an orthodox system of warrant and non-commissioned ranks. Private soldiers in the Home Guard were styled 'Volunteer' until the spring of 1942, when powers were taken to direct enrolment into the Home Guard and the force lost its exclusively volunteer character. At the same time the title 'Home Guard' was confirmed as the only title of the force, which it had effectively been since August 1940.

With the successful advance of the Allies across Europe in the summer of 1944, the requirement for the Home Guard greatly diminished and 'Stand-Down' was ordered to take effect on 1st November 1944, with final parades held on 3rd December. Formal disbandment became possible once the 'present emergency', for which members had enrolled, was over, and took effect from 31st December 1945.

The Home Guard was an exclusively infantry force until early 1942, and, indeed, even after the authorisation of various forms of specialist unit, the 'general service battalion' (frequently more than one thousand strong) remained the back-bone of the force.[1] Home Guard units were affiliated to their local infantry regiments and at no stage was any element of the Home Guard ever 'badged Royal Artillery'. However, this did not prevent the Home Guard from undertaking a number of roles which in normal circumstances might, or would, have fallen to the Gunners. 'Heavy weapons', generally known as 'sub-artillery', integral to general service battalions included the 29-mm. spigot mortar (or 'Blacker Bombard'), which, by analogy with the 3-in. mortar platoons of infantry battalions, could have been held to be an infantry responsibility, despite the 20-pound projectile. The 2-pdr. anti-tank gun, issued to the Home Guard from September 1943, had been both a battalion and an anti-tank regiment weapon, whereas there was no orthodox infantry equivalent to Ordnance, Smooth-Bore, 3-in. (otherwise known as the 'Smith Gun'), available to the Home Guard in increasing quantity from late 1942. Members of infantry battalions in coastal areas were trained to man coast artillery and organised in specialist groups to do so, but no specifically coast artillery units or sub-units were formed.

It was, however, as part of the anti-aircraft defences that the Home Guard came closest to being 'real Gunners'. From anti-aircraft light machine-guns, issued in the late summer of 1940 for the defence of aircraft factories, they graduated through rocket projectors to the 3.7-in. and 4.5-in. guns that were the principal armament of Anti-Aircraft Command, forming, eventually, 28 Home Guard Anti-Aircraft Regiments. In addition, there were more than 250 light anti-aircraft troops for the close air defence of vulnerable points. The history of these units will be outlined in greater detail in a further volume.

*The Home Guard in Hertfordshire*

 The original scheme for the raising of the Local Defence Volunteers in Hertfordshire in May

Plate 177 *The 29-mm. Spigot Mortar or 'Blacker Bombard' on mobile mounting. The loading number* (left foreground) *is fitting the hollow tail-shaft of the practice bomb on to the spigot. The weapon had an effective range with the 20-pound anti-tank bomb of between one and two hundred yards.* (Fox Photos Ltd.)

1940 provided for a county headquarters and nineteen companies based in the principal urban and rural areas. By July 1940, many of the companies had grown to a strength of over five hundred and the unwieldy organisation was rationalised by grouping companies geographically into seven battalions and forming new companies by division of the original ones. Two months later the 6th Battalion at Watford was split to form in addition the 8th, 9th and 10th Battalions. By the end of 1940, the ten battalions comprised 35 individually numbered companies. The ten-battalion organisation continued until July 1942, with a further nine companies being raised and with some switching of companies between battalions. Sweeping changes in organisation took place between July and September 1942, when five additional battalions were formed. At the same time, the individual company numbers were discarded and companies were lettered within their battalions.

Sub-division of Hertfordshire for purposes of tactical command began in March 1941, when the ten battalions were divided into two 'Groups', covering the Watford area and the rest of the county. Following the reorganisation in the summer of 1942, fourteen battalions were placed under command of three groups – Eastern Group (1st, 3rd, 11th and 12th Battalions), Central Group (2nd, 4th, 5th, 13th, 14th and 15th Battalions) and Western Group (7th, 8th, 9th and 10th Battalions) – and the 6th Battalion was transferred to London District. (Some parts of south and east Hertfordshire which fell within the Metropolitan Police District – Bushey, Borehamwood, Barnet, Cheshunt and Waltham Cross – had always been in London District and were included in the recruiting area of the Middlesex Home Guard.) Groups were redesignated 'Sectors' in February 1943.[2]

*Home Guard artillery and sub-artillery in Hertfordshire*

The capabilities and tactical handling of artillery and sub-artillery in use by the Home Guard in the autumn of 1943 were set out in Home Guard Instruction No. 51[3] and they are incorporated in the summaries below:

*29-mm. Spigot Mortar (Blacker Bombard)*

In its primary, anti-tank role this weapon had a maximum range, with the 20-pound high-explosive anti-tank bomb, of two hundred yards, and a 'best' range of one hundred yards. With the 14-pound high-explosive anti-personnel bomb its maximum range was 750 yards and 'best' range four hundred yards. It was officially described as the "most destructive of all the Home Guard anti-tank weapons" and tactical handling instructions emphasised the anti-tank role, requiring that mortars should be 'spared' for the anti-personnel role only when all likely tank approaches were well covered. Issues to the Home Guard in Hertfordshire began in May 1942 and continued at intervals as supplies increased. According to Brock (see Bibliography) the 7th Battalion received an initial issue of ten mor-

Plate 178 *The 29-mm. Spigot Mortar in the hands of the Home Guard in Hertfordshire.* Top – *One of the 2nd Hertfordshire Battalion's static mountings, a standard-pattern concrete emplacement in Stevenage* (Hertfordshire Pictorial Archives – Hitchin Museum); Bottom – *Mobile mountings manned by the 19th Middlesex Battalion at Borehamwood.* (Private Collection)

tars between May and August 1942 and by Stand-Down the battalion had thirty on charge. Mortar positions, many of them of the standard concrete pattern, were incorporated into all battalions' defence schemes as soon as the weapons were available. Spigot mortar sections were initially incorporated in the support platoons of sector mobile reserve companies but they were quite quickly replaced by the more mobile Smith Guns or 2-pdr. anti-tank guns. Thereafter, they reverted to the static anti-tank role with mobility limited to movement between positions in the battalion area. A number of concrete emplacements for the 29-mm. spigot mortar can still be seen in Hertfordshire.

Despite the instructions that priority was to be given to defence, and especially to anti-tank defence, a three-page document, apparently locally produced and entitled 'Drill for spigot mortar troops acting in support of infantry in the attack', survives. This document assumes a four-gun troop using indirect fire and in Gunner terminology covers deployment drills, simple fire discipline and instruction for application of fire to the target. The spigot mortar was not equipped with a dial sight but indirect fire could be achieved with aiming

Plate 179 *Ordnance, Smooth Bore, 3-in. – the 'Smith Gun' – used exclusively by the Home Guard. The gun was capable of firing an 8-pound high explosive shell to a maximum range of 500 yards. With its rudimentary ammunition limber, it could be towed behind a small car or van and was brought into action by tipping it on to one wheel.*
Top left – *Limber in the travelling position* (I.W.M. – MH 12984);
Top right – *Gun and limber in the firing position* (I.W.M. – M.H. 12987);
Bottom – *Gun and detachment in action.* (Fox Photos Ltd.)

posts and the 'prongs' on the foresight that were used for aiming off when sighting directly on a moving target. Unfortunately there is no record of whether these drills were put into effect.

*Ordnance, Smooth-Bore, 3-in. (Smith Gun)*

The Smith Gun fired a 6-pound high-explosive anti-tank shell to a maximum range of two hundred yards ('best' range: one hundred yards) and an 8-pound high-explosive anti-personnel round to a maximum range of 650 yards ('best' range : 150 yards). The gun had a low trajectory, which made for 'crest clearance' problems as close as twenty yards from the muzzle, and it was generally held to be difficult to conceal. It was, however, very mobile. Tactical handling instructions covered defence (including indirect fire), reserve (rapid deployment to reinforce a threatened area) and counter-attack. Special attention was paid to the use of the Smith Gun in built-up areas.

Brock records that the Smith Gun "made its appearance in 1942, but, as it was considered that this weapon might most usefully be employed in street fighting in large built-up areas, its issue was restricted to Home Guard units in large towns". Issues of the Smith Gun to the Home Guard in Hertfordshire began in the autumn of 1942 and by the end of August 1943 28 guns had been delivered. Although they were subject to the over-riding 'built-up areas' policy, some were used in a more mobile role. Waters (see Bibiliography) shows that, certainly by June 1943, Central Sector Mobile Reserve Company (15 E Company) had a 'half troop' (two guns) and there are indications that Eastern Sector Mobile Reserve Company may have had as many as five Smith Guns.

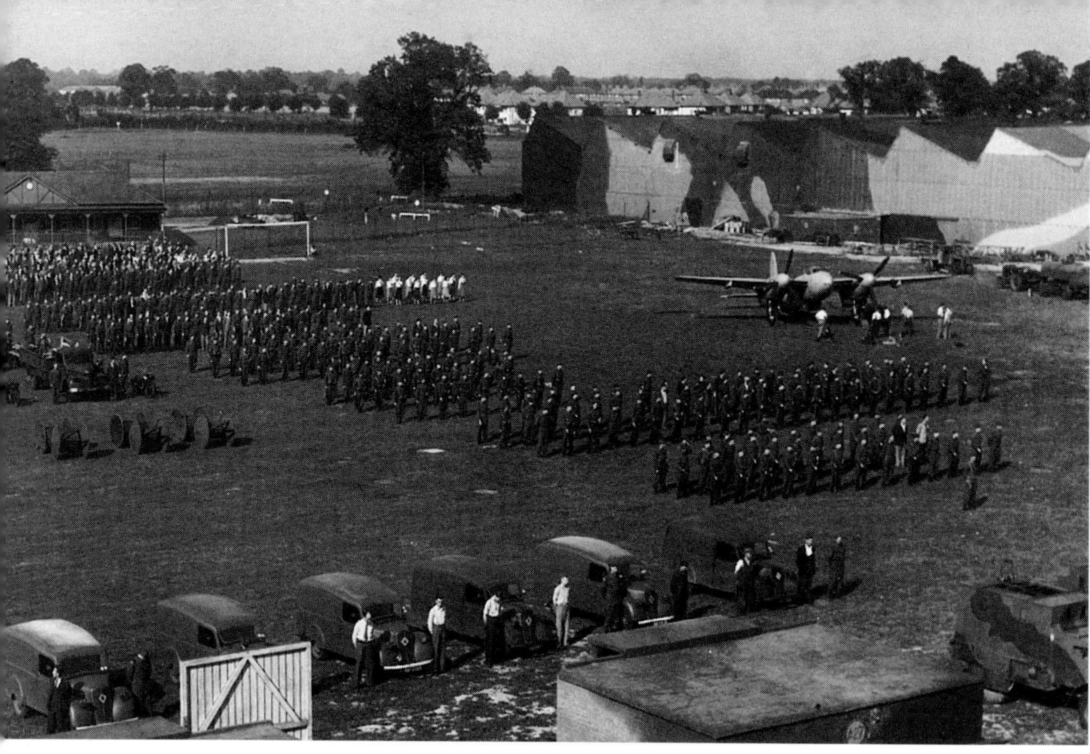

Plate 180 *The first Smith Guns (O.S.B. 3-in.) to be issued to the Hertfordshire Home Guard on parade with 19 Company at the de Havilland factory at Hatfield, summer 1942.* (British Aerospace)

In consequence of the issue of anti-tank shells for the Smith Gun, the policy covering its tactical employment was revised in August 1943 and the gun's potential as a close support weapon for counter-attack sub-units was recognised.[4] The guns were authorised to be used "in support of local reserves within defended areas and in conjunction with any mobile sub-units which have the role of reinforcing vulnerable points in defended localities within a short distance from their homes". At the same time, however, supplies of the 2-pdr. anti-tank gun (see below) became available and the Smith Gun was removed from the establishment of mobile companies in Hertfordshire and deployed to defensive tasks within battalion areas. A final eight guns were delivered before the end of 1943, bringing the total number in Hertfordshire Sub-District to 36.

*2-pdr. Anti-Tank Gun*

At the end of August 1943, 2,400 2-pdr. anti-tank guns were declared surplus to the requirements of the field army in Europe and available for use by the Home Guard. Adequate supplies of operational and training ammunition were assured, but no anti-personnel round was available. With armour-piercing solid shot the maximum effective range of the 2-pdr. was five hundred yards but the 'best' range was much lower, at two hundred yards. The effectiveness of the 2-pdr. round against armour plate was a great deal less than that of the high explosive anti-armour rounds fired by the 29-mm. spigot mortar or the Smith Gun. Home Guard Instruction No. 51 accordingly appears optimistic in its tactical handling instructions, which concentrate on an anti-tank, rather than an anti-vehicle, role. Nevertheless, the 2-pdr. was still a useful weapon against soft-skinned vehicles and was highly mobile and accurate, with a good rate of fire.

Instructions for the employment of the 34 2-pdr. anti-tank guns allocated to Hertfordshire Sub-District were issued in November 1943.[5] Priority was given to the provision of two guns each to the support platoons of the sector mobile reserve companies and battalion mobile companies, where they replaced spigot-mortars or Smith Guns. The remaining guns were to be incorporated in battalion defences. Steps were taken to provide towing vehicles, or at least to earmark them for use on call-out, but it was considered likely that there would only be enough vehicles for the mobile companies. Those guns assigned to 'battalion defences' would, according to the instructions, "be moved to alternative positions by drag ropes". The 2-pdr. remained in service with the Home Guard in Hertfordshire until Stand-Down and was enthusiastically fired on local ranges during the spring and summer of 1944.

All the evidence, and particularly their organisation into separate sub-units, their mobility, potential for indirect fire and proposed tactical employment in support of 'other arms' (in this

Plate 181 *A 2-pdr. anti-tank gun displayed in Stevenage by 2nd Hertfordshire Battalion, May 1944. The gun fired armour-piercing solid shot to a maximum effective range of 500 yards.* (Hertfordshire Pictorial Archives – Hitchin Museum)

case Home Guard infantry), points to the artillery and sub-artillery elements of the Home Guard in Hertfordshire being Gunners in all but name. They were without doubt successors to the troop of 'Horse or Flying Artillery' that was raised in 1797 and later incorporated in the South Hertfordshire Legion – the county's first force of all arms. They were, too, closer in spirit to Hertfordshire's Yeoman Gunners, mobilised and on active service in various theatres, than perhaps either party realised at the time.

NOTES

1. Order of battle and titles and designations of Home Guard units can be traced in the *Home Guard List* and in Whittaker (see Bibliography).
2. For fuller details of order of battle, etc. of the Home Guard in Hertfordshire see *Hertfordshire's Soldiers from 1757* and *The Hertfordshire Regiment – An Illustrated History* (see Bibliography – Sainsbury).
3. Home Guard Instruction No. 51 – Battlecraft and Battle Drill for the Home Guard: Part IV – The Organisation of Home Guard Defence (G.H.Q. Home Forces, November 1943)
4. Eastern Command file 'Home Guard Weapons and Equipment' (1942–1944) (P.R.O. : W.O. 199/2492)
5. Hertfordshire Sub-District Operational Instruction No. 23 dated 21st November 1943 (Hertfordshire Archives and Local Studies)

# Bibliography and Guide to Sources

PRINTED BOOKS

ALEXANDER, S. C. *Sweet Kwai Run Softly*, Bristol, Merriotts Press, 1995.

BALDWIN, M. and MILLER, K. *The Gunners' Favourite – The 25-Pounder Gun – A Brief History*, London, National Army Museum, 1993 (2nd Edition).

BARNETT, C. *Britain and Her Army 1509–1970 – A Military, Political and Social Survey*, London, Alan Lane (The Penguin Press), 1970.

BEALE, P. *Tank Tracks – 9th Battalion Royal Tank Regiment at War, 1940–45*, Stroud, Gloucestershire, Alan Sutton Publishing Ltd., 1995.

BECKETT, I.F.W. *The Amateur Military Tradition 1558–1945*, Manchester, Manchester University Press, 1992.

BELCHEM, D. *Victory in Normandy*, London, Chatto and Windus Ltd., 1981.

BHARGAVA, K.D. and SASTRI, K.N.V. *Official History of the Indian Armed Forces in the Second World War 1939–1945: Campaigns in South-East Asia 1941–1942*, Combined Inter-Services Historical Section India and Pakistan, 1960.

BIDWELL, R.G.S. *The Development of British Field Artillery Tactics – Part I: 1920–1939, Reform and Reorganisation; Part II: 1940–1942, The Desert War; Part III: 1940–1943, Old Principles – New Methods*, Royal Artillery Journal, Vol. XCIV, Nos. 1 and 2, 1967; Vol. XCV, No. 1, 1968.

BIDWELL, R.G.S. *Gunners at War – A Tactical Study of the Royal Artillery in the Twentieth Century*, London, Arms and Armour Press, 1970.

BINGHAM, J.K.W. *Crusader – Cruiser Mk. VI*, Windsor, Berkshire, Profile Publications Ltd. (A.F.V. Profile No. 8), 1970 [For details of Covenanter and Crusader O.P. Tanks].

BROCK, A.St.H. (Ed.) *7th Hertfordshire Battalion Home Guard – A History of the Battalion, 1940–1944*, Berkhamsted, Hertfordshire, Clunbury Press [Printers], 1945.

CAMPBELL, D.A. *The Dress of the Royal Artillery*, London, Arms and Armour Press, 1971.

CAPLAN, J. *From Gorbals to Jungle*, Glasgow, William MacLellan and Co. Ltd., 1960.

CHAMBERLAIN, P. and CROW, D. *Carriers*, Windsor, Berkshire, Profile Publications Ltd. (A.F.V. Profile No.14), 1970.

CHAMBERLAIN, P. and ELLIS, C. *British and American Tanks of World War II*, London, Arms and Armour Press, 1969.

CHAMBERLAIN, P. and ELLIS, C. *Making Tracks – British Carrier Story 1914 to 1972*, Windsor, Berkshire, Profile Publications Ltd., 1973.

CHAMBERLAIN, P. and GANDER, T. *Light and Medium Field Artillery*, London, Macdonald and Co. Ltd., 1975.

CHAPPELL, M. *British Infantry Equipments 1908–1980*, London, Osprey Publishing Ltd., 1980.

CHAPPELL, M. *British Cavalry Equipments 1800–1941*, London, Osprey Publishing Ltd., 1983.

CLAY, E. W. *The Path of the 50th – The Story of 50th (Northumbrian) Division in the Second World War 1939–45*, Aldershot, Hampshire, Gale and Polden Ltd., 1950.

COLLIER, B. *History of the Second World War – United Kingdom Military Series: The Defence of the United Kingdom*, London, H.M.S.O., 1957.

CONNIFORD, M.P. *British Army Transport 1939–45 – Part Two: Gun Tractors ........*, Hemel Hempstead, Hertfordshire, M.A.P. Publications, 1971.

CONNIFORD, M.P. *British Light Military Trucks 1939–45*, King's Langley, Hertfordshire, Argus Books Ltd, 1976.

COUSINS, G. *The Defenders – A History of the British Volunteer*, London, Frederick Muller Ltd., 1968.

DAVIES, P.N. *The Man behind the Bridge – Colonel Toosey and the River Kwai*, London, Athlone Press Ltd., 1991.

DAVIS, B.L. *British Army Uniforms and Insignia of World War Two*, London, Arms and Armour Press, 1983.

DENNIS, P. *The Territorial Army 1906–1940*, Woodbridge, Suffolk, Boydell Press (for the Royal Historical Society), 1987.

DEWEY, J. and S. and WILDER, W. *P.O.W. Sketchbook – A Story of Survival*, Cholsey, Oxfordshire, Pie Powder Press, 1985.

DUNCAN, W.E. and others [Eds.] *The Royal Artillery Commemoration Book, 1939–1945*, London, G. Bell and Sons Ltd. (for the Royal Artillery Benevolent Fund), 1950.

DUNLOP, J.K. *The Territorial Army Today*, London, A. and C. Black, 1939.

ELLIS, C. and CHAMBERLAIN, P. *American Half-Tracks of World War Two*, Watford, Hertfordshire, Argus Books Ltd., 1978.

ELLIS, C. and CHAMBERLAIN, P. *Ram and Sexton*, Windsor, Berkshire, Profile Publications Ltd. (A.F.V. Profile No. 13), 1970.

ELLIS, L. F. *History of the Second World War – United Kingdom Military Series: Victory in the West 1944–45 (Vol. 1 – June–August 1944; Vol. 2 – September 1944–May 1945)*, London, H.M.S.O., 1962 and 1968.

ESSAME, H. *The 43rd Wessex Division at War, 1944–1945*, London, William Clowes and Sons Ltd., 1952.

FARNDALE, Sir M. *History of the Royal Regiment of Artillery – The Years of Defeat: Europe and North Africa 1939–1941*, London, Brassey's (U.K.) Ltd., 1996.

FORBES, P. *6th Guards Tank Brigade – The Story of Guardsmen in Churchill Tanks*, London, Sampson Low, Marston and Co. Ltd., n.d.

FREDERICK, J.B.M. *The Lineage Book of British Land Forces 1660–1978* (2 Vols.), Wakefield, Yorkshire, Microform Academic Publishers, 1986.

GANDER, T. *The 25-pounder Gun* (2 parts), London, Outline Publications, 1983.

GEE, P.W. *A History of the Essex Yeomanry 1919–1949*, Colchester, Benham and Co. Ltd., 1950 [For history of 191st Field Regiment, R.A.].

GILL, R. and GROVES, J. *Club Route in Europe – The Story of XXX Corps in the European Campaign*, Hanover, H.Q. XXX Corps, 1946.

GRAVES, C. *The Home Guard of Britain*, London, Hutchinson and Co. Ltd., 1943.

GRIFFITH, A.L.P. *A Brief Record of the Hertfordshire Yeomanry and the Hertfordshire Artillery*, Hertford, G. Creasey and Sons, 1927.

HARCELRODE, P. *'Go to it!' – The Illustrated History of the 6th Airborne Division*, London, Bloomsbury Publishing Ltd., 1990.

HODGES, P. and TAYLOR, M.D. *British Military Markings, 1939–1945*, Retford, Nottinghamshire, Cannon Publications, 1994.

HOGG, I.V. *A History of Artillery*, London, Hamlyn Publishing Group Ltd., 1974.

HOGG, I.V. *British and American Artillery of World War Two*, London, Arms and Armour Press, 1978.

HOWARD M. and SPARROW, J. *The Coldstream Guards 1920–1946*, London, Oxford University Press, 1951.

HUGHES, B.P. (Ed.) *The History of the Royal Artillery 1919–1939*, Woolwich, Royal Artillery Institution, 1978.

HUGHES, B.P. (Ed.) *History of the Royal Regiment of Artillery – Between the Wars, 1919–39*, London, Brasseys (U.K.) Ltd., 1992.

HUGHES, F.K. *A Short History of 49th (West Riding and Midland) Infantry Division, Territorial Army*, Barnet, Hertfordshire, The Stellar Press Ltd. [Printers], 1958.

ICKS, R.J. *Hellcat, Long Tom and Priest*, Windsor, Berkshire, Profile Publications Ltd., (A.F.V. Profile No. 26), 1971.

JEWELL, B. *British Battledress 1937–61*, London, Osprey Publishing Ltd., 1981.

KILN, R.J. *D-Day to Arnhem with Hertfordshire's Gunners*, Welwyn Garden City, Hertfordshire, Castlemead Publications, 1993.

KIRBY, S.W. *History of the Second World War – United Kingdom Military Series: The War against Japan (Vol. 1 – The Loss of Singapore)*, London, H.M.S.O., 1957.

LAMB, D.A. *View from the Bridge: The Story of the 191st Field Regiment of the Royal Artillery 1942–1944*, [Published privately], 1970.

LONGMATE, N.R. *The Real Dad's Army – The Story of the Home Guard*, London, Arrow Books Ltd., 1974.

LOWE, P.A. *The Development of Artillery Tactics since 1900*, Tactics Wing, Royal School of Artillery, 1976.

MACKENZIE, S.P. *The Home Guard – A Military and Political History*, Oxford, Oxford University Press, 1995.

MARTIN, H.G. *A History of the Fifteenth Scottish Division, 1939–1945*, Edinburgh, William Blackwood and Sons Ltd., 1948.

MEAD, P. *Gunners at War, 1939–45*, London, Ian Allan Ltd., 1982.

MEULSTEE, L. *Wireless for the Warrior* (2 Vols.), Broadstone, Dorset, G.C. Arnold Partners, 1995 and 1997.

PEMBERTON, A.L. *The Development of Artillery Tactics and Equipment*, London, War Office, 1950.

POWELL, G. *The Devil's Birthday – The Bridges to Arnhem, 1944*, London, Buchan and Enwright, 1984.

ROSSE, Earl of, and HILL, E.R. *The Story of the Guards Armoured Division*, London, Geoffrey Bles Ltd., 1956.

SAINSBURY, J.D. *Hertfordshire's Soldiers from 1757*, Hitchin, Hertfordshire, Hertfordshire Local History Council, 1969.

SAINSBURY, J.D. *Roll of Honour of Officers and Men of Hertfordshire Yeomanry and Artillery Units who lost their lives on active service in South Africa and in the two World Wars*, Digswell, Hertfordshire, Hertfordshire Yeomanry and Artillery Historical Trust, 1972 (First Supplement, 1977; Second and Final Supplement, 1982).

SAINSBURY, J.D. *A Record of Honours and Awards to Officers and Men of Hertfordshire Yeomanry and Artillery Units*, Digswell, Hertfordshire Yeomanry and Artillery Historical Trust, 1977 (First Supplement, 1984; Second and Final Supplement in preparation).

SAINSBURY, J.D. *A Short Account of the Volunteer Artillery*, Journal of the Royal Artillery, Volume XCIII, No. 1 – Spring 1966.

SALMOND, J.B. *The History of the 51st Highland Division 1939–1945*, Edinburgh, William Blackwood and Sons Ltd., 1953.

SANDARS, J. *British Guards Armoured Division 1941–45*, London, Osprey Publishing Ltd., 1979.

SANDARS, J. *The Sherman Tank in British Service 1942–45*, London, Osprey Publishing Ltd., 1980.

SAUNDERS, H. St. G. *The Green Beret – The story of the Commandos 1940–1945*, London, Michael Joseph Ltd., 1949.

SAUNDERS, H. St. G. *The Red Beret – The story of the Parachute Regiment at war 1940–1945*, London, Michael Joseph Ltd., 1950.

SCARFE, N. *Assault Division – A History of the 3rd Division from the Invasion of Normandy to the Surrender of Germany*, London, Collins, 1947.

SELLWOOD, A.V. *The Saturday Night Soldiers – The Stirring Story of the Territorial Army*, London, White Lion Publishers Ltd., 1974 (2nd Edition).

STACEY, C.P. *Official History of the Canadian Army in the Second World War: The Victory Campaign – The Operations in North-West Europe, 1944–1945*, Ottawa, Canada, The Queen's Printer, 1960.

TOOSEY, P.J.D. *Diary of 135th (Hertfordshire Yeomanry) Field Regiment, R.A. in Malaya and Singapore, January–February 1942*, Welwyn Garden City, Hertfordshire, Hertfordshire Yeomanry and Artillery Historical Trust [typescript, duplicated], 1963.

VENTHAM, P. and FLETCHER, D. *Moving the Guns – The Mechanisation of the Royal Artillery, 1854–1939*, London, H.M.S.O., 1990.

WEBSTER, F.A.M. *The History of the 5th Battalion The Bedfordshire and Hertfordshire Regiment (T.A.)*, London, F. Warne & Co. Ltd., 1930.

WHITE, B.T. *Valentine – Infantry Tank Mk. III*, Windsor, Profile Publications Ltd. (A.F.V. Profile No. 6), 1970. [For details of Bishop S.P. 25-pdr.].

WHITTAKER, L.B. *Stand-Down – Order of Battle ... of the Home Guard ... November 1944*, Newport, Gwent, Ray Westlake Military Books, 1990.

WISE, T. *Military Vehicle Markings – Part Two: Tactical Signs and National Indentification Marks*, Hemel Hempstead, Hertfordshire, Model and Allied Publications Ltd., 1973.

WISE, T. *D-Day to Berlin: Armour, Camouflage and Markings of the United States, British and German Armies June 1944–May 1945*, London, Lionel Leventhal Ltd., 1979.

*The Citizen Soldier*, London, Hutchinson and Co. Ltd., n.d. [1939].

*Taurus Pursuant – A History of 11th Armoured Division*, no imprint [1945].

*The Territorial and Auxiliary Forces of Hertfordshire*, London, Reid-Hamilton Ltd., n.d. [1950].

*The 59th Division – Its War Story*, London, Frederick Muller Ltd., 1954.

*The Story of 34 Armoured Brigade* no imprint [Germany, 1945].

WAR OFFICE PUBLICATIONS

*Reports of Proceedings at a Conference between the Secretary of State for War and Representatives of the Territorial Force Associations* (3 pamphlets recording conferences which took place on 1st April 1919, 1st May 1919 and 30th January 1920).
*Reorganisation of the Territorial Force* (4-page leaflet outlining the arrangements. Printed for the War Office, February 1920).
*Revised Titles and Designations of Major Units of the Territorial Army, 1951*. (W.O. Code No. 6724), 1952.
*Regulations for the Territorial Army.*
*Establishments* and *War Establishments.*
*Army Lists*, especially the *Monthly Army List.*[1, 2]
*Army Orders* (formerly *General Orders*).[2]
*Army Council Instructions.*[2]
*Home Guard List.*

OTHER OFFICIAL PUBLICATIONS

*The London Gazette.*[3]

NOTES
1. Details of the various Army Lists and lists covering the Auxiliary Forces are given in WHITE, A.S. 'The Army List', Journal of the Society for Army Historical Research, Vol. XXV, No. 103 – Autumn 1947 and Vol. XLV – No. 181, Spring 1967.
2. *Army Lists* and the *Orders* and *Instructions* mentioned above were published by H.M.S.O. for the War Office and on publication were subject to varying degrees of security classification, and hence availability. In general these security classifications have now been removed and such copies as have reached public reference libraries are available without restriction. Readers requiring advice on these specialised sources are recommended to consult the National Army Museum (Department of Archives).
3. The *London Gazette* is registered as a newspaper and is held by a number of major public reference libraries.

NEWSPAPERS, ETC.

*The Times.*
Local newspapers published in Hertfordshire, especially the *Hertfordshire Mercury* (Hertford), *Hertfordshire Advertiser* (St. Albans), *Watford Observer* and *Hertfordshire Express* (Hitchin).

OTHER SOURCES

*Public Record Office*
War Diaries 1939–1945.
*Imperial War Museum*
HARRISON, A.M.L. *History of the 11th Indian Division in Malaya* (Unpublished typescript; also in the Regimental Collection).
WATERS, R.S. *Reminiscences of the Mobile Reserve, 13 Company and E Company, 15th Battalion Hertfordshire Home Guard* (Duplicated typescript; also in Hertfordshire Archives and Local Studies).
*Hertfordshire Archives and Local Studies*
Hertfordshire Territorial Force Association (later Territorial and Auxiliary Forces Association) – Minute Books and related Committee Papers 1908–1947.
*Royal Artillery Institution, Woolwich*
The extensive collections of the Royal Artillery Institution include duplicate war diaries for 1939–45, records of formation, disbandment, etc. of batteries and regiments, equipment handbooks and training publications and a wealth of other material relating to the Royal Regiment of Artillery, both Regular and Reserve.
*The Regimental Collection*
A substantial collection including private correspondence, diaries, etc. and photographs has been deposited at Hertfordshire Archives and Local Studies, at County Hall, Hertford by the Herfordshire Yeomanry and Artillery Historical Trust. It is catalogued under reference D/EYO.

*About the Author*

John Sainsbury was born in Hitchin in 1938 and educated first at local schools, including Hitchin Grammar School, and later at Eton. He was commissioned in the Royal Artillery during National Service, which he spent with a field regiment in Germany. On release from full-time service he joined the Bank of England, where he worked, initially in the Overseas and Economic Intelligence Departments, then in the Corporate Services Department, until retiring a few years early in 1989. He then spent nearly ten years as archivist in the Honours and Awards Branch of the Military Secretary's Department of the Ministry of Defence. As a Territorial Army officer he has served in local field artillery units and in a variety of staff jobs. He was appointed O.B.E. (Military Division) in the 1997 New Year Honours.

His interest in military history goes back to his school days but gained real purpose when, on joining the Hertfordshire Yeomanry – by then a field regiment of the Royal Artillery – he discovered how little had been published on the units of the Auxiliary Forces raised in the county. His first book – *Hertfordshire's Soldiers* – appeared in 1969 and several others have followed. This first part of *The Hertfordshire Yeomanry Regiments, Royal Artillery – An Illustrated History*, joins similar works on Hertfordshire's Territorial Infantry, the Hertfordshire Yeomanry and the Hertfordshire Batteries of the Royal Field Artillery in a series which the author regards as a major step towards increasing public awareness of the continuing history and achievements of local units. He looks forward to producing a final volume on Hertfordshire's Territorial Gunners and then turning to the Home Guard and the Cadets. He indulges in occasional diversions from Hertfordshire's military history, and has written two small but important books on specialised aspects of British decorations for gallantry and contributes to the *Journal of the Orders and Medals Research Society*. After completing the Roll of Honour used for Special Operations Executive's F Section Memorial at Valençay in France, which was inaugurated in 1991, he edited a commemorative booklet published in both English and French. In recognition of his work in preserving and recording the history of military units raised in Hertfordshire, he was elected a Fellow of the Society of Antiquaries of London in 1991.